THE INTERNATION.
BESTSELLING AUTHOR C
PRESENTS A SWEEPING AND IN-DEPTH
HISTORY OF THE KNIGHTS TEMPLAR,
THE MOST SUCCESSFUL CHRISTIAN
INVADERS EVER TO VENTURE INTO
THE HOLY LAND.

In 1099, THE CITY OF JERUSALEM, a possession of the Islamic Caliphate for over four hundred years, fell to an army of European knights intent on restoring the Cross to the Holy Lands. From the ranks of these holy warriors emerged an order of monks trained in both scripture and the military arts, an order that would protect and administer Christendom's prized conquest for almost a century. They were known as the Knights of the Temple of Solomon, or the Templars.

In this articulate and engaging history, Piers Paul Read explores the rise, the catastrophic fall, and the far-reaching legacy of these knights who took, and briefly held, the most bitterly contested citadel in the monotheistic West. Drawing on the most recent scholarship, and writing with authority and candor, Read chronicles the history of the blood-splattered monks whose legend persists in modern literature and culture, inspiring secret societies and the backyard fantasies of any child with access to a stick and a garbage can lid.

More than armed holy men, the Templars also represented the first uniformed standing army in the Western world. Sustaining their military order required

(continued on back flap)

the templars

Also by Piers Paul Read

FICTION

Game in Heaven with Tussy Marx
The Junkers
Monk Dawson
The Professor's Daughter
The Upstart
Polonaise
A Married Man
The Villa Golitsyn
The Free Frenchman
A Season in the West
On the Third Day
A Patriot in Berlin
Knights of the Cross

NON-FICTION

Alive: The Story of the Andes Survivors
The Train Robbers
Ablaze: The Story of Chernobyl

the templars

Piers Paul Read

St. Martin's Press

NEW YORK

www.stmartins.com

ISBN 0-312-26658-8

First published in Great Britain by Weidenfeld & Nicolson

10 9 8 7 6 5 4 3 2

Contents

Acknowledgements

I am grateful for permission to reproduce passages from *The Jewish War* by Josephus, translated and with an introduction by G. A. Williamson, Penguin Books, 1959 (Copyright © G. A. Williamson, 1959); *The Rule of the Templars* by J. M. Upton-Ward, The Boydell Press, 1992 (Copyright © J. M. Upton-Ward 1992); and *The Murdered Magicians* by Peter Partner (Copyright © Peter Partner 1981) by permission of A. M. Heath & Co. Ltd on behalf of Professor Peter Partner.

Maps

Preface

Who were the Templars? One view of this military order comes from the novels of Sir Walter Scott. The Templar knight in *Ivanhoe*, Brian of Bois-Guilbert, is a demonic anti-hero, 'valiant as the bravest of his Order; but stained with their usual vices, pride, arrogance, cruelty, and voluptuousness; a hard-hearted man, who knows neither fear of earth, nor awe of heaven'. The two Templar Grand Masters are little better. Giles Amaury in *The Talisman* is treacherous and malevolent while Lucas of Beaumanoir in *Ivanhoe* is a bigoted fanatic.

In Wagner's opera *Parsifal*, by contrast, Templar-like knights appear as the chaste guardians of the Holy Grail. The nineteenth-century libretto was based on the thirteenth-century epic poem by Wolfram of Eschenbach in which the *Templeisen* bear only a superficial resemblance to the Knights of the Temple but the germ of fact has been enough to persuade posterity that there is truth in the fiction. Thus, in the nineteenth-century imagination, the depraved brutes of *Ivanhoe* and *The Talisman* coexisted with the chivalrous brotherhood of *Parsifal*.

In the twentieth century, there emerged a more sinister image of the Templars as the prototypes of the Teutonic Knights who, in the late 1930s, were the historical models for Himmler's SS. Coupled with a common perception of the crusades as an early example of west European aggression and imperialism, the Templars came to be perceived as brutal fanatics imposing an ideology with the sword. Or, quite to the contrary, it is said they were seduced from their commitment to the Christian cause by their contact with Judaism and Islam in the east, forming a secret society of initiates through which the arcane mysteries of ancient Egypt, conveyed to the masons of the Temple of Solomon, were passed on to the Free Masonic lodges of modern times. It has also been claimed that the Templars were infiltrated by the heretical Cathars after the Albigensian Crusade; that they protected throughout the centuries the royal descendants of a union between Jesus and Mary Magdalene; that their stupendous treasure was discovered by a priest in south-west France in the nineteenth century; and that they were the custodians of fabulous relics, among them the embalmed head of Christ and the Shroud of Turin.

My aim in this book has been to uncover the truth about the Order, avoiding fanciful speculation and recording only what has been established by the research of reputable historians. I have set the story in a wide perspective: histories of the Templars that begin with its founding by Hugh of Payns in 1119, or even with the proclamation of the First Crusade at the Council of Clermont in 1095, often assume a background knowledge that the general reader may not possess. To my mind, it is difficult to understand the mentality of the Templars without examining the significance attached to the Temple in Jerusalem by the three monotheistic relgions – Judaism, Christianity and Islam – and recalling why it has been a point of conflict from the beginning of recorded history to the present day.

There are other pertinent questions that can only be answered by looking back from the early medieval period into the swirling chaos of the Dark Ages. At a time when it has been proposed that the present Pope should apologise for the crusades, it is appropriate to examine the motives of his predecessors in initiating these Holy Wars. To those already familiar with the history of the crusades, some of what I have written will seem repetitious; but in retelling it I have taken advantage of the researches of a new generation of crusade historians. My debt to these and other scholars will become apparent to anyone who reads this book.

I also felt that what a contemporary chronicler called 'God's deeds done by the Franks' are worth retelling not just for their intrinsic interest but also for their relevance to many of the dilemmas we face today. The Templars were a multinational force engaged in the defence of the Christian concept of a world order: and their demise marks the point when the pursuit of the common good within Christendom became subordinate to the interests of the nation state, a process that the world community is now trying to reverse.

There are remarkable parallels in the Templars' story between the past and the present. In the Emperor Frederick II of Hohenstaufen we find a ruler whose idiosyncratic amorality harks back to Nero and forward to

Hitler. The medieval concept of a Holy Roman empire is remarkably similar to the founders' aspirations for the European Union. The Assassins in Syria are both the descendants of the Jewish Sicarii and the ancestors of the suicide-bombers of Hezbollah. The attitude of many Muslims in the Middle East to the modern state of Israel is very like that of their ancestors to the crusader Kingdom of Jerusalem. How many Arab leaders, one wonders, from Abdul Nasser to Saddam Hussein, have aspired to become a latter-day Saladin, defeating the infidel invaders at another Hattin or, like the Mameluk Sultan, al-Ashraf, driving them into the sea?

My gratitude goes to all those historians whose works have taught me what I know about the Templars. More specifically, I should like to thank Professor Jonathan Riley-Smith for his early encouragement and advice; and Professor Richard Fletcher for reading the manuscript and alerting me to a number of errors. Neither of these eminent historians should be held responsible for the shortcomings of my work.

I should like to thank Anthony Cheetham who first suggested that I should try my hand at history and proposed a book on the Templars; my agent, Gillon Aitken, for urging me to pursue the project; my editor, Jane Wood, for her constant encouragement and invaluable work on the first draft; and Selina Walker for her help with the maps and illustrations. I am also grateful to Andrew Sinclair who lent me his library of books on the Templars; to Charles Glass for introducing me to the Memoirs of Usamah Ibn-Munqidh; and to the Librarian and staff of the London Library for their courteous help with my research.

part one

THE TEMPLE

one

The Temple of Solomon

On maps drawn on parchment in the Middle Ages, Jerusalem is shown at the centre of the world. It was then, as it remains today, a city sacred to three religions – Judaism, Christianity and Islam. For each, Jerusalem was the site of momentous events that formed the bond between God and man – the first being the preparations by Abraham to sacrifice his son Isaac on the outcrop of rock now covered by a golden dome.

Abraham was a rich nomad from Ur in Mesopotamia who, around 1,800 years before the birth of Christ, moved at God's command from the valley of the Euphrates to territory inhabited by the Canaanites lying between the River Jordan and the Mediterranean Sea. There, as a reward for his faith in the one true God, he was endowed with this land 'flowing with milk and honey' and promised innumerable descendants to inhabit it. He was to be the father of a multitude of nations; and, to seal this covenant, Abraham and all the men in his tribe were to be circumcised, a practice that was to continue 'generation after generation'.

This promise of posterity was problematic because Abraham's wife Sarah was barren. When she realised that she was past the age of child-bearing, Sarah persuaded Abraham to father a child by her Egyptian maidservant, Hagar. In due course, Hagar gave birth to a son Ishmael. Some years later, three men appeared as Abraham was sitting by the entrance of his tent during the hottest part of the day. They told him that Sarah, then over ninety, would have a child.

Abraham laughed. Sarah, too, took it as a joke. 'Now that I am past the age of child-bearing, and my husband is an old man, is pleasure to come my way again!'[1] But the prediction proved to be correct. Sarah conceived and gave birth to Isaac. She then turned against Ishmael, seeing him as a rival for Isaac's inheritance, and asked Abraham to send him and his

3

mother away. God sided with Sarah and, ever-obedient to God's command, Abraham dispatched Hagar and Ishmael into the wilderness of Beersheba with some bread and a skin of water. When the skin was empty, Hagar, because she could not bear to watch Ishmael die of thirst, meant to abandon him under a bush: but God directed her towards a well and promised that her son would found a great nation in the deserts of Arabia.

It was now that God set a final test for Abraham, ordering him to offer 'your only child Isaac, whom you love ... as a burnt offering on a mountain I shall point out to you'. Abraham obeyed without demur. He took Isaac to the spot designated by God, an outcrop of rock on Mount Moriah, placed wood on this makeshift altar, and laid Isaac on the pile of wood. But just as he took the knife to kill his son, he was commanded to desist. 'Do not raise your hand against the boy ... Do not harm him, for now I know you fear God. You have not refused me your son, your only son ... and because you have done this ... I will shower blessings on you, I will make your descendants as many as the stars of heaven and the grains of sand on the seashore ... All the nations of the earth shall bless themselves by your descendants as a reward for your obedience.'[2]

Did Abraham exist? In modern times, scholarly views of his historicity have vacillated between the scepticism of German exegetes who dismissed him as a mythical figure and more positive judgements made as a result of archaeological discoveries in Mesopotamia.[3] In the Middle Ages, however, no one doubted that Abraham had existed, and almost all those living between the Indian subcontinent and the Atlantic Ocean claimed descent from this patriarch from Ur – figuratively by Christians, literally by the Muslims and Jews. The Jews had a pedigree to prove it – the collection of Jewish texts combined in the Torah that tell the story of Abraham's descendants.

Around 1300 BC, these records tell, famine drove the Jews out of Palestine into Egypt. There they were welcomed as guests by Joseph, a Jew, the chief minister of the Egyptian Pharaoh, who in his youth had been left to die in the desert by his jealous brothers; but after Joseph's death and the accession of a new Pharaoh, the Jews were enslaved and used as forced labour to build the residence at Pi-Ramases for the Pharaoh, Rameses II.

Moses, the first of the great prophets of Israel, led them out of Egypt and into the desert. There, on Mount Sinai, God transmitted his com-

THE TEMPLE OF SOLOMON

mandments to Moses engraved on tablets of stone. To house them, the Jews constructed a portable shrine which they called the Ark of the Covenant. After many years of meandering through the Sinai Desert, they reached the promised land of Caanan. As punishment for a past transgression, Moses was permitted only to see it from afar. It was left to his successor, Joshua, to reclaim the birthright of the Jews. Between 1220 and 1200 BC they conquered Palestine. The contest with the indigenous inhabitants was not a fair one; God took the side of the Jews. Their victory was never absolute; there were constant wars with the neighbouring tribes of Philistines, Moabites, Ammonites, Amalekites, Edomites and Arameans; but the Jews survived because of their unique destiny, as yet undefined.

The marriage between God and his chosen people was not an easy one. He was a jealous God, angered when the Jews turned to other gods, or broke the strict code imposed upon their behaviour – demanding rituals and detailed laws that followed the Ten Commandments that Moses had been given by God on the summit of Mount Sinai. The Jews in their turn were fickle: they turned away from God to worship idols such as the Golden Calf[4] or pagan gods such as Astarte and Baal.[5] They misused the prophets sent by God to chastise them. Even their kings, God's anointed, were sinners. Saul disobeyed God's command to exterminate the Amalekites,[6] and David seduced Bathsheba, wife of Uriah the Hittite, and subsequently instructed Joab, the commander of his army, to 'station Uriah in the thick of the fight and then fall back behind him so that he may be struck down and die'.[7]

It was David who at the turn of the first millennium BC conquered Jerusalem from its indigenous inhabitants, the Jebusites. Below the citadel, on Mount Moab, close to the spot chosen by God for Abraham's sacrifice of Isaac, there was a threshing floor owned by a Jebusite, Onan. At God's command, David bought it as a site for a temple to house the Ark of the Covenant. David assembled the materials for the Temple that was finally built by his son Solomon around 950 BC.

The reign of Solomon marked the apogee of an independent Jewish state. After his death, Israel was conquered by the powerful nations to the east – the Assyrians, the Chaldeans, the Persians. Solomon's Temple was destroyed by the Chaldeans under their king Nebuchadnezzar in 586 BC and the Jews transported to Babylon as slaves. The Chaldeans were in turn conquered by the Persians whose king, Cyrus, allowed them to return to Jerusalem and rebuild their Temple in 515.

In the fourth century BC, the tide of conquest ebbed in the East and flowed in from the West: the Persians were defeated by the Macedonian Greeks under their young king, Alexander the Great. After Alexander's premature death, his empire was divided among his generals and for a time Palestine was contested by the rival Ptolemies based in Egypt and Seleucids based in Mesopotamia. In the absence of a king, the High Priest in Jerusalem assumed many of his functions among the Jews.

In 167 BC a revolt against the Greeks on religious issues developed into a successful struggle for political independence. Its leaders, three Maccabean brothers, founded the Hasmonean dynasty of Jewish kings who recovered most of the territory that had been ruled by David and Solomon. In the course of their constant conflicts with the neighbouring states, an appeal was made to the new and rising power of Rome. The Judaean King Hyrcanus, and his minister Antipater, placed themselves under the protection of the Roman general who had conquered Syria, Gnaeus Pompeius, or Pompey the Great.

Jerusalem was held by Aristobulus, the rival claimant to the throne. After a three-month siege, the city was taken by Pompey's legions. The Romans suffered few casualties but the conflict left 12,000 Jewish dead. According to the Jewish historian Josephus, however, this loss of life was a lesser calamity than the desecration of the Temple by Pompey.

Among the disasters of that time nothing sent a shudder through the nation as the exposure by aliens of the Holy Place, hitherto screened from all eyes. Pompey and his staff went into the Sanctuary, which no one was permitted to enter by the high priest, and saw what it contained – the lamp-stand and the lamps, the table, the libation cups and censers, all of solid gold, and a great heap of spices and sacred money . . .

The Romans were now the arbiters of power in the Jewish state. Pompey reinstated Hyrcanus as high priest but, seeing that he was an ineffective ruler, put political power into the hands of his first minister, Antipater. Julius Caesar, when he came to Syria in 47 BC, conferred Roman citizenship on Antipater and appointed him Commissioner for all Judaea: Antipater's eldest son Phasael became governor of Judaea and his second son, Herod, then aged twenty-six, governor of Galilee. Caesar's fellow consul, Mark Antony, became Herod's lifelong friend.

In 40 BC, the Parthians invaded Palestine. Herod escaped via Arabia and Egypt to Rome. There the Roman Senate equipped him with an army and appointed him King of Judaea. Herod vanquished the Parthians and, despite siding with his friend Mark Antony against Octavian, was confirmed by Octavian as the King of Judaea after his victory over Mark Antony at the Battle of Actium.

Now at the height of his glory, Herod embellished his kingdom with magnificent cities and imposing strongholds, many of them named after his patrons and members of his family. On the coast between Jaffa and Haifa, he built a new city which he named Caesarea and in Jerusalem the fortress called the Antonia. He extended the stronghold at Masada where his family had taken refuge from the Parthians; and built a new stronghold in the hills facing Arabia which he named Herodium after himself.

A man of exceptional courage and ability, Herod understood that his hold on power in Palestine depended upon meeting the expectations of the Romans without upsetting the religious susceptibilities of the Jews. To the Romans, control of Syria and Palestine was considered essential for the security and well-being of their empire. It straddled the land routes between Egypt and Mesopotamia, and dominated the eastern Mediterranean. The city of Rome itself depended upon the regular supply of grain from Egypt, which would be threatened if the ports on the eastern coast of the Mediterranean should fall into the hands of the Parthians.

The Jews were more problematic. Culturally dominated by the Greeks since the time of Alexander the Great, and now politically subservient to the Romans, they retained their sense of destiny as God's chosen people. Their extraordinary fidelity to their beliefs and practices at once impressed and exasperated their pagan contemporaries. Pompey, when besieging the rump of Jewish resistance in the Temple,

was amazed at the unshakeable endurance of the Jews, especially their maintenance of all the religious ceremonies in the midst of a storm of missiles. Just as if deep peace enfolded the City the daily sacrifices, offerings for the dead, and every other act of worship were meticulously carried out to the glory of God. Not even when the Temple was being captured and they were being butchered around the altar did they abandon the ceremonies ordained for the day.[8]

However, their exclusiveness – their belief that they were defiled by contact with Gentiles – antagonised their neighbours. By now, the Jews were no longer confined to Palestine: substantial communities existed in many of the major cities of the Graeco-Roman world and in the Persian empire beyond the Euphrates. In Alexandria, there are criticisms of Jewish exclusivity as early as the third century BC. In Rome, where they won unique exemptions from taking part in pagan cults and permission to observe the Sabbath, Cicero, in his *Pro Flacco*, complained of their clannishness and undue influence; and Tacitus, in his *Histories*, of what he saw as the misanthropy of the Jews: 'Toward every other people they feel only hatred and enmity. They sit apart at meals, and they sleep apart, and although as a race they are prone to lust, they abstain from intercourse with foreign women; yet among themselves nothing is unlawful.'[9]

It was in their homeland, however, that the Jews' sense of superiority to all pagan nations had grave political implications. Time and again, after being conquered by their larger and more powerful neighbours – the Egyptians, the Persians, the Greeks, and now the Romans – they would rise against their oppressors in the belief that God was on their side. Time and again, an initial triumph would be followed by a savage repression.

Herod, although a Roman citizen and of Arab origin, was scrupulous in his observance of the Jewish Law; and to further endear himself to the adherents of his adopted religion, he announced that he would rebuild the Temple. The Jews' reaction was one of suspicion: to reassure them that he would complete this ambitious project, Herod had to promise not to demolish the old Temple until he had assembled all the materials to build the new. Since only priests could enter the Temple precincts, he trained a thousand Levites as masons and carpenters. The foundations of the Second Temple were greatly enlarged by the construction of huge retaining walls to the west, south, and east. Along the edges of the large platform, sustained by landfill or arched supports, ran covered galleries. A fence surrounded the sacred area, and at each of its thirteen gates was an inscription in Latin and Greek to warn that any Gentile who passed beyond it would be punished with death.

In the centre, framed by the colonnades, was the Temple itself. On one side was the Court of the Women and, on the other side of the Beautiful Gate, the Court of the Priests. Two golden doors led into the Sanctuary: in front of these was a curtain of Babylonian tapestry embroidered with blue, scarlet and purple designs symbolising all creation. The inner sanctum, shrouded by a huge veil, was the Holy of Holies into which only the High Priest could venture on certain days of the year. The rock upon which Abraham had prepared Isaac for sacrifice was the altar upon which kids or doves were killed: the cavity still to be seen on the north end of the rock was used to collect the sacrificial blood.

The scale of the Temple was stupendous and, where it towered above the Kidron valley, rose to a dizzying height. Its splendour could not fail to impress upon Herod's subjects that their king, despite his Arab origin, was a worthy Jew. But Herod left nothing to chance. The Antonia fortress formed part of the north wall of the Temple compound and was permanently garrisoned by a contingent of Roman infantry. During major festivals, this was deployed, fully armed, along the colonnades.

The Temple was the culminating achievement of one of the most extraordinary figures of the ancient world. Herod in his prime raised the state of Israel to a level of splendour that it had not seen before and has not seen since. His munificence extended to foreign cities – Beirut, Damascus, Antioch, Rhodes. Skilled in combat, an able huntsman, a keen athlete, Herod patronised and presided over the Olympic Games. He used his influence to protect the Jewish communities in the Diaspora, and was generous to those in need throughout the eastern Mediterranean. Yet he failed to establish a stable dynasty because, as his life progressed, he became possessed by a paranoia that turned the benevolent despot into a tyrant.

There can be little doubt that Herod was surrounded by conspiracy and intrigue. Both his father and his brother had met violent ends, and he had powerful enemies both among the Pharisee faction of Jews who resented the rule of a foreigner subservient to a pagan emperor in Rome, and among the adherents of Hasmonean claimants to the crown of Judaea. To placate the latter, Herod divorced Doris, the bride of his youth, and married Mariamme, the granddaughter of Hyrcanus the high priest.

Hyrcanus had been taken prisoner by the Parthians when they had overrun Palestine, but he had been freed on the intercession of the Jews living beyond the Euphrates. Encouraged by the marriage of his granddaughter to Herod, he returned to Jerusalem where he was immediately executed by Herod, not, as Josephus puts it, because he claimed the throne 'but because the throne was really his'.[10] Another potential rival was his wife's brother Jonathan who, at the age of seventeen, Herod made high priest; but when the young man had put on the sacred vestments and approached the altar during a feast, all those in attendance wept with emotion and so Herod had him drowned by his bodyguard of Gauls.

What might have been politically expedient was domestically disastrous. Herod had fallen deeply in love with Mariamme who, after his treatment of her brother and her grandfather, hated him with an equal passion. Added to her resentment was the disdain of a royal Jewish princess for an Arab upstart, which both tormented Herod and infuriated his family, in particular his sister Salome. Playing the role of Iago to Herod's Othello, Salome persuaded her brother that Mariamme had been unfaithful with her husband, Joseph. Herod ordered the immediate execution of both. His paranoia turned next to his two sons by Mariamme: convinced that they were conspiring against him, he had them strangled at Sebaste in the year 7 BC. Towards the end of his life, as he lay dying with 'an unbearable itching all over his body, constant pains in the lower bowel, swellings on the feet as in dropsy, inflammation of the abdomen, and mortification of the genitals producing worms', Herod was told that his eldest son and heir, Antipater, had planned to poison him. Antipater was executed by his father's bodyguard. Five days later, Herod himself was dead.

It was not merely these domestic tragedies that turned a potentially great king into a tyrant but, more significantly, the impossible task of reconciling God's chosen people to pagan rule. At the time of a census in 7 BC, six thousand Pharisees had refused to take an oath of loyalty to Octavian, now the Emperor Augustus; and, shortly before Herod's death, around forty followers of two rabbis in Jerusalem, well known as exponents of Jewish tradition, had lowered themselves on ropes from the roof of the Temple to remove a pagan idol, the golden eagle that Herod had placed above the Temple's Great Gate. For this the two rabbis had been arrested and, on Herod's orders, burned alive.

Herod's successors were less successful than he was at keeping this incipient rebelliousness under control. Under Herod's will, which he had changed a number of times, his kingdom was to be divided between three of his sons – Archelaus, Herod Antipas and Philip. The Emperor Augustus confirmed this arrangement but denied the title of king to Archelaus, making him merely ethnarch, or governor, of Judaea and Samaria until, after nine years of incompetent government, he dismissed him altogether and exiled him to the city of Vienne in Gaul. Judaea was placed under the direct rule of a Roman procurator – first Coponius, then Valerius Gratus and, in AD 26, Pontius Pilate.

This settlement did not ensure the stability of Palestine. While the Jewish aristocracy and the Sadducee establishment did what they could to contain the resentment of their people, the heavy taxation imposed by the Romans and their insensitivity to the religious beliefs of the Jews led to sporadic revolts and finally to outright war. Masada was taken by Jewish insurgents and the Roman garrison killed. In the Temple, Eleazar, the son of the high priest Ananias, persuaded the ministers of the Temple to abolish the sacrifices offered for Rome and for Caesar. This gesture of defiance developed into a general insurrection: the Antonia was captured, Ananias murdered and the Romans driven back into the fortified towers of Herod's palace. In Caesarea, the Romans' administrative capital on the coast, the Gentile inhabitants attacked the Jewish colony and massacred them all. This atrocity enraged the Jews throughout Palestine, who sacked Greek and Syrian cities such as Philadelphia and Pella, killing their inhabitants in revenge.

In September 66, the Roman legate in Syria, Cestius Gallus, set out from Antioch with the Twelfth Legion to restore order in Palestine. The Jewish insurgents in Jerusalem prepared to resist. After some skirmishes outside the city, Cestius withdrew. His retreat turned into a rout. The Jews were left masters in their own land, and set about organising their defences against the Romans' return.

In view of the catastrophe that was to overwhelm them, it seems astonishing that the Jews imagined that they could defy the power of Rome. Certainly there were some 'who saw only too clearly the approaching calamity and openly lamented';[1] but the great majority were wholly convinced that their moment of destiny had come. They were, after all, God's chosen people, and from the earliest times their prophets had promised not just deliverance but a deliverer referred to as 'the anointed' or, in Hebrew, *Messiah*. God's promises to Abraham and Isaac had been that salvation of an unspecified kind should come through their seed, but subsequently this concept of salvation had been combined with the idea of a king descended from David whose reign would be eternal. He was to be a specifically Jewish hero ('See, the days are coming ... when I will raise a virtuous Branch for David, who will reign as true king and be wise, practising honesty and integrity in the land. In his days Judah will be saved and Israel dwell in confidence')[12] but his sovereignty would be universal ('his empire shall stretch from sea to sea, from the river to the ends of the earth ... all kings will do him homage, all nations become his servants').[13] It was the powerful sense of Messianic expectation among the Jews in first-century Palestine that emboldened them to defy the power of Rome.

The main division among the Jews was between the Sadducees and the Pharisees: the Sadducees were the establishment party which controlled the Temple and were easier-going in their interpretation of the Law; the Pharisees were stricter, more radical and more austere, using the oral tradition to impose legalistic minutiae upon every aspect of Jewish life. A major difference in the beliefs of the two factions concerned the afterlife – the Sadducees agnostic, the Pharisees insisting upon the immortality of the soul, a personal resurrection and divine rewards for virtue and punishment for sin in the world to come.

It was the Pharisees who were most vociferous in their opposition to Roman rule; and among the Pharisees there were austere and fanatic sects such as the Essenes who lived in quasi-monastic communities, and the Zealots, a terrorist faction who despised not just the Romans but any collaborating Jews. They sent out assassins known as Sicarii (from the Greek word *sikarioi* meaning 'dagger men') to mingle in a crowd and assassinate their enemies. A contingent of Galilean Zealots that took refuge in Jerusalem waged class war on their hosts.

Their passion for looting was insatiable: they ransacked rich men's houses, murdered men and violated women for sport, and drank their spoils washed down with blood: through sheer boredom they shamelessly gave themselves up to effeminate practices, adorning their hair and putting on women's clothes, steeping themselves in scent and painting under their eyes to make themselves attractive. They copied not merely the dress but also the passions of women, and in their utter filthiness invented unlawful pleasures; they wallowed in slime, turning the whole city into a brothel and polluting it with the foulest practices. Yet though they had the faces of women they had the hands of murderers; they approached with mincing steps, then in a flash became fighting-men, and drawing their swords from under their dyed cloaks ran every passer-by through.[14]

When news of the defeat of Cestius Gallus reached the Emperor Nero, he turned to a veteran general, Vespasian, and put him in command of the Roman forces in Syria. Vespasian sent his son Titus to Alexandria to fetch the Fifteenth Legion and join him at Ptolemais. This combined army moved into Galilee and with great difficulty reduced the strongholds held by the Jewish insurgents and slaughtered or enslaved their inhabitants. Each city was fiercely defended, in particular Jopata commanded by Joseph ben-Matthias who later went over to the Romans, changed his name to Josephus, and wrote an account of the conflict in his *Jewish War*.

In the middle of this campaign, the Emperor Nero was murdered and his successor Galba assassinated in his turn. A civil war followed between rival claimants, Otho and Vitellius, from which Vitellius emerged triumphant. In Caesarea, the legions repudiated Vitellius and proclaimed Vespasian emperor. The governor of Egypt, Tiberius Alexander, supported him: so did the legions in Syria. In Rome, Vespasian's adherents ousted Vitellius and proclaimed Vespasian the heir to the imperial throne. The news reached him in Alexandria from whence he embarked for Rome, leaving his son Titus to complete the subjugation of the rebellious Jews.

The Jews' redoubts were now only a number of outlying fortresses and the city of Jerusalem itself, already invested by the Roman legions. Resistance was ferocious: when the renegade Josephus toured the city walls, calling upon his compatriots to surrender, he was answered with derision and abuse. Yet the city was in the grips of famine and Josephus, who in his history wanted to establish that the depravity of the rebels vitiated the righteousness of their cause, relates with some relish how hunger led wives to rob their husbands, children their fathers, and 'most horrible of all – mothers their babes, snatching the food out of their very mouths; and when their dearest ones were dying in their arms, they did not hesitate to deprive them of the morsels that might have kept them alive'. The culmination of this unnatural behaviour was the story of a certain Mary from the village of Bethezub who killed her own baby, 'then roasted him and ate one half, concealing and saving up the rest'.[15]

The final outcome was not in doubt, but every section of the city was fiercely contested. First the Antonia fortress fell to the Romans but the Temple held out. For six days the battering-rams of the Roman legions pounded away at the Temple walls but made no impression on the huge blocks so smoothly shaped and tightly knit by Herod's masons. An attempt to undermine the northern gate was equally fruitless. Not wanting to risk further casualties on an all-out assault over the walls, Titus ordered his men to set fire to the doors. The silver cladding melted in the heat: the timber was set alight. The fire spread to the colonnades, clearing a path through smouldering masonry for the Roman soldiers. Such was their rage against the Jews that civilians were slaughtered alongside the combatants. According to Josephus who was keen to exculpate his patron in the eyes of the Jews in the Diaspora, Titus did everything he could to save the sanctuary; but his men put it to the torch. Thus what Josephus describes as 'the most wonderful edifice ever seen or heard of, both for its size and construction and for the lavish perfection of detail and the glory of its holy places' was destroyed.

Such was the strength of its fortifications and the determination of its defenders, it had taken Titus and his legions six months to capture Jerusalem – from March to September, AD 70. The population was all but annihilated. Those who had taken refuge in the city's sewers either died of starvation, killed themselves or were killed by the Romans when they emerged. Josephus estimated that over a million people died in the siege of Jerusalem and any survivors were enslaved. Leaving a garrison in the citadel, Titus commanded that the rest of the city including what remained of the Temple be razed. Retiring to Caesarea, he celebrated his birthday on 24 October by watching the Jewish prisoners die in the arena, killed either by wild animals, or by one another, or by being burned alive. When he returned to Rome, Vespasian and Titus, wearing scarlet robes, celebrated their triumph. Wagons loaded with the magnificent treasures looted from Jerusalem were dragged through the streets, among them the golden lampstand from the Temple, together with columns of prisoners in chains. When the procession reached the Forum, the surviving leader of the Jewish insurgents, Simon ben-Gioras, was ceremoniously executed after which the victors retired to enjoy the sumptuous banquet prepared for them and their guests.

In Palestine, bands of insurgents still held out in Herod's impregnable fortresses – Herodium, Machaerus and Masada. Herodium fell without difficulty; Machaerus surrendered; but Masada remained in the hands of the Zealots under Eleazar ben-Jair, a descendant of Judas the Galilean. In this extraordinary fortress, built on an isolated mountain plateau 1,440 feet above the western shore of the Dead Sea, were a thousand men, women and children. The Roman governor, Flavius Silva, encircled the fortress with a wall and built a ramp to enable a battering-ram to make a breach in the wall.

The Zealots at first resisted but, when it became clear that the Romans would breach the wall the next day, Eleazar persuaded his followers that it was better to die at their own hands than be killed by the Romans. Having burned their possessions, each father killed his immediate family; then ten men were chosen by lot to dispatch their companions; and finally one, again chosen by lot, killed the other nine before himself falling on his sword.

two

The New Temple

The hopes of the Jews living in Palestine for an independent nation did not end with the fall of Masada. Some sixty years later, there was a second rebellion against Roman rule led by Simeon ben-Koseba who was acknowledged by the Rabbi Akiba as the promised Messiah. As before, the revolt met with an initial success: the forces of the Roman legate in Judaea, Tineius Rufus, were defeated. The Emperor Hadrian sent the legate in Britain, Julius Severus, to Palestine and in AD 134 Severus recaptured Jerusalem. The war continued for a further eighteen months until August 135, when Bether, the last of around fifty strongholds held by insurgents, fell to Severus and Simeonen ben-Koseba was killed.

The Romans' punishment for this second rebellion was severe. The Jewish captives were either killed or enslaved. Judaea was abolished; it became the province of Syria-Palestine. The city of Jerusalem became a Roman colony from which all Jews were excluded. On the Temple Mount were built sanctuaries to the god-emperor, Hadrian, and the father of all the gods, Zeus.

However, by this time there were other sites in Jerusalem sacred to another religion that Rufus, the Roman Legate, felt he must cauterise by the superimposition of pagan temples. Over the ground that had been used for public executions a century before and a nearby tomb he built temples to Jupiter, Juno and Venus, the goddess of love. They had no significance for the Jewish nation but were sacred to the followers of another claimant to the title of Messiah, Jesus of Nazareth or Jesus the Christ.

Jesus has remained a controversial figure throughout the twenty centuries since he lived and died, as much today as in the past. The traditional teaching of most Christian churches is that his coming was foretold by the nation's prophets, most specifically by his cousin, a popular preacher called

John the Baptist; that he was miraculously conceived in the womb of a virgin, was born in a stable in the village of Bethlehem, preached in Galilee and Judaea and performed a number of spectacular miracles starting with changing water into wine at a wedding in Cana. These miracles included many instances of healing the sick, but Jesus also demonstrated a power over nature by walking on water and calming storms. Like John the Baptist before him, he called for repentance and warned of judgement and eternal punishment for those who died in their sins.

In contrast to the brutality that was all around him in Palestine under Roman occupation, Jesus extolled gentleness and simplicity: he blessed the poor and the meek; he said we should aspire to the innocence of a child. The values he promoted reversed those of what he called 'the world' – the culture of egoism and self-indulgence. We should not strive for wealth, power and social advancement but take the lowest place at table. We should not retaliate against acts of justice but if struck on the face, 'turn the other cheek'. It was not simply a matter of passivity: an enemy's hatred must be met with love. Time and again, Jesus insisted that virtue did not lie in external observances of the kind practised by the Jews but depended upon our internal disposition – our feelings and fantasies as much as our deeds.

This denigration of ritual and observance, together with Jesus's claims to be the Messiah and Son of God, to forgive sins and to embody the only means to eternal life, was considered both blasphemous and seditious by the Jewish leaders – the Pharisee scribes and Sadducee elders. They successfully persuaded the Roman procurator, Pontius Pilate, to have Jesus crucified. After his death he was taken down from the cross and laid in a nearby tomb but three days later, according to his disciples, he rose from the dead.

Even at this distance in time, and if treated as a character in work of fiction, the person of Jesus as depicted in the Gospels has a powerful effect on the reader. Unlike the books of the Old Testament which demonstrate the majesty of God through 'the complexity of life, of emotions and desires beyond the range of intellect and language', the Gospels are spare narratives virtually devoid of characterisation that nevertheless persuade us 'that this and no other way was how it was'.[16] To the literary critic Gabriel Josipovici, Jesus comes across 'as a force, a whirlwind which drives all before it and compels all who cross his path to reconsider their lives from the root up. He has access, not so much to a secret of wisdom as to a source of power.'

Jesus speaks with exceptional assurance and authority yet makes the kind of claims for himself that one would expect from a lunatic. But as G. K. Chesterton pointed out, 'he was exactly what the man with a delusion never is: he was a good judge. What he said was always unexpected; but it was always unexpectedly magnanimous and often unexpectedly moderate.'[17]

How historically accurate are these depictions of Jesus? Attempts to reach an objective view are frequently hampered by prejudice either in favour or against the Christian religion. The biblical scholar E. P. Sanders thinks it is possible to arrive at a core of historical fact.

> We know that he started under John the Baptist, that he had disciples, that he expected the 'kingdom', that he went from Galilee to Jerusalem, that he did something hostile against the Temple, that he was tried and crucified. Finally we know that after his death his followers experienced what they described as the 'resurrection': the appearance of a living but transformed person who had actually died. They believed this, they lived it, and they died for it.[18]

This faith in Jesus in those who knew him proved contagious. 'Whatever significance is ultimately ascribed to the title "the Christ",' writes Geza Vermes in *Jesus the Jew*, 'one fact is at least certain: the identification of Jesus, not just with *a* Messiah, but with *the* awaited Messiah of Judaism, belonged to the heart and the kernel of the earliest phase of Christian belief.'[19] However, this Messiah was not a warrior king who would lead the Jews to triumph and ascendancy in this world, but something far more profound and paradoxical – a sacrificial scapegoat who through his suffering would confound Satan and conquer death.

The most specific predictions of this saviour, so different to what most Jews expected, are found in prophecies of Isaiah made in the Temple in 740 BC. 'Here is my servant,' says God in his vision, 'whom I uphold, my chosen one in whom my soul delights.' God will make him the 'light of nations so that my salvation may reach to the ends of the earth'; yet he will be 'a thing despised and rejected by men, a man of sorrows and familiar with suffering, a man to make people screen their faces; he was despised and we took no account of him. And yet ours were the sufferings he bore, ours the sorrows he carried.'[20]

In the Psalms, too, we find the kind of lament that is echoed many centuries later in Christ's suffering prior to his crucifixion. 'I have become an object of derision, people shake their heads at me in scorn.'[21] And in the Gospels, the evangelists quite specifically point to the episodes in the life of Christ that fulfil the prophets' predictions. When, after they have nailed Christ to his cross, the Roman soldiers share out his clothes and throw dice for the seamless undergarment, it is, the Evangelist John points out, to fulfil Psalm 22, verse 18: 'they divide my garments among them and cast lots for my clothes'. Some of today's sceptical scholars believe that the facts were added after the event to match the prophecies; that, for example, the birth of Jesus of Nazareth was placed in Bethlehem, not Nazareth, because this was foretold by the prophet Micah. The historian Robin Lane Fox, despite the distance in time, feels sufficiently confident in his own researches to decide that 'Luke's story is historically impossible and internally incoherent ... It is, therefore, false.'[22]

Can we discover anything about Jesus from sources other than the Gospels? The only references to him by a near contemporary are found in Josephus's *Antiquities*, and in a version of his *History of the Jewish War*, probably written in Aramaic for a Jewish leadership beyond the Euphrates. These passages are themselves controversial: one theory holds that they were removed from the Greek edition published in Rome so as not to antagonise the Emperor Domitian who was persecuting the Christians at the time; another that they are interpolations forged many years later by Byzantine monks. However, one disputed passage in Josephus's *Antiquities* is quoted in the earliest history of the Christian Church, written by Eusebius in the fourth century: and, improbably if they were added by Christians, the passages in *The Jewish War* say as much about John the Baptist as about Jesus. John is 'a strange creature, not like a man at all'. His face is 'like a savage's'. 'He lived like a disembodied spirit ... he wore animal hair on those parts of his body not covered by his own.'

Jesus, Josephus reported, was notable for his miracles: 'he worked such wonderful and amazing miracles that I for one cannot regard him as a man; yet in view of his likeness to ourselves I cannot regard him as an angel either ...' Josephus describes how:

Many of the common people flocked after him and followed his teaching. There was a wave of excited expectation that he would enable the Jewish tribes to throw off the Roman yoke ... When they saw his ability to do whatever he wished by a word, they told him that they wanted him to enter the City, destroy the Roman troops, and make himself king; but he took no notice.[23]

According to Josephus, the Jewish leaders bribed the Roman governor of Judaea, Pontius Pilate, to allow them to crucify Jesus because they were envious of his popularity. He also describes how, at the very moment of Christ's execution, the veil of the Temple was 'suddenly rent from top to bottom'; and, in his lengthy description of the Temple, Josephus mentions an inscription stating that 'Jesus, the king who never reigned, was crucified by the Jews because he foretold the end of the City and the utter destruction of the Temple'.[24]

We find the same prophecy in the Gospels. 'When some were talking about the Temple, remarking how it was adorned with fine stonework and votive offerings, he [Jesus] said, "All these things you are staring at now – the time will come when not a single stone will be left on another: everything will be destroyed."'[25] More audaciously, in the Gospel of John, Jesus suggests that the Temple, once destroyed, will subsist in him. 'Destroy this sanctuary, and in three days I will raise it up,'[26] a claim that was deemed blasphemous and later formed part of the charge against him. 'This man said, "I have power to destroy the Temple of God and in three days build it up."'[27]

Again, there are conflicting theories about Christ's predictions that not just the Temple but Jerusalem itself would be destroyed. Christians think it explains why the incipient Christian community in Jerusalem moved to Pella before the Romans besieged the city; sceptics suggest that these 'prophecies' were added by the evangelists after the event. What is clear, however, is that the early Christians regarded the destruction of the Temple in Jerusalem as both a necessary part of the new covenant between God and man, and as God's punishment for the Jews' repudiation of his only begotten Son. After the passage I have quoted above, describing a mother devouring her own child during the siege of Jerusalem, Eusebius, the earliest Christian chronicler, adds:

> Such was the reward for the Jews' iniquitous and wicked treatment of God's Christ ... After the Saviour's passion, and the cries with which the Jewish mob clamoured for the reprieve of the bandit and murderer [Barabbas], and begged that the Author of Life should be removed from them, disaster befell the entire nation.[28]

From the perspective of the twentieth century, which has seen an attempt to exterminate the Jewish people more ruthless and systematic than that undertaken under Vespasian and Hadrian, it is difficult not to see such a judgement as one of the sources of anti-Semitism in the style of the Gospels themselves. Saint Matthew, for example, has Pontius Pilate protest: '"I am innocent of this man's blood. It is your concern." And the people, to a man, shouted back, "His blood be on us and on our children!"'[29] But this did not signify, so far as one can judge, a condemnation of the Jews as a race of the kind we find in the cult of *limpieza de sangre* in Spain in the sixteenth century, or in the racial theories of a Houston Stewart Chamberlain in the nineteenth. Crude racial prejudice seems remarkably absent both in antiquity and in the Middle Ages. After all, Christ's disciples, the apostles and the evangelists, were all Jews.

The enmity that arose between the Jews and Christians was not racial but religious and, given the inherent contradictions, it is difficult to see how it could have been avoided. The destruction of the Temple, which Christ predicted, was more than a physical fact; it was a metaphor for the demise of Judaism. God had chosen the Jewish people as a chrysalis for the Messiah: once he had been born, it had served its purpose.

It is quite apparent from the Gospels that this was understood by the Jewish leaders in the Sanhedrin at the time. Whether or not their fear that Christ would provoke the Romans was sincere (given Pilate's reluctance to become involved it was probably not), their alarm at his growing popularity seems reasonable in view of the import of his teaching. They may have been over-optimistic in believing that it would die with him; but if that was their judgement, then it was not unreasonable for the chief priest Caiaphas to decide that 'it is better for one man to die for the people, than for the whole nation to be destroyed'.[30]

However, Christ's claims did not die with him: they came to be accepted by an increasing number of Jews. Leaving aside the questions of whether or not Christ rose from the dead, or a 'holy spirit' descended upon the rump of his followers in the form of tongues of fire, there is no doubt that the crucifixion of Jesus of Nazareth did not deter his disciples from preaching openly that he was 'both Lord and Christ'.

It is equally clear that the Jewish leaders did what they could to suppress this nascent movement of seditious Jews. Peter was arrested; Stephen was stoned to death. Herod Agrippa I, the grandson of Herod the Great, beheaded the apostle James, the brother of John. Only the powers reserved by the Roman Procurator inhibited an all-out persecution; but in AD 62, during the brief interregnum between the death of Porcius Festus and the arrival of Lucceius Albinus, the high priest Anan condemned a second apostle called James, known as 'the brother of the Lord', to be thrown down from the wall of the Temple and clubbed to death.

The real *bête noire* of the Jewish leaders, however, was not one of Christ's original twelve apostles, but Paul of Tarsus, a man who had never known Jesus and was zealous in persecuting Christians until, on his way to Damascus with warrants to arrest Christians signed by the high priest, Jesus appeared to him in a vision and appointed him his 'chosen instrument to bring my name before pagans and pagan kings and before the people of Israel'.[31] It was not just that Paul was a turncoat but that he took the repudiation of Judaism one step further, insisting upon a point that was not at all clear to Christ's original apostles – namely, that you could be a Christian without first becoming a Jew.

Controversy about Paul continues to this day. He is charged with inventing Christianity – elevating 'a Galilean exorcist' into the founder of a world religion.[32] The animosity of the Jewish leaders at the time, however, was provoked by the remarkable success he met in his preaching tours around the Roman Empire. The letters Paul wrote to those he had converted in cities like Ephesus, Corinth and Rome show a great respect for the Jewish tradition but an inflexible insistence that the Mosaic Law is now redundant, that we can only be saved by faith in Christ.

This radical repudiation of the Jews' *raison d'être* antagonised many of the Jews among his fellow Christians; and it was not immediately accepted by the early Church. It was also used against Paul by the Jewish leaders who brought him before Gallio, the Proconsul of Achaea, charging him with 'persuading people to worship God in a way that breaks the Law'. With an exasperation that reflects that of Pilate Gallio dismissed the charges: '"Listen, you Jews. If this were a misdemeanour or a crime, I would not hesitate to attend to you; but if it is only quibbles about words and names, and about your own Law, then you must deal with it yourselves – I have no intention of making legal decisions about things like that."'[33]

Returning to Jerusalem, Paul was again arrested and was taken before the Sanhedrin but, claiming his rights as a Roman citizen, he was put under the protection of a Roman tribune, Lysias. Realising that they could not get rid of him by legal means, a group of Jews planned to assassinate him; but the plot was leaked to Lysias who then sent Paul to Caesarea escorted by seventy cavalry and two hundred infantry. There he appeared before the legate Felix together with his accusers – the high priest Ananias with some of the elders and an advocate called Tertullus who charged him with making trouble 'among Jews the world over' and being 'a ringleader of the Nazarene sect'.[34] Paul claimed his right as a Roman citizen to appeal to Caesar, and Felix therefore sent him in chains to Rome.

According to Christian tradition, Paul was eventually beheaded in Rome not as a result of the charges brought by the Jewish leaders but as a victim of the pagan Romans' first persecution of Christians under Nero in the year AD 67. The Roman historian Cornelius Tacitus considered that this first assault upon Christians was not the product of a considered policy of the imperial government but a whim of the Emperor Nero. After the fire which in July 64 had burned a large part of the city of Rome, Nero deflected the suspicion that he himself had started the fire by blaming the adherents of this troublesome sect. The initial execution of suspects was followed by a general round-up of Christians who were then put to death in a variety of refined ways: men were nailed to crosses, doused with pitch and set on fire, or wrapped in the skins of animals to be torn apart and devoured by dogs.

Although Tacitus thought that Nero's cruelty went too far, and in fact provoked compassion in the citizenry, he had no doubt that the Christians merited 'extreme and exemplary punishment' because of their 'hatred of humanity'. Their disdain for the material world, their refusal to bear arms or to take part in either the major or minor pagan rituals that were an integral part of Roman life, the secret meetings and obscure ceremonies where they 'ate' their god and, above all, their confidence that their pagan neighbours were destined to eternal torment while they would inherit eternal bliss, had a similar effect on the Romans as the aloofness of the Jews.

The Jews, however, were a known quantity, and they were seen as a nation, not a sect. Once the revolt in Palestine had been suppressed, the special privileges previously held by the Jews – the right to worship in their synagogues, to circumcise their male children, to rest on the Sabbath – were restored. The exclusiveness of Christians, on the other hand, was seen not just as offensive but as seditious; and, consequently, over the next two-

and-a-half centuries they were intermittently suppressed. 'Whatever may be the principle of their conduct,' wrote Pliny the Younger, 'their inflexible obstinacy appeared deserving of punishment.'[35] As a result, in his capacity as an official of the imperial government, Pliny, whose writings show him to be a kind, cultivated and magnanimous man, ordered the execution of those who professed the Christian religion.

'The more you mow us down the more we grow,' wrote Tertullian, a Christian writer of the second century, 'the seed is the blood of Christians.' Although there were certainly a number of apostates who, when faced with a choice between being torn to pieces by lions and tigers in the arena or sprinkling a handful of incense on an altar in honour of Zeus, chose the latter, the sustained persecution of Christians did not prevent the growth of the Church. Far from shunning martyrdom, many of them embraced it as an imitation of the suffering of Christ. Ignatius, the third Bishop of Antioch, when arrested, forbade his followers to do anything to save him and implored the Romans to throw him to the lions. 'Encourage the beasts to become my sepulchre, leaving no part of me behind.' Polycarp, the Bishop of Smyrna, was more judicious but equally inflexible when given the choice between worshipping Caesar and being burned to death. 'The fire burns for an hour, and is speedily quenched,' he said to the Roman governor Titus Quadratus, 'but you know nothing of the fire of the coming Judgement and the eternal punishment reserved for the wicked,' after which Quadratus passed sentence and 'the crowds rushed to collect logs and faggots from workshops and public baths, the Jews as usual joining in with more enthusiasm than anyone.'[36]

Such atrocities were repeated in all corners of the Empire. In Phrygia (in Asia Minor) a small town was surrounded by legionaries:

who then set it on fire and completely destroyed it, along with the entire population – men, women, and children – as they called on Almighty God. And why? Because all the inhabitants of the town without exception – the mayor himself and the magistrates, with all the officials and the whole populace – declared themselves Christians and absolutely refused to obey the command to commit idolatry.[37]

The persecution was particularly harsh in two Roman cities on the River Rhône, Vienne and Lyons. First pagan servants were induced to accuse their Christian masters of incestuous and cannibalistic orgies to incite the populace against them; then the most atrocious deaths were inflicted upon those who would not abjure Christ and worship the pagan gods. Not only the leaders of the community such as the bishop Pothinus, but even the meanest, were subjected to torture. In Vienne, a maidservant, Blandina, perhaps rather plain, ('through her Christ proved that things which men regard as mean, unlovely, and contemptible are by God deemed worthy of great glory') was so resilient that 'those who took it in turns to subject her to every kind of torture from morning to night were exhausted by their efforts and confessed themselves beaten – they could think of nothing else to do to her'. Finally 'after the whips, after the beasts, after the griddle, she was finally dropped into a basket and thrown to a bull'.[38]

In the nineteenth century Friedrich Nietzsche was to denigrate Christianity for its appeal to servants like Blandina, and above all to the enormous number of slaves to whom its assurance of spiritual parity made up for their lack of civic worth. However, Christianity was not limited to the uneducated; it spread to the families of senators and even the emperors themselves. Formidable philosophers and scholars such as Justin, Origen, Tertullian and Clement of Alexandria not only embraced Christianity but, in their own writing, deepened the Church's understanding of Christian belief. Origen purged the scriptures of the apocryphal Gospels and established the authenticity of the New Testament as we know it today. Apollonius, described by Eusebius as 'one of the most distinguished for learning and philosophy of the Christians of the time', was given a hearing before the Roman Senate which nevertheless condemned him to be beheaded because no other verdict was possible under the statute: 'It is unlawful for a Christian to exist.'

Before his arrest, Apollonius had been vigorous in refuting the heresy of a certain Montanus who denied that the Church had the authority to absolve penitents of serious sins. This heresy was just one among many which from its earliest days and throughout its history were to bedevil the Christian Church. The apostle Peter himself had warned that, 'As there were false prophets in the past history of our people, so you too will have your false teachers, who will insinuate their own disruptive views ...';[39] and Paul of Tarsus condemned the Gnostics and Docetics in his Epistle to the Colossians. Ignatius of Antioch used the word heretic as a term of bitter reproach. Tertullian who, ironically, was later to join the Montanists, defined a heretic as one who puts his own judgement above that of the Church, either founding a sect or joining one that deviates in its teaching from the doctrines which the apostles received from Christ.

To refute false teaching, the successors to the apostles held councils – the first in Jerusalem in AD 51, another in Asia Minor fifty years later. Each of these 'bishops' also had authority within his own community, with pre-eminence given to those in the major cities of the Empire such as Jerusalem, Antioch, Alexandria and Rome, the patriarchs of the nascent religion. A first among equals among these bishops and patriarchs emerged in the successor to Peter, the leader of the apostles, who had presided over the Christian community in Rome. Clement, who is thought to have been consecrated bishop by Peter, wrote in the year 96 to resolve a dispute in the Church in Corinth. Victor, Bishop of Rome towards the end of the second century, ruled on the date for the celebration of Easter and excommunicated a leather-seller called Theodotus who taught that Jesus had been a mere man.

Victor is also the first bishop known to have had dealings with the Emperor's household: he supplied Marcia, the Christian mistress of the Emperor Commodus, with a list of Christians condemned to the mines of Sardinia and secured their release. Commodus, the son of Marcus Aurelius, though an unsatisfactory ruler, tolerated Christians because of the influence of Marcia. Persecution was resumed under his successor, Septimius Severus. It was sporadic, depending upon the view of the current Emperor: some of the most sagacious and enlightened, like the Antonine emperors and Marcus Aurelius, were rigorous in their suppression of Christians. Persecution became severe under the emperors Maximin, Decius and above all Diocletian who in 303 embarked upon what came to be called 'The Great Persecution' which only ceased when Diocletian abdicated and retired to his palace at Split on the Dalmatian coast.

Before his retirement, Diocletian, deciding that the Roman Empire was too large to be governed by one man, had appointed four to a ruling body or tetrarchy, one of them Constantius Chlorus. Chlorus was assigned the northern quarter of the Empire which included Britain and Gaul. When Diocletian abdicated in 305, Chlorus became the senior Caesar in the west but died a year later in York. His son Constantine was proclaimed emperor by the legions in Britain and, after a series of victories over rival claimants, established his rule over the whole Empire.

Constantine believed that he had come to power with the help of the Christians' God. On the eve of the critical battle against the rival Emperor Maxentius at the Milvian Bridge outside Rome, he had been told in a dream (or possibly a vision) to paint a Christian monogram on the shields of his soldiers: 'In this sign conquer'. Persecution had been lax under his father Chlorus in the western provinces: now it ceased altogether throughout the Empire. Under the Edict of Milan in 313, all penal edicts against Christians were rescinded; Christian captives were released and their property was restored. But Constantine's policy towards the Christians went beyond toleration. Bishops were made his counsellors and were allowed to use the imperial postal service, an invaluable privilege at a time when overland travel was both dangerous and expensive. A law of 333 ordered imperial officials to enforce the decisions of bishops, and to accept the testimony of bishops over other witnesses. Constantine donated the imperial property of the Lateran to the Bishop of Rome as a site for a basilica and he promulgated laws giving the Christian clergy fiscal privileges and legal immunities 'for when they are free to render supreme service to the Divinity, it is evident that they confer great benefit upon the affairs of state'. He enjoyed the company of Christian bishops, called them his brothers, entertained them at court and, when they had been scourged and mutilated in past persecutions, reverently kissed their scars.

Like Herod, Constantine suffered from tragedy in his immediate family. His second wife Fausta accused Crispus, his son by his first wife, of making improper advances. Crispus was executed before Helena, Constantine's mother, was able to prove to the Emperor that the charges were false. Fausta was then suffocated in a superheated bath.

In the wake of this tragedy, Helena – converted to Christianity by Constantine – set out on a penitential journey to Palestine. There Constantine had ordered the demolition of the temples and the construction of churches over the sites of Christ's nativity in Bethlehem, his crucifixion in Jerusalem, and the tomb from which he had risen from the dead. In the course of the excavations, there was uncovered the timber of a cross bearing the inscription 'Jesus of Nazareth King of the Jews'. Whether or not this was what it purported to be, or a forgery passed off on a gullible old woman, it was accepted by Helena and faithful Christians as the supreme relic of their

Salvation; and, upon its completion, was placed in the church built over the Holy Sepulchre in Jerusalem.

The conversion of Constantine was of momentous consequence for Christianity. Equally significant for the future of the Empire was his decision to move its capital from Rome to Byzantium on the Bosphorus. It had been clear for some time that Rome was poorly placed as a strategic centre for a state whose most vulnerable frontiers and most prosperous provinces lay in the east. The emperors had become first and foremost military commanders, no longer dependent either for their power or for their legitimacy on the Senate and people of Rome. Byzantium, with its strategic position between Europe and Asia, the Black Sea and the Mediterranean, and its natural harbour known as the Golden Horn, was ideally suited to this role. Within three weeks of his victory over Licinius, one of his rivals, at nearby Chrysopolis in 324, Constantine laid the foundations of this 'new Rome'. The city, already enlarged by one of his predecessors, Septimius Severus, was tripled in size, endowed with magnificent public buildings such as the Hippodrome, begun under Severus, an imperial palace, public baths and halls, and streets adorned with numerous statues taken from other cities. Full citizenship and free bread were offered as an inducement to settlers: there was a policy of tolerance towards pagans and Jews.

Renamed Constantinople after its founder, the city became a centre for his favoured religion. A number of great churches were built by the Emperor, and in 381 it became the seat of a patriarch who joined those of Rome, Antioch, Alexandra and later Jerusalem. Many early Councils of the Church were called by Constantine to meet in Constantinople, or nearby cities such as Nicaea and Chalcedon.

The ascendancy of Christianity was not yet assured. During the reign of Constantine's nephew, Julian, later known as 'the apostate', paganism was reinstated and the Church subjected to a form of renewed persecution. Significantly, one of the measures initiated by Julian to antagonise the Christians, whom he called 'the Galileans', was the rebuilding of the Temple in Jerusalem; but natural calamities hampered the project (considered miraculous interventions by the Christians) and it was abandoned upon the death of the Emperor in 363.

Julian was the last of the pagan emperors. Under his successor, Jovian, the Church was restored to the privileged position it had enjoyed under Constantine. and became as intolerant of paganism as paganism had been of Christianity. Already, under Constantine's son Constantius, the pagan temples had been closed and sacrifices to the pagan gods forbidden under pain of death. Now the prohibition was made absolute, and pagan ceremonies continued only in secret, frequently in the guise of carnivals or seasonal celebrations. The old temples were abandoned and became derelict or were destroyed.

The same intolerance was shown towards the Jews. Having aided and abetted the pagan persecution of Christians, and welcomed the counter-reformation of Julian the Apostate, they were now subject to oppression by imperial statutes and harassment by Christian mobs. The Emperor Theodosius, one of the last to rule an undivided empire, issued a decree in 380 prescribing the Nicene Creed as binding on all subjects. This was directed as much against heretical Christians as against pagans and Jews, but it encouraged excesses among Christian zealots. In 388, in Callinicum on the River Euphrates, the Jewish synagogue was burned down by a Christian mob. Theodosius ordered it rebuilt at Christian expense but was persuaded by Ambrose, the Archbishop of Milan, to rescind the command. 'What is more important?' the prelate asked the Emperor. 'The parade of discipline or the cause of religion?'[40] A further demonstration of the kind of power now exercised by bishops came two years later when a punitive massacre in Thessalonika ordered by Theodosius was condemned by a Church Council at Ambrose's instigation, and the Emperor was only readmitted to communion after public penance.

Ambrose, the Archbishop of Milan, shows how while Rome became Christian, Christianity became Roman, adopting a system of administration and a body of law like those of the Empire, and employing the same personnel. Ambrose was the son of a Roman prefect and a member of the senatorial class. He had been educated at Rome and employed as an imperial civil servant, around 371 serving as governor of the provinces of Aemilia and Liguria whose administrative headquarters was then Milan. Mediating in his official capacity in a disputed episcopal election in 373, he was unexpectedly chosen by popular acclamation to be bishop himself. Although his family was Christian, he had not yet been baptized. He was received into the Church on 24 November and ordained priest and consecrated bishop on 1 December.

It was the sermons of Ambrose, delivered in Milan, that persuaded a young teacher of rhetoric in the city, Augustine, to become a Christian. The son of a pagan father and a Christian mother, both of Berber extraction, Augustine had lived in North Africa until moving to Milan. The salient features of his youth were intellectual curiosity and sexual licence. At one time believing in Manichaeism, the belief that God and the Devil are equal powers, God the creator of spirit, the Devil of matter, and later a Neoplatonist, Augustine was persuaded by Ambrose of the truth of Christian teaching. But he was ambitious and had a powerful sexual drive. He gave up his mistress of long standing, by whom he had had a son, for the prospect of an advantageous marriage; and while waiting for his future bride to come of age, he had affairs with a number of other women. His love of women had always been an impediment to his conversion. As an adolescent he had prayed to God: 'Grant me chastity and continence, but not yet.' He had been afraid that God might grant his prayer too quickly – 'that you might too rapidly heal me of the disease of lust which I preferred to satisfy rather than suppress'.[41] Now in his early thirties, Augustine's 'old loves' held him back. He was in a state of paralysing indecision until one afternoon, in the garden of his lodging, he heard an ethereal voice ('it might be of a boy or a girl') chanting, 'take and read, take and read'. He opened a book of the epistles of Paul of Tarsus at random, and his eyes fell on Paul's Letter to the Romans: 'Let us live decently as people do in the daytime: no drunken orgies, no promiscuity or licentiousness, and no wrangling or jealousy. Let your armour be the Lord Jesus Christ; forget about satisfying your bodies with all their cravings.'[42]

Augustine was baptized by Ambrose in 387 and returned to North Africa where he became a priest. At first he lived in a secluded community but after five years was made Bishop of Hippo. The remaining thirty-five years of his life were spent fulfilling his duties as a diocesan bishop and writing works of supreme importance for the future of the Church. As we shall see when we come to the founding of the Templars, it was the rule established by Augustine for his community of Christians that the Order initially adopted; and it was Augustine's theory of a just war that was used to defend the crusades.

There are two further developments notable in the time of Ambrose and Augustine that were to shape Europe in the Middle Ages. The first was the division of the Roman Empire into two. The eastern half became the Byzantine Empire and in time abandoned the use of Latin for Greek. The western half was ruled notionally from Rome, but at times from Milan or Ravenna. The line of demarcation was the Adriatic Sea, and a line through modern Yugoslavia which remains problematic to this day.

Both empires were constantly at war with the tribes and peoples beyond their borders – in Asia the Persians, in Europe across the Danube and the Rhine, the barbarian tribes of Sarmatians, Ostrogoths, Visigoths, Franks, Burgundians, Alamanni, Quadi, Vandals and behind them, pushing forward for unknown reasons from the steppes, the ferocious tribe of Huns.

The line could not be held but what came to be described as the 'Fall' of the Roman empire was not a single dramatic defeat or even a sequence of defeats of imperial armies followed by a systematic colonisation by the barbarian victors. 'These invasions were not perpetual, destructive raids; still less were they organised campaigns of conquest. Rather they were a "gold rush" of immigrants from the underdeveloped countries of the north into the rich lands of the Mediterranean.'[43]

Some tribes, such as the Franks and Alamanni, had already been permitted to settle within the frontiers of the empire in north eastern Gaul; and the Ostrogoths and Greutingi, pushed west by the Huns, were allowed to move into Thrace. So-called 'barbarians' came to be recruited into the Roman army and even to command it. A half Vandal, Stilicho, married the niece of the emperor Theodosius and took charge of the Empire after Theodosius's death. But it was a time of violence, confusion and disorder when fearful and frequently hungry hordes ranged around Europe in search of security and food. In 406, the Vandals and Sueves, followed by the Burgundians and Alamanni, fled from the advancing Huns across the frozen River Rhine and entered Gaul. In 407, the Romans withdrew their legions from Britain, leaving the Britons to defend themselves against the Picts and Scots in the north, and piratical raids on the eastern coast by Angles, Saxons and Jutes. In 410 Alaric and his Visigoths captured and sacked Rome, then moved back north along the coast of the Mediterranean to settle in south-western France and later in Spain. In 429, 80,000 Vandals swept through Spain and over the Straits of Gibraltar into the Roman provinces of North Africa: Augustine died in 430 while they were besieging his city of Hippo.

Attempts were made, particularly by the Roman general Aetius, to bring some order into the settlement of the barbarian tribes. There were some transitory triumphs: Aetius defeated an army of Huns under Attila which then moved south into Italy, sacking cities on the plain of the Po, and only holding back from an attack on Rome in return for tribute paid by the Pope. But after the death of Aetius, the western Roman emperors were mere figureheads, real power lying in the hands of Germanic tribal chiefs. One of these, Odoacer, deposed the last Emperor, Romulus Augustus, and ruled Italy as a barbarian king. Notionally, he did so as regent for the eastern emperor in Constantinople but in reality the western Roman Empire as a distinctive political entity had come to an end.

However, this did not mean 'the disappearance of a civilisation: it was merely the breaking down of a governmental apparatus that could no longer be sustained'.[44] The barbarians, who remained minorities in the lands they conquered, felt no antagonism to the empire and the idea of abolishing it never crossed their mind: 'the conception of that empire was too universal, too august, too enduring. It was everywhere around them, and they could remember no time when it had not been so'.[45] The social organisation and cultural traditions of the Roman Empire survived the demise of the single centralised administration in the counties, as duchies and kingdoms started to take shape – the Ostrogothic principality in Italy; a Visigothic state in Spain and in Gaul as far as the Loire; and further north, the kingdom of the Salian Franks. By the end of the fifth century, the Franks under their king Clovis had become the dominant power north of the Alps. After defeating the Alamanni and the Visigoths, Frankish dominion was established between the Rhine and the Pyrenees. Around 498, Clovis became a Christian together with all his barons: it was said that he had witnessed a miracle at the tomb of Martin of Tours.

The baptism of Clovis, like the conversion of Constantine, was of momentous significance for the future of the Christian Church. However, the portions which each party now brought to this marriage between the secular and spiritual were very different from what they had been a century-and-a-half before. Clovis was not the chief executive of a huge, well-regulated state but the leader of a horde of ferocious, uneducated fighting men. He could not give the bishops, as Constantine had done, lavish endowments, fiscal privileges and the perquisites of senior civil servants.

All he could offer was the souls of his savage people, and a commitment to protect the universal or 'Catholic' Church.

The Church, on the other hand, had much to offer the barbarian chieftain, having an intact organisation modelled on that of the Roman state. At the apex of the hierarchy was the Patriarch of the West, the Bishop of Rome, now called the Pope from the Greek *pappas*, meaning father, with cardinals as the departmental heads of his administration. Below him, in what remained of the larger cities of the ruined Empire, were the archbishops; and in most towns of any stature, a bishop with a corps of literate deacons and priests. The Church was also rich, having been generously endowed with large landholdings by Christian emperors: it was therefore able, following the collapse of both commerce and legality, to see to the material as well as the moral well-being of the people under its care. With the collapse of the political and administrative institutions of the Roman world, the episcopate became the sole moral force, and, thanks to its landed possessions, the sole economic resource that remained for the people. The bishop replaced the state as the provider of public services, feeding the poor, ransoming captives and seeing to the welfare of the imprisoned. Hospices, hospitals, orphanages, even inns, were annexes of the churches and the monasteries.

The Church took on more than the functions of the defunct Empire; it *was* the Roman Empire in the minds of the people. To be a Roman was to be a Christian: to be a Christian was to be a Roman. After Justinian, 'the Mediterranean world came to consider itself no longer as a society in which Christianity was merely the dominant religion, but as a totally Christian society. The pagans disappeared in the upper classes and even in the countryside ... the non-Christian found himself an outlaw in a unified state'.[46]

In a real and self-conscious sense, the bishops of the Catholic Church took on the mantle of the Roman senatorial class: this was 'the basic assumption behind the rhetoric and ceremonial of the medieval papacy'.[47] Already, from the earliest days of the Christian Church, the Bishop of Rome had claimed an ascendancy in spiritual matters not merely as Patriarch of the West, but as the successor of Peter to whom Christ himself had given the keys to the kingdom of heaven, and the power to 'bind and loose', viz. define what was true and what was false; and by the time of the barbarian invasions, Roman jurisdiction was accepted in all the diocese of the western empire. Now to the Pope's spiritual supremacy was added, in the absence of an emperor, the authority of the chief magistrate of the city of Rome.

Although for some time the city had been in decline, it remained by far the largest and most populous city in the west. Some of the majestic buildings and splendid monuments had been stripped by its inhabitants for building materials, but much remained of its glorious past. Its people were conservative; the old senatorial families were still pre-eminent; and pagan influences remained strong. When Alaric and his Visigoths threatened to attack the city in 408, the Prefect and Senate proposed sacrifices to the pagan gods.

Their invocations failed; but then so too did the diplomatic initiative of Pope Innocent I. The Visigoths under Alaric captured and plundered Rome. However, almost fifty years later Pope Leo I went to Mantua where he successfully persuaded Attila, the leader of the Huns, to stay away from Rome. In 455, he met Gaiseric, the leader of the Vandals, outside the walls of the city; and while he failed to prevent them from plundering the city, they desisted at his request from harming the people.

More than a hundred years after this, another pope, Gregory, who like Leo was to earn the appellation of 'the Great', faced a Lombard invasion and made himself responsible for the welfare of the citizens of Rome. Coming from a rich and aristocratic family, and related to two previous popes, Gregory not only used his own resources to mitigate the suffering of the poor, but he appointed rectors to maximise receipts from the 'patrimony of St Peter' – large estates all over Europe that belonged to the papacy. In 593, when the Lombard King Agilulf besieged the city, Gregory took command of the garrison and bribed the Lombards to leave.

In the absence of any effective secular authority, Gregory became the *de facto* ruler of Italy. He raised troops, appointed generals and made treaties. This was not perceived as a radical departure from tradition. 'In Gregory's time, the distinction later drawn between spiritual and secular matters was not clear: men had never thought of political authority being divorced from a religious basis.'[48] He was equally zealous in pursuing the well-being of the Church, imposing celibacy on the clergy and a strict code for the election of bishops. He was tolerant towards the Jews: in 599 he ordered restitution after the desecration of a synagogue in Caraglio in northern Italy, and he reprimanded the bishops of Arles and Marseilles for allowing the compulsory baptism of Jews in their diocese. Like Leo before him, he insisted upon the universal authority of the Bishop of Rome, fought against heresy, and was said to have been moved by the sight of blond pagan Angles being sold as slaves in Rome to dispatch Augustine and a band of forty Benedictine monks to preach the Gospel in their homeland.

Gregory the Great was the first pope who was a monk; and the growth of monasticism is the second development in the history of the Christian Church that affects our understanding of the Templars. The word 'monk' comes from the Greek *monos* meaning 'alone' or 'solitary'. It was not used by Christians until the fourth century because until the middle of the third Christian monks were unknown. The early Church was mostly found in the cities and, to judge from the Acts of the Apostles, its members held their goods in common. 'We share everything,' Tertullian wrote, 'except our wives.'

However, not all men and women among the early Christians married. From the first, virginity was esteemed as a mark of total dedication to God. Paul of Tarsus, who is generally credited with a dislike of women, thought it was good to marry but better to remain celibate: he expected an imminent end to the world and therefore saw marriage as a pointless distraction. He also pointed out that those who were married must consider the well-being of their spouses while those who were unmarried could dedicate themselves wholly to God. An unprejudiced reading of his epistles suggests that he was neither as puritanical nor as misogynistic as he is usually portrayed. In the context of sexual relations, he enjoined husbands and wives to give to one another what they had the right to expect. Though initially ruling that widows should not remarry, he later reversed his judgement saying that it is better to marry than to live tormented by sexual desire ('better to marry than to burn').

Yet it seems certain that Paul and the early Christians considered marriage an impediment to perfection. This esteem for celibacy, though possibly found in the Essene sects, was a departure from the Jewish teaching that men and women should obey God's command in the Book of Genesis to 'be fruitful, multiply, fill the earth and conquer it'; but it came from the advice of Christ himself when he commended 'eunuchs who have made themselves that way for the sake of the kingdom of heaven', adding 'Let anyone accept this who can.'[49] This led to a cult of virginity in the early Church which sometimes went too far; the young Origen in the third century was censured for putting a literal interpretation on what Christ had said, a self-mutilation which he later regretted.

Eusebius, in his history, describes with approval how young Christian women, during periods of persecution, preferred death to dishonour. Dominina and her two daughters, 'in the full flower of their girlish charm', apprehended as Christians and sent under escort to Antioch, 'when they had travelled half way ... modestly requested the guards to excuse them a moment, and threw themselves into the river that flowed by'.[50]

The canon of saints has many such 'virgins and martyrs' from this period, but there were as yet no nuns or monks. Living as a Christian, and being ready to die for your beliefs, was considered enough. It was only after the conversion of Constantine, and the transformation of the Church from a persecuted sect into a rich and privileged institution that it became advantageous to be Christian, and possible to practise that religion with a minimal zeal. Among the majority of Christians, standards of piety declined; but there remained a small number who retained the fervent spirit of the early Church and sought to escape from the material and political preoccupations of the world. The growing wealth of the Church seemed to contradict Christ's recommendation to the rich young man: 'Sell all that you own and distribute the money to the poor.' And subsequently: 'How hard it is for those who have riches to make their way into the kingdom of God.'[51]

The first instances of Christians taking Christ at his word are found in Upper Egypt – first Paul, who at the age of fifteen, to escape from the persecution under the Emperor Decius, went to live in a cave close to a palm tree and a spring of water. He remained there for the next ninety years without any human company until he was found by a fellow hermit, Antony, shortly before he died. Antony, a young man from Hieracleus, also in Upper Egypt, on the death of his parents around 273, made provision for his sister's education, then sold all his remaining property and gave the proceeds to the poor. He too went to live in a cave in the nearby desert, existing on bread and water which he consumed only once a day. A number of admirers joined him and he eventually founded two monasteries for which he drew up a rule of life. His fame was such that the Emperor Constantine asked for his prayers while Athanasius, the Bishop of Alexandria, wrote an account of his life.

Antony's example was infectious. The decades following his death saw a veritable exodus into the desert of men seeking to come close to God by living alone in remote places, in caves, makeshift huts or abandoned buildings, eating only enough for bare survival, inflicting upon themselves severe penances, and devoting their waking life to prayer. At first, these hermits would only gather to hear Mass and receive advice from older hermits; but subsequently communities were formed which accepted the rule of a chosen leader or 'father'. Pachomius, who lived from AD 286–346, headed a group which added the vow of obedience to poverty and chastity and drew up a penal code for transgressions. He is deemed the first abbot, the word coming from *abba*, the Hebrew for father.

The example of the Egyptian hermits was followed in Syria and Palestine. In Syria, some chained themselves to the rock walls of their caves, or lived in the open air unprotected from the elements. Their reputation for sanctity attracted crowds of followers seeking their prayers and advice. To escape them, they would retreat yet further into the desert or, in the case of Simeon the Stylite, escape vertically by living on a platform on top of a pillar built to the height of sixty feet. From here could be heard not the ravings of a fanatic but words of sympathy and common sense. The Emperor Marcian visited him incognito, and under Simeon's influence the Empress Eudoxia ceased to support the heretical Monophysites and returned to orthodox belief.

Jerome, a Roman scholar who translated the Bible into Latin and served as secretary to Pope Damasus, lived among the hermits in the desert east of Antioch. Basil, coming from a rich and distinguished family in Cappadocia in Asia Minor, travelled throughout Egypt, Syria and Palestine to visit the numerous communities before returning to found his own monastery on his family estate at Annesi on the River Iris close to a community of nuns already established by his sister Macrina. He rejected the individual feats of asceticism of the hermit in favour of a communal life where prayer was mixed with physical labour and works of charity: an orphanage and workshop for the unemployed were attached to his monastery. Although he wrote no Rule, Basil is regarded as the founder of monasticism in the Eastern Church.

The monastic movement spread to the West. John Cassian, a monk first in Bethlehem and later in Egypt, was sent by the Patriarch of Constantinople on a mission to Rome and thereafter remained in the West, settling in Marseilles. He founded two monasteries, one on the Ile de Lérins, and wrote two works on monastic life, *Institutes* and *Conferences*, which were used by the father of Western monasticism, Benedict of Nursia, in the formulation of his Rule.

Augustine of Hippo, as we have seen, thought that wholehearted conversion to Christianity led inevitably to some form of monastic life but was called out of monastic seclusion to help govern the Church. It was the same with Martin of Tours, the son of an officer in the Roman army and himself a soldier who though born in Hungary was stationed in Amiens in northern France where, after giving half his cloak to a beggar, saw it covering the shoulders of Christ in a vision. Leaving the army around 355/6, Martin lived for a time as a hermit, first on an island off the Italian coast, subsequently in a small community of hermits near Poitiers.

His holiness, and the miracles he was said to have performed, led to his election as the Bishop of Tours. He was consecrated on 4 July 371, despite the objections of some other bishops and the local nobility that he was not a gentleman and looked 'contemptible with dirty clothes and unkempt hair'. Even as a bishop, he lived a form of hermit's life in a monastery that he founded outside Tours. He was assiduous in the suppression of paganism, destroying sanctuaries and chopping down sacred trees. The miraculous powers ascribed to him continued after his death and supposedly led, as we have seen, to the conversion of Clovis. Martin was the first Christian who had died a natural death to inspire the cult of a saint.

However, Martin was the exception, not the rule among the bishops; and the progressive entanglement of the regular clergy with secular affairs in the last years of the Roman Empire together with the savagery that prevailed after the collapse of the Empire in the west, led those of a gentle and pious disposition to form numerous small communities set apart from the world:

> with no interests outside its walls, save that of helping neighbours and travellers, materially and spiritually. Even within the walls there was no specific work. The monks at first were neither priests nor scholars, and there was no elaboration of chant or ritual. They lived together to serve god and save their souls.[52]

This monastic pluralism was changed through the influence of Benedict of Nursia, the most significant figure in the establishment of monasticism in western Europe. He was born around the year 480 into a family of minor gentry living south of Rome in the Sabine Hills. Sent to be educated in Rome, he was so appalled by the dissipation of the Romans that he fled from the city and lived as a hermit in a cave on a mountainside at Subiaco. Soon he was joined by other young men who wanted to share his way of life. Some time between 520 and 530, as a result of an intrigue, he left the community at Subiaco with a group of his supporters and moved to Cassinum where, demolishing a temple to Apollo that he found on the summit of a mountain, he established the monastery of Monte Cassino.

It was here that he wrote his Rule, a code of conduct for his monks that was to set the pattern for religious life in western Europe for the next six hundred years. In composing it, Benedict drew on the experiences of Basil and the works of John Cassian; but the tenor of the work reflects his own remarkable personality. In its judiciousness, it draws on his Roman heritage; in its fervour, on his strong faith. The Rule demonstrates a sound appreciation of the realities of living in a community, and a true understanding of the strengths and weaknesses of human nature. Absolute authority was vested in the abbot, chosen by the community, but in exercising that authority he is enjoined to 'so temper all things that the strong may still have something to long for, and the weak may not draw back in alarm'. The regulations for everyday living govern what the monks should eat and drink and what they should wear. Their habit was black, and could vary in material at the discretion of the abbot according to the climate and season.

The monks' diet was meagre: Benedict insisted upon a perpetual abstinence from meat and he set periods of rigorous fasting. The monks were to sing the divine office – prayers and psalms – at specified moments of the day and night and, when not at prayer or at table or in bed, they were to use their time in studying, teaching and, above all, in manual labour. *Laborare est orare*: to work is to pray. The monks laboured in the fields, making each monastery self-sufficient, and in the scriptorium, copying texts on to vellum, not just the books of the Bible but also the works of classical authors. Every monastery was to have a library, and every monk was to possess a pen and tablets.

Benedict lived in sombre times. The Goths had established a kingdom in Italy and were struggling to defend it from the forces of the eastern Emperor Justinian under his great general Belisarius. In 546, the year before Benedict's death, the Goths captured Rome and left it in ruins: the city was totally deserted for forty days. It was retaken by Belisarius, fell again to the Goths, and its final deliverance by Justinian's army caused such devastation that Gibbon considered it 'the last calamity of the Roman people'. In Benedict's lifetime, Italy had passed from the twilight of the ancient world into the gloom of the Dark Ages; but in that obscurity, the Benedictine monasteries of western Europe 'became centres of light and life ... preserving and later diffusing what remained of ancient culture and spirituality'.[53] In the process, they became an integral part not just of European culture but of the European economy because, while kingdoms were fought over and great estates broken up, the monasteries often remained intact.

Before he died, Benedict was said to have sent one of his monks called Maur to found a monastery at Glanfeuil, near Angers, in France. Benedictine monasteries now grew up alongside the existing foundations of the Celtic missionary Columban in Annegray, Luxeuil and Fontaine in the Vosges which, together with the Abbey of Bobbio in Italy, also founded by Columban, eventually abandoned the rigorous and inflexible code that Columban had brought from Bangor in Ireland in favour of the gentler rule of Saint Benedict.

In 596, as we have seen, Pope Gregory I, himself a Benedictine monk, dispatched Augustine, the Prior of Saint Andrew's in Rome with forty of his Benedictine brethren on a mission to Ethelbert, the pagan King of Kent. In 633, Benedictines went to Spain. In England the Benedictine missionaries made contact with the Celtic Catholics who had been cut off from Rome by the barbarian invasions; and in 664, at the Synod of Whitby, they returned to the Roman fold. There followed a surge of religious enthusiasm in northern England. Benedict Biscop, a warrior-companion of King Oswy of Northumbria, abandoned his military career to become a priest and, after visiting Rome and becoming a monk on the Ile des Lérins, returned to England in 669 to found monasteries at Jarrow and Wearmouth. In 690, an English Benedictine, Willibrord, also a Northumbrian, sailed to what is now the Netherlands to preach to the pagan Frisians. He was followed by Boniface, another English Benedictine, this time from Devon, who preached the Gospel to the heathen tribes in Germany. He was killed by pagan Frisians and is buried at the monastery he founded at Fulda in Hesse.

The achievements of these Benedictine missionaries were secured by the monastic foundations that followed in their wake. In the two centuries after the death of Benedict of Nursia, these changed radically from remote refuges for communities of hermits to large complexes administering extensive estates. In areas such as Burgundy and Bavaria, the monasteries became major civic centres and were often elevated to episcopal sees in which both political and spiritual authority were combined in the monk-bishop. Principalities such as Cologne, Mainz and Würzburg were to be ruled by their bishops until they were secularised by Napoleon in 1802.

The pagans had their martyrs too, and in some instances it was difficult to distinguish conversion from conquest. Following the conversion of Clovis, the Franks had become the champions of the Church and the Church the patron of the Franks. By now a fusion had taken place between the Gallo-Romans and their Frankish conquerors. Mixed marriages had become frequent, and increasingly 'Romans' had changed their Latin names to Frankish ones. By the seventh century there had come into being a 'French' aristocracy described by the historian, Ferdinand Lot, as 'a turbulent, pugnacious and ignorant class, scornful of things of the mind, incapable of rising to any serious political notion and fundamentally selfish and unruly'.[54]

In contrast to the sagacity and dedication of the imperial officials of antiquity, this new ruling class sought only its own aggrandizement and was indifferent to the public good. With the collapse of commerce, land was the only source of wealth and therefore its ownership the sole basis of power. There were customs but no law that could limit the powers of kings. The barbarism of the Franks, described with a certain relish by the chronicler Gregory of Tours, reached its nadir under the Merovingian successors of Clovis when, writes Ferdinand Lot, 'the king wallowed in debauchery and his courtiers imitated him. In the second half of the seventh and in the eighth century it was even worse; the sovereign was literally a vicious degenerate who died young, a victim of his own excess.'[55]

Because of the inadequacy of these Merovingian monarchs, actual power passed into the hands of the kings' first ministers, known as 'mayors of the palace', most notably Charles Martel. His son, Pepin the Short, was encouraged by Pope Zacharias to depose the last Merovingian King, Childeric III, and was crowned King of the Franks at Soissons in November 751 by Boniface, the missionary from Devon, now Archbishop and Papal Legate.

This compact between the Papacy on the one hand, and the Frankish kings on the other, was to remain in force for the next five hundred years. The monasteries, too, benefited from the alliance. The baronial class lived lives steeped in violence, treachery and lust; yet they believed implicitly in Christian teaching and, fearing damnation, endowed communities of monks whose prayers and austerities would atone for their sins. The same sentiment led bishops, compromised by their entanglement in the secular world, to found monasteries in their diocese and grant them privileges and exemptions. 'From the seventh century there was not a single nobleman or bishop who did not wish to ensure the salvation of his soul by a foundation of this kind.'[56] Abbeys such as Saint Germain-des-Prés outside Paris had become enormously rich by the end of the Merovingian period.

And just as the Frankish warriors made use of the monks' prayers, so the monks made the most of the warriors' prowess. The wars waged by the Franks against the Saxons east of the Elbe in the eighth century were not simply to secure their frontier and exact tribute but 'as wars of Christians against barbarians who were also pagans, they had from the outset a religious tinge'.[57] Saxon resistance both to the Franks and to Christianity was more stubborn than had been anticipated, and harsh measures were taken to persuade them of the advantages of submission and conversion. Now for the first time we enter an age 'where monasteries are fortresses and baptism the badge of submission'.[58] In 782, the Franks massacred 4,500 of their Saxon prisoners and deported or enslaved the rest. Three years later, the Saxon King Widukind surrendered and was baptized, an event celebrated by the Pope with three days of thanksgiving.

The King of the Franks who ordered this slaughter was Charles, the grandson of Pepin the Short who, like the popes Leo and Gregory, was to earn the title of the Great. With him, the compact between the kings of the Franks and the popes of Rome reached its fullest fruition. In the year 800, Charles, a prodigy of piety, courage and learning and now master of most of Europe, came to Rome at the head of his army where he was received with ceremony and respect by the man who had ascended the papal throne five years before, Leo III.

For the past three hundred and twenty-four years no emperor had reigned in Rome; and now in Byzantium the throne was deemed vacant because its present incumbent, the Empress Irene, had deposed and blinded her son, Constantine VI, and, more significantly, was a woman. On Christmas Day Charles came to hear Mass at the basilica built over the tomb of Christ's apostle Peter wearing the white robes and sandals of a Roman patrician. As the reading of the Gospel ended, Pope Leo rose from his throne, crossed to the kneeling Frankish chieftain, and placed on his head the imperial crown. From the packed congregation of Romans and Franks, a tumultuous cry arose: 'To Charles Augustus, crowned by God, the great and peace-giving Emperor, long life and victory!' The supreme pontiff bowed in obeisance to the new Caesar. 'From that moment,' writes Sir James Bryce, 'modern history begins.'[59]

three

The Rival Temple

One of the principal reasons why it was thought necessary that Christendom should have a strong leader was the growing menace of a rival religion, Islam. Its origins lay beyond the far south-eastern corner of the Roman Empire where the frontiers were ill-defined and nomadic tribes of pagan Arabs, the descendants of Ishmael, lived according to their own codes and customs beyond the reach of Byzantine jurisdiction. A number had settled in cities on the trade routes of the Arabian peninsula such as Mecca, some of which included communities of Christians and Jews.

The religion of the Arabs has been described as 'tribal humanism'.[60] The meaning of life lay in membership of a tribe possessing the qualities that reflect the Arab's idea of manliness – courage, virility, munificence. Solidarity with other members of one's tribe was all-important, and morality applied only to one's kin.[61] The gods worshipped by the Arabs were stars, idols and sacred stones, in particular a black stone of great antiquity sacred to a deity known simply as Allah – 'the god' – housed in a temple, the Ka'bah, in Mecca. The Quraysh, the most prominent of the settled tribes, controlled Mecca and had successfully established the Ka'bah among all the Arabs as something so sacred that Mecca became a centre for pilgrimage and immune from attack. The pilgrims brought trade while the special status of Mecca protected the Quraysh from the *razzias*, or predatory raids, of other tribes.

Muhammad, the founder of Islam, came from one of the lesser clans forming the tribe of Quraysh. He was born in Mecca around 570. His father died before he was born, and his mother when he was still a child. He was brought up first by his grandfather, the head of his clan; then by his uncle, Abu Talib, whom he accompanied on trading caravans to Syria. There he became familiar with the teachings of both Judaism and Christianity whose

44

one God was already associated in the minds of some Arabs with the Allah of the Ka'bah.

When he was around the age of twenty-five, Muhammad went on a trading mission on behalf of a rich widow called Khadijah, and so impressed her with his honesty and acumen that she proposed marriage. Despite the fifteen years' difference in their ages, Muhammad accepted and thereby acquired the capital to trade on his own behalf. However, he was more than a competent businessman: he showed an interest in religion and would withdraw to a cave in the mountains outside Mecca to meditate and pray to Allah.

One night around AD 610, while engaged in one of these nocturnal meditations, Muhammad fell into a trance and had a vision of an ethereal being whom he later identified as the Angel Gabriel. He heard a voice saying 'You are the messenger of God,' and there began a series of revelations that were to continue until his death. These he memorised and repeated to his followers who wrote them down. Around 650 they were assembled in written form in the Qur'an or Koran. To Muhammad and those who came to believe in him, they were the Word of God.

At first confused by his vision, Muhammad was encouraged by the faith in their veracity of his wife Khadijah and her Christian cousin, Waraqah. Waraqah convinced him that he was the last in the line of the prophets who had spoken to the Jews and Christians. A group of supporters formed around him and in 613 Muhammad started to preach openly the message of uncomplicated monotheism – there was only one God and Muhammad was his prophet.

'The connection between religion and politics ... is an important point to keep in mind in trying to understand the career of Muhammad.'[62] Muhammad was an orphan and, in a society with no patrilineal rights of inheritance, had been without property until he had married Khadijah. He also came from one of the poorer clans within the tribe of the Quraysh and lived at a time when the pursuit of individual interests by the merchants of Mecca was destabilising the old tribal society. Muhammad's denunciation of riches, call for justice and compassion, and his denigrating pagan idols, antagonised the richer merchants. Their inducements to the Prophet to tone down his teaching were rejected.

Until now, Muhammad had been protected from his enemies by the solidarity of his clan; but around 619 his wife Khadijah and his uncle Abu

Talib both died. A second uncle who succeeded Abu Talib as head of the clan was persuaded by the Meccan merchants to withdraw his protection. Muhammad was obliged to leave Mecca, going first to Ta'if and later, at the invitation of its inhabitants, to Medina. This was the emigration, or *hijrah*, of 622 – year 0 of the Muslim era.

Muhammad established his authority in Medina only over a number of years, and then as a result of the raids he organised and later led on the caravans of the merchants of Mecca. At first these were small-scale skirmishes: in April 623, a group of sixty Muslims went to intercept a caravan on its way from Syria to Mecca. One of them shot some arrows at the escort, the first act of aggression on behalf of Islam. In the following year, a force of 800 Meccans moved against Muhammad but was defeated at the Battle of Badr with the loss of 45 killed and 70 taken prisoner. This victory enhanced his authority and prestige. Whether or not, as Muhammad believed, his victory was a proof of God's favour, it persuaded some of the uncommitted to accept Islam. At the same time Muhammad forged links with the indigenous tribes of Medina by marrying a number of wives.

Two of the captives taken at Badr were poets: the supreme cultural achievement of the nomadic Arabs of this period were their oral epics, accounts of the brave deeds of their heroes spoken under the stars. The misfortune of these two particular poets was that they had written verse critical of Muhammad: one had said that his own stories were as good as those in the Koran. They were executed at Muhammad's command. The Jewish clan of Qurayzah was severely punished for conspiring against Muhammad – the men executed, the women and children sold as slaves. Subsequently, in so far as the Jews abandoned their opposition to Islam, Muhammad allowed them to live in Medina unmolested.

In 630, Mecca finally capitulated. Muhammad with ten thousand followers was admitted to the holy temple, the Ka'bah: veneration of the black stone was the only concession he made to the Arabs' ancient beliefs.[63] All other pagan idols were destroyed. Though not all the Meccans embraced Islam, two thousand joined the army that he led against a coalition of hostile nomads and, when it was defeated, shared the booty. The tribes of Arabia were now united under Muhammad and subject to the discipline of Islam; but, since this meant that they could no longer profit from pillaging each other, they were forced to look for plunder and converts elsewhere.

In 630 Muhammad led 30,000 warriors north to secure the submission of the rulers of Eilat, Adhruh and Jarba on the borders of Syria. He realised that 'for its continuing welfare the Islamic state must find an outlet northwards for the energies of the Arabs'[64] and that this meant challenging the Byzantine Empire. He returned to Arabia where, in 632, after leading a pilgrimage to Mecca, he died.

How do we account for the appeal of Muhammad? Unlike Jesus, he performed no miracles. His vision in the year 620, in which he rode on a heavenly steed, el-Buruq, with the Angel Gabriel to the Temple Mount in Jerusalem to meet Abraham, Moses and Jesus, and from there ascended past the seven heavens to the throne of God, is comparable to the account of Christ's transfiguration and was one reason why Jerusalem became a city sacred to Islam; but it 'seems to have been a personal experience for Muhammad himself because it contained no revelation for inclusion in the Koran'.[65]

Rather, Muhammad's success came not from the exercise of a supernatural power over nature but from his adroit appeal to both the spiritual and the material self-interest of the Arabs of his time. Muhammad promised paradise for those who died in battle and plunder for those who did not. When his forces reached a critical mass, it became advantageous for other tribes to join them; and his straightforward monotheism was easy to comprehend. The authority of the Prophet not only ended the incessant feuding of the tribes; it also gave a sense of identity to the Arabs like that already possessed by the Abyssinians, Persians, Byzantine Christians and Jews. Islam was an Arab religion, not, like the other faiths on offer, an import from abroad.

The political stability brought about by Islam had advantages for all: even the Jews and Christians, 'the Peoples of the Book', could secure the Prophet's protection by the payment of a tax. To them, however, the creed of Islam was less appealing. The Jews were scornful of Muhammad's use of their scripture and found the improvisation of the Angel Gabriel self-evidently absurd. Initially Muhammad had told his followers to pray facing Jerusalem; later, after the Jews' rejection of his message, he accused them of falsifying scripture to conceal that the Ka'bah had in fact been built by Abraham and instructed Muslims to pray facing Mecca. To Muhammad,

'Islam was the resurrected uncontaminated religion of Abraham, which the Jews had deserted.'[66]

Christians, too, found it impossible to give credence to revelations that so arbitrarily and naively rewrote history. Most offensive of all was Muhammad's insistence that Jesus was not the son of God; indeed, that it was blasphemous to suggest that God would deign to appear in human form. It was not that he dismissed Christ as a fraud; quite to the contrary, he was a prophet like Abraham and Moses, his mother Mary, a virgin. It was because God so loved the son of Mary that his crucifixion had been an illusion: God would not permit such a painful and ignoble fate.

There were other aspects of Islam that the Christian apologist contrasted unfavourably with his religion. Where Jesus had preached love and non-violence, Muhammad converted with the sword. Where Jesus had blessed the meek and poor in spirit, Muhammad honoured the triumphant warrior. Where Jesus insisted that his kingdom was not of this world, Muhammad founded a theocratic empire. Where Jesus asked his followers to take up their cross and embrace suffering, Muhammad offered booty, concubines and slaves. Jesus promised paradise in an afterlife, Muhammad prosperity in this life *and* paradise in a world to come.

There is no more stark a contrast between the two religions than in their teaching on sexual morality. Jesus insisted upon lifelong monogamy; Muhammad allowed a man to have up to four wives and any number of concubines. Where Jesus had rescinded the Law of Moses and forbade divorce, Muhammad allowed a man to end a marriage with a simple declaration. Jesus esteemed celibacy and was celibate: Muhammad condemned it, and had a Christian concubine and nine wives.

No doubt many of his marriages were of convenience, made to form bonds with hitherto hostile clans. None the less, it shocked his contemporaries that one of Muhammad's wives had been married to his adopted son. Another, A'ishah, he married when he was fifty-three and she was only nine. He had a separate room or small suite built for each of his wives around the courtyard of his house in Medina, and was reputedly proud of his ability to satisfy all his wives on a single night. When one of them became jealous at his dalliance with an Egyptian captive, the Angel Gabriel commanded Muhammad to rebuke her. 'God's interest in detail, and particularly in detail concerning the Prophet's personal life, occasionally bewildered the faithful ... but Allah supported the Prophet and silenced his critics.'[67]

Christian propagandists were to make much of these aspects of Muhammad's life, as well as certain instances of treachery which suggest that, in the cause of Islam, he believed the end justified the means: but it is clear that he was not considered immoral by his contemporaries and in fact raised the ethical standards of the society into which he was born. He enjoined honesty, humility and frugality. He forbade infanticide and insisted on the care of vulnerable members of the community, in particular widows and orphans. He created a family structure and a form of social security that were a major advance on what went before, and made a nation out of the nomadic tribes of Arabia that conquered a vast empire and founded a great civilisation.

The choice of a successor to Muhammad (caliph, from the Arabic *khalifah*) was disputed between different members of his family and was to lead to the division of Islam into the Sunnis, the followers of Abu Bakr, the father of Muhammad's young wife A'ishah; and the Shia, the followers of Ali, the husband of Muhammad's daughter Fatimah. At first Ali and his supporters accepted the election of Abu Bakr and on his death, two years after Muhammad, another of the Prophet's fathers-in-law, Umar. It was Umar who led the Muslims on a triumphant campaign of conquest. Byzantine Syria capitulated in 636 and Iraq in the same year. In 641, Egypt fell to Umar's army and in the following year he was master of Persia.

How was it that the two ancient empires of Persia and Byzantium were unable to resist the onslaught of Islam? Both were enfeebled after a long war against one another and, in the case of Byzantium, against the encircling tribes of barbarians to the north, in particular the Avars. Substantive changes had by now taken place in this, the eastern half of the Roman Empire. The Latin language had been replaced by Greek and, under the Emperor Justinian in the sixth century, a swathe of the Western Empire covering parts of Italy, Sicily and North Africa had been retaken from their barbarian conquerors by Byzantine armies.

It was the prefect, or exarch, of the North African province, Heraclius, who with the gruesome bloodshed that invariably accompanied a Byzantine succession, had mounted the imperial throne in 610. In the first years of his reign, Asia Minor and Palestine were overrun by the Persians. In 614 they captured Jerusalem with the help of the Jews who, in retaliation for their mistreatment by the Byzantines under Justinian, joined the Persians in destroying Christian homes and churches.[68] The relic of the True Cross was removed to Persia as a trophy of war.

In 626 Constantinople itself was besieged by a combined army of Persians and Avars. At this low point in their fortunes, the Christian faith of the Byzantines came to their rescue; for in the course of the sixth and seventh centuries, the alliance of Church and state had become so close that it amounted to a virtual merger. In many parts of the empire, patriarchs, bishops and clergy had taken over the functions of the imperial civil service; and the Emperor, while distinct from the Patriarch, saw himself as head and champion of the Church. 'The key to understanding the Byzantine empire is the notion that the emperor was the divinely appointed instrument of God for the achievement of His purposes on earth through the diffusion of the orthodox . . . Christian faith.'[69]

This profound faith was held by rulers and ruled alike. A sung liturgy and the composition of hymns, together with the depiction of Christ, the Virgin Mary, the Apostles and Saints in striking icons, stimulated a fervour among the populace that was now harnessed by the Emperor Heraclius when pagan Avars and Zoroastrian Persians were at the gates of Constantinople. The Patriarch processed along the walls of the city holding high an icon of Christ; and to deflect the projectiles of the enemy, images of the Virgin and the child Jesus were painted on the walls. The siege was raised and, in a campaign that can legitimately be described as a crusade, the Byzantine armies chased the Persian army back to Nineveh in Mesopotamia where it was finally defeated in 627. In 630, in a triumph worthy of the emperors of antiquity, Heraclius returned the True Cross to Jerusalem.

Yet only eight years later, Jerusalem surrendered to the armies of Islam. After their victory over the Persians, the Byzantine army had been demobilised, and what forces were gathered to resist the Muslim onslaught were defeated at the Battle of the Yarmuk River. But there were also groups who welcomed the invader – the Jews who preferred the relative tolerance extended by the Muslims to the persecution of the Orthodox Christians, but also the majority Monophysite Christians who rejected the Orthodox teaching on the dual nature of Christ, had their own patriarch and hierarchy, and had also been persecuted for their heretical beliefs.

Moreover, in return for the surrender of the city the caliph had guaranteed the lives and property of its Christian inhabitants, and left their churches and shrines intact. True to the precepts of the Prophet, the yoke he imposed on the Peoples of the Book was a light one. If they paid the requisite tax, which was often lower than that hitherto imposed by the Byzantine rulers, the conquered communities were left to follow their own religions and live by their own laws. The Muslim Arabs remained the ruling caste, and were sustained by their subjects' taxes, but they continued to occupy fortresses on the borders of their empire.

This regime was also a reason for the Copts, the Monophysite Church in Egypt, to welcome the Muslim invaders. Alexandria, the Greek-speaking metropolis on the Mediterranean that was the Byzantine capital of the province and seat of an Orthodox patriarch, finally capitulated in 646. From there the Arab armies moved east along the deserts of North Africa. By 714 they had reached Central Asia and northern India in the East; while in the West they had crossed over the Straits of Gibraltar and, welcomed as liberators by the Jews, had overrun most of Visigothic Spain. In 732, under Abd ar-Rahman, they crossed the Pyrenees into France. After sacking Bordeaux and burning its Christian churches, they moved on to Poitiers. Here, outside the city, they met an army of Franks led by Charlemagne's grandfather, mayor of the palace of the Merovingian monarchs, Charles Martel. The Muslims were routed and driven back into Spain.

Although the Battle of Poitiers was to mark the furthermost advance of Islam into western Europe, it did not end its progress to the north and the east. Having secured a naval base at Alexandria, Muslim fleets were sent to blockade Constantinople – first in 669, then between 673 and 677, and again from 717 to 718, and it was only with great difficulty that the Byzantines were able to defeat them. In 846, less than half a century after the crowning of Charlemagne by Pope Leo III, a Muslim expeditionary force of five thousand cavalry and ten thousand infantry landed on the coast of Italy near Ostia, the port that served Rome. The garrison of Ostia fled, and a defending force composed mainly of pilgrims, among them Anglo-Saxons, was massacred when it tried to impede the march on Rome of these 'Saracens', the name now used by the Latins for their Islamic adversaries. On the outskirts of the city, the basilicas of Saint Peter on the Vatican Hill and Saint Paul without the walls were both looted while the Pope, Sergius II, and the Roman people looked on helplessly from behind the Aurelian walls.

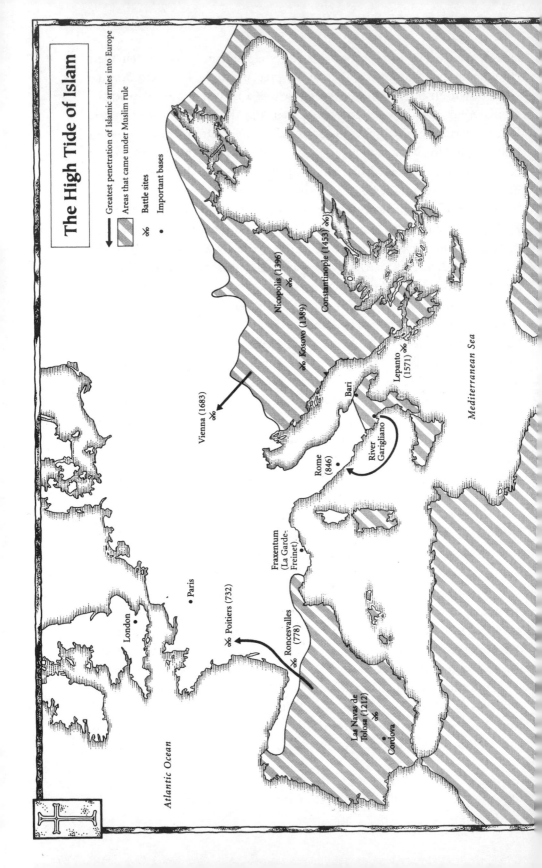

The High Tide of Islam

→ Greatest penetration of Islamic armies into Europe

▨ Areas that came under Muslim rule

⚔ Battle sites

• Important bases

Atlantic Ocean

London •

• Paris

⚔ Poitiers (732)

Roncesvalles
(778) ⚔

Fraxentum
(La Garde-
Freinet) •

Las Navas de
Tolosa (1212) ⚔

Córdova •

Vienna (1683) ⚔

Nicopolis (1396) ⚔

Kosovo (1389) ⚔

Constantinople (1453) ⚔

Lepanto
(1571) ⚔

Bari •

Rome •
(846)

River
Garigliano

Mediterranean Sea

A Saracen base was established at Fraxentum (modern La Garde-Freinet) on the coast of Provence from which marauders threatened the Alpine passes and raided Christian cities on the Mediterranean coast. Bari, on the coast of the Adriatic, was taken by the Saracens and became the seat of an emirate, and in the middle years of the ninth century they gained control of Sicily, culminating in the fall of Syracuse in 878.

By this time the Islamic family or *ummah* had fragmented into different sects, notably the majority Sunnis and the minority Shia – and by the end of the tenth century there were three different caliphates named after the families of their founders: the Abbasids in Baghdad, the Fatimids in Damascus and Cairo; and the Umayyads in Cordova in Spain. The ascendancy of the Arab and Bedouin warrior caste had given way to a more heterogeneous elite.

> Imperceptibly, Arabic civilisation became Muslim civilisation, and it is the spontaneous collaboration of the best minds of all the Empire's nationalities that accounts for the stupendous rise of this civilisation in those two hundred years, from 750–950, so breathlessly crowded with cultural exploits in the most disparate areas of human accomplishment.[70]

The one enduring mark of Islam's origins was the adoption of the Arabic language in the conquered lands. In Syria and Palestine, Arabic gradually replaced Greek as the official language in the course of the seventh century, and by around 800 was in common use, with Greek or Aramaic spoken only in parts of the north and Hebrew in parts of the south.[71] Although a basic tolerance of 'the Peoples of the Book' remained a principle of Islamic governance, it did not ensure equal treatment before the Law, or the right to participate on equal terms in the civic life of the community. The early bias in favour of Christians as against Jews slowly altered so that, for example, the Caliph al-Mutawakkil who reigned between 847 and 851 expressed his dislike of Christians by making them 'bind bandlets of wool around their heads ... and if any man among them had a slave, he was to sew two strips of cloth of different colours on his tunic from the front and from behind'.[72] On occasions, the persecution was more extreme. Gibbon records how in southern Italy 'it was the amusement of the Saracens to profane, as well as to pillage, the monasteries and churches'; and how, at the siege of Salerno, 'a Musulman chief spread his couch at the communion table and on the altar sacrificed each night the virginity of a Christian nun'.[73]

Christian proselytism was forbidden, and a public denunciation of Muhammad was punished by death, but such martyrdom seems only to have come to those who courted it, for example Peter of Capitolias, a hermit from Transjordan, who in 715 was stoned to death for preaching openly against Islam; and the fifty men and women who in Cordova in 850 publicly preached the superior truth of Christianity and suffered the same fate.

Christian pilgrims were allowed to visit the Holy Land and, with occasional lapses by particular rulers, went unmolested. Pilgrims from western Europe would travel to Palestine either by land through the Byzantine Empire, or on the ships of the mercantile republic of Amalfi in southern Italy. The Amalfi merchants built a hospice in Jerusalem for the care of sick pilgrims. Although trade was a mere trickle if compared to the strong flow in the heyday of the Roman Empire, 'velvet and silk from the Orient were ... on sale in the markets of Pavia in the 780s; and a hundred years later, at the height of the Viking invasions, the monk Abbo of Fleury was able to pour scorn on those whose manners had been "softened by eastern luxuries, rich attire, Tyrian purple, gems and Antioch leather".[74]

In Jerusalem the Church of the Holy Sepulchre remained in Christian hands. However, a shrine was built to rival the site of Christ's Resurrection, the Dome of the Rock. Already, when he entered Jerusalem on foot (it was the turn of his servant to ride his horse), the Caliph Umar had gone to pray on the Temple Mount, abandoned since Julian the Apostate had attempted to rebuild the Temple, and used by the Byzantine inhabitants to dump their rubbish. To the Muslims, however, the rock was sacred not so much as the 'furthermost Temple' of the Prophet's Night Journey as described in 17:1 of the Koran, in Arabic the *masjid el-aksa*, but as the Temple of the Prophets of Israel. He therefore built the al-Aqsa mosque on the south-western corner of the Temple Mount, and Jerusalem became, with Mecca and Medina, one of the three places of Muslim pilgrimage.

Fifty years later the Umayyad Caliph, Abd al-Malik, decided to build a second mosque over the rock itself upon which Abraham had prepared Isaac for sacrifice, and from which Muhammad had ascended to heaven. This was the first major shrine built by Islam, and remains one of the architectural wonders of the world. With a mathematical design comparable to Diocletian's mausoleum in Dalmatia, and following the same principles used in the construction of some sixth-century churches in Ravenna, it was decorated by Christian Syrian craftsmen with a splendour that was to overawe those who saw it, and impress upon Jews and Christians that their faiths had been superseded by Islam. Because the Prophet had condemned the depiction of living things as idolatrous, vegetation and geometric motifs form the rich background to the mosaic representation of the imperial jewels of Byzantine rulers and the ornaments worn in Christian images of Christ.

These symbols of another faith are there as the trophies of a triumphant Islam: and to bring home the message to anyone who might have missed it, there is an inscription which states:

> Oh you people of the Book, overstep not bounds in your religion, and of God speak only the truth. The Messiah, Jesus, son of Mary, is only an apostle of God, and his Word which he conveyed into Mary, and a Spirit proceeding from him. Believe therefore in God and his apostles, and say not Three. It will be better for you. God is only one God. Far be it from his glory that he should have a son.

As Jerome Murphy-O'Connor writes in quoting this inscription in his invaluable guide to the Holy Land. 'An invitation to abandon belief in the Trinity and in the divine Sonship of Christ could hardly be put more clearly.'[75]

four

The Temple Regained

On the Iberian Peninsula, the Muslim conquest was no sooner completed than the Christian counter-attack or *Reconquista* began. Visigothic nobles who had retreated into the mountains of Asturias joined forces with the native inhabitants to resist the invaders, and around 722, ten years before the rout of the Muslim army at Poitiers by Charles Martel, they defeated an Islamic force at Covadonga under their leader Pelayo. They later occupied Galicia in the north-western corner of the peninsula and established a frontier along the Douro river between Christian and Muslim Spain.

In the west of Spain, the fierce tribe of Basques regained their independence and towards the end of the eighth century Charlemagne's Franks invaded Catalonia, capturing Barcelona in 801. However, the chief additions to Western Christendom in the ninth and tenth centuries came from the defeat and conversion of pagan tribes in northern and eastern Europe – the Saxons, the Avars, the Wendts, the Slavs. Byzantine Christendom also expanded through a mix of conquest and conversion. Though there was as yet no open division between the Byzantine Orthodox and Roman Catholic churches, there was a certain competition for the allegiance of convert kings. The Kingdom of the Rus with its capital in Kiev went to the Patriarch of Constantinople together with Bulgaria and Serbia; Hungary and Poland went to the Pope.

Christianity, despite the missionary efforts of Anskar and Rembert in the ninth century, did not take root in Scandinavia until the tenth. The Vikings, whose piratical raids had all but destroyed Celtic Christianity, were late converts; among the first was Rollo who in 918, with a group of followers, had founded a colony in the valley of the lower Seine with the sanction of the King of France. Because of their provenance they were known as the men of the north – *Nordemann* in German: *Normand* in French.

The menace of Islam was ever present in the minds of the Christian leaders but their martial energies were largely dissipated in fighting one another. In Gaul, under the Merovingian kings, where quarrels among the nobility 'resembled nothing as much as the fighting of wild beasts',[76] the state had been powerless to ensure even the most rudimentary public order. For his own security and that of his family, a man had no alternative but to buy the protection of a powerful neighbour with some form of service, usually as a warrior in his private wars. It was also the only way to protect his land which, with the collapse of commerce and a paid administration, was the sole source of livelihood. The term used for the subordinate's commitment was vassalage, and that for his 'pay' was a benefice, usually a grant of land but sometimes the income of ecclesiastical institutions. The contract was sealed with solemn vows and, while using the language of servitude, became 'a coveted status, a mark of honour, at any rate where direct vassalage to the king was concerned'.[77]

In theory, this feudal system was a pyramid that covered at its base the entirety of Western society. In reality, the position at the apex was disputed between popes and emperors; the link was notional between emperors and kings, and problematic between kings and their barons. The most effective bonds were formed between the great dukes, counts and princes – descendants of the vassals of the Carolingian sovereigns – whose territorial holdings were sufficiently large to sustain an effective force of vassals and therefore remain independent of the state. Their vassals in turn would command the allegiance of lesser knights whose wordly possessions might amount to no more than a horse, a lance, a sword and a shield; but whose descent from the caste of Carolingian warriors ensured membership of the social elite. In theory if not in practice, this allegiance was a matter of choice: however meagre his resources or humble his origin, the knight remained a free man under the law and had the right of trial in a public court.

Some vassals depended entirely upon their liege lord, even for their horse and armour. Others, though they received property as a benefice, might also own land in their own right or as a tenant of an ecclesiastical foundation. Although he might feel great loyalty to the lord whose 'man' he was, and feel honour bound to join in his vendettas, his commitment was not open-ended but was governed by custom and law: for example, his obligation to provide military service was limited to forty days. His allegiance could also shift if either party was unable to fulfil his obligation; knights took service under different princes who could provide them with horses or with pay. The bond between lord and vassal was not necessarily hereditary but tended to become so: intermarriage created a *cousinage* that formed the basis of loyalty to a clan.

Violence was also endemic in the eastern empire and the caliphates of Islam where each succession was usually the occasion for a civil war; but whereas a Byzantine emperor or a caliph could gather into his hands all the reins of power of a unified state, the different principalities that had come into being in the Western Empire would never, after Charlemagne, combine under a single sovereign.

This had grave consequences for the Papacy which, with the dis-integration of Charlemagne's Empire under his quarrelling successors, 'was left defenceless in the snakepit of Italian politics'.[78] The last effective Pope of this period was Nicholas I (858–67). During the hundred years which followed his death, the position of successor to Saint Peter became the disputed gift of powerful Roman families such as the Theophylacts. In 882 John VIII became the first pope to be assassinated – beaten to death by his own entourage. Stephen VI had the corpse of his predecessor but one, Pope Formosus, disinterred and enthroned in his pontifical robes so that he could be condemned for perjury and misuse of his powers. The three fingers of his right hand which he had used to bless his flock were hacked off and his body was thrown into the River Tiber. Shortly afterwards, Stephen was deposed by the supporters of Formosus, incarcerated and subsequently strangled.

The personal depravity of many of these popes did not necessarily mean that they were incompetent in their government of the Church. John X, brought to the throne of Saint Peter by the powerful Theophylact family, organised a coalition of Italian states against the Muslims who had harassed Roman territory for the past sixty years and led the force that after a three-month siege took their stronghold at the mouth of the River Garigliano. Two of the popes appointed by the Roman despot Alberic II (Leo VII and Agapitus II) were sincere and effective reformers. Even John XI, the bastard son of Marozia Theophylact, sanctioned a reform in the Church that is germane to the story of the Templars: he took under the direct protection of the Roman pontiff a community of Benedictine monks from an abbey in Burgundy called Cluny.

Cluny was established in 910 by the Duke of Aquitaine, William the Pious, to atone for the sins of his youth and ensure his salvation in the world to come. The man he chose to lead the community was Berno who came from the Burgundian nobility and was then the abbot of the remote Abbey of Baume. With Berno, the duke chose a fine site for his foundation in the hills to the west of the River Saône.

Over the previous century, Benedictine monasticism had gone into decline. The generous endowments of past generations had made the monasteries rich and therefore vulnerable to the demands of the descendants of their former benefactors. Their revenues were used to provide for the younger sons of the local nobility who, with no religious vocation, would be foisted on the religious communities as priors or abbots. Local bishops, often related to the secular lords, would also exploit these monastic offices to reward their dependants.

To ensure the free election of their abbot, the community of Cluny was placed by Duke William under the direct protection of the Pope in Rome while Berno put through reforms to arrest the decline in monastic practice and restore the rigours of Benedict of Nursia's original Rule. The movement flourished, and a network of subsidiary houses was founded that remained under the direction of the community at Cluny. It was Berno's successor as Abbot of Cluny, Odo, who petitioned the dissolute Pope John XI to extend papal protection to a new monastery at Deols. Odo, like Berno, came from the Frankish nobility and he established the Cluniac tradition of monks who were aristocratic but genuinely humble, shrewd but utterly devout, learned but also simple, and always humorous and cheerful.

Odo's noble birth enabled him to confer easily with popes and princes, and they in turn looked to him. Pope Leo VII invited Odo to Rome where he negotiated a settlement between Alberic II and King Hugh of Italy and initiated reforms of the monastic communities in Rome and the Papal States, among them Benedict of Nursia's first Abbey of Subiaco. He was succeeded by a series of able, holy and long-lived abbots – Aymard, Mayeul, Odilo, Hugh, Pons and Peter the Venerable – who together covered a span of two hundred and eleven years. Like Odo, they became the friends and counsellors of emperors, kings, dukes and popes. In 972 the revered Abbot Mayeul of Cluny was captured as he crossed the Alps by Saracen raiders from their base at Fraxentum in Provence. He was later ransomed but this scandalous act of brigandage provoked a response that finally drove the last Muslims out of France.[79]

The influence of Cluny in the century that followed its foundation was to be immense: of the six popes who were monks between 1073–1119, three were from Cluny; however, it was not the reforming zeal of the Cluniac Benedictines that pulled the papacy out of the mire of corruption but the intervention of German emperors. After Charlemagne's death, the Teutonic principle of equal division among a king's heirs had triumphed over the Roman one of the transmission of an indivisible empire. His heritage had therefore been split into three – France in the west, Germany in the east, and between them a long and narrow middle kingdom stretching from Flanders to Rome which came to be called Lotharingia – in German Lottringen, in French Lorraine – because it was given to his eldest son Lothar who also inherited the imperial crown.

The century which followed the death of Charlemagne saw 'the nadir of order and civilisation',[80] and it was not until the German princes chose the Saxon dukes as their leaders that Pope Leo III's concept of a new Roman *imperium* was revived in a modified form with sovereignty over Germany and parts of Italy vested in a German prince. This 'Holy Roman Empire' was essentially the brainchild of the Duke of Saxony, Otto I or Otto the Great who, having defeated the Magyars, marched across the Alps in 951 to assert his claims over Italy. Having been acknowledged as King of Italy at Pavia, he led his army to the gates of Rome. There, after pledging himself to respect the liberties of the city and protect the Holy See, he ascended the altar of the Church of Saint John Lateran with his queen, Adelheid, and was crowned emperor by the corrupt and youthful Pope, John XII.

This revival of the Roman Empire was not just a political expedient or a picturesque fiction. Western Europe had arrived at an understanding of itself as 'a single society, in a sense in which it was not before, and has not been since'.[81] Although a man's immediate loyalty went to his feudal lord, he defined himself not as an Englishman, a Frenchman or a German but as a Christian whose faith's universal dominion was visible in both Church and state. 'The first lesson of Christianity was love, a love that was to join in one body those whom suspicion and prejudice and pride of race had hitherto kept apart. There was thus formed by the new religion a community of the faithful, a Holy Empire ...' that made 'the names of Roman and Christian convertible'.[82] There could be no national churches because there were as yet no nations: if the unpolitical man of the Middle Ages had been capable of conceptualising his sense of community, he would have said that he lived in a world-state.

Unfortunately, the co-operation of pope and emperor upon which this universal government depended was rarely achieved: and as the Cluniac reformers gained ground within the Church, their determination to emancipate the clergy from the interference of lay powers confronted the authority of the emperors. A complicating factor was the importance attached by the popes in Rome to their standing as secular princes. The legal basis to their claim to a large swathe of central Italy was the supposed 'Donation of Constantine' who in return for a miraculous cure from leprosy at the hands of Pope Silvester I had bequeathed Rome and undefined parts of Italy to the successors of Saint Peter. The document that established this donation was forged in the middle of the eighth century when the Frankish King Pepin had saved Pope Stephen II from the Lombards and confirmed the Donation of Constantine as the Donation of Pepin. Whatever the legality of the forgery, it was accepted as valid by the Franks; and it could be thought that the right of conquest made the Papal States Pepin's to give. However, it was vehemently contested by the eastern Byzantine emperors who, as we have seen, were to reclaim large parts of Italy and rule through their exarchs from Ravenna; and it also came to be disputed by western emperors who regarded themselves as the heirs to the Caesars and, consequently, overall sovereigns of all those territories that had once formed part of the Roman Empire.

As a result of these counter-claims by the eastern and western emperors, the policy of the popes in Rome was always to maintain a balance of power in Italy which enabled them to tip the scales in their favour. But sovereignty over the Papal States was by no means the only difference between the popes and the German emperors. More acute was the power of secular princes to make ecclesiastical appointments within their domains. In theory, an abbot was chosen by his community and a bishop by his diocesan clergy but, as we saw in the case of Martin of Tours, their election was frequently contested. It was not simply a matter of a candidate's spiritual calibre but, more significantly, his political loyalties and affiliations. Bishops throughout the former Roman Empire had often taken up the task of secular administration within their diocese. They had also, thanks to past endowments, become powerful landowners with armed vassals at their command. Particularly in Germany, dioceses like Cologne, Münster, Mainz, Würzburg and Salzburg were sovereign principalities. The loyalty of the man who brandished the crozier was therefore of critical importance to the Holy Roman Emperor and the German princes; but the right to the crozier came with the pallium, the band of white wool worn over the shoulders that was the symbol of his office and in the gift of the Pope.

The growing differences between pope and emperor came to an open rupture during the pontificate of Hildebrand, a man from a modest family in Tuscany who had been the indispensable counsellor of the four previous popes before being chosen as pope himself by popular acclaim in 1073, taking the name of Gregory as a tribute to Gregory the Great. Like his illustrious predecessor, this Gregory was a man of exceptional intelligence and ability, with long experience in the administration of the Church. He was energetic in promoting reform, issuing decrees against simony (the sale of ecclesiastical appointments) and clerical marriage, but also in forbidding the lay investiture of bishops, a measure that brought him into direct conflict with the Emperor, Henry IV. Henry convened a synod of German bishops to depose Gregory; Gregory in turn excommunicated Henry and released his subjects from their vows of allegiance; for among the claims he made for the Roman pontiff in his *Dictatus papae* was a supreme legislative and judicial power over all temporal as well as spiritual princes.

The Pope's dispensation of their vows of fealty was seized upon by Henry's opponents and obliged the Emperor, in 1077, to seek out Gregory at the castle of Canossa in northern Italy and profess repentance and seek forgiveness, standing barefoot in the snow at its gate. But Henry's humiliation at Canossa did not end the conflict which, partly because of Gregory's uncompromising nature, continued throughout his reign. In 1084 he lost Rome to Henry's forces and was only rescued by a new power that had arisen to the south of the Papal States – the Norman kingdom of Sicily.

*

'The establishment of the Normans in the kingdoms of Naples and Sicily', wrote Gibbon, 'is an event most romantic in its origin, and in its consequences most important both to Italy and the Eastern empire.'[83] Only a few generations after Rollo and his Vikings had settled in northern France, the Christian and French-speaking Duchy of Normandy had become a European power. In 1066 Rollo's great-great-great grandson, William, defeated King Harold of England at the Battle of Hastings and secured his claim to the English throne.

Unlike the Norman conquest of England, the Norman incursion into southern Italy was a private initiative taken at a shrine to the Archangel Michael on Monte Gargano which juts out into the Adriatic Sea in Apulia – the spur, as it were, of the Italian boot. Here, early in the eleventh century, a group of Norman pilgrims met a Greek exile from the nearby city of Bari, then held by the Byzantine Empire. He persuaded them to take up his cause. Returning to Normandy, the pilgrims recruited an army of adventurers who crossed the Alps disguised as pilgrims and, though they failed in their assault on Bari, became a formidable band of mercenaries much in demand by the conflicting powers in the bottom half of the Italian peninsula – their courage, energy, aggression and fighting skills leading them to overwhelm, time and again, the considerably larger forces deployed against them by the Lombard dukes of Naples, Salerno and Benevento or the agents of the emperors in Constantinople.

To the tough northerners, these rich territories ruled by 'effeminate tyrants' were ripe for the taking; and over a few decades they established their dominance over southern Italy with only the coastal cities remaining in Byzantine hands. After at first assisting the Byzantines in their attempts to reconquer Sicily from the Muslims who had held it now for two hundred years, the Normans made the project their own. The extended family from the minor Norman nobility, the Hautevilles, gained ascendancy over their fellow barons. In 1060, Roger Guiscard captured Reggio and Messina on the coast of Sicily and, after thirty years of fighting against the Muslims, subdued the entire island; while on the Italian mainland the cities of Bari and Salerno fell to his brother Robert.

The popes in Rome were at first alarmed by the rise of these Norman states and in 1053 Pope Leo IX led an army against them which was defeated at the Battle of Civitate. Pope Leo was taken prisoner but was well treated by the Normans because the crown they coveted was within his gift. Seeing an advantage in a power that might counterbalance that of the German emperors, the policy of the popes was reversed. Pope Nicholas II, advised by Hildebrand, the future Pope Gregory VII, invested the Normans with their principalities in Apulia and Sicily in return for the recognition of his overall suzerainty and a promise of military assistance. Pope Alexander II, again on Hildebrand's advice, sent banners and granted indulgences to Norman and French knights fighting against the Muslims in Sicily and Spain. The policy bore fruit when the Normans under Robert Guiscard saved Hildebrand from the army of the German Emperor, Henry IV. However, the Normans so antagonised the citizens of Rome that the Pope had to flee from the city to Monte Cassino and then Salerno where he died, insisting that he died in exile only because he had 'loved justice and hated iniquity'.

Hildebrand's claims to an overall authority over secular as well as spiritual powers for the office of pope brought with it a sense of responsibility for the fortunes of Christendom; and one of his unfulfilled ambitions was the dispatch of a Christian army against Islam. Until now, the Saracen threat had been sufficiently close to Rome for the popes to leave the Byzantines to fight the war on the eastern front. There was, moreover, both an endemic rivalry with, and contempt for, the Byzantine Greeks. It was not just the propensity of Byzantine emperors to put out the eyes of their rivals that affronted the Catholic Christian; the popes themselves had resorted to barbarities of the same kind. But the Greeks were seen as a treacherous people corrupted by the decadence of the East. The Byzantine emperors employed eunuchs not simply as guardians of their wives, but as high officials in both Church and state: only four offices were denied to them, and 'many an ambitious parent would have a younger son castrated as a matter of course'.[84] The Italian bishop Liudprand of Cremona who was sent on a diplomatic mission to Constantinople by the western Emperor Otto I, described it as 'a city full of lies, tricks, perjury and greed, a city rapacious, avaricious and vainglorious'; but in all these western judgements of the Byzantine capital there was no doubt a measure of resentment at the Byzantines' arrogance, and envy of a metropolis that surpassed Rome in size and splendour, had never been sacked by a barbarian army and, for all the occasional cruelty employed in the exercise of power, was a deeply religious society in which intellectual skills were highly esteemed and illiteracy among the middle and upper classes virtually unknown.

In other words, the Eastern Empire, despite its susceptibility to Oriental influences, had kept more of the strengths of the unified Roman state of antiquity than had the empire in the west. It had retained a salaried civil service and a disciplined, professional standing army. Unlike the *ad hoc* armies of unruly individuals found in western Europe, gathered for limited periods in accord with feudal custom, the regular units of the Byzantine army could be trained to respond to complex commands of a strategist trained in military science. The world's best-run state had at this time its most efficacious army.

Grave differences had arisen between the eastern and western branches of the Christian Church on issues such as the primacy of the two patriarchal sees, the religious allegiance of newly converted peoples such as the Bulgarians, and on doctrine – not just the notorious *filoque* clause in the Creed that remains esoteric to all but the most erudite theologians, but, more significantly, on the veneration of images or icons of Christ and the saints. In the eighth century, the eastern emperors had moved towards the Muslim position that the veneration of icons was indistinguishable from the worship of graven images and should therefore be forbidden. The subsequent controversy led to a century of violence and persecution: the popes in Rome had condemned iconoclasm which, if it had triumphed throughout Christendom, would have killed in embryo the pictorial art that was to be one of the finest manifestations of Western civilisation – there would have been no Fra Angelico, no Raphael, no Leonardo da Vinci. None the less, the conflict had adversely affected relations between the Greek and Latin branches of Christendom which reached their nadir with the exchange of anathemas and excommunications in 1054.

However, when it came to the endemic conflict between Byzantium and Islam, there was never any doubt that Latin loyalties lay with their fellow Christians in the east. For a time, after the first wave of Muslim conquest, a frontier had been established between the Byzantine Empire and the Abbasid calpihate of Baghdad in the Taurus Mountains above Antioch in the southern corner of Asia Minor. In the early tenth century, under two Armenian generals, the imperial forces embarked upon a campaign of reconquest which led to the recapture of Cyprus and northern Syria including the city of Aleppo. Although Jerusalem still remained in the hands of the Fatimid caliphs who ruled from Cairo, the much larger city of Antioch, also the seat of a patriarch, was back in Christian hands. By 1025, the Byzantine Empire stretched from the Straits of Messina and the northern Adriatic in the west to the River Danube and Crimea in the north, and to the cities of Melitine and Edessa beyond the Euphrates in the east.

However, this military supremacy was not sustained. Internally, a social shift in favour of the great landed magnates of the Empire had led to the disappearance of the class of smallholders in Anatolia who had hitherto provided troops for the Byzantine army, and consequently to an increasing reliance on mercenary troops; and externally there appeared on the eastern frontiers of the Byzantine Empire a new wave of Islamic conquerors, the Seljuk Turks.

The Seljuks were a tribe of nomadic marauders from the steppes of Central Asia who in the tenth century had conquered the territory of the Baghdad caliphate and, embracing Islam, proclaimed themselves the champions of the Sunni Muslims. Further waves of related Turkoman tribesmen, inspired by the same mix of religious zeal and love of plunder as the Arab founders of Islam, approached with predatory intent the eastern frontiers of the Byzantine Empire.

In 1071 under their Sultan Alp Arslan, the Seljuks came up against an enormous Byzantine army at Manzikert near Lake Van in Armenia composed largely of mercenaries that had been assembled by the Emperor, Romanus IV Diogenes. The Byzantines were defeated, the Emperor himself taken prisoner by Alp Arslan. Nothing now stopped the Turkish advance: the Turkoman tribes swept across Asia Minor and by 1081 had taken Nicaea, less than a hundred miles from Constantinople, and established a province in Asia Minor which, because it had formed part of the Roman Empire, was called the Sultanate of Rum.

The strength of the Byzantines had been sapped by their need to fight a war on a second front. In the same year as the Battle of Manzikert, Bari, their last stronghold in Italy, had fallen to the Normans from Sicily under Robert Guiscard who had then crossed the Adriatic, taken the port of Dyrrhachium, and planned an advance towards Thessalonika. The Byzantines were powerless to resist them. Asia Minor, now held by the Seljuk Turks, had been their main source of corn and had provided half their manpower. The once mighty Eastern Empire had been reduced to a small Greek state facing annihilation. In this crisis, the Byzantines had the good sense to elevate their ablest general, Alexius Comnenus, to the imperial throne. Providence also came to their assistance with the deaths of the Normans' leader, Robert Guiscard, and the Seljuk Sultan, Alp Arslan. None the less, the Byzantines' predicament remained acute and so the Emperor Alexius appealed to his fellow Christians in the West.

Alexius's first approach to Western Christendom was to Robert, Count of Flanders, who around 1085 had sent a small contingent of knights to Constantinople. It was perhaps Robert who advised Alexius that the Pope now carried greater weight in western Europe than the western Emperor, and in the spring of 1095 Byzantine delegates arrived at the Church Council being held at Piacenza in northern Italy.

The Pope who presided over the Council of Piacenza was a Burgundian called Odo of Lagery, the son of a family of minor Burgundian nobility living in Châtillon-sur-Marne. His background was therefore the same as the leaders of the Cluniac reform, and his upbringing, too, had imbued him with religious zeal. He was taught at the cathedral schools in Rheims by the exceptional Bruno who in 1084 had founded a community of monks at a remote spot in the Alps near Grenoble, the mother house of the Carthusian order, La Grande Chartreuse. Odo of Lagery had been ordained priest at Rheims, and had risen through the ranks of the archiepiscopal administration to become archdeacon of the cathedral; but then in 1070 had left the regular clergy to become a monk at Cluny. For a time he served as prior under the Abbot Hugh, but was subsequently called to Rome where Hildebrand, then Pope Gregory VII, appointed him Cardinal-Bishop of Ostia. In 1088 he was elected pope and took the name Urban II.

A courteous, conciliatory and good-looking man, Urban shared the same high estimate of his office as his mentor, Gregory VII, but was far more tactful in the exercise of his authority in the difficult circumstances of the time. His policy of conciliation extended to Byzantium: in 1089, at the Council of Melfi, he had raised the ban of excommunication on the Emperor Alexius and had been rewarded with equally conciliatory moves in Constantinople. The rapprochement encouraged Alexius to appeal to the Latin Church for aid. His ambassadors were admitted to the Council at Piacenza and the Council fathers listened to their eloquent depiction of the suffering of their fellow Christians in the East. At the close of the Council, the bishops dispersed with a clear understanding of the threat posed by the infidels' advance; while Urban II, as he moved on to France, carried with him the full burden of his personal responsibility as the Prince of the Apostles for the fate of Christ's universal Church.

Having crossed the Alps, Urban II went first to Valence on the Rhône, then on to Le Puy where another aristocratic prelate, Adhemar of Monteil, was the bishop. Adhemar had been on pilgrimage to Jerusalem some years before and could give the Pope the benefit of his experience. From Le Puy, Pope Urban summoned the bishops of the Catholic Church to meet him at Clermont in November of the same year. He then travelled south to Narbonne, only a hundred miles or so from Christendom's western front on the other side of the Pyrenees. He was now in Provence, then ruled by an experienced campaigner against the Saracens in Spain, Raymond of Saint-Gilles, Count of Toulouse and Marquis of Provence. From Narbonne, Urban II moved east along the coast of the Mediterranean to Saint-Gilles on the estuary of the Rhône, then north again up the Rhône valley to Lyons which he reached in October. From Lyons he moved on to Cluny in Burgundy where he had once been prior, and consecrated the high altar of the great church that for many years was to be the largest in western Europe. From Cluny he continued north to Souvigny to pray at the tomb of the abbot, Mayeul, who had been kidnapped by the Saracens as he crossed the Alps in the previous century, had refused the papal tiara, and was now acknowledged as one of the holiest of the abbots of Cluny.

What were Urban's thoughts as he prayed at Mayeul's tomb? No doubt, he felt that something must be done to aid the Byzantine Empire in its struggle against the Seljuk Turks. But there was also a pressing interest of the Western Church – the free passage of pilgrims to the Holy Land. For many centuries now, pilgrimage had been an integral part of the devotional life of the Christian. Every year, many thousands travelled across Europe to pray at favoured shrines – of Michael the Archangel on Mount Gargano which drew the Norman knights to southern Italy; of the apostle James at Compostella at Galicia in north-western Spain, sometimes starting at the Abbey of Vézelay in Burgundy which housed the relics of Mary Magdalene, or at the Abbey of Cluny itself. Or they went to Rome to pray at the tombs of the apostles Peter and Paul: as we have seen, it was a party of Anglo-Saxon pilgrims who were hacked to pieces when marauding Saracens made their attack on Rome in the ninth century.

However, the prize destination for all pilgrims was the Holy Land –

the ground trodden by God made Man, his home town of Nazareth, his birthplace of Bethlehem, and above all the site of his resurrection from the dead, the Church of the Holy Sepulchre in Jerusalem. The journey was an expensive and hazardous undertaking. The easiest way to travel to Palestine was by sea in a vessel of the Amalfi merchants but that ran the risk of piracy and shipwreck. The journey by land was made easier with the conversion of Hungary to Christianity in the early years of the eleventh century; and, until the Seljuk invasion, the 1,500-mile route across the Byzantine Empire from Belgrade to Antioch was relatively secure; but once entering Islamic Syria, the Christian could be subject to harassment and onerous tolls.

None of this deterred the pilgrims, to whom the very hazards and suffering incurred on their journey were part of the point. For many, 'pilgrimage was a form of martyrdom'[85] that would ensure the salvation of the pilgrim's soul. Sometimes it was imposed as a form of penance that would atone for the most serious sins; 'the most important expression of the renewed spirituality in the eleventh century – which originated in Cluny – was the penitential pilgrimage';[86] and one finds some of the most notorious villains of the period such as Fulk Nerra of Anjou or Robert the Devil, Count of Normandy, going to Jerusalem to escape divine punishment for their crimes — Fulk, like Chaucer's Wife of Bath, three times.

Such penitenital pilgrimages were encouraged and organised by the Church. The monks of Cluny presented the pilgrimage to Jerusalem as the climax to a man's spiritual life – a severing of the ties that bound him to the world, with Jerusalem the Holy City as an antechamber to the world to come. Just as the good Muslim was obliged to go on pilgrimage to Mecca at least once in his lifetime, so the ambition of many a pious Christian was to touch Christ's Holy Sepulchre before he or she died. 'In fact the attitude of the eleventh-century Christians towards Jerusalem and the Holy Land was obsessive.'[87]

On the whole, in the course of the four centuries during which Palestine had been ruled by the successors of the Prophet, access to their sacred shrines had been allowed to the Peoples of the Book. The only outright persecution of Christians had taken place at the start of the eleventh century during the reign of the fanatical Egyptian Caliph, al-Hakim, who had ordered the destruction of all Christian churches in his domain, among them the Church of the Holy Sepulchre in Jerusalem; but his successor had permitted it to be rebuilt. However, only thirty years or so before the moment when Pope Urban knelt at the tomb of Abbot Mayeul, the Archbishop of Mainz, together with the bishops of Utrecht, Bamberg and Ratisbon, had led a group of seven thousand pilgrims from the Rhine to the Jordan which, when ambushed by a party of Muslims near Ramleh in Palestine, had been obliged to fight in self-defence.

A further consideration that may have been in the mind of Pope Urban, although this has never been established and remains essentially a matter of conjecture, was the need to find an outlet for the surplus energies of the Frankish warrior class. Coming from this background, Urban II was well acquainted with the problem posed by quarrelsome knights whose only talent was their skill with the lance and the sword. Descended from the battle companions of the Merovingian and Carolingian kings, they were now a distinct caste in society – a military elite. But the cost of the necessary equipment for a knight was considerable – the chain-mail tunic, shield, sword, lance, steel cap and horse. Although some customs and precedents from the barbarian past mitigated the rule of force, most disputes were settled with the sword. The raid on a neighbour's crops and livestock was as common to the Christian knights of the Middle Ages as it was to the Arab tribes prior to the advent of Muhammad. 'Violence was everywhere, impinging on many aspects of daily life.'[88] Even when differences were brought before a court, they often let God settle the matter by way of a duel or trial by ordeal.

To limit the endemic conflict between the different groups among Christendom's rapacious nobility, and in particular to keep its hands off the property of the Church, popes and bishops had tried to impose its usual sanctions of interdict (a ban on Mass and withholding the sacraments) and excommunication (expulsion from the Church); but also, more recently, the concept of a 'Truce of God' – the designation of certain holy days or penitential times of year such as Lent when fighting was forbidden. However, this device had been only partially successful. Western Christendom remained scandalously afflicted by fratricidal strife. How much wiser if a lesson could be learned from the example of Normans like the Hautevilles whose aggression had been channelled into conquering new kingdoms at the expense of Islam.

With such thoughts in his mind, Pope Urban II rose from the tomb of the Abbot Mayeul and turned south towards Clermont to meet the three hundred or so bishops who had obeyed his summons. From 19–26 November the Council, meeting in the cathedral, passed a number of decrees against the usual abuses of lay investiture, simony and the marriage of priests. King Philip of France was excommunicated for his adulterous liaison with Bertrada de Montfort and the Council endorsed the idea of a Truce of God.

On Tuesday, 27 November, the Council fathers were summoned to meet in a field outside Clermont's eastern gate for a session that was open to the public. Here the papal throne had been set on a platform to enable Pope Urban II to address the huge crowd that had gathered to hear what he had to say. Although the accounts of his speech were written after the event, and were possibly coloured by what it inspired, it appears that the Pope first told of the reverses of the Byzantine Christians in the East and the suffering they had endured at the hands of the Seljuk Turks; then went on to describe the oppression and harassment of Christian pilgrims to the holy city of Jerusalem, conjuring up images of Zion that would have been wholly familiar to his audience from the constant singing of the Psalms. With the winning eloquence and genuine fervour of an experienced preacher, he reminded his audience of the example set by their ancestors under Charlemagne. He exhorted them to stop fighting one another for base motives of vengeance and greed, and to turn their weapons instead on the enemies of Christ. He in his turn, as the successor to Saint Peter with his God-given powers to 'bind and loose' on this earth, promised that those who committed themselves to this cause in a spirit of penitence would be forgiven their past sins and earn full remission of the earthly penances imposed by the Church.

Urban's appeal was received with enthusiastic cries of '*Deus le volt*' – 'God wills it' – and, in a dramatic gesture that had almost certainly been rehearsed by the two church leaders, Adhemar of Monteil, Bishop of Le Puy, went down on his knees before the Pope and asked to be allowed to join this Holy War.[89] A cardinal in the Pope's entourage also fell to his knees and led Urban's audience in the *Confiteor*, the confession of their sins, after which the supreme pontiff granted absolution.

One twentieth-century writer has described Pope Urban's appeal as a 'combination of Christian piety, xenophobia and imperialistic arrogance'.[90] Others have suggested that, in proclaiming Jerusalem as the crusade's objective when Emperor Alexius's appeal had been for military assistance in Anatolia against the Seljuk Turks, the Pope was taking advantage of the

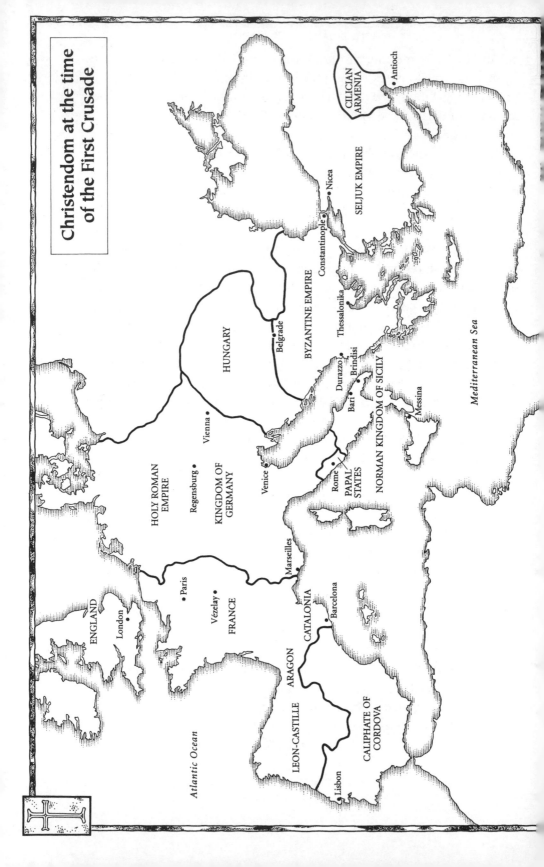

Christendom at the time of the First Crusade

Antioch

CILICIAN ARMENIA

SELJUK EMPIRE

Nicea

Constantinople

BYZANTINE EMPIRE

Thessalonika

Belgrade

HUNGARY

Durazzo

Bari

Brindisi

NORMAN KINGDOM OF SICILY

Messina

Mediterranean Sea

Vienna

HOLY ROMAN EMPIRE

Regensburg

KINGDOM OF GERMANY

Venice

Rome

PAPAL STATES

Paris

Vézelay

FRANCE

Marseilles

CATALONIA

Barcelona

ARAGON

ENGLAND

London

LEON-CASTILLE

Atlantic Ocean

CALIPHATE OF CORDOVA

Lisbon

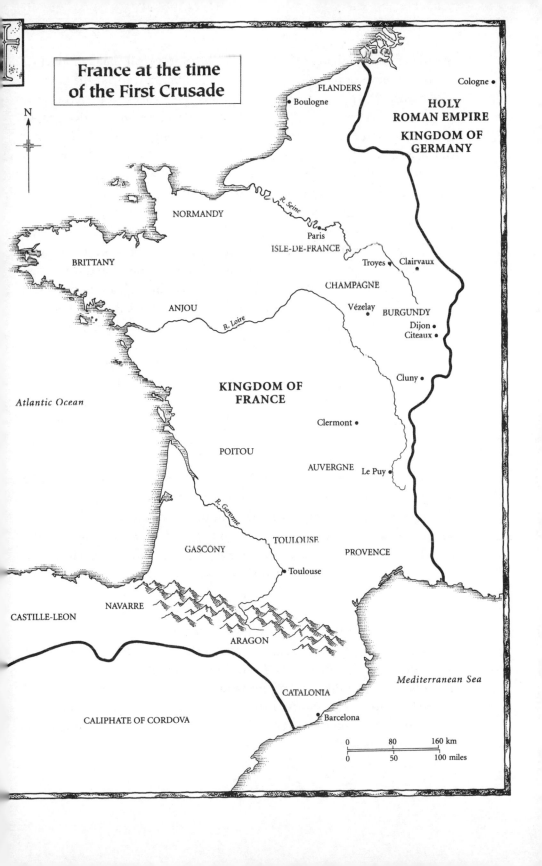

France at the time of the First Crusade

N

HOLY ROMAN EMPIRE

KINGDOM OF GERMANY

Cologne •

FLANDERS

• Boulogne

R. Seine

NORMANDY

Paris •

ISLE-DE-FRANCE

Troyes • • Clairvaux

BRITTANY

CHAMPAGNE

ANJOU

Vézelay • BURGUNDY

R. Loire

Dijon •

Citeaux •

Cluny •

KINGDOM OF FRANCE

Atlantic Ocean

Clermont •

POITOU

AUVERGNE Le Puy •

R. Garonne

TOULOUSE

GASCONY PROVENCE

Toulouse •

NAVARRE

CASTILLE-LEON

ARAGON

Mediterranean Sea

CATALONIA

CALIPHATE OF CORDOVA

Barcelona •

| 0 | 80 | 160 km |
| 0 | 50 | 100 miles |

ignorance and gullibility of his flock. However, it is clear that spin doctors are not an invention of the late twentieth century: already at the Council of Piacenza, the ambassadors of the Emperor Alexius had played up the plight of Jerusalem precisely because 'it would prove an effective propaganda slogan in Europe'.[91] Moreover, the Pope's objective was 'the defence of Christians wherever they were being attacked. "For it is not service to liberate Christians from the Saracens in one place and to deliver them in another to Saracen tyranny and oppression."'[92]

Did the Pope have any qualms of conscience about the use of violence? In the early Church, Jesus's injunction to turn the other cheek had on the whole been taken at face value and violence was therefore deemed sinful in any circumstances. It was Augustine of Hippo who considered it justified in legitimate defence, and his teaching, scattered through a number of his works, had been assembled in the eleventh century by Anselm of Lucca. It had been absorbed into papal thinking during the pontificate of Gregory VII in relation to the reconquest of Sicily and Spain; and, indeed, at the news of the Byzantine defeat at Manzikert when in the name of the apostle Peter he twice appealed to the faithful to sacrifice their lives to 'liberate' their brothers in the east.

Now Augustine's teaching was attached to the concept of a penitential pilgrimage, making the 'culminating surge towards the Holy Land of a cult of the Holy Sepulchre which had regularly spawned mass pilgrimages to Jerusalem throughout the eleventh century ...'.[93] The pilgrims would be armed to ensure, in the words of Pope Urban, that the Saracens 'would not further grind under their heels the faithful of God'. The indulgences he promised, and privileges granted to the crusaders, were almost indistinguishable from those given to pilgrims: 'when the march began it seemed ... to belong entirely to the traditional world of the pilgrimage to Jerusalem'.[94]

In this the Pope, true to his Cluniac vocation, showed that he was as interested in what the crusade could do for the crusader as in what the crusader could do for 'the Asian Church'. He frequently referred to Christ's injunction, which would have been familiar to all who heard him, to abandon wives, families and property for his sake, take up their cross and follow him. To give substance to the symbol, cloth crosses were distributed at Clermont to all those who vowed to go on crusade. These were sewn on to their surcoats at the shoulder not simply to signify this holy commitment, but also to show that the crusader was entitled to certain legal privileges and exemptions. The crusader's family and possessions were to be protected by the Church. He was exempt from taxes and granted a moratorium on his debts. In return, he was expected to fulfil his obligation: the man who reneged on his vow was subject to automatic excommunication.

Although, as we have seen, precedents had been set in Sicily and Spain for a holy war fought by Christians against Muslims, it is clear that the appeal made by Pope Urban at Clermont was seen as momentous, 'a shock to the communal system' and 'something different from anything that had been attempted before'.[95] To Urban's consternation, the most immediate and radical response was not among the class of knights that he had in mind, but among the poor. While Urban continued on a preaching tour of France, steering clear of the territories controlled by the French King Philip whom the Council had condemned, a number of popular preachers ignited the excitable and idealistic riff-raff of northern Europe and formed an ill-armed and undisciplined army that set off without further ado to vanquish the Saracens and liberate Jerusalem.

Their leader was a charismatic preacher from Picardy known as Peter the Hermit who claimed to have had a letter from Heaven authorising the crusade. The bishops did what they could to deter the old and the sick, and specifically forbade monks and clergy from going on the crusade without the permission of their superiors; but the movement got out of control. The lure of adventure and promise of spiritual reward proved irresistible. As we can still see from the carved images in the statuary of medieval cathedrals, people lived in real fear of the torments of Hell. Here was a chance to wipe the slate clean. Married men were forbidden to leave without their wives' permission, but many ignored the ban. One wife locked her husband in his home to prevent him hearing the preaching of the crusade, but when he heard through the window what was on offer, he jumped out and took the Cross.

The crusade got off to a catastrophic start. The forces led by Peter the Hermit and a knight called Walter Sans-Avoir passed through Germany and Hungary in reasonable order; but contingents of Germans under a priest called Gottschalk, and a minor baron, Count Emich of Leinigen, as they marched down the Rhine, attacked the Jewish communities they came across in cities such as Trier and Cologne. This was probably not the undisciplined rabble that was once supposed. 'These armies contained crusaders from all parts of western Europe, led by experienced captains.'[96] However, they were almost certainly unable to make a meaningful distinction between Muslims and Jews; would almost certainly have counted on pillage *en route* to finance the journey to Palestine; and could only conceive of the crusade in the familiar terms of a vendetta which obliged them to avenge the suffering of their fellow Christians in the East. In consequence, there followed a series of pogroms – massacres, forced conversions, and collective suicide by the Jews in sanctification of their faith (*kiddush ha-shem*) like that of the zealots in Masada twelve centuries before.

Earlier in the century, the Church had clearly been aware of the danger posed to Jewish communities in circumstances of this kind: Pope Alexander II had written to the bishops of Spain ordering them to protect the Jews in their diocese 'lest they be killed by those who are setting out to fight against the Saracens in Spain'.[97] Now, in some German cities, the Prince Bishops and local nobility took the Jews under their protection and the clergy threatened the miscreants with excommunication. To little avail. In Mainz, the Christian chronicler, Albert of Aix, describes how the would-be crusaders,

> having broken the locks and knocked in the doors ... seized and killed seven hundred who vainly sought to defend themselves against forces far superior to their own; the women were also massacred, and the young children, whatever their sex, were put to the sword. The Jews, seeing the Christians rise as enemies against them and their children, with no respect for the weakness of age, took arms in turn against their co-religionists, against their wives, their children, their mothers, and their sisters, and massacred their own. A horrible thing to tell of – the mothers seized the sword, cut the throats of the children at their breast, choosing to destroy themselves with their own hands rather than to succumb to the blows of the uncircumcised.[98]

The atrocities were not confined to the Rhineland: in Speyer, Worms, and as far away as Rouen in the west and Prague in the east, the crusaders fell on the Jews. No doubt, the religious zeal of the murderous mob 'was merely a feeble attempt to conceal the real motive: greed. It can be assumed that for many crusaders the loot taken from the Jews provided their only means of financing such a journey.'[99] Nor were the Jews the only victims of their criminality: in Hungary the predatory rabble set about plundering the local inhabitants and were all massacred in their turn. Albert of Aix later wrote that this was believed by many Christians to be God's punishment of those 'who sinned in his sight with their great impurity and intercourse with prostitutes and slaughtered the wandering Jews ... more from avarice for money than for the justice of God'.[100]

Meanwhile, the force led by Peter the Hermit and Walter Sans-Avoir had reached Constantinople escorted by the cavalry of the recently conquered Pechnegs whom the Emperor Alexius used as military police. Although advised to await the rest of the crusading army, Peter's followers grew restless and started to ravage the suburbs of the city. Alexius arranged for their transfer across the Bosphorus and billeted them in a military camp close to the territory controlled by the Seljuk Turks. A successful raid by a French contingent encouraged some Germans to follow suit. When trapped by the Turks, the main force went to rescue them and was annihilated by the Turks on 21 October 1096. This marked the ignominious end of the 'People's' Crusade.

Two months after the rout of this undisciplined vanguard at Xerigordon in the vicinity of Nicaea, the first contingents of the kind of army that Pope Urban had envisaged began to assemble at Constantinople. First to arrive was Count Hugh of Vernandois, a cousin of the King of France, who had come by sea with a small group of knights and men-at-arms. On 23 December, a far larger force arrived led by Godfrey of Bouillon, Duke of Lower Lorraine; his brothers Eustace, Count of Boulogne, and Baldwin of Boulogne; and their cousin Baldwin of Le Bourg.

Descended on both sides of their family from Charlemagne (and, according to later legend, from a swan), these four were classic exemplars of Frankish warrior-champions of the Church. Their retinue embodied the diversity of the old Frankish empire with both German-speaking and French-speaking knights. Godfrey had held the dukedom of Lower Lorraine under the Emperor Henry IV, but the fact that he sold all his estates and his castle at Bouillon to finance his participation in the crusade suggests that he did not mean to return home; though whether his objective was an eastern principality or the crown of martyrdom remains unclear.

Next came a contingent of Normans from southern Italy led by the forty-year-old Bohemond of Taranto, the eldest son of Robert Guiscard. Here there was less ambiguity: the Norman record suggested that they had predatory intentions and with good reason gave the Emperor Alexius some cause for disquiet. However, Bohemond had taken the Cross while besieging Amalfi with the outward signs of sincere conviction, personally handing out cloth crosses to those who wanted to join him. Among them was his dashing young nephew Tancred. With their contingent, they had crossed the Adriatic from Italy to Greece, and then had proceeded in good order to Constantinople.

The same route had been followed by a group of powerful nobles from northern Europe – Robert II, Count of Flanders, whose father had fought for the Emperor Alexius; Robert, Duke of Normandy, brother of the English King, William Rufus; and Stephen, Count of Blois, the son-in-law of William the Conqueror; while the largest contingent of all, Provençals and Burgundians under Count Raymond of Toulouse, took an intermediate route down the Dalmatian coast, then across from Dyrrhachium to Thessalonika and on to Constantinople. With him came Adhemar of Le Puy, appointed by Urban II as his legate and the spiritual leader of the crusade.

Adhemar's influence was invaluable in settling the differences between the Frankish princes and negotiating the passage of the crusading army through the Byzantine Empire. The Emperor Alexius had not anticipated a force of this size and would only allow its leaders to enter Constantinople, keeping the troops outside its walls. In April 1097, the crusading army crossed the Bosphorus unopposed. The Turkish Sultan, Kilij Arslan, lured into a false sense of security by his earlier victory over the army of Peter the Hermit, attacked the crusaders outside Nicaea. He learned too late that he was up against something more formidable – the heavy cavalry made up of Western knights. Anna Comnena, the daughter of the Emperor Alexius, was to write in her memoir of her father that 'the irresistible first shock' of a charge by Frankish knights 'would make a hole through the walls of Babylon'.[101]

The defeat of their sultan, followed by the investment of Nicaea not just by the Frankish army but also by a Byzantine fleet brought overland to the lake adjoining the city, led the Turkish garrison of Nicaea to surrender to the Byzantine admiral, Butumites. Although they had done a large part of the fighting, the crusaders kept the promises they had made to the Emperor Alexius to return his former possessions and remained outside while his troops entered the city. Although they were given gifts of considerable value, there was no question of the kind of plunder that a victorious army might have expected as the spoils of war.

However, their spirits were high. 'Unless Antioch proves a stumbling block,' Stephen of Blois wrote in a letter to his wife, 'we hope to be in Jerusalem in five weeks' time.' But the going was harder than they had anticipated. They were unused to the heat of the Anatolian summer: there was a shortage of water and, since the Turks had scorched the earth in front of them, a lack of food as well. As they approached Dorylaeum, the vanguard made up of the Italian and French Normans, a Byzantine contingent and some Flemings was attacked by the army of Kirij Arslan. The Turks had learned from their experience of Nicaea and manoeuvred to avoid a frontal attack by the crusaders' cavalry. Their mounted archers circled the crusaders. The Christian foot-soldiers were sheltered by the army of Bohemond and his knights who held firm until the rearguard under Godfrey of Bouillon, Raymond of Toulouse and Adhemar of Le Puy came to their rescue and routed the Turks. The Turkish camp, abandoned by the fleeing army, was taken by the crusaders and this time the booty was theirs.

After this second triumph the army resumed its march across Anatolia. Hunger and thirst continued to torment, and it had to fight two further battles before reaching a safe haven in the Christian kingdom of Cilician Armenia – an anomalous state in the south-east corner of Anatolia: Armenians had first been settled there by Byzantine emperors as a reward for military service, and had been joined by their compatriots ousted from the Armenian homeland near Lake Van by the Turks.

After a period of rest and recreation as guests of the Armenians at their capital of Marash, the crusading army, led by Adhemar of Le Puy, came down from the hills, fought its way across the River Orontes and on 21 October 1097 reached the city of Antioch. Antioch was a daunting sight – a city almost three miles long and one mile deep, built half on the plain of the Orontes, half on the precipitous slopes of Mount Silpius with four hundred towers punctuating the walls built by the Emperor Justinian and reinforced by the Byzantines a hundred years before; and, at its highest point, a citadel a thousand feet above the town. It had been one of the major metropolises of the Roman Empire and remained not just the strategic key to the whole of northern Syria but a rich and powerful principality in itself, still with a largely Christian population but garrisoned by the Turks who had captured it from the Byzantines twelve years before.

The Latin leaders could not agree upon whether to attempt to storm the city or to wait for reinforcements. Taking advantage of the crusaders' hesitation, the Turks made sorties, attacking the groups sent out to forage for food. The siege dragged on. Cold, wet and hungry, the Christian army found its morale declining to the point where the crusaders began to wonder whether God had not abandoned them as punishment for their misdeeds. Having already lost a large number of their horses and mules on the march across Anatolia, so that three-quarters of the knights had to travel on foot, they now ate those that remained to stay alive. The price of food brought from Armenia made it accessible only to the rich: some impoverished Flemings who had followed Peter the Hermit, known as Tafurs, ate the Turks they killed. 'Our troops', wrote Radulph of Caen, 'boiled pagan adults in cooking pots: they impaled children on spits and devoured them grilled.'[102] In January 1098, Peter the Hermit was caught by Tancred trying to desert and forced to return. In February, the Byzantine contingent abandoned the siege. To make matters worse, news reached the crusaders that a large army was marching to the relief of Antioch led by Kerbogha of Mosul.

In this moment of crisis, Bohemond of Taranto showed his hand. He had a tame traitor inside Antioch but he wanted the other crusaders' assurance that if he captured the city it would be his. The council of princes, overriding the objections of Bohemond's chief rival, Raymond of Toulouse, agreed. Sensing that the city's surrender was imminent, Stephen of Blois left for home. On the same day, the rest of the crusading army feigned a retreat from the walls of the city but returned under cover of darkness and were let in by Bohemond's spy. The city was taken. When Kerbogha of Mosul reached Antioch, the besiegers became the besieged but, inspired by the miraculous discovery beneath the cathedral of the Holy Lance that had pierced the side of Christ, they made a sortie that put the Saracens to flight.

Because it was thought inadvisable to continue towards Jerusalem in the heat of the summer, the crusading army remained in Antioch: the date for their departure was fixed for All Saints Day, 1 November. Meanwhile, the more adventurous set out to emulate Baldwin of Boulogne who earlier that year had established the first Latin state in the area at Edessa. Entering the city with a force of only eighty knights, he had been welcomed by the

Armenian ruler, Thoros, and adopted as his son. However, Thoros was unpopular with his Monophysite subjects and only a month later, probably with Baldwin's connivance, he was deposed and killed, leaving Baldwin the sole ruler of Edessa.

In July, Antioch was afflicted by the plague which on 1 August claimed the life of Adhemar of Le Puy. As Papal Legate and spiritual leader of the crusade, and with a wise and conciliatory nature, he had played an invaluable role in smoothing the ruffled feathers of the quarrelling and vainglorious princes. To escape the plague, many of them had left Antioch and the morale of the army again declined. The bad blood that existed between Bohemond and Raymond was reflected in a growing antagonism among their Norman and Provençal followers: a favourite gibe of the Normans was to say that the Holy Lance was a fake.

In September, after returning to Antioch, the princes wrote to Pope Urban asking him to come out in person to lead the crusade. The feast of All Saints came and went. Raymond at last agreed that Bohemond should keep Antioch on condition that he took part in the assault on Jerusalem. To this, Bohemond agreed; but apathy seemed to paralyse the leaders. There were weeks of procrastination. It was only at the insistence of an increasingly exasperated rank and file that the princes finally agreed to appoint Raymond of Toulouse their commander-in-chief.

The crusading army set out from Antioch on 13 January 1099, marching between the mountains and the Mediterranean coast. Most of the local emirs, rather than block their progress, preferred to pay protection to the advancing horde of monstrous *Franj*. The more significant powers in Damascus, Aleppo and Mosul watched and waited: it was not in their interest, as they saw it, to come to the aid of the Fatimid caliphs in Egypt who the year before had reoccupied Jerusalem.

On 7 June 1099, the crusading army struck camp before the walls of the Holy City. Although smaller than Antioch, and far less significant in political and strategic terms, Jerusalem had remained well fortified ever since the Emperor Hadrian had rebuilt the city. The Byzantines, the Ommayads and the Fatimids had all renewed its defences; and the Fatimid governor of the city, Iftikhar, had had ample warning of the crusaders' approach. The Christian inhabitants had been expelled but not the Jews. The city's cisterns were full of water and there were plentiful supplies of food, while the wells outside the city had been blocked or poisoned. The ramparts were manned by the garrison of Arab and Sudanese troops, and help had been summoned from Egypt.

Aware of their vulnerability to a relieving force, short of food and water, and lacking in heavy equipment such as towers and mangonels, the crusaders understood that they could not afford a protracted siege. Only one-third of those who had departed from western Europe two years before remained alive: discounting non-combatant pilgrims, among them women and children, this meant a fighting force of around twelve thousand foot-soldiers and twelve or thirteen hundred knights. They knew they could expect no help from the Byzantines: indeed, Emperor Alexius, instead of aiding them, was actually parleying with the Caliph in Cairo.

Providentially, ships from England and two galleys from Genoa had arrived at the port of Jaffa which the Muslims had abandoned. Their cargo supplied the army with food, and also nails and nuts and bolts. Tancred and Robert of Flanders went as far as Samaria to find suitable wood, returning with tree-trunks on the backs of camels. Carpenters from the Genoese galleys went to work constructing mobile towers, catapults and ladders to scale the walls.

On the night of 13 July the assault began. The first tower to reach the walls was that of Raymond of Toulouse but the defence of that sector was directed by the Muslim governor, Iftikhar, and the Provençals could not gain a foothold on the ramparts. On the morning of 14 July, Godfrey of Bouillon's tower was brought up against the north wall, and around midday a bridge was made from its upper storey, from which Godfrey himself and Eustace of Boulogne directed the assault. First across the bridge were two Flemish knights, Litold and Gilbert of Tournai. Behind them came the leading knights of the Lotharingian contingent, followed closely by Tancred and his Norman knights. While Godfrey sent his men to open the gates to the city, Tancred fought his way through the streets to the Temple Mount which some of the Muslims intended to make their redoubt. Tancred was too quick for them. He took the Dome of the Rock and pillaged its precious contents and, in exchange for the promise of a considerable ransom from the capitulating Muslims, allowed them to take refuge in the al-Aqsa mosque, displaying his banner as a pledge of his protection.

Iftikhar and his bodyguard withdrew into the Tower of David which he subsequently surrendered to Raymond of Toulouse in exchange for the city's treasure and a safe-conduct out of Jerusalem for himself and his entourage, Raymond accepted the terms, took possession of the citadel and escorted Iftikhar and his bodyguard out of the city. They were the only Muslims to escape with their lives. Intoxicated by their victory, and still charged with the passions of battle, the crusaders set about the slaughter of the city's inhabitants with the same indifference to their victims' age or sex as had been shown more than a thousand years before by Titus's legionaries. Tancred's banner on the al-Aqsa mosque was not enough to save those who had taken refuge inside. They were all killed. The Jews of Jerusalem fled to their synagogue for safety. The crusaders set it on fire: the Jews were burned alive.

Raymond of Aguilers, chaplain of Raymond of Toulouse, made no attempt to play down the horror of what he had seen when he subsequently described the capture of Jerusalem in his chronicle. When visiting the Temple Mount, he had walked up to his ankles in blood and gore. 'In all the ... streets and squares of the city, mounds of heads, hands and feet were to be seen. People were walking quite openly over dead men and horses.' But to him, the Muslim defenders had only got what they deserved. 'What an apt punishment! The very place that endured for so long blasphemies against God was now masked in the blood of the blasphemers.'

Muslim apologists were quick to point to the contrast between the savagery of the Franks and the courtesy and humility of the Caliph Umar when he had captured Jerusalem in 638: Christians would counter that the Byzantines had surrendered without a fight. But such polemic was to come later. Now there was only jubilation that Pope Urban's mission had been accomplished, and the crusaders' vows fulfilled. After three years of suffering and hardship, and a journey of two thousand miles, in savage climates and through inhospitable terrain, the pilgrims had reached their journey's end. On 17 July, the princes, barons, bishops, priests, preachers, visionaries, warriors and camp-followers processed through the streets of the deserted city to the Church of the Holy Sepulchre. There they gave thanks to God for their extraordinary victory and celebrated the sacrifice of the Mass at the holiest shrine of their religion – the tomb from which Jesus of Nazareth, the living Temple of the New Covenant, had risen from the dead.

part two

THE TEMPLARS

fIVE

The Poor Fellow-
Soldiers of Jesus Christ

In the years which followed the capture of Jerusalem, four different states were established in the conquered territories which came to be known in western Europe as 'Outremer' – overseas. In the north was the Principality of Antioch ruled by the Norman from southern Italy, Bohemond of Taranto. To the east, on the other side of the Euphrates, was the County of Edessa ruled by Baldwin of Boulogne. South of Antioch was the County of Tripoli, appropriated by Raymond of Saint-Gilles, Count of Toulouse, who died while besieging the city in 1105. Further south again, reaching from Beirut in the north to Gaza in the south, was the Kingdom of Jerusalem, ruled by Godfrey of Bouillon who, unwilling to call himself King where Christ had worn a crown of thorns, took the title of 'Defender of the Holy Sepulchre' instead.

Pope Urban II had died in Rome two weeks after the crusaders' triumph but before the news had reached the West that the city was taken. Prior to his death, he had appointed a Pisan archbishop, Daimbert, to succeed Adhemar of Le Puy as Papal Legate to the crusade. Daimbert became Patriarch of Jerusalem and on Godfrey's death in 1100 tried to establish himself as a theocratic sovereign in his place. The Frankish knights would not have it and instead summoned Godfrey's brother, Baldwin of Boulogne, from Edessa. Baldwin was less scrupulous about taking a royal title and on Christmas Day 1100, at the Church of the Nativity in Bethlehem, the defeated Daimbert crowned him King of Jerusalem.

The social order that now prevailed in Latin Syria and Palestine was based on the feudal system of western Europe. But while a conquering army with a strong leader such as William the Conqueror in England or Roger of Hauteville in Sicily had enabled that leader to retain control over his vassals, the way in which Godfrey of Bouillon and then Baldwin of Boulogne were chosen as first among equals by the leaders of the crusade led them to emphasise the rights of vassals and a codification of those rights unknown in the West. The allegiance of the princes of Tripoli and Antioch, and the counts of Edessa, to the kings of Jerusalem was as tenuous as that of the great counts and dukes to the kings of France: they only placed themselves under his authority when they felt their own security was threatened by a Muslim coalition. Bohemond's young nephew, Tancred, who had conquered Galilee and Sidon, held it as a vassal of King Baldwin but acted as a sovereign prince. There were also transfers of the leading princes from one principality to another, like pieces on a chess board: when Bohemond was captured on an expedition against the Danishmend Turks, Antioch was ruled in his absence by Tancred. When Baldwin of Boulogne, was summoned to the throne in Jerusalem, his cousin Baldwin of Le Bourg became Count of Edessa. After Bohemond had been ransomed, it was Baldwin of Le Bourg's turn to be captured, after which Tancred took over Edessa, but went back to Antioch as regent when his uncle Bohemond returned to Europe for reinforcements.

A shortage of manpower was endemic in Outremer from the start. In the autumn of 1099, after defeating the Egyptian army sent to relieve Jerusalem, most of the surviving crusaders began their journey home. In Jerusalem, Godfrey of Bouillon was left with around three hundred knights and a thousand foot-soldiers. Baldwin I, on his accession, had no more. While there was no imminent threat of a Fatimid invasion, and some support from the indigenous Christians, the tenuous position of the Kingdom of Jerusalem could only be secured by further expansion, and in particular by taking the Mediterranean ports. Aware of the need, and hoping for both the glory and spiritual rewards that had accrued to the successful first crusaders, further contingents set out from Europe – Frenchmen, Lombards, Bavarians. These were all attacked and defeated while crossing Anatolia, with only a small number escaping back to Constantinople.

More useful to King Baldwin were the naval squadrons of the Italian maritime republics – Pisa, Venice and Genoa – which, seeing the opportunities offered by the Latin possession of the eastern littoral of the Mediterranean, bartered their support in the siege of the ports in return for commercial privileges when they were taken. Haifa, Jaffa, Arsuf, Caesarea, Acre, Sidon – one by one they fell to the Latin forces until, finally, with the

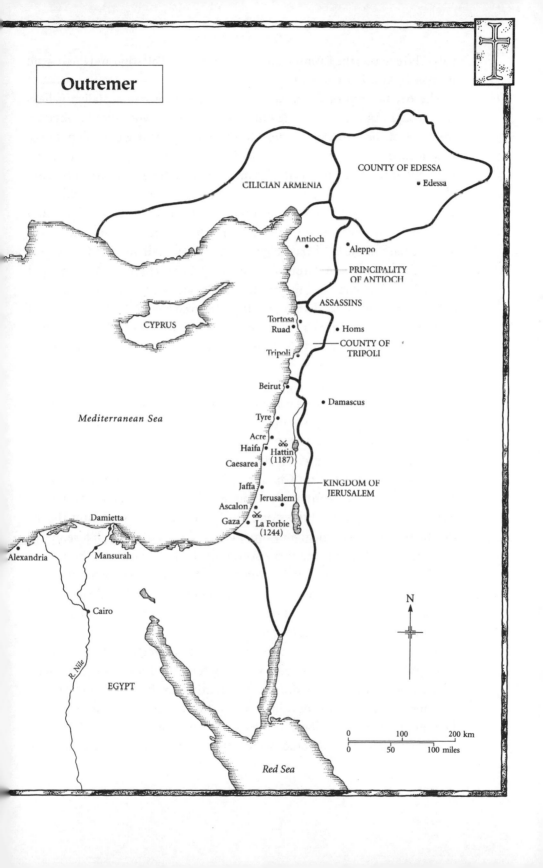

Outremer

COUNTY OF EDESSA

CILICIAN ARMENIA

• Edessa

Antioch •

• Aleppo

PRINCIPALITY
OF ANTIOCH

ASSASSINS

CYPRUS

Tortosa
Ruad •

• Homs

Tripoli •

COUNTY OF
TRIPOLI

Beirut •

• Damascus

Mediterranean Sea

Tyre •

Acre •
Haifa •
Hattin
(1187)

Caesarea •

KINGDOM OF
JERUSALEM

Jaffa •

Ascalon • Jerusalem •

Gaza • La Forbie
(1244)

Damietta •

Alexandria • • Mansurah

N

Cairo •

R. Nile

EGYPT

0   100   200 km
0   50   100 miles

Red Sea

fall of Tyre in 1124 the Fatimid navy lost any base in Palestine and the coastal frontier of Outremer was secure.

The pacification of the interior was more problematic. Italian galleys also brought out an increasing number of pilgrims who were inspired by the news of the crusaders' victory to make the pilgrimage to Zion. Some were armed but others were equipped only with the pilgrim's pouch and staff: the distinction between pilgrim and crusader remained imprecise. These not only prayed in the Church of the Holy Sepulchre to fulfil their vows, but set out on a tour of the numerous shrines of Judaea and Samaria which a familiarity with the Scriptures and indifference to historicity made a theme park of the Christian religion. In Jerusalem there was the Dome of the Rock, now converted from a mosque into a church, sanctifying the spot where Jesus had chastised the moneylenders and known by the crusaders as the Temple of the Lord. In the south-eastern corner of the Temple Mount there was the house of Saint Simeon containing the bed of the Virgin, and the cradle and bath of the baby Jesus; and north of the Gate of Jehoshaphat a church built on the site of the house of the Virgin Mary's parents, Joachim and Anne. In the vicinity of the Holy City there was the house of Zacharius where John the Baptist had been born; Mary's well, where Mary and Joseph had turned back to find Jesus in Jerusalem; the site where the tree had been felled that made up the Cross used in Jesus's crucifixion; and the place where Jesus taught his disciples the Lord's Prayer.

A well-trodden route for Christian pilgrims led east from Jerusalem to Jericho and the River Jordan where many went for a ritual rebaptism in its waters. Here they passed the stone block used by Jesus to mount the ass that he rode into Jerusalem on Palm Sunday; the pit into which Joseph had been thrown by his brothers; the stump of the tree which Zacchaeus had climbed to see Jesus; the bend in the road where the Good Samaritan had found the victim of a mugging; the spot where the Holy Family had rested on the flight into Egypt; and finally the shallows where John had baptized Jesus with the waters of the Jordan.

Because of the nature of the terrain and the disaffection of the Muslims among the inhabitants, the route was no safer than it had been in the days of the Good Samaritan. From the moment when they landed at Jaffa or Caesarea, the pilgrims were vulnerable to attack by Saracen marauders and Bedouin brigands who lived in the caves of the Judaean Hills. Those pilgrims who were armed could defend themselves, but there was no protection for those who were not. The forces at King Baldwin's disposal were already fully stretched securing strategic fortresses and the Mediterranean ports.

In 1104 Count Hugh of Champagne came to the Holy Land with a retinue of knights. From Troyes on the upper reaches of the River Seine he ruled a large and rich principality that had formed part of the West Frankish kingdom left by Charles the Bald. Hugh was pious and unhappily married – unsure whether or not he was really the father of his eldest son. Among his vassals was a knight called Hugh of Payns. Payns, a few miles downstream from Troyes on the Seine, was probably his birthplace; he was related to the Count of Champagne, had the benefice of Montigny and served as an officer in the count's household.

In 1108, Count Hugh returned to Europe but was back in Jerusalem in 1114. Whether or not Hugh of Payns had accompanied him on his first pilgrimage, or came to the Holy Land only now, he seems to have remained there when Count Hugh again returned to Europe. By now the childless King Baldwin I had been succeeded by his cousin, Baldwin of Le Bourg, and the Patriarch Daimbert by Warmund of Picquigny. It was to them that Hugh and a knight called Godfrey of Saint-Omer proposed the incorporation of a community of knights that would follow the Rule of a religious order but devote themselves to the protection of pilgrims. The Rule they had in mind was that of Augustine of Hippo, followed by the canons of the Church of the Holy Sepulchre in Jerusalem.

Hugh's proposal was approved by the King and the Patriarch; and on Christmas Day, 1119, Hugh of Payns and eight other knights, among them Godfrey of Saint-Omer, Archambaud of Saint-Aignan, Payen of Montdidier, Geoffrey Bissot, and a knight called Rossal or possibly Roland, took vows of poverty, chastity and obedience before the Patriarch in the Church of the Holy Sepulchre. They called themselves 'The Poor Fellow-Soldiers of Jesus Christ', and at first they wore no distinctive habit but kept the clothes of their secular profession. To provide them with a sufficient income, the Patriarch and the King endowed them with a number of benefices. King Baldwin II also provided them with somewhere to live, finding room in the palace which he had made out of the al-Aqsa mosque on the southern edge of the Temple Mount, known by the crusaders as the *Templum Salomonis* – the Temple of Solomon. As a result, they came to be known successively as 'The Poor Fellow-Soldiers of Jesus Christ and the Temple of Solomon', 'The Knights of the Temple of Solomon', 'The Knights of the Temple', 'the Templars' or simply 'The Temple'.

It is possible that the original intention of Hugh of Payns and his companions was simply to withdraw into a monastery, or perhaps found a lay confraternity comparable to the hospice of Saint John that had been founded by the merchants of Amalfi to care for pilgrims before the First Crusade. Michael the Syrian, a medieval chronicler, suggested that it was King Baldwin, only too aware of his inability to police his kingdom, who persuaded Hugh of Payns and his companions to remain knights rather than become monks 'in order to work to save his soul, and to guard these places against robbers'. Another medieval historian of the crusades, James of Vitry, describes the dual nature of their commitment: 'to defend pilgrims against brigands and rapists', but also to observe 'poverty, chastity and obedience according to the rules of ordinary priests'.

The decision to remain under arms may have been prompted by the growing insecurity of the Latins in Outremer. A party of 700 unarmed pilgrims travelling from Jerusalem to the River Jordan in Holy Week of 1119 was ambushed by Saracens: 300 were killed and 60 taken off as slaves. Marauding Saracens had reached as far as the walls of Jerusalem, and it had become dangerous to leave the city without an armed escort. Later in the year, news reached the kingdom of a catastrophe in the principality of Antioch: Roger, the cousin of Bohemond, acting as regent for Bohemond's son Bohemond II, had been killed in an ambush and his forces annihilated on what came to be called the 'Field of Blood'. This led to urgent pleas for help to the Pope, Callixstus II, to the Venetians, and even to the Archbishop of Compostella in north-western Spain. As always, setbacks were seen as divine chastisement: it was felt that some of the Latins who had settled in the Holy Land had been softened and corrupted by the lax ways of the Orient. A gathering of lay and spiritual leaders in Nablus in January 1120 welcomed Hugh of Payns's project as much for its spiritual as its practical potential.

It is not known whether any reference to the founding of this confraternity was made to Pope Callistus II in Rome though, as the son of Count William of Burgundy, he would probably have been sympathetic to the knights' aspirations. Nor does what must have seemed like a good idea at the time – the fusing of military skills with a religious vocation – appear to have been regarded as a radical departure from any norm. We have already seen how Catholic theologians' endorsement of fighting in a just cause had grown into a sanctification of the crusade: it would seem almost inevitable that the 'nomadic monastery'[103] would sooner or later take the form of a military order.

In 1120, the powerful magnate from central France, Fulk of Anjou, came on pilgrimage to the Holy Land and enrolled as an associate of the Poor Fellow-Soldiers of Jesus Christ. It seems that he had formed a high estimation of their Master, Hugh of Payns, and on his return endowed the Order with a regular income. A number of other French magnates did the same. In 1125, Hugh, Count of Champagne, returned to Jerusalem for the third and last time. He had repudiated his unfaithful wife, disinherited the son whom he believed was not his and made over his county of Champagne to his nephew, Theobald.[104] Hugh now renounced all his worldly wealth and took the vows of poverty, chastity and obedience as a poor fellow-soldier of Jesus Christ.

This was not the most significant of Count Hugh's penitential deeds. Some ten years before, he had given a tract of wild, afforested land about forty miles east of Troyes to a group of monks led by a young Burgundian nobleman, Bernard of Fontaines-les-Dijon. This foundation at Clairvaux was an offshoot from the Abbey of Citeaux from which a new order of monks, the Cistercians, took their name. Citeaux had been founded in 1098 by a Benedictine abbot, Robert of Molesme, who felt that the Cluniac communities had abandoned the rigours and simplicity of Benedict of Nursia's rule. With their massive endowments and consequent powers and responsibilities, the Cluniac abbots and priors had been drawn into affairs of the secular world. Leaving serfs to till their land, the monks had abandoned manual labour and served either as administrative officials or as 'choir monks' devoted to a superb liturgy elaborated with a plethora of new devotions. The abbey church at Cluny, the largest in Europe, was richly decorated and fabulously adorned. Money poured into the monastic coffers not just from rents, tithes and feudal rights but from the stream of pilgrims who set off from Cluny and passed the Cluniac staging posts on their way to the shrine of Saint James at Compostella in north-western Spain.

A brief account of this new phase of monastic renewal reveals the close links of those involved in the early days of the Templars. Robert of Molesme, like Hugh of Payns, was born near Troyes. He became a Benedictine monk at the age of sixteen, and was later made abbot of the Cluniac monastery of Saint Michael of Tonnerre, about thirty miles from Châtillon-sur-Seine where Bernard went to school. At the request of a group of hermits living in the nearby forest of Colan, Robert left this post to teach them how to live according to the Benedictine Rule. Later he led this community to land belonging to his family on a bluff overlooking the small River Laignes between Tonnerre and Châtillon-sur-Seine. Here they founded the monastery of Molesme.

Two other monks searching for a harsh path to perfection passed through Molesme. One was Bruno, born in Cologne, who had studied and subsequently taught at the cathedral school in Rheims. Among his pupils was the young Burgundian nobleman, Odo of Lagery, who went on to become a monk at Cluny and then the Pope who preached the First Crusade, Urban II. Falling out with the Archbishop of Rheims, Bruno fled from the world to live as a hermit close to Molesme but, finding this refuge insufficiently remote, went south to Savoy and founded a cluster of hermitages in the Chartreuse mountains. La Grande Chartreuse became the mother house of the most rigorous of all the monastic orders, the Carthusians, with its offshoots, or Charterhouses, throughout the world.

A second monk who passed through Molesme was an Englishman, Stephen Harding, a member of the Anglo-Saxon nobility whose family had been ruined as a result of the Norman Conquest in 1066. Fleeing first to Scotland, and then to France, Stephen studied in Paris and in 1085, aged twenty-five, he made a pilgrimage to Rome where he took the tonsure of a Benedictine monk, then returned over the Alps to join the community at Molesme.

Here, Robert's reputation for sanctity had attracted endowments which in turn had bred a laxity in many of the monks that their abbot found incompatible with his concept of the Benedictine life. In 1098, the year before Jerusalem fell to the crusaders, Robert left Molesme with around twenty supporters, among them Alberic and Stephen Harding, and, after a brief stay in the diocese of Langres, went south to found a community at Citeaux about fifteen miles south of Dijon. Here they were able to live according to their concept of Benedict of Nursia's Rule. They dropped the long litanies and prayers that filled the days of the choir monks of Cluny. They rejected all links with the local nobility. The community was to be self-sufficient: hard manual labour became part of the monk's daily routine.

As a symbol of their dedication to a life of purity, they changed the colour of their habit from black to white. They refused to accept child oblates and would not employ serfs, but they admitted lay brothers to work on their properties who, if these were some distance from the monastery, would live in a 'grange'.

In Robert's absence, Molesme had gone into decline. Pope Urban II ordered him to return. He was succeeded as Abbot at Citeaux first by Alberic of Aubrey and then by Stephen Harding. Impressed by their austerity, popes were subsequently to grant the Cistercians exemptions from the payment of tithes and manorial dues; but their aloofness alienated the Burgundian nobility, and the austerity which impressed popes deterred those with a monastic vocation. In the early years of the abbacy of Stephen Harding, it seemed that the project would fail. Then, in 1113, the charismatic young Bernard arrived from Fontaines-les-Dijon with thirty-five of his relatives and friends. The Cistercian order was rejuvenated. By the end of the century there would be twelve hundred communities affiliated to Citeaux throughout Europe.

Three years after his admission at Citeaux, Bernard himself led twelve other monks to start a monastery in the wooded Valley of Wormwood, known as a refuge for robbers, given by Hugh, Count of Champagne. They changed the name to Valley of Light, Clairvaux, and themselves set about clearing the ground and building a church and dwelling. Soon, Clairvaux attracted a strong flow of zealous young men.

It is difficult, in the late twentieth century, when a monk is seen as an oddity on the margins of society, to understand how so many belonging to their country's elite should have chosen a life of self-abnegation. Without necessarily doubting the sincerity of each one's conviction that he was responding to a call from God, it should be borne in mind that the choice for a scion of a noble house, or even the minor gentry, was then, and was to remain for some time, between fighting and praying, warfare and ministry, the scarlet and the black.

Thus a young man with a sensitive or studious nature, or simply an aversion to violence and bloodshed, might well be directed by a pious and loving mother towards a religious vocation: this would seem to have been the case with Bernard and his mother, Aleth of Montbard. Those entering an easier-going monastery such as Cluny could envisage a career as an ecclesiastical administrator or statesman, ending up, like Odo of Lagery, as pope. Or they would be free to pursue scholarship and learning: Stephen Harding was a scholar of the first rank, revising the text of the Latin Bible and calling on Jewish rabbis to help him understand the Hebrew of the Old Testament.

Bernard's decision to choose the narrowest gate and steepest path to the Kingdom of Heaven at Citeaux demonstrates the purity of his vocation. It also betrays a measure of self-knowledge: by his own account, his passionate, even violent nature could only be tamed by the austere life followed by the Cistercians. Evidence of that nature is found in his quarrel over a young monk with Peter the Venerable, Abbot of Cluny. In his letter to Peter, Bernard scornfully contrasted the pleasant, easy, luxurious life at Cluny with the spare diet and harsh regime at Clairvaux. Carried away by his own rhetoric, Bernard castigates the moral degeneracy of Peter's community. He is ardent, provocative, uncompromising, revolutionary: even the beauty of Cluny is a symptom of corruption. Peter, in his rejoinder, is conservative, moderate, conciliatory, gentle.

Another aspect of the monastic vocation that surprises, even offends, the accepted norms of the late twentieth century is the high value put on chastity. It is difficult not to feel sorry for the aristocratic young women in Burgundy and Champagne as their potential husbands retreated behind the walls of the Cistercian foundations. Christ had commended those who 'made themselves eunuchs' for the sake of the Kingdom; and the apostle Paul, in the early days of the Church, had written that, while it was good to be married, to remain unmarried was better. Augustine of Hippo, as we have seen, thought a wholehearted commitment to Christ was incompatible with marriage; and one of the major campaigns of the Papacy in this period was to insist upon celibacy for the clergy.

A number of factors go to explain what might appear in the twentieth century as a neurosis. First of all, the fundamental equation of the eremitic life was that the indulgence of atavistic instincts shut off the conduits to the spirit of Christ. The very power and intensity of sex, and the way in which it engages the will, made it an impediment on the path to sanctity. There was also the idea put forward by Augustine of Hippo, never developed and later retracted, that the Original Sin of Adam and Eve had something to do with sex, and that it was transmitted by the act of coition. A sense of disgust with our reproductive apparatus is found in Judaism in the ritual uncleanness of a woman during her period, and in the distaste expressed by Augustine in his *Confessions* for his involuntary nocturnal emissions.

Did this mean that sex, even within marriage, was wrong? By the eleventh century, there were two contradictory streams of thought found in Church teaching. On the one hand, there were monastic moralists who thought that conjugal coition could only be justified if its purpose was to have children; and even then, the carnal enjoyment contained a measure of sin. The most extreme exponent of this view was Peter Damian, one of the chief ideologues of the Gregorian reforms – a monk who rose through the papal administration to become Cardinal Bishop of Ostia, lived on a diet of coarse bread and stale water, wore an iron girdle around his loins and submitted to frequent and severe flagellation. He regarded marriage 'as a doubtful cover for sin, and rejoiced in any device which discouraged men on whom the divine image had been stamped from engaging in anything so degrading'.[105]

At the same time there was a growing insistence by the Papacy upon the sacramental nature of marriage as a holy state that depended for its validity on free consent. The English Pope, Adrian IV, in the mid-twelfth century, ruled that this right even applied to slaves; and 'even though it took many long years for Western society to believe its ears – his ruling won the day in the end'.[106]

Inevitably, if sex was a sin outside marriage, and a source of imperfection even within, it was better to avoid the source of temptation. It was axiomatic that monks should not mix with women, whose come-hither looks had lured many a good man to perdition. 'No religious body was more thoroughly masculine in its temper and discipline than the Cistercians, none that shunned female contact with greater determination or that raised more formidable barriers against the intrusion of women.'[107] Equally tempting, of course, were handsome young men to women, and it was no doubt with the salvation of their souls in mind, but also to provide for the spinsters among his own and his monks' families, that Bernard established a community of sisters, among them his own younger sister Humbeline, at Jully close to Molesme.

Did these young women willingly take the veil? According to the *Vita prima* of Bernard of Clairvaux, Humbeline had been married and led a worldly life before being persuaded by her brother to repent and, with her husband's consent, become a nun.[108] It was the same with Bernard's elder brother, Guy; he was married and had two daughters, yet was persuaded by Bernard to renounce them and join the community at Clairvaux. Clearly, here was a prophet fully recognised in his own country. What was the nature of Bernard's charisma? His biographer in the *Vita prima* considered him good-looking: his body was slim and fragile, his physique average, his skin soft, his hair fair, beard reddish, his complexion fresh and pink. But clearly his power over others came from his personality and conviction. 'His face radiated with a bright splendour, which was not of earthly but of heavenly origin ... even his physical appearance overflowed with inner purity and an abundance of grace.'[109] Fruitless to wonder how he would have appeared on television; all we need know in relation to the Templars is that Bernard of Clairvaux, as summarised by Dom David Knowles, a Benedictine historian of our own time, was:

> one of the small class of supremely great men whose gifts and oppor-
> tunities have been exactly matched. As a leader, as a writer, as a preacher
> and as a saint his personal magnetism and his spiritual power were far-
> reaching and irresistible. Men came from the ends of Europe to Clairvaux,
> and were sent out again all over the continent ... For forty years, Citeaux-
> Clairvaux was the spiritual centre of Europe, and at one time Saint
> Bernard had among his ex-monks the pope, the archbishop of York, and
> cardinals and bishops in plenty.[110]

In 1127 Hugh of Payns was sent by King Baldwin II with William of Bures on a diplomatic mission to western Europe. Its purpose was to persuade Fulk of Anjou to marry King Baldwin's daughter Melisende and become heir to the throne of Jerusalem; and to raise forces for a projected attack on Damascus. Hugh had a third objective: to gain recruits and papal sanction for his Order, the Knights of the Temple. The size of the Order at this point is unclear: chroniclers mention only the nine founders, but the very fact that the Master should have been chosen by King Baldwin for this important mission, and that he felt able to bring a number of knights in his entourage, suggests that the Order had already achieved a certain standing in Outremer.

King Baldwin II no doubt felt that his offer to Fulk and the European nobility was attractive: five years earlier, his position had been desperate but now he could make his appeal from a position of strength. With Tyre in the hands of the Latins, he could contemplate an assault on the Muslim heartland. In 1124 he had besieged Aleppo; in 1125 he had defeated a Saracen army at A'zaz, and had raided the territory of Damascus. In early 1126, with the full complement of his kingdom's military strength, he had penetrated even deeper into Damascene territory with considerable success. Damascus itself must have seemed within his grasp: with reinforcements and one last push, it could fall, removing a threat from the Muslim hinterland, creating a new principality for the Latins and providing fabulous amounts of booty.

With three daughters but no son, it was clearly vital for the long-term stability of the kingdom that Baldwin's eldest daughter Melisende should be married to a man of some standing. Whatever popes might say about the validity of a marriage depending upon the free consent of the pair, it was essential to the security of Outremer that every fief should have a strong leader. As a concession to the greater probability of dying young, it had been agreed that a fief could be inherited by a man's wife and children. However, neither a woman nor a child could lead knights into battle. It was therefore imperative that, on the death of a baron, his wife should immediately marry someone who could. There is no evidence that the wives themselves questioned this necessity although, as we shall see, their feelings sometimes affected the choice.

Hugh's trip to Europe was a great success. In April 1128, we find him in Anjou visiting Fulk in Le Mans. In June, Fulk's son Geoffrey was married to Matilda, the heiress of Henry I of England, leaving Fulk free to move to Jerusalem and marry Melisende. King Henry I responded generously to Hugh's fund-raising, giving him 'great treasures, consisting of gold and silver', which no doubt paved the way for Hugh's successful tour of England, Scotland, France and Flanders, picking up small donations of armour and horses, and more significant endowments from the counts of Blois and Flanders; and from William II, Castellan of Saint-Omer in Picardy, the father[iii] of Godfrey of Saint-Omer who had been the co-founder with Hugh de Payns of the Poor Fellow-Soldiers of Jesus Christ.

It is not entirely clear whether Hugh's fund-raising was specifically for his Order, or more generally for King Baldwin II's projected campaign against Damascus. The *Anglo-Saxon Chronicle* reported, no doubt with some exaggeration, that Hugh managed to recruit more people than had Pope Urban II for the First Crusade. Numerous charters show Frankish noblemen selling their property or raising loans to fund their participation in a crusade.

The authority given to Hugh of Payns by Baldwin II, and his success in recruiting significant magnates for the assault on Damascus, suggests that he was a more authoritative figure than was once assumed. The early seal of the Templars showed two knights riding a single horse to symbolise their poverty; there is nothing to suggest that Hugh travelled around Europe in this fashion. Although political turbulence in Europe may have prevented monarchs of the first rank such as the kings of England and France, and the Count of Flanders, from taking the Cross, they had responded enthusiastically to his appeal for support for his military Order.

More important still, however, was the endorsement of the Church of the new Order: as the historian Joshua Prawer points out, 'in medieval usage *ordo* meant far more than an organisation or a corporate body, because it included the idea of a social and public function. Men who belonged to an *ordo* not merely followed their personal destiny, but filled a place in a Christian polity.'[112] To secure this endorsement, Hugh appeared before the Church Council assembled at Troyes in January 1129. Host to the venerable churchmen was Count Theobald of Champagne and presiding over the Council was the Papal Legate, Matthew of Albano. Most of the prelates who attended were French – two archbishops, of Rheims and Sens, ten bishops, and seven abbots, among them Stephen Harding, Abbot of Molesme, and Bernard, Abbot of Clairvaux.

Despite the earlier endorsement of the Patriarch of Jerusalem, the Council's approval was not a foregone conclusion. A letter of encouragement, thought to have been written by Hugh while he was in Europe to the brothers in Jerusalem, suggests a crisis in their morale. There were, and there continued to be, doubts in the minds of some prominent churchmen about the morality of war: some held that Christ's rebuke of Peter when he cut off the ear of the chief priest's servant meant that the use of violence was incompatible with the life of a professed religious. The learned Lombard, Anselm, Archbishop of Canterbury, had considered taking the Cross to go on crusade vastly inferior to a monastic vocation: 'For him the important choice was quite simply between the heavenly Jerusalem ... which was to be found in the monastic life, and the carnage of the earthly Jerusalem in this world, which under whatever name was nothing but a vision of destruction...'[113]

However, Anselm was now dead and the pre-eminence he had earned by his sanctity and wisdom had now passed to Bernard of Clairvaux.

Despite his enclosed life in Clairvaux, Bernard knew of the founding of the Templar Order from his friend and patron, Count Hugh of Champagne. On hearing that Hugh had joined the Order in Jerusalem, Bernard wrote to congratulate him, regretting at the same time that he had not chosen to become a monk at Clairvaux. Because of his earlier patronage, Bernard must have felt some sense of obligation to this great magnate who had renounced the world. An even more intimate connection to the Templars was Andrew of Montbard, Bernard's younger uncle, his mother's half-brother. Both must have kept him informed of the needs of Outremer: in 1124, when the Cistercian Abbot of Morimond had proposed founding a monastery in the Holy Land, Bernard dismissed the idea on the grounds that 'the necessities there are fighting knights not singing and wailing monks'.[114]

To enlist Bernard's support, Hugh of Payns had written to him from Jerusalem to ask for his help in obtaining 'apostolic confirmation' and in drawing up a Rule of Life. He sent the appeal with two knights, Godemar and Andrew – Andrew being possibly Bernard's uncle whom Bernard would find it difficult to refuse. Although down with a fever, Bernard obeyed an imperative summons to attend the Church Council at Troyes and clearly dominated the proceedings: Jean Michel who kept the minutes of the Council said that he did so 'by order of the council and of the venerable father Bernard, abbot of Clairvaux'[115] whose words were 'praised liberally' by the assembled prelates. The only opposition came from John, the Bishop of Orleans, described by the chronicler Ivo of Chartres as a 'succubus and sodomite', and known by the nickname 'Flora'.[116] The reasons for his opposition are not known.

Hugh of Payns, accompanied by five members of the Order, Godfrey of Saint-Omer, Archambaud of Saint Armand, Geoffrey Bisot, Payen de Montdidier and a certain Roland, described the founding of their Order and presented their Rule. Scrutinised and revised by the Council fathers, this was transcribed by Jean Michel in a document of seventy-three clauses. The Cistercian influence is immediately apparent. The prologue has nothing good to say about the secular knighthood: it 'despised the love of justice that constitutes its duties and did not do what it should, that is defend the poor, widows, orphans and churches, but strove to plunder, despoil and kill':[117] but now those who joined the Templars were given the opportunity to 'leave the mass of perdition' and 'revitalise' the order of knighthood and at the same time save their own souls. It meant total self-abnegation and, when not engaged in military duties, leading the life of a monk. 'You who renounce your own wills ... for the salvation of your souls ... strive everywhere with pure desire to hear matins and the entire service according to canonical law ...'; and if circumstances should make that impossible, 'he should say instead of matins thirteen paternosters; seven for each hour and nine for vespers'.

Just as a distinction was made in the Benedictine and Cistercian orders between the monk and the lay brother, so the difference between a knight of the Temple and a sergeant or squire was to be made apparent by their dress. 'We command that all the brothers' habits should always be of one colour, that is white or black or brown.' White could only be worn by a fully professed knight 'so that those who have abandoned the life of darkness will recognise each other as being reconciled to their creator by the sign of their white habits; which signifies purity and complete chastity'. Chastity, i.e. celibacy, was the *sine qua non* of the knight's commitment. 'Chastity is certitude of heart and healthiness of body. For if any brother does not take the vow of chastity he cannot come to eternal rest nor see God, by the promise of the apostle who said ... "Strive to bring peace to all, keep chaste, without which no-one can see God".'

Married men were allowed to join the Order with the permission of their wives, but they were not to wear the white habit and widows, though supported by the Order from the benefice brought by their husbands, were, like the knights' other female relatives, to be banned from the Templar houses.

The company of women is a dangerous thing, for by it the old devil has led many from the straight path to Paradise ...

We believe it to be a dangerous thing for any religious to look too much upon the face of a woman. For this reason none of you may presume to kiss a woman, be it widow, young girl, mother, sister, aunt or any other; and henceforth the Knighthood of Jesus Christ should avoid at all costs the embraces of women, by which men have perished many times, so that they may remain eternally before the face of God with a pure conscience and sure life.[118]

Following the Rule of Benedict of Nursia, possibly as a precaution against other forms of sexual sin, the dormitory where the knights slept was to be 'lit until morning'; and the Templars were to sleep 'dressed in shirt and breeches and shoes and belt'. This was perhaps to enable them to fight at short notice: 'we command all to have the same, so that each can dress and undress, and put on and take off his boots easily'. The Order's Draper was to make sure that their clothes fitted the knights, and that the hair on their heads be cut short: however, they were not permitted to shave. All Templar knights wore beards. There were to be no fashionable variations to their attire – 'no brother will have a piece of fur on his clothes ... We prohibit pointed shoes and shoe-laces and forbid any brother to wear them ... for it is manifest and well known that these abominable things belong to pagans.'

Like monks, the knights were to eat in silence in the refectory. Because 'it is understood that the custom of eating flesh corrupts the body', meat was permitted only three times a week: to abstain altogether, as did the Cistercians, would enfeeble them as fighting men. On Sundays, the knights and clergy were allowed two meat meals while the squires and sergeants 'shall be content with one meal and be thankful to God for it'. On Mondays, Wednesdays and Saturdays, the brothers were to eat two or three meals of vegetables and bread. They were to fast on Fridays, and for the six months between All Saints (1 November) and Easter eat a minimal amount of food. The sick were excused from fasting. One-tenth of the Templars' food, and all the leftovers, went to the poor.

One can sense in this primitive Rule of the Templars the fear of Bernard of Clairvaux and the Council fathers that, without the safeguard of monastic enclosure, the Templar knights would slip back into the ways of the world. The Order could own land and benefit from the labour of tenants and villeins whom they were to govern justly. They were also permitted to receive tithes as part of a lay or clerical endowment. Falconry and hunting were prohibited, except of the lion which like Satan 'comes encircling and searching for what he can devour'. Not only were pointed shoes and shoelaces forbidden to the Templar knight, but also gold or silver decorations on his bridle, and a food bag made of linen or wool.

The brothers were to avoid levity in their conversation – 'idle words and wicked burst of laughter' – nor should they while away their time chatting, 'for it is written ... that too much talk is not without sin'. They were not to boast of their past prowess: 'we prohibit and firmly forbid any brother to recount to another brother nor anyone else the brave deeds he has done in secular life, which should rather be called follies committed in the performance of knightly duties, and the pleasures of the flesh that he has had with immoral women'. They were to avoid 'the plague of envy, rumour, spite, slander'; and, presumably a practical injunction against envy, 'no brother should explicitly ask for the horse or armour of another' and, if the Master should choose to give these away to another, he 'should not become vexed or angry'.[119]

It was understood that the knights would have some contact with the world, but they were not 'to go out into the town or city without the permission of the Master ... except to pray at night to the Sepulchre and the places of prayer that lie within the walls of the city of Jerusalem'. Even there, the brothers were to go in pairs and, if obliged to stop at an inn, 'neither brother nor squire nor sergeant may go to another's lodging to see or speak to him without permission'. As with an abbot in a monastic community, the power of the Master was absolute. 'In order to carry out their holy duties and gain the glory of the Lord's joy and to escape the fear of hell-fire, it is fitting that all brothers who are professed strictly obey their master. For nothing is dearer to Jesus Christ than obedience. For as soon as something is commanded by the Master or by him to whom the Master has given the authority, it should be done without delay as though Christ himself had commanded it.' The Master, if he so wished, could take counsel from the wiser brothers, and on serious matters 'assemble the entire congregation to hear the advice of the whole chapter'. The Master and chapter were authorised to punish those brothers who transgressed.

Of the seventy-three clauses in this Rule approved by the Council of Troyes for the Knights of the Temple, around thirty are based on the rule of Benedict of Nursia. Bernard and the Council fathers seemed more anxious to make monks out of knights than knights out of monks. There are some references to the brothers' military calling, for example, stating the number of horses to be made available to each knight; and one concession to the conditions in Outremer: they were to be permitted to change their woollen shirts for linen ones in the summer months. But in general, the focus of the Rule seems to have been on the saving of the knights' souls, not on the efficacy of a fighting force. The Council fathers do not seem to have foreseen that the application of monastic discipline to a military unit would, for the first time since the collapse of the Roman Empire in the west, result in disciplined, uniformed heavy cavalry taking the field that was not subject to shifting personal loyalties or the uncertainties of the feudal levy.[120]

However, the Order of the Knights of the Temple might well have been stillborn had it not received the Church's endorsement at the Council of Troyes, subsequently confirmed by Pope Honorius II. That endorsement was due largely to the support of Bernard of Clairvaux which he reinforced, upon his return to Clairvaux, by writing a treatise *De laude novae militae*, 'In Praise of the New Knighthood'. Was this promoted by criticism of the Order? Hugh de Payns, on returning to Jerusalem, had received a letter from Guigo, the fifth Prior of La Grande Chartreuse. He was a highly respected monk and clearly felt it was his duty to impress upon the Templars that they must see their vocation first and foremost as a spiritual, not a martial one. 'It is useless indeed for us to attack exterior enemies if we do not first conquer those of the interior.'[121] He sent copies of this letter by two messengers and asked Hugh to ensure that it was read to all the members of his Order.

It was no doubt to allay any doubts in the minds of existing Templars and potential recruits that Hugh badgered Bernard to write *De laude*: Bernard states in the introduction that it was only after three requests that he had picked up his pen. It is addressed to the brothers and warns them at the outset that the Devil will attempt to undermine their resolve, impugning their motives in killing the enemy and taking the spoils of war, luring them away from their chosen calling with the chimera of a greater good. They were, he acknowledged, a novelty in the life of the Church, 'clean different from the ordinary way of knighthood',[122] whose pure motives transformed *homicide*, which was evil, into *malecide* – the killing of evil – which was good. There was no doubt in Bernard's mind that the Holy Land was the patrimony of Christ unjustly seized by the Saracens: much of the treatise was taken up with a description of the scenes of his life and Passion. It was to the spiritual benefit of the Templars that they would tread the same ground as their saviour. Above all, to encounter the physical reality of the Holy Sepulchre reminds the Christian that here he too will conquer death.

Go forward in safety, knights, and with undaunted souls drive off the enemies of the cross of Christ, certain that neither death nor life can separate you from the love of God which is in Christ Jesus, repeating to yourself in every peril, Whether we live or whether we die we are the

Lord's. How glorious are the victors who return from battle! How blessed are the martyrs who die in battle! Rejoice, courageous athlete, if you live and conquer in the Lord, but exult and glory the more if you die and are joined to the Lord. Life indeed is fruitful and victory glorious, but ... death is better than either of these things. For if those are blessed who die in the Lord, how much more blessed are those who die for the Lord?

SIX

The Templars in Palestine

After the Council of Troyes, Hugh of Payns returned to Palestine. A number of his lieutenants, however, remained in western Europe to raise recruits, solicit donations and establish an administration. Although the titles and functions of the Templar officials at this stage are imprecise, records refer to 'procurators', 'seneschals' and provincial masters. Payen of Montdidier, one of the nine founders of the Order, appears to have been put in charge of France north of the Loire; Hugh of Rigaud received donations in the area of Carcassonne, Peter of Rovira in Provence, and a future Master of the Order, Everard of Barres, in Barcelona. Donations could be as little as one denier or the rent of a small parcel of land; a horse, a sword, a suit of armour, chain-mail shirt, even a pair of breeches; or they could be substantial gifts of land or the valuable rights to hold markets or run mills given by magnates such as the Duke of Brittany or Eleanor of Aquitaine. Eleanor also exempted the Templars from paying harbour dues at La Rochelle.

In England, as we have seen, the Templars were given a warm welcome by King Henry I and on his death had established their headquarters in the parish of Saint Andrew in Holborn near to the north end of the present Chancery Lane. The most extensive donations of land were made in Lincolnshire and Yorkshire. These varied in size, and the Templars sensibly sublet the smaller holdings and managed only the larger holdings themselves. In both Yorkshire and Lincolnshire, the Order followed the profitable example of the Cistercians in breeding sheep whose wool was exported to the weavers of Flanders. Whether or not it was understood at the time of the Order's foundation, a large part of the funds raised by the Templars and the Hospitallers was used to maintain these houses, called preceptories: the norm was not military service in Palestine but estate management and semi-monastic life in western Europe. The financial and administrative organisation of a Templar preceptory, like that of a Cistercian monastery, was simple; and 'some Templars placed in charge of estates lived almost alone'.[123]

Unlike monastic foundations, however, the endowment was not to a particular house but to the Order represented by its chief house, the Temple, in London. That such a considerable proportion of its resources should have been spent on the establishment and staffing of what was, in essence, an early multinational corporation did not initially provoke any resentment among the donors whose gifts to the Templars sprang from the same pious impulse as their donation to the monastic orders. For example, in the parish of Helmsley in North Yorkshire thirty acres was given to the Order by the Norman baron, Walter l'Espec; he also gave land on the River Rye two or three miles from his castle to monks from Bernard's community at Clairvaux who named their monastery Rievaulx. A minor baron in nearby Stonegrave, the village where I lived as a child, gave three bovates of land in his parish which was let for 40 pence.[124] A Roger de Staingrive was to be captured by the Saracens in a later crusade.

On the Continent, substantial benefices came from princes already familiar with the needs of Outremer such as Alfonso-Jordan, Count of Toulouse, son of Raymond and half-brother of Bertrand, Count of Tripoli; and from those engaged in fighting the Muslims on the Iberian Peninsula. Aragon under King Alfonso I, known as 'the Battler', was pursuing a determined policy of Christian reconquest, and granted privileges to the Templars as early as 1130. Clearly, Alfonso's interest was not just in how he could help the Templars but in how the Templars could help him. To some extent, he had anticipated the Templar Order by creating confraternities of knights to fight against the Moors. These had links with the Cistercians but, in the case of the Order of Santiago in the Kingdom of León, married men were admitted as members and they were allowed to sleep with their wives.[125]

The advantage to Alfonso of the military orders was that he would not lose control of the newly conquered territories to his barons. The Templars' first loyalty, however, was to the Holy Land and they were initially unwilling to commit the Order to the war against Islam on a second front; but it proved difficult to resist the Iberians' embrace. In Portugal, the Countess Teresa promised them the castle of Soure. In Catalonia, in 1134, Raymond Berenguer IV, Count of Barcelona, and a party of his vassals pledged themselves to serve with the Templars for a year. He also ruled that the Templars together with their dependants should be exempt from the jurisdiction of the lay courts.

Also drawn into the Iberian *Reconquista* was a second order of military monks with roots in the Holy Land – the Knights of the Hospital of Saint John. This had been founded not as a military order but as a lay community devoted to the care of poor pilgrims by the monks of Saint Mary of the Latins, a monastery established in Jerusalem before the First Crusade by merchants from Amalfi who at that time exercised a monopoly in western trade with the Levant. Like the early Templars and the canons of the Church of the Holy Sepulchre, the knights followed the rule of Augustine of Hippo and built their hospice on the site where the conception of Saint John the Baptist had been announced by an angel.

A papal bull of 1113 endorsing the Hospital names their founder as a Brother Gérard. After the capture of Jerusalem in 1099, his piety, combined with an exceptional competence as 'the most efficient billeting officer the crusaders had encountered'[126] led to endowments by Godfrey of Bouillon and his successors, and by pious Europeans impressed by what they heard from the returning soldiers and pilgrims. By 1113, the Hospital had established a number of houses in Europe to care for pilgrims on their way to the Holy Land.

Brother Gérard died in 1120 and was succeeded by Raymond of Le Puy, by tradition a Frankish knight who had remained in Jerusalem after the First Crusade. Clearly, the imperative need for a force to protect the pilgrims was as apparent to him as to Hugh of Payns. If Raymond and his *confrères* had given up their sword and armour, they now retrieved them. Although the Hospital never abandoned its original vocation of caring for pilgrims and the sick, it now became a military order. In 1128, while Hugh of Payns was in Europe, Brother Raymond of Le Puy is found accompanying King Baldwin II on a campaign against Ascalon.

The two orders expanded side by side: the administrative structure developed by the Templars in Europe was based on that already established by the Hospitallers; while the Church's endorsement of the Templar Rule at the Council of Troyes, and Bernard of Clairvaux's treatise in their defence, sanctioned and encouraged the Hospital's evolution into a comparable military order. The Hospitallers retained the milder rule of the Augustinian canons but took the title of Master for their superior from the Templars. Their quarters by the Church of the Holy Sepulchre soon absorbed the monastery of Saint Anne, and included a great hall with a capacity for two thousand pilgrims and several hundred knights, 'a building so great and marvellous that it would seem impossible unless one saw it'.[127]

King Alfonso of Aragon, 'the Battler', for all his prowess as a hammer of the Moors, proved unable to father any children. His marriage to Urraca of Castile was dissolved in 1114. With no heir, and possibly hoping to prevent a divisive scramble for his kingdom after his death, Alfonso drew up a will in October 1131, leaving his kingdom to the Canons of the Holy Sepulchre in Jerusalem and the two military orders – the Hospitallers and the Templars. 'To these three I concede my whole kingdom ... also the lordship which I have in the whole of the lands in my kingdom, both over clerics as well as over laity, bishops, abbots, canons, monks, magnates, knights, burgesses, peasants and merchants, men and women, the small and the great, rich and poor, also Jews and Saracens, with such laws as my father and I have had hitherto and ought to have.'[128]

The motive for this settlement is unclear, but when Alfonso died in 1134 it was ignored and, despite the support of Pope Innocent II, the three beneficiaries were unable to enforce it. However, when a settlement was finally reached at Gerona ten years later with Raymond Berenguer of Barcelona, the Templars were compensated with the lordship of half-a-dozen fortresses, a tenth of royal revenues, exemption from a number of taxes and a fifth of all lands conquered from the Moors.[129] Thus, despite their earlier reluctance, they were drawn into the *Reconquista* and became one of the most formidable powers in both Portugal and Spain.

The very fact that the Order of the Temple was able to take on such a military commitment on a second front in 1144 demonstrates its success in the recruitment of knights. Their reasons for joining varied but it would be wrong to underestimate religious zeal. The consensus among historians, which once saw crusading as a feeble pretext for pillage and rapine, has now shifted in favour of penitential motivation. 'A commitment to crusade ... involved heavy expenses and real financial sacrifices, and burdens on families were even heavier if several members chose to go.'[130] The same was true for a knight who joined the Templars: 'postulants were expected to provide their own clothing and equipment when they joined the order"[131] and the cost was often met by their family or friends.

Frequently, endowment and commitment were combined. Hugh of Payns and Geoffrey of Saint-Omer were praised for bringing their property with them. In northern Provence, Hugh of Bourbouton joined the Templars in 1139, endowing it with sufficient land to establish the preceptory of Richerenches which remains one of the best preserved to this day: he did so, he stated, in obedience to Christ's injunction in the Gospel of Saint Matthew: 'If anyone wants to be a follower of mine, let him renounce himself and take up his cross and follow me. For anyone who wants to save his life will lose it; but anyone who loses his life for my sake will find it.'[132] Six years later, he was followed by his son Nicholas who gave all his property to the Temple except for his sheep, which were to provide for his mother; and 'I render myself to the same knighthood of God and the Temple to serve as servant and brother, although unworthy, all the days of my life, that I might merit the indulgence of my sins and by inheritance [be] with the elect in eternity.'[133]

The Bourbouton family came from a social class just below, but on familiar terms with, the great magnates of western Europe. So too did Hugh of Payns, Geoffrey of Saint-Omer and most of those who provided the leadership of the Order. However it also appealed to poorer knights, and at its inception, knightly descent does not seem to have been a necessary qualification for admission. Clearly a postulant would have to be trained in fighting on horseback, with either experience in the field or at least in jousting. The military orders were in fact less exclusive than the monasteries:[134] literacy was not a requirement – few of the knights could read or write, certainly not in Latin. It was left to the chaplains to recite the office and all that was demanded of the brothers was that they say the prescribed number of paternosters at the appointed hours.

There were no doubt postulants whose motives were mixed. Grandees like Hugh, Count of Champagne, or Harpin of Bourges, joined the Temple late in life after losing their wives – one through separation, the other through death. Younger knights with limited resources were drawn by 'prospects of travel and promotion in the world'.[135] There was also the magnetic attraction of the Holy Land. There are cases of knights who had travelled to Palestine on their own resources, for example the cousin of

Roger, Bishop of Worcester, joining a military order when those resources ran out.

As the Order grew in power and wealth, it offered a career structure comparable to that of the Church. Quite quickly, the Masters of the military orders became significant figures not just in Syria and Palestine, but in western Europe as well. The provincial masters and other officials, with enormous resources at their disposal, became the equals of the highest peers in the realm. Their reputation for honesty and good judgement made them the trusted counsellors of popes and kings.

There may have been more romantic motives: ballads and *chansons de gestes* liked to suggest that knights joined the Templars because of unrequited love. As we shall see, Gérard of Ridefort, the tenth Master, was said to have enlisted because he was turned down as a husband for an heiress, but here a broken heart may have been less significant than disappointed expectations; however, it would not be fanciful to draw at least a partial analogy between the Order of the Temple and the French Foreign Legion. Although a probationary period was written into the early Rule, this was discarded under pressure caused by attrition; and even at the Order's inception, provision had been made to recruit among excommunicated knights. 'Where you know excommunicated knights to be gathered, there we command you to go.'[136] A knight accused of murder could join the Templars to expiate his sin. The penance imposed on the knights who murdered the Archbishop of Canterbury, Thomas à Becket, was fourteen years' service in the Templars.

Finally, there was the perennial appeal of male comradeship in dangerous and demanding conditions. This certainly was an important feature of crusading, and undoubtedly attracted men to the military orders. The Benedictine and Cistercian drive for detachment from the world did not extend to friendship between men. Quite to the contrary, the great abbots such as Anselm of Canterbury, Bernard of Clairvaux and Aelred of Rievaulx saw it as one of the greatest goods that this life had to offer. Aelred wrote a treatise on the subject, *De spirituali amicitia*: Bernard, 'though he did not exclude women from his friendships, still less refuse to allow that the love of a husband and wife could partake of the quality of true human friendship', nevertheless thought that 'human love was infinitely less than the love of God, [and] married love less than the love between male friends'.[137] In a society where violence was endemic and the Crown was unable to control the fractious barons, bonds of kinship and friendship were all-important, and we find that *cousinage* frequently defined who joined a monastery or went on crusade. Over two generations, twenty-five descendants of Guy of Monthéry took the Cross; and we have seen how Bernard appeared at the gates of Citeaux with thirty-five relatives and friends.

Was there a sexual element in this male bonding? Certainly, among monks there was no prohibition of the kind of *amitié particulière* that was frowned on later in the history of the Church. Some of the letters written by Anselm, the Benedictine Archbishop of Canterbury, read like love letters: 'Most beloved . . . since I do not doubt that we both love the other equally, I am sure that each of us equally desires the other, for those whose minds are fused together in the fire of love, suffer equally if their bodies are separated by the place of their daily occupations . . .'; or, 'If I were to describe the passion of our mutual love, I fear I should seem to those who do not know the truth to exaggerate. So I must subtract some part of the truth. But you know how great is the affection that we have experienced – eye to eye, kiss for kiss, embrace for embrace.'

Although Anselm was writing around half-a-century before the founding of the Templars, his case is pertinent to our consideration of the Templars' quasi-monastic way of life. The inferences drawn by the American academic, John Boswell,[138] from passages such as those quoted above, that Anselm regarded homosexual acts as 'common failings with which almost anyone could empathise', have been convincingly refuted by the eminent historian, Sir Richard Southern. Southern points out that 'no one knew anything about, or had any interest in, innate homosexual tendencies; in so far as they were known to exist, they were seen simply as symptoms of the general sinfulness of mankind.' The only recognised form of homosexuality in the eleventh century was sodomy, 'and this was roughly equated with another form of unnatural sex, copulation with animals'.[139]

The Church's unequivocal condemnation of sodomy as a sin against both God and nature was founded on the teaching of Paul of Tarsus[140] and Augustine of Hippo[141] which would have been well known to the literate Benedictines. It no doubt meant less to the illiterate knights and barons, and sodomy was certainly practised at the time of Anselm in the court of King William Rufus. 'It must be recognised that this sin has become so common', wrote Anselm, 'that hardly anyone blushes for it, and many, being ignorant of its enormity, have abandoned themselves to it.' As a result of what he saw, Anselm, as Archbishop of Canterbury, 'was notable for his condemnation of this sin and of any behaviour, such as long hair and effeminate clothes, which might encourage it'.[142]

It would therefore seem certain that, while the opportunity for homosexual *amours* was not a reason for joining the Templars, the fathers of the Council of Troyes were aware of the danger: hence the rule that the brothers' dormitory should remain lit throughout the night. The ban on sharing beds, sleeping naked or in the dark was 'lest the hostile enemy give them occasion to sin'.[143] It is also clear that there were cases where individual knights or sergeants succumbed to temptation. The offence was included in the detailed schedule of penances drawn up by the Order around 1167, described as 'the filthy, stinking sin of sodomy, which is so filthy and so stinking and so repugnant that it should not be named'.[144] It was of the same order of seriousness as killing a Christian man or woman – and was regarded as more serious than sleeping with a woman.

Upon the return to Jerusalem of his emissaries, Hugh of Payns and William of Burres, with forces they had recruited in Europe, King Baldwin II immediately embarked upon his projected assault on Damascus. Baldwin led his army, which included a contingent of Templars, from the frontier fortress of Banyas early in November and got within six miles of Damascus. William of Burres set off on a foraging expedition with the contingent from Europe which, impatient to plunder, got out of control. Twenty miles from the main camp, it was attacked by Damascene cavalry: only forty-five survived. Baldwin, hoping to catch the enemy off-guard as they were celebrating this victory, ordered his army to attack; but as it did so it began to rain and water poured down in such torrents that the roads became impassable and the move against Damascus had to be abandoned.

There is little information on the activities of Hugh of Payns and the early Templars over the next few years. The first fortress to be assigned to a military order, Bethgibelin, situated between Hebron in the Judaean hills and Ascalon on the coast, went to the Hospitallers in 1136. It is likely that the Templars concentrated their resources on the task for which they had been originally intended – guarding the routes commonly taken by pilgrims. At the Cisterna Rubea, midway between Jerusalem and Jericho, the Templars built a castle, a road-station and a chapel. There was a Templar tower closer to Jericho at Bait Jubr at-Tahtani; a castle and priory on the summit of Mount Quarantene where Jesus fasted for forty days and was tempted by Satan; and a castle by the River Jordan at the spot where Jesus was baptised by John the Baptist.[145]

The first major fortress assigned to the Templars was not in the Kingdom of Jerusalem but on the northernmost frontier of the Latin possessions in the Amanus Mountains. This narrow range runs south from Asia Minor and, rising to peaks of between two and three thousand metres, creates a natural barrier between the Armenian kingdom of Cilicia and the principality of Antioch; and also between Aleppo and the Syrian hinterland and the Mediterranean coast.

The road through these mountains from either Aleppo or Antioch to the ports of Alexandretta and Port Bonnel (Arsuz) is by the Belen Pass, otherwise known as the Syrian gates. In the 1130s the Templars were given the responsibility for securing the mountainous frontier region between the Kingdom of Cilicia and the Principality of Antioch – the Amanus march. To guard the Belen Pass through the Amanus range they occupied the stronghold of Barghas, which they called Gaston, a castle 'towering on an impenetrable summit, rising on an impregnable rock, its foundations touching the sky'.[146] Gaston was on the eastern side of the range and looked down over the plain of Aleppo to Antioch. Further north, to guard the Hajar Shuglan Pass, they occupied the castles of Darbsaq and la Roche de Roussel.

In 1130 the Prince of Antioch, Bohemond II, was killed fighting the Danishmend Turks and his embalmed head was sent by the Danishmend Emir Ghazi as a gift to the Caliph in Baghdad. His widow, Alice of Jerusalem, was the second of the three formidable daughters of Baldwin of Le Bourg and Morphia, an Armenian princess: her elder sister, Melisende, the heir to Jerusalem, was now married to Fulk of Anjou. Alice's daughter Constance now inherited her father's throne at Antioch but, upon hearing of the death of her husband, Alice usurped this role. It quickly became apparent that this was not the limit of her ambitions: she planned to disinherit her own daughter and to frustrate a move by her father, King Baldwin of Jerusalem, to exercise his rights as regent. Alice sent an emissary to Zengi, the Saracen governor of Aleppo, asking for his help.

This unfortunate messenger was intercepted by Baldwin and hanged. Alice shut the gates of Antioch to her father, probably with the support of the indigenous Christians among its citizens; but the French barons would not support her and reopened the gates. Father and daughter were reconciled; Alice was banished to the port of Latakia; but her disloyalty to her father no doubt hastened his end. Returning to Jerusalem a sick man, Baldwin was admitted as a canon of the Church of the Holy Sepulchre and in August 1131 died wearing the habit of a monk.

Five more years saw the death of Hugh of Payns. The general chapter of Templar knights assembled in Jerusalem to elect a new Grand Master, Robert of Craon, who, although known as 'the Burgundian', was in fact from Anjou and so was undoubtedly the favoured candidate of Fulk. However, he had also established a reputation as an outstanding administrator, and immediately proved his grasp of the needs of the Templar Order by obtaining additional and exceptional privileges from Pope Innocent II in a bull published in 1139, *Omne datum optimum.*

Addressed to 'our dear son Robert', this ruled that the Order of the Temple should be exempt from all intermediary ecclesiastical jurisdiction and be subject only to the Pope. Even the Patriarch of Jerusalem, before whom the founding knights had taken their vows, lost any authority over the Order. The bull allowed the Temple to have its own oratories, and permitted priests to join as chaplains which made the Templars wholly independent of the diocesan bishops both in Outremer and in the West. The Temple was entitled to receive tithes but need not pay them – an exemption that had hitherto only applied to the Cistercian Order; it could have cemeteries attached to its houses and bury travellers and their *confrâtres* – rights with a considerable pecuniary value. They were also entitled to booty taken from the enemy, and were to be answerable only to their Master who must be one of their number and chosen by the chapter without any pressure from secular powers.

What was behind this papal largesse? Innocent II, born Gregorio Papareschi, came from the Roman upper classes but his election had been contested and a rival candidate, taking the name Anacletus II, was backed by the Norman King of Sicily, Roger II. Innocent had fled to France where he won the support of Bernard of Clairvaux whose influence was sufficient to bring Louis VI of France and Henry I of England on to his side. Norbert, the Archbishop of Magdeburg, persuaded the German bishops and King Lothair III to back him, and finally only the Church in Scotland, Aquitaine and Norman Italy acknowledged Anacletus II.

Anacletus died in 1138 and in 1139 Innocent returned to Rome, the eight-year schism at an end. Was *Omne datum optimum* Bernard's reward for his support? Gratitude may have been a factor; however, bulls reinforcing the privileges of the Templars issued during the subsequent pontificates of Celestine II and Eugenius III – *Milites Templi* in 1144 and *Militia Dei* in 1145 – suggest that support for the Order was now the established policy of the Roman Curia. Holding the Holy Land remained a priority whoever happened to be wearing the papal tiara, and the Order of the Temple which had started as the charism of a few pious knights had already become a mainstay of Christendom's war against Islam.

If anyone doubted the need for increased aid to Outremer, it was demonstrated shortly after the publication of *Milites Templi*, on Christmas Eve, 1144, by the fall of Edessa to the army of the governor of Mosul, Imad ad-Din Zengi. News of this catastrophe reached the newly elected Pope, Eugenius III, in Viterbo in the autumn of 1145. An Italian from a humble background, Eugenius had once been a monk at Clairvaux, drawn into the community by the magnetism of Bernard, and at the time of his election he was Abbot of the Cistercian house Saints Vincenzo and Anastasio outside Rome. In response to this setback in the East, Eugenius addressed a bull, *Quantum praedecessores*, to Louis VII, the King of France, appealing to him to take the Cross.

Now, for the first time, an European monarch took up the challenge of a crusade. Louis was the direct descendant of Hugh Capet, elected King of the Franks by the Frankish barons in 987. Inheriting the throne of his father, Louis the Fat, at the age of seventeen, he was married to Eleanor, the daughter and heiress of William, Duke of Aquitaine. Still only twenty-five when he received the Pope's appeal, he summoned his barons to join him at Bourges for Christmas, 1145. There he told them that he planned to go on crusade and invited them to do the same. Louis made no mention of the Pope's appeal, nor of his encyclical *Quantum praedecessores*, but presented the initiative as his own.

The response was poor. The leading barons had little respect for Louis who, three years before, had precipitated a war by siezing land belonging to his most powerful vassal, Theobald of Champagne. At Bourges even his own chief counsellor, Abbot Suger of Saint-Denis, argued against the idea of a crusade: a far-sighted statesman who saw the value of a strong monarchy, Suger feared that the French barons would make trouble in their king's absence. The most Louis could achieve at Bourges was an agreement to postpone a decision on the matter until the following Easter when the court would reassemble at Vézelay in Burgundy.

Undaunted by this initial setback to his plan, King Louis turned to the one man in France whose authority and prestige exceeded that of Abbot Suger – Bernard of Clairvaux. It was now thirty-two years since Bernard had appeared at the gates of Cîteaux; and thirty since he had founded the Cistercian community at Clairvaux. In those years, as we have seen, he had established a unique position as the mentor of popes and kings. Not only had Eugenius III been one of his monks but that very year Louis VII's brother, Henry of France, had joined the community at Clairvaux.

Bernard's power did not stem simply from these influential connections: in a world where so many preached but so few practised the Christian virtues, his piety and asceticism qualified him to act as the conscience of Christendom, constantly chastising the rich and powerful and championing the poor and the weak. To some modern historians, living in a period when most are indifferent to what awaits them after death, Bernard comes across as a self-righteous zealot – someone who 'saw the world with the eye of a fanatic'[147] and 'had a disquieting tendency to take it for granted that his contemporaries were evil-doers who needed to repent'.[148] However, to Bernard, surrounded by secular brutality and clerical corruption, and utterly convinced of the reality of Hell, it was impossible to do too much to save an imperilled soul.

The glamour of evil, in his perception, lay not just in the obvious lure of wealth and worldly power, but in the subtler and ultimately more pernicious attraction of false ideas. Besides his piety, Bernard was renowned for his outstanding intellect which he demonstrated in his sermons on Grace, Free Will and the Book of the Old Testament, the Song of Songs. He was quick to recognise heretical ideas and implacable in his pursuit of those who taught them. In 1141, at the Council of Sens, he had accused the celebrated theologian (and lover of Elouise) Peter Abelard of heresy and had persuaded the assembled bishops to condemn Abelard's overly rationalistic teaching.

In 1145, even as Eugenius III was contemplating a new crusade, Bernard was in Languedoc preaching against the heretical ideas of a popular preacher, Henry of Lausanne. Having been instrumental in reconciling King Louis VII with Count Theobald of Champagne, Bernard listened sympathetically to the young King's request. However, he did not like to see a spiritual venture led by a secular lord and so referred the matter back to Pope Eugenius who, on 1 March 1146, reissued his bull *Quantum praedecessores* and gave Bernard the task of promulgating it in France.

On 31 March, Louis VII and the French nobles gathered in Vézelay, as had been arranged. Already the knowledge that Bernard was to preach had drawn admirers from all over France. As with Pope Urban II at Clermont in 1095, the church which housed the relics of Mary Magdalene was not large enough to hold the crowd: a platform had to be built on the outskirts of the town. Bernard's eloquence had the desired effect. When he had finished his address, so many were ready to take the Cross that Bernard had to cut his habit into strips of cloth.

First came King Louis, and after him his brother Robert, Count of Dreux. Many of those who followed the Capetian princes 'were following, or were intending to follow, in the footsteps of fathers and grandfathers',[149] such as Alfonso-Jordan, Count of Toulouse, who had been born while his father was besieging Tripoli; William, Count of Nevers, whose father had taken part in the disastrous expedition of 1101; Thierry, Count of Flanders, who was married to the stepdaughter of Queen Melisende; and Henry, heir to the Count of Flanders. They were joined by Amadeus, Count of Savoy; Archimbald, Count of Bourbon; and the bishops of Langres, Arras and Lisieux. A few days later, Bernard wrote to the Pope: 'You ordered; I obeyed; and the authority of him who gave the order has made my obedience fruitful ... Villages and towns are now deserted. You will scarcely find one man for every seven women. Everywhere you will see widows whose husbands are still alive.'[150]

Bernard's preaching was not confined to Vézelay. From there he went north to Châlons-sur-Marne, then on to Flanders. Those potential recruits he could not meet face to face, he addressed by letter. To the English people he wrote:

The Lord of heaven is losing his land, the land in which he appeared to men, in which he lived amongst men for more than thirty years ... Your land is well known to be rich in young and vigorous men. The world is full of their praises, and the renown of their courage is on the lips of all ...[151]

He stressed their good fortune in being given this chance to save their souls.

You now have a cause for which you can fight without endangering your soul; a cause in which to win is glorious and for which to die is but gain … Do not miss this opportunity. Take the sign of the cross. At once you will have indulgence for all the sins which you confess with a contrite heart. It does not cost you much to buy and if you wear it with humility you will find that it is the kingdom of heaven.

At first, no similar appeal was made to the Germans because Pope Eugenius wanted King Conrad III to help him against the Norman King of Sicily, Roger II. However, Bernard was summoned to the Rhineland by the Archbishop of Mainz to stop the unauthorised preaching of a Cistercian monk called Rudolf which was inciting pogroms against the Jews. Bernard had already condemned such atrocities in his letters. 'The Jews are not to be persecuted, killed or even put to flight … The Jews are for us the living words of Scripture, for they remind us always what the Lord suffered.'[152]

The monk Rudolf was put in his place, but the enthusiasm for the crusade which he had aroused could not now be assuaged. It was therefore decided to include the Germans, and Bernard travelled from city to city advertising this wonderful opportunity for the remission of sins. His emphasis was always on the spiritual advantage to the sinner – the exceptional opportunity to escape punishment for one's sins – and God seemed to validate what he offered by working miracles in his wake.

Bernard's most important task was to persuade a reluctant King Conrad to lead the German crusaders. He failed at his first attempt at Frankfurt in November 1146; but he was given a second chance at Speyer at Christmas. Here, though an interpreter, he asked Conrad to imagine Christ on the Day of Judgement comparing what he had done for Conrad with what Conrad had done for him. 'Man, what ought I to have done for you that I have not done?' The King's answer was to kneel and take the Cross.

In January 1147, Pope Eugenius III crossed the Alps to France. He was met by King Louis in Dijon and proceeded to Clairvaux, the abbey where he had once been a monk. From Clairvaux he went on to Paris, spending Easter at the Abbey of Saint-Denis. On Easter Day he presented King Louis with the royal standard, the *oriflamme*, and a pilgrim's stick; then, on 27 April, the octave of Easter, he attended the chapter meeting of the French Templars in their new enclave built just to the north of the city of Paris.

It was a solemn and magnificent occasion that established the importance of the Order. Eugenius appointed Brother Aymar, the Templar Treasurer in Paris, to receive the proceeds of a one-twentieth tax on all Church goods that the Pope had instituted to pay for the crusade.[153] Accompanying the Pope were King Louis of France, the Archbishop of Rheims, four other bishops and one hundred and thirty knights. The Master of the Order, Everard of Barres, had recalled his best men from Portugal and Spain. With them were at least as many sergeants and squires. The sight of the bearded knights in their white habits impressed all the chroniclers who recorded the event; and it was almost certainly here that Pope Eugenius gave them the right to wear a scarlet cross over their hearts, 'so that the sign would serve triumphantly as a shield and they would never turn away in the face of the infidels': the red blood of the martyr was superimposed on the white of the chaste.[154]

A number of German magnates had followed Conrad's example in taking the Cross but some of those with lands in the East such as Henry the Lion, Duke of Saxony, and Albert the Bear, Margrave of Brandenburg, were granted the same privileges by Pope Eugenius for a crusade against the pagan Wends on the eastern marches of Christian Europe. Despite these defections, an army of around twenty thousand men set off from Regensburg in May 1147 to follow the overland route taken by the First Crusade. The French army that had assembled at Metz followed few weeks later, King Louis accompanied by his spirited wife, Eleanor of Aquitaine.

Unlike his predecessor, Alexius Comnenus, the Byzantine Emperor Manuel Comnenus had not asked for help from western Europe and was suspicious of its intentions. He was at war with Roger of Sicily and had felt obliged to conclude a treaty with the Seljuk Turks to cover his rear. To the western crusaders, this pact with the infidel was only comprehensible as a symptom of treachery and Manuel's suspicion of them was returned tenfold.

Impatient to proceed, Conrad crossed the Bosphorus with his army of Germans. At Nicaea they split up. Otto, Bishop of Freising, set off with all the non-combatants on the longer coastal route still controlled by the Byzantines while Conrad led the army on the direct route across Anatolia. At Dorylaeum it was attacked and defeated by the Seljuk Turks. The survivors, Conrad among them, returned to Nicaea where they were joined by the French. The two kings now led their forces south to Ephesus, constantly skirmishing with the Byzantines in their search for food.

At Ephesus, Conrad fell ill and returned by sea to Constantinople. The French proceeded inland along the valley of the Meander. Already, King Louis had learned the value of the Master of the French Templars, Everard of Barres, sending him as one of his three ambassadors to treat with the Byzantine Emperor, Manuel Comnenus. Now he came to appreciate the value of his knights. As they marched through the bitter winter weather – the Queen and her ladies-in-waiting shivering in their litters – the crusaders were constantly harassed by the Turks' light cavalry, horsemen with a particular talent for firing arrows while on the move. The Franks' heavy cavalry, so effective in a pitched battle, could not be deployed in the narrow passes of the Cadmus Mountains. Here the Turks intensified their attacks and the French army was in danger of disintegration. In this extremity, Louis turned to Everard of Barres. Everard divided the army into different units, each led by a Templar knight: 'a form of communal organisation retrieved the situation; the crusaders formed a fraternity with the Templars, whose commands they swore to obey'.[155] In this way the column reached the Byzantine port of Attalia from where King Louis sailed to Antioch with the cream of what remained of his army, leaving the rest to proceed to Syria as best they could.

A warm welcome awaited King Louis and the French crusaders when they reached Antioch. The reigning prince was now Raymond of Poitiers, a younger son of Duke William of Aquitaine who had been married to Constance, the young heiress to the principality, some years before. He was therefore the uncle of Eleanor of Aquitaine and now rode down to the port of Saint-Symeon to greet his royal niece and the French crusaders. For Raymond and the Latin barons, the French party was considerably enhanced by the presence of the young queen with her ladies-in-waiting: and Eleanor, too, was pleased to see her courageous uncle Raymond. Beautiful, intelligent, vivacious, high-spirited and around twenty-five years old, she found that her feelings for her petulant and indecisive young husband had not been improved by the terrible journey across Anatolia.

Louis's position at this juncture was made worse by lack of money: he had spent all his treasure on food and transport supplied at extortionate prices by his Byzantine allies. Again, he turned to the French Master of the Templars. Everard of Barres sailed to Acre where he used the Temple's resources to raise the sum required. The King wrote to Abbot Suger instructing him to repay the Temple two thousand silver marks, a sum equivalent to half the annual income of the royal demesne,[156] demonstrating not just the high cost of crusading but also the considerable financial resources of the Temple.

Eleanor's flirtatious gaiety was clearly appreciated by her uncle and gossip began to circulate in his court at Antioch that their affection for one another had transgressed the bounds of propriety. The feelings of Raymond's wife Constance are not known: she was later to demonstrate that she too was capable of passion but at this stage was perhaps still too young to be aware of what was going on. Not so King Louis, whose jealousy was aggravated by Eleanor's outspoken support for Raymond's ideas about what should be done with the French expeditionary force.

Raymond wanted Louis to attack Aleppo to relieve the pressure on his forces confronting the Seljuk Turks in the north. He argued that it was also the best preliminary to a reconquest of Edessa whose fall had led to the crusade. Louis might have agreed, had it not been for his suspicion that Raymond was sleeping with his wife. Hearing that Conrad, now recovered, had reached Acre, he announced that it was only in Jerusalem that his vow could be fulfilled. He gave orders for his army to march south. Eleanor, with the self-assurance of a woman who knows that she is richer than her husband, said that she would stay and petition for their marriage to be annulled. Louis took her with him by force.

Despite the losses suffered by the German and French armies as they crossed Anatolia, a considerable force from western Europe assembled at Acre in June 1148. The two kings Conrad and Louis had been joined by troops under the Marquis of Montferrat and the counts of Auvergne and Savoy. A Provençal force had arrived by sea under Alfonso Jordan, the Count of Toulouse. Also by sea came what remained of a contingent of English, Flemish and Frisian crusaders: it had been diverted *en route* by Afonso Henriques, King of Portugal, to help him take Lisbon from the Moors.

On 24 June the assembly of Latins from Europe and Outremer was presided over by the young King of Jerusalem, Baldwin III, who ruled jointly with his mother, Melisende. Attending him were the principal barons and bishops of his kingdom. The local team was outranked by the visitors, which included King Conrad and two of his half-brothers, the

Duke of Austria and the Bishop of Freisingen, his nephew Frederick of Swabia, Welf of Bavaria, and the powerful bishops of Metz and Toul. With King Louis were his brother Robert of Dreux, Henry of Champagne (son of his old enemy, Theobald), and Thierry, Count of Flanders. Also present were the Grand Masters of the Temple and the Hospital. Notable for their absence were Raymond of Poitiers, Prince of Antioch, in a huff after the fracas with Louis; and Alfonso-Jordan, Count of Toulouse, who had died suddenly while at Caesarea.

What was to be done with this powerful army? Sage counsel would have concurred with Raymond of Antioch that the greatest threat to the Franks came from Aleppo, ruled by Zengi's son, Nur ed-Din. His defeat was also the necessary preliminary to the recovery of Edessa. To the south, the road to Egypt was blocked by the stronghold of Ascalon, still in the hands of the Fatimid caliphs. The third possible objective was Damascus, but Damascus was the only Muslim power in the region that had shown itself willing to join with the Franks against Nur ed-Din. This consideration was dismissed, either by the local barons who had their eye on the large swathe of fertile land controlled by the Damascenes, or by the European monarchs who felt that Damascus, a city with biblical resonance, would bring them not just booty but also renown.

Like the force led by King Baldwin II twenty years before, the crusading army marched through Banyas and reached Damascus on 24 July. It pitched camp in the orchards south of the city and prepared for the siege. The Damascenes made sorties and attacked the Franks with irregular forces hidden in the orchards. Deciding that this ground cover was helping the enemy, the two European monarchs moved their camp to the open ground to the east of Damascus. Here they could deploy their heavy cavalry but there was no water and they faced the best-fortified section of the city walls.

Muslim reinforcements entered Damascus from the north and joined the native forces in repeated forays. While the leaders of the crusaders' invincible army bickered over who would rule the city once it was captured, their forces were obliged to go on the defensive and rumours started to circulate that they had been betrayed. Word reached their camp that Nur ed-Din was on his way to relieve Damascus on the understanding that he would be permitted to enter the city. The local barons now realised the folly of their strategy and on 28 July persuaded the European monarchs to abandon the siege. Harassed by Damascene light cavalry, the once invincible army limped back to Galilee. The humiliation of the crusaders was complete.

Inevitably, after a débâcle of this kind, its authors looked for scapegoats and found them in many different and contradictory guises. The crusaders blamed the barons of Outremer who had previously been on such friendly terms with the Damascenes. They had taken their money before; was it not likely that they had taken it again? Even the Templars came under suspicion. In November, King Conrad left the Holy Land in disgust. With his entourage, he took ship from Acre to Thessalonika from whence he was lured back to Constantinople by the Emperor, Manuel Comnenus. If he harboured suspicions of Greek treachery, he suppressed them: the Greek Emperor and the German King had a common enemy in Roger of Sicily and an alliance was sealed with the marriage of Conrad's brother to Manuel's niece.

To King Louis VII, the Byzantines had been the cause of all their misfortunes and they now joined the Saracens as the enemies of Christendom. Despite the pleas of Abbot Suger for him to return, Louis lingered in Palestine, brooding on the catastrophe, his hatred of the Greeks moving him towards an alliance with King Roger. When he finally decided to return to western Europe, he chose a Sicilian ship. Off the Peloponnese, the flotilla was attacked by a Byzantine squadron: when Louis's standard was raised, his boat was allowed to sail on but some of his company and most of his possessions in a second Sicilian ship were captured and taken as booty to Constantinople.

This final humiliation brought Louis's simmering hatred of the Greeks to the boil. At Potenza, with King Roger, Louis planned a new crusade that would include Constantinople among its objectives. He continued to promote the idea upon his journey north, ignoring the scepticism expressed by Pope Eugenius, and recruiting several curial cardinals, the Abbot of Cluny, Peter the Venerable, and even his chief mentor, Abbot Suger of Saint-Denis.

No doubt Louis' vengeful frame of mind came partly from the knowledge that he had lost much more in the East than a fine army and the laurels of victory: he had also lost his wife, and with his wife a dowry greater than the Kingdom of France. When they passed through Rome on their way back from the crusade, Pope Eugenius attempted to reconcile the royal couple, whose problematic marriage was by now common knowledge, insisting upon them sleeping in the same bed, and weeping as he blessed them when they departed.[157]

Despite the Pope's counselling, the marriage never recovered from Louis's humiliation during the Second Crusade. Among the memories of the still young King, responsibility for the fiasco before the walls of Damascus had at least been shared with others: but that dreadful march across Anatolia, his army constantly harassed, saved from annihilation not by his leadership but by the discipline of the Templars; his abandonment of a large part of his army in the port of Attalia; and the final disgrace of finding himself a cuckold in the court of his wife's uncle – all this was surely more painful and, in his own mind, stemmed from the treachery of the Greeks.

Driven to prove himself and seek revenge, Louis appealed yet again to Bernard of Clairvaux to preach this new crusade. As before, Bernard felt he could not refuse. Always longing for the peace of the cloister, he nevertheless felt compelled to try and salvage something from what had been lost. He had corresponded with Queen Melisende in Jerusalem, and with his uncle Andrew of Montbard, the Templar Seneschal in Outremer, and so knew well of their need for help. He was also aware that many of those who had taken the Cross at his prompting held him responsible for the disaster. He defended himself in the second book of his *De consideratione*. The scapegoats here were not treacherous barons or scheming Greeks: to Bernard the débâcle was God's punishment for men's sins. To his critics, this hypothesis made God too inscrutable by half: some, like Gerhoh of Reichersberg, preferred to see the crusade as the work of the Devil.

At a Church Council held in Chartres in 1150, Bernard was asked not just to preach but to lead a new crusade. 'I expect you must have heard by now', he wrote to Pope Eugenius,

> how the assembly at Chartres, by a most surprising decision, chose me as the leader and commander of the expedition. You may be quite sure that this never was and is not now by my advice or wish, and that it is altogether beyond my powers, as I gauge them, to do such a thing. Who am I to arrange armies in battle order, to lead forth armed men? I could think of nothing more remote from my calling, even supposing I had the necessary strengths and skill. But you know all this, it is not for me to teach you.[158]

In the event, the Council's command was scotched by the Cistercian

Order. Nor did the nobility of western Europe respond to the Abbot of Clairvaux's appeal. Too many had died too recently and to no avail. King Louis's zeal was counterbalanced by King Conrad's scepticism. The idea of a new crusade was abandoned and, within three years, five of the principal players had left the stage. Abbot Suger of Saint-Denis died in January 1151; King Conrad III died in February 1152. Later in the same year, the Grand Master of the Templars, Everard of Barres, resigned his post to become a monk at Clairvaux. Pope Eugenius III died in July 1153; and Abbot Bernard of Clairvaux one month later.

seven

Outremer

The disillusion in Europe that followed the fiasco of the Second Crusade obliged the Latins in the Holy Land to reach the kind of accommodation with the infidel that would have seemed sacrilegious to the previous generation of crusaders. This was also the consequence of a process of cultural acclimatisation that had occurred over half a century of living in the East. The early crusaders had expected to encounter wild savages and depraved pagans in Syria and Palestine: but those who had remained in the Middle East had been obliged to recognise that the culture of Arab Palestine – Muslim, Christian, and Jewish – was more evolved and sophisticated than that at home.

Some had quickly adopted Eastern customs. Baldwin of Le Bourg, having married an Armenian wife, took to wearing an Eastern kaftan and dined squatting on a carpet; while the coins minted by Tancred showed him with the head-dress of an Arab. The Damascene chronicler and diplomat, Usamah Ibn-Munqidh, describes a Frankish knight reassuring a Muslim guest that he never allowed pork to enter his kitchen and that he employed an Egyptian cook.[159]

The Franks employed Syrian doctors, cooks, servants, artisans, labourers. They clothed themselves in eastern garments, included in their diets the fruits and dishes of the country. They had glass in their windows, mosaics on their floors, fountains in the courtyards of their houses, which were planned on the Syrian model. They had dancing girls at their entertainments; professional mourners at their funerals; took baths; used soap; ate sugar.[160]

Coming from a cold climate where fresh produce was unavailable during winter, and where even the potato was as yet unknown, the encounter not

128

just with sugar but also with figs, pomegranates, olives, rice, hummus, peaches, oranges, lemons and bananas, the spices indigenous to the region, and delicacies such as sherbet whose names have since entered the gastronomic vocabulary of the West, must have convinced the crusaders that it was not just in a spiritual sense that this was the promised land. Certainly, the hot climate was debilitating and indeed in some cases proved fatal; but among those who survived, many adopted the scented, sensuous lifestyle which they had thought *effete* in the Byzantines.

Not only were the Franks softened by the style of life they encountered in Syria and Palestine; they were also obliged to reach a *modus vivendi* with the Muslims who remained a majority of the population. As long as they paid their taxes, the Frankish overlords were prepared to permit the Muslim communities to choose their own administration. As in the reconquered territories in Spain, there were insufficient Christian immigrants to replace the Muslims; it was therefore important for the fief-holders to persuade them to stay. A baron's wealth depended upon their prosperity. Nor did his principal revenue come from the land, as in Europe. 'The Holy Land was an urbanised area *par excellence*[161] and a baron's income came from rents on properties, tolls, licences for public baths, ovens and markets, port dues and levies on goods.[162]

By the standards of the day – and even by those of today – these charges and exactions were not severe: the tax on a peasant's produce (*terrage*) was fixed at around one-third. Although the Muslims' first loyalty was always to Islam, there is evidence that they were not dissatisfied with Latin rule. The rule of Frankish overlords was in fact lighter than in the former period of Muslim domination.[163] The Franks' respect for feudal law contrasted favourably with the capricious demands of Muslim princes. Certainly, Muslims were second-class citizens; they were forbidden to wear Frankish dress; but they had their own courts and officials. Conversion to Christianity brought with it full civil rights and led to assimilation into the Christian Syrian population. Among the Franks themselves there were no serfs, a fact that distinguished it from the feudal societies in western Europe. 'Though hierarchic, it was a society of free men, where even the poorest and most destitute were not only free, but enjoyed a higher legal standing than the richest among the conquered native population.'[164]

Despite the anti-Semitic atrocities that had accompanied the First Crusade, there was a large measure of tolerance of the Jews in the crusader states: they were treated much better than their counterparts in western Europe and could practise their religion in relative freedom.[165] Jewish pilgrimages to the holy places and Jerusalem became more frequent from as far off as Byzantium, Spain, France and Germany.[166] No attempt was made by the Catholic Latins to convert the Muslims or the Jews: there was a remarkable lack of any kind of missionary activity. The religious disputes that did take place were rather between the Catholics and Orthodox Christians, exacerbated by Latin rivalry with Byzantium; or between both Catholic and Orthodox and the Jacobite, Armenian, Nestorian and Maronite churches.

The indigenous population – both Muslim and Christian – also benefited from the prosperity that came with the increase in trade. Prior to conquest by the crusaders, a small flow of commerce in oriental products such as silks and spices found its way to the West via the merchants of Amalfi. With the capture of the ports on the Mediterranean coast and the granting of concessions to the growing maritime powers from Italy – Venice, Genoa and Pisa – considerable trade was stimulated with the Muslim hinterland financed by a Latin currency, the *besant* – 'the first Christian coin in wide circulation, struck a hundred years before the *florins* and *ducats* of Italy'.[167]

The Templars benefited from this prosperity through their fiefs, and they also came to extend a tolerance to the indigenous Muslims which shocked those newly arrived from Europe. There was a celebrated incident when Usamah Ibn-Munqidh came to Jerusalem to negotiate a pact against Zengi, the Saracen governor of Aleppo.

> When I was visiting Jerusalem, I used to go to the al-Aqsa mosque, where my Templar friends were staying. Along one side of the building was a small oratory in which the Franj had set up a church. The Templars placed this spot at my disposal that I might say my prayers. One day I entered, said *Allahu akbar* and was about to begin my prayer, when a man, a Franj, threw himself upon me, grabbed me, and turned me toward the east, saying, 'Thus do we pray.' The Templars rushed forward and led him away. I then set myself to prayer once more, but this same man, seizing upon a moment of inattention, threw himself upon me yet again, turned my face to the east, and repeated once more, 'Thus do we pray.' Once again, the Templars intervened, led him away, and apologised to me, saying, 'He is a foreigner. He has just arrived from the land of the

Franj and he has never seen anyone pray without turning to face the east.'[168]

Despite his friendship with the Templars, the attitude of Usamah towards the Franks was one of contempt. He ridicules trial by combat and trial by ordeal as a form of justice, and is scornful of their medical practices. In fact, the Franks developed a pragmatic approach towards disease: the kind of religious hysteria provoked by the epidemic in Antioch during the First Crusade was not repeated, 'perhaps because prayer and penance had not worked'; and subsequently the crusaders 'seem to have approached medicine in a very practical way, and may have had less to learn from the native practitioners than had been assumed'.[169] By and large, the only Latin quality deemed worthy of respect by Muslims was their military prowess. They despised the Christians' culture and beliefs. 'According to the *Bahr al-Fava'id*, the books of foreigners were not worth reading ... [and] anyone who believes that his God came out of a woman's privates is quite mad; he should not be spoken to, and he has neither intelligence nor faith.'[170]

This contempt for the religious beliefs of the enemy was, by and large, returned. The Templars might have permitted their Muslim guest to pray in their chapel, but they used the al-Aqsa mosque as an administrative centre and a store. Theoderich, a German monk on pilgrimage to Jerusalem in the 1170s, calling it the palace of Solomon, describes how it was used for 'stores of arms, clothing and food they always have ready to guard the province and defend it'. Below the mosque were the Templars' stables 'erected by King Solomon' with space, he estimated, for ten thousand horses. Adjacent to the al-Aqsa was the palace originally occupied by King Baldwin I, and a number of other:

> houses, dwellings and outbuildings for every kind of purpose, and it is full of walking-places, lawns, council-chambers, porches, consistories and supplies of water in splendid cisterns ... On the other side of the palace, that is on the west, the Templars have built a new house, whose height, length and breadth, and all its cellars and refectories, staircase and roof are far beyond the custom of this land ... There indeed they have constructed a new Palace, just as on the other side they have the old one. There too they have founded on the edge of the outer court a new church of magnificent size and workmanship.[171]

It is difficult to know how many lived in this compound. At most, there

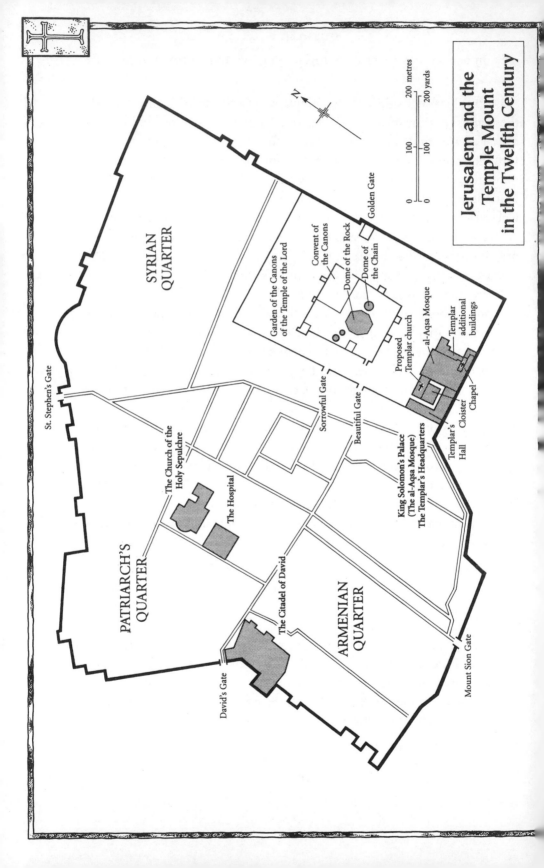

Jerusalem and the
Temple Mount
in the Twelfth Century

SYRIAN
QUARTER

PATRIARCH'S
QUARTER

ARMENIAN
QUARTER

St. Stephen's Gate

The Church of the
Holy Sepulchre

The Hospital

The Citadel of David

David's Gate

Mount Sion Gate

Sorrowful Gate

Beautiful Gate

King Solomon's Palace
(The al-Aqsa Mosque)
The Templar's Headquarters

Garden of the Canons
of the Temple of the Lord

Convent of
the Canons

Dome of the Rock

Dome of
the Chain

Proposed
Templar church

al-Aqsa Mosque

Templar
additional
buildings

Templar's
Hall

Cloister

Chapel

Golden Gate

N

200 metres
200 yards

0   100
0   100

were probably around 300 knights in the Kingdom of Jerusalem and around 1,000 sergeants.[172] There would have been an irregular and indeterminate number of knights serving for a set period in the Order, and there were the Templar Turcopoles – native Syrian light cavalry employed by the Order. Beyond this, there would been a large number of auxiliaries of one sort or another – armourers, grooms, blacksmiths, stonemasons and sculptors: Templar sculptors 'prepared the most elaborately decorated of all royal tombs' for King Baldwin IV.[173] The Templars therefore participated in the extraordinary boom in building that took place in the Holy Land under the crusaders – fortresses, palaces and above all churches: 'not even Herod built as much'.[174] Among the major architectural accomplishments were the new Church of the Holy Sepulchre, dedicated in 1149, and the redecoration of the Church of the Nativity in Bethlehem – 'a milestone in crusader artistic development because many artists from a variety of backgrounds took part'.[175]

Despite this cultural refinement, and the sensuous blandishments that came with the climate, the Templars appear to have kept to their Rule and retained a quasi-monastic way of life. When not in the field, the Templars followed the same kind of timetable as Benedictine or Cistercian monks. At four in the morning, they rose for matins after which they went to take care of their horses before returning to bed. The further offices of Prime, Terce and Sext preceded their breakfast which, like all their other meals, was eaten in silence while listening to a reading from the Bible. At 2.30 p.m. there was Nones and their evening meal followed Vespers which was at 6.00 p.m. They retired to bed after Compline and remained silent until the next day. Orders were given after each office except Compline. When in the field, every attempt was made to follow the same regime.

There were more than six hundred clauses in the Templar statutes, some elaborations on those of the primitive Rule, others drawn up to deal with questions that had arisen since the Council of Troyes. The original seal of the Order had shown two knights riding on a single horse. Now, the Master was permitted to have four horses, and could have in his entourage one chaplain, one clerk, one sergeant and one valet with a horse to carry his shield and lance. He should also be accompanied by a blacksmith, an interpreter, a turcopole and a cook. There were clear limits to his powers: he was not to have the key to the treasury, and he could only lend large sums with the consent 'of a group of the worthy men of the house'. Limits were also set to his munificence: he could give a noble friend of the house a gold or silver goblet, a squirrel-hair robe or some other item worth no more than one hundred besants, and these gifts should only be made with the consent of his companions and for the benefit of the house.

The Rule reflects some of the prejudices of the period; for example, despite the commitment to humility, it became necessary by the mid-twelfth century for a Templar knight to be 'the son of a knight or descended from the son of a knight' (rule 337). The white habit that had been chosen to symbolise purity now became a mark of prestige: the tunics of the squires and sergeants were brown or black. The knights ate at the first sitting, the sergeants and squires at the second. Given the fact that almost none of the knights or sergeants could read, it seems likely that most of the statutes simply reflected the practices that had evolved, and were picked up by new recruits like new boys at a public school. And like the punishments meted out in public schools in the past, the penances inflicted on erring Templars seem savage – whipping, being put in irons, or being obliged to eat like a dog off the floor. Such penances were similar to those imposed on monks, and were normal for the time.

Every aspect of the Templar's daily life was regulated down to the smallest detail. When he should eat, how much he should eat, how he should comport himself while eating – even how he should cut cheese (371) – is specified in the Rule. He could not rise from table without permission unless he had a nosebleed, there was a call to arms (and then he had to be sure that the call was made by a brother or 'a worthy man'), a fire or a disturbance among the horses. He had no private property: 'all things of the house are common, and let it be known that neither the Master nor anyone else has the authority to give a brother permission to have anything of his own ...' If any money was found in a brother's possession on his death, he was not to be buried in hallowed ground.

The care of horses was clearly of cardinal importance: the number allocated to the Master is stated in the first statute and horses are mentioned in around a hundred of those that follow. There were several different sorts: warhorses for the knights; lighter, swifter steeds for the turcopoles; palfreys; mules; packhorses and rouncies – transport for men-at-arms. Each knight was allowed his own horse, while the others were kept in a general pool in the charge of the Marshal of the Order. Horses were bred on stud farms both in the Kingdom of Jerusalem and in western Europe – for example, at the Temple commandery at Richerenches in northern Provence. There were precise regulations for the care of the horses, and one of the only excuses for missing prayers was taking a horse to the blacksmith for shoeing.[176]

Few clauses in the Rule pertain to training: a knight was expected to be adept at mounted combat before he joined the Order. Given the weight of the accoutrements of combat, each must have been immensely strong. A knight was expected to bring his own horse and equipment. If he was serving as a *confrère* for a limited term, they would be returned when it ended or, if his horse died in Templar service, he would be given another from the pool. True to the spirit of Bernard of Clairvaux, saddles and bridles were not to be adorned; permission had to be obtained to race and the placing of wagers on the outcome was forbidden.

Although the way of life suggested by the Templar Rule is imbued with Christian religiosity, and the monastic practices given an equal standing to the military regulations, there is a shift in emphasis in comparison with the primitive Rule from the quest for individual salvation to a regimental *esprit de corps.* 'Each brother should strive to live honestly and to set a good example to secular people and other orders in everything ...' (340): the unspecified 'other orders' were principally the Hospitallers and later the Teutonic knights. The Temple's two-pointed black-and-white banner, the *confanon baucon,* was their rallying point in battle. It was held by the Marshal and ten knights were assigned to guard it, one of whom kept a spare banner furled on his lance. While this banner was still held aloft, no Templar could leave the field of battle. If a knight was cut off from his contingent, he was allowed to regroup around the Hospitaller or another Christian banner (167).

The monastic vow of obedience was invaluable in a military context: severe penalties were imposed on a knight who succumbed to the impetuosity so common among the Frankish knights and charged at the enemy on his own initiative. The only occasions upon which he was permitted to break rank were to make a brief sortie to ensure that his saddle and harness were secure or if he saw a Christian being attacked by a Saracen. In any other circumstances, the punishment was to be sent back to the camp on foot (163).

In the same way no distinction was made between military and religious transgressions. Of the nine 'Things for which a Brother of the House of the Temple may be Expelled from the House', four were sins that had nothing as such to do with life under arms: simony, murder, theft and heresy. Revealing the proceedings of the Temple chapter, conspiracy between two or more brothers, and leaving a Templar house other than by the prescribed gates are infringements that would have applied to any monastic institution. Only the punishment of cowardice and desertion to the enemy relate specifically to conditions of war.

Thus the regimental ethos was never distinct from the Christian ethos of the Temple as a religious community. The regulations governing fasts and feast-days, the saying of office and prayers for the dead, were quite as precise as those concerned with saddles and bridles. The Templars showed a particular devotion to Mary, the Mother of Jesus: 'And the hours of Our Lady should always be said first in this house ... because Our Lady was the beginning of our Order, and in her and in her honour, if it please God, will be the end of our lives and the end of our Order, whenever God wishes it to be' (306). A number of beliefs arose which linked Mary with the Temple: for example, it was said that the Annunciation had taken place in the Temple of the Lord (the Dome of the Rock) and a stone on which Mary rested was outside the Templar fortress of Castle Pilgrim. There were Lady chapels in many of the Templar churches and a number of their houses, such as that at Richerenches, were dedicated to Mary: Richerenches was referred to by a number of donors not as the Temple but as 'the house of the Blessed Mary'.[177]

One of the more revealing clauses in the Templar Rule (325) concerns the wearing of leather gloves, which was allowed only to the chaplain brothers, 'who are permitted to wear them in honour of Our Lord's body, which they often hold in their hands'; and to the 'mason brothers ... because of the great suffering they endure and so that they do not easily injure their hands; but they should not wear them when they are not working'.[178] The number of these mason brothers is not known, but because of the importance of the fortresses in Outremer their skills would have been highly valued. A castle built by the Templars or the Hospitallers 'showed itself as a fortress without, while within it was a monastery'.[179] With a relatively small garrison, a well-provisioned castle could withstand a siege of a considerable army. Should that army ignore it, it could make sorties to attack its rear. Sieges tied down large armies which could often only be held together for a limited period of time. Non-mercenary troops had to think of the harvest and the protection of their families from marauders who took advantage of their absence: and in the case of the Franks, the feudal levy was restricted to a period of forty days. The conflict between Christians and Muslims in the Holy Land 'rarely afforded the spectacle of two armies bent on mutual destruction; the true end of military activity was the capture and defence of fortified places'.[180]

A prime example was the great fortress of Ascalon, held by the Fatimid caliphs in Egypt. Supplied by land across the Sinai peninsula and by sea from Alexandria, it protected the coastal road leading to Egypt and pro vided a base for raids against Christian settlements. In an attempt to contain Ascalon, King Fulk had surrounded it with a ring of fortresses at Ibelin, Blanchegarde and Bethgibelin: Bethgibelin had been assigned to the Hospitallers and Ibelin to a knight, probably of Italian extraction, who came to be known as 'Balian the Old'.

In 1150, the encirclement was completed with the construction of a fortress on the ruins of Gaza, the city to the south of Ascalon where in the Old Testament Samson had been imprisoned by the Philistines. This was given to the Templars, who successfully repelled an attempt by the Egyptians to take it. The south of the Kingdom of Jerusalem was now secure and King Baldwin III could proceed to besiege Ascalon itself. In January 1153, he assembled his forces before the city, including a force of Hospitallers under their Master, Raymond of Le Puy, and Templars under Bernard of Trémélay: Bernard was a Burgundian from near Dijon, no doubt known to Bernard of Clairvaux, who had been chosen to replace Everard des Barres as Grand Master when, the year before, Everard had retired to Clairvaux as a monk.

Supplied from the sea, the Egyptians in Ascalon could not be starved into surrender: the city had to be taken by assault. The Franks built a wooden tower that rose higher than the ramparts which was positioned at the sector manned by the Templars. On the night of 15 August, a group of the defenders made a sortie from the city and set fire to this tower; but when it was ablaze, the wind changed direction and blew the flames against the walls. The masonry cracked and crumbled and part of the wall collapsed. Bernard of Trémélay, the Master of the Templars, seized this opportunity and led forty of his men through the breach: however, the main force failed to follow them and the Templars were surrounded and cut down by the defenders. The next day, their headless bodies were dangled from the walls – among them, that of the Grand Master, Bernard of Trémélay.

In his account of this misfortune, the Latin chronicler, William of Tyre, wrote that the Templars had fallen victim to their own greed: Bernard of Trémélay had ordered his knights to prevent anyone else from joining them in this initial assault because he wanted to reserve for his Order the glory of taking the city and a lion's share of the booty. The most recent research suggests, however, that 'William's version of this incident seems to be distorted,' being based on the defensive accounts of the Latin commanders who had been criticised 'for failing to follow the Templars into the breach':[181] however, the calumny was widely circulated and damaged the Order's reputation in western Europe.

The loss of the Templars did not affect the outcome of the siege. On 19 August the city surrendered to King Baldwin and was evacuated by the Egyptians, its inhabitants being permitted to take their moveable belongings with them. Prodigious amounts of treasure and supplies of arms were left behind. For King Baldwin, Ascalon was a remarkable prize and its capture marked the high point of his reign. It was given as a fief to his brother Amalric, Count of Jaffa. The mosque was consecrated as a cathedral dedicated to the apostle Paul.

To replace Bernard of Trémélay, the Templar chapter elected Andrew of Montbard, the uncle of Bernard of Clairvaux who until then had held the office of Seneschal of the Kingdom of Jerusalem. Despite the loss of forty knights, they continued to garrison their fortress at Gaza, using it as a base from which to patrol the routes taken by caravans travelling between Cairo and Damascus. In 1154, the year after the fall of Ascalon, a Templar contingent ambushed an Egyptian force that was escorting the Egyptian Vizir, Abbas, and his son Nasir al-Din – both fleeing with a large amount of treasure after the failure of a coup against the Caliph. Abbas was killed in the attack but Nasir al-Din was taken prisoner by the Templars. It was later claimed by William of Tyre that in their custody he learned Latin and was ready to become a Christian but that this was not thought a good enough reason for the Templars to forgo the substantial sum of money offered for him by his enemies in Egypt. He was duly returned to the partisans of the Caliph and once in Cairo was first 'personally mutilated' by the Caliph's four widows,[182] then 'torn to pieces by the mob'.[183]

Such charges of greed against the Templars were made by chroniclers who had an axe to grind, such as William of Tyre and Walter Map, and are difficult either to verify or to refute from this distance in time. It should also be borne in mind that booty was considered a legitimate form of income and provided the means to further the work of their Order. The costs incurred by the military orders were stupendous: the Hospitallers faced bankruptcy in the 1170s.

Andrew of Montbard died in 1156 after only three years as Grand Master. In 1158, his successor, Bertrand of Blanquefort, with 87 brothers and 300 secular knights, was ambushed by a Saracen force as they passed down the Jordan valley and Bertrand captured.

Because of the mountainous terrain in Syria and Palestine, and because the Saracens' intelligence was generally better than the Christians' (they used carrier pigeons and the rural population was mostly Muslim), it was difficult to guard against setbacks of this kind. Despite their occasionally insensate courage, no doubt inspired by confidence that God would weigh in on their side, the Templars in particular, and the Frankish knights in general, became more circumspect in battle as time went on. They had learned from experience that the Saracens were also skilled fighters who often exploited the Franks' courage with their guile. They appreciated 'that they must stand firm in the face of archery and encirclement, ignore the temptation offered by ... simulated flight, preserve their solidarity and cohesion until they could choose the moment at which to deliver their charge with the certainty of striking into the main body of the enemy...'[184] Gone was the wild impetuosity of the early crusaders. 'Of all men,' wrote the Damascene diplomat Usamah, 'the Franks are the most cautious in warfare.'

The same circumspection was apparent in the diplomacy of King Baldwin III, the most sagacious of the kings of Jerusalem. His father Fulk had been killed out hunting when Baldwin was still a child and, although crowned king in 1143 at the insistence of the barons, he had only broken loose from the tutelage of his mother Melisende with great difficulty. The eldest of the three formidable daughters of King Baldwin II of Jerusalem, Melisende, like her sister Alice in Antioch, had refused to accept that as a woman she lacked the competence to rule. In the 1140s she had brought the Kingdom of Jerusalem to the brink of civil war in a struggle with her husband, Fulk of Anjou, preferring her childhood friend, the handsome Lord of Jaffa, Hugh of Le Puiset, to the 'short, wiry, red-haired, middle aged man whom political advantage had forced upon her'.[185] It was also said that, as a favour to her sister Hodierna, she had commissioned the poisoning of Alfonso-Jordan, the young Count of Toulouse, who had died suddenly at Caesarea at the time of the Second Crusade: he had a better hereditary claim to the County of Tripoli than Hodierna's husband, Count Raymond.

In 1152 it was the turn of Melisende's son, King Baldwin III, to antagonise his mother when, nine years after his coronation, he tried to govern on his own. Melisende was no more willing to abdicate her share of power to her son than she had been to her husband. Their differences led to a breach with, first, a *de facto* division of the kingdom and, subsequently, open conflict between mother and son. Besieged by Baldwin's forces in the citadel in Jerusalem, Melisende was eventually persuaded to surrender and live with her sister, the Abbess Joveta, in her convent in Bethany.

Both Melisende's contemporaries and later historians have been impressed by this 'truly remarkable woman who for over thirty years exercised considerable power in a kingdom where there was no previous tradition of any woman holding public office'.[186] William of Tyre judged that 'she was a very wise woman, full experienced in almost all spheres of state business, who had completely triumphed over the handicap of her sex so that she could take charge of important affairs ... she ruled the kingdom with such ability that she was rightly considered to have equalled her predecessors in that regard.' Baldwin himself came to recognise her qualities and, his confidence bolstered by the capture of Ascalon, treated his mother with considerable respect and involved her in state affairs.

Even before the fall of Ascalon, she was summoned to join the principal dignitaries of Outremer to consider the future of her niece Constance, the widowed Princess of Antioch. Three years before, her handsome husband Raymond of Poitiers, the uncle and reputed lover of Eleanor of Aquitaine, had been killed while on a raid to the north of his principality, and it was deemed vital that Constance should marry a credible leader in war: the widower brother-in-law of the Byzantine Emperor, a Norman, John Roger, was proposed. It was also hoped that she might reconcile her sister Hodierna to her husband, Count Raymond II of Tripoli, but in the event she failed on both counts: Constance refused to consider the middle-aged John Roger and Raymond II was murdered as he rode into his city of Tripoli.

Raymond's murderer was a member of a fanatic sect of Shia Muslims, the Assassins, who, like the Sicarii among the Jewish Zealots, pursued their objectives by the covert killing of their enemies. Their name comes from the word hashish, the narcotic which, according to the crusaders, induced a trance which made the killers oblivious to danger. The Shia were originally a political faction who believed that Ali, Muhammad's son-in-law, was his true successor; but after the death of Ali in 661 it had developed into a radical Islamic sect dedicated to the overthrow of the Sunni caliphate in Baghdad. Persecuted for their beliefs, the Shia developed mystical notions, revolutionary methods and messianic aspirations, and split into further factions, the most radical being the Ismailis who 'elaborated a system of religious doctrine on a high philosophic level and produced a literature which, after centuries of eclipse, is only now once again beginning to achieve recognition at its true worth'.[187]

Central to the Ismaili system was the idea of the Imam, the inspired and infallible descendant of Ali and Fatima through Ismail. He had access to special knowledge and was to be obeyed without question. In the early tenth century, a claimant to this descent seized power in North Africa and established the Fatimid (after Fatima) caliphate in Cairo in rivalry to the Sunni caliphate in Baghdad. By the time of the crusades the Fatimid empire was in decline. However, in the Elburz Mountains in northern Persia, overlooking the shore of the Caspian Sea, a group of intransigent Ismailis under Hasan-Sabbah established themselves in the impregnable fortress of Alamut. From here Hasan sent out his devotees to murder the Sunni sultans and their viziers. He also sent missionaries to Syria to win converts but also to take fortresses as bases for his campaign of terror. In 1133 the Assassins purchased the castle of Qadmus from the Muslims who had taken it from the Franks. Shortly afterwards, they acquired al-Kahf; in 1137 they took Khariba from the Franks; and in 1142 the major stronghold of Masyaf was taken from the Damascenes. Other fortresses fell into their hands at around the same time and brought them face to face with the castles of the military orders at Kamel, La Colée and Krak de Chevaliers, and in the coastal cities of Valania and Tortosa.

The hatred of the Assassins for their Muslim enemies made them amenable to forming alliances with the Franks. At the Battle of Inab in 1149, an Assassin leader, Ali ibn-Wafa, died fighting alongside Raymond of Poitiers: yet only three years later a member of the same sect murdered Raymond II of Tripoli for no known reason. Since Queen Melisende was suspected of ordering the poisoning of the young Alfonso-Jordan, Count of Toulouse, it is not impossible that she also commissioned the Assassins to get rid of Hodierna's difficult husband.

In this way, theological differences among the followers of Muhammad, combined with the passions of strong-willed women, came to affect the destiny of the Latins in Outremer. The most fateful instance of the latter came in 1153 when Constance returned to the principality of Antioch. Now it became clear why she had turned down the bridegroom proposed by the King of Jerusalem and Emperor of Byzantium. Her eye had fallen on another man – a French knight, Reginald of Châtillon. Reginald was the younger son of Geoffrey, Count of Gien-sur-Loire, and took his title from Châtillon-sur-Loire. Thought to have come east with King Louis VII on the Second Crusade, he had remained in the retinue of King Baldwin III. To judge from his subsequent behaviour, he was ruthless, audacious, exceptionally brave and almost certainly handsome – qualities that won the love of Constance and led to the *mésalliance* of the century: it was quite astonishing, wrote the Archbishop of Tyre, 'that such a famous, powerful and well-born woman, the widow of such an outstanding husband, should condescend to marry a kind of mercenary knight'.[188]

Baldwin III, acknowledging Reginald's abilities as a soldier, recognised him as Prince of Antioch. So too, albeit with reluctance, did the Byzantine Emperor Manuel in exchange for Reginald's help against the Armenians in Cilicia. Aided by the Templars, Reginald marched north and took the port of Alexandretta which he gave to the Templars. He now quarrelled with the Emperor Manuel over the subsidies he felt were his due. Encouraged by the Templars, he made peace with the Armenians and decided to recover from the Byzantines what he felt was his due by plundering the island of Cyprus. He needed funds for this expedition and decided to extract them from Aimery, the Latin Patriarch of Antioch, whom Reginald loathed because Aimery had vociferously opposed his marriage to Constance. Aimery refused to give him any money, whereupon Reginald had him thrown into prison, brutally beaten, then pinioned on the roof of the citadel with honey rubbed into his wounds to attract the flies.

This treatment had the desired effect: the Patriarch gave over his money to Reginald who used it to equip a fleet. In the spring of 1156, with the Armenian King Thoros, he landed with an army on Cyprus, until then one of the most peaceful provinces of the Byzantine Empire and the source of supplies to the starving army of the First Crusade. Defeating and capturing the island's governor, the Emperor's nephew John Commenus, and its military leader, Michael Branas, the army of Reginald and Thoros proceeded to pillage the island 'on a scale that the Huns and Mongols might have envied'.[189] Indifferent to the fact that the Cypriots were Christian, their women were raped, their children and old people murdered, their churches and convents robbed, their cattle and crops sequestered. The prisoners either bought their own freedom, were taken in chains to Antioch, or were mutilated and sent to Byzantium as a living gesture of defiance and disdain.

Reginald's brutal and piratical behaviour caused consternation in Jerusalem. On hearing of the incarceration of the Patriarch Aimery, King Baldwin III sent emissaries to insist upon his release and, once it was secured, to bring him to Jerusalem. The plunder of Cyprus was even more grave because it placed in jeopardy Baldwin's policy of an alliance with the Byzantine Empire. To seal the pact, Baldwin had been promised a Byzantine princess, Theodora, the Emperor's fifteen-year-old niece, with a huge dowry that would replenish the depleted treasury of the kingdom. The wedding took place in Jerusalem in 1158.

The diplomatic objective of this alliance was Byzantine assistance against Nur ed-Din and, for the Emperor Manuel, the punishment of Thoros and Reginald. At the approach of a powerful Byzantine army, Thoros fled into the mountains while Reginald made an abject submission. Before an assembly of visiting princes and courtiers gathered before the walls of Mamistra, Reginald advanced, barefooted and bareheaded, and prostrated himself in the dust before the Byzantine Emperor. After savouring his enemy's humiliation, and imposing certain conditions, Manual permitted the penitent to rise and return to Antioch.

This degradation of Reginald, although recognised by the Latins as well deserved, was felt as a humiliation to them all. Baldwin had hoped that Reginald would not be so easily forgiven. For Manuel, however, it was better to have Antioch ruled by a man who, when Manuel made his triumphal entry into the city, was prepared to walk beside him leading his horse than another prince less amenable and certainly less visibly his vassal. Though Manuel developed a warm personal regard for Baldwin, his nephew by marriage, the two men's strategic priorities were not the same, as Manuel demonstrated by making a pact with the Latins' arch-enemy, Nur ed-Din, against the Seljuk Turks in Anatolia. To the Latins, this was yet another instance of Greek perfidy; however, among the benefits of this treaty to the

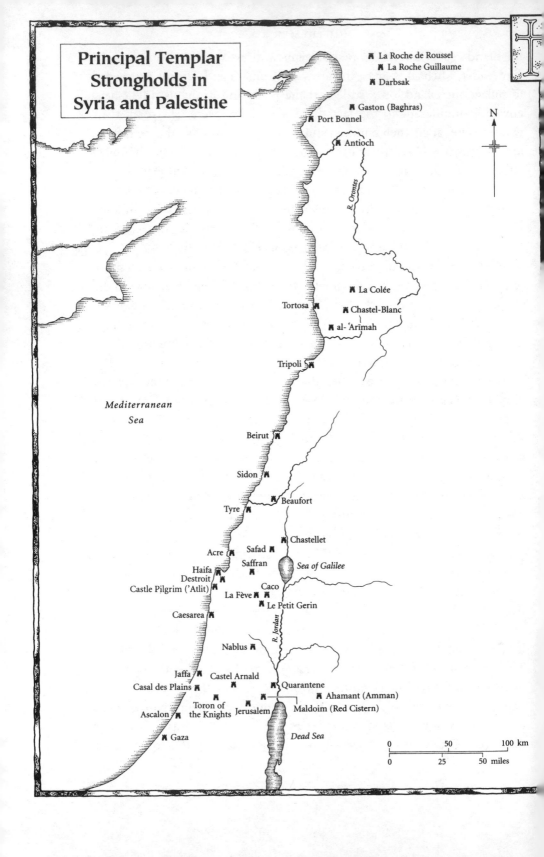

Principal Templar Strongholds in Syria and Palestine

La Roche de Roussel
La Roche Guillaume
Darbsak

Gaston (Baghras)
Port Bonnel
Antioch

R. Orontes

N

La Colée
Tortosa
Chastel-Blanc
al-'Arīmah

Tripoli

Mediterranean
Sea

Beirut

Sidon

Beaufort
Tyre

Safad
Chastellet
Acre
Saffran
Sea of Galilee
Haifa
Destroit
Caco
Castle Pilgrim ('Atlit)
La Fève
Le Petit Gerin

Caesarea

R. Jordan

Nablus

Jaffa
Castel Arnald
Casal des Plains
Quarantene
Ahamant (Amman)
Toron of
the Knights
Maldoim (Red Cistern)
Ascalon
Jerusalem

Gaza
Dead Sea

| 0 | | 50 | | 100 km |

| 0 | 25 | | 50 miles |

Latins was the release of Christian captives, among them the Master of the Temple, Bertrand of Blanquefort.

Any expectation among the Christian princes that Reginald of Châtillon would have learned by his mistakes would soon be shown to be misplaced. In November 1160, Reginald had set out on a raid on the herds of cattle mostly owned by Christian Syrians. On his way back to Antioch with his four-footed booty, he was ambushed by a Muslim force under the governor of Aleppo. Reginald was captured and taken on the back of a camel to Aleppo. No one came forward to offer a ransom. He was to remain incarcerated for the next sixteen years.

In February 1160, King Baldwin III died at the age of only thirty-three – a man of great charm, intelligence and learning who was mourned even by his Muslim subjects and by the governor of Aleppo, Nur ed-Din. He had no heir: his wife, Queen Theodora, was still only sixteen and now retired to Acre, given to her as part of the marriage settlement.

Baldwin was succeeded by his brother Amalric, aged twenty-five, as tall and good-looking as Baldwin but lacking both his learning and his charm. Amalric, who had been Lord of Jaffa and Ascalon, was content to leave the Byzantines to protect the northern frontiers of his kingdom and directed his attention south towards Egypt. There, as a result of a sequence of sanguinary coups and counter-coups, the Fatimid caliphate was disintegrating and the government of the country was in confusion. Few of the cities in Sinai or the Nile Delta were fortified and the potential booty was stupendous; but there was also the more pressing strategic reason for moving against Cairo; for if the Latins did not fill the vacuum, then Nur ed-Din surely would.

In 1160, a projected invasion by Baldwin III had been bought off by the promise of a yearly tribute that was never paid. Using this default as a pretext, Amalric led a force into Egypt in the autumn of 1163 which included a large contingent of Templars; but by breaching dykes in the Nile Delta the Egyptians forced the Franks to retire. In the following year, to pre-empt a take-over in Cairo by Nur ed-Din's protégé, Shawar, Amalric was back in Egypt: he reached an agreement with Shawar that both armies should retire.

Taking advantage of Amalric's absence, Nur ed-Din had attacked the principality of Antioch, laying siege to the fortress of Harenc. Bohemond, the young son of Constance and Raymond of Poitiers, now reigning as

Prince Bohemond III, set off with a combined Antiochene, Armenian and Byzantine army to relieve Harenc. In this force there was a contingent of Templar knights and their accompanying sergeants, squires and turcopoles. At its approach, Nur ed-Din raised the siege and retired. Against the advice of his more experienced companions, Bohemond went after this much larger army. He caught up with them on 10 August. Using their favourite tactic, the Muslims feigned retreat. Bohemond and his knights charged after them, were ambushed and either taken prisoner or killed. Of the Templar knights, sixty fell in the battle and only seven escaped.

This setback was no doubt one of the factors that led the Templars to prefer their own judgement on military matters to that of the Latin princes. Although committed by their statutes to the defence of the Holy Land, the Grand Master was subject to the Pope, not the King of Jerusalem. To Amalric, however, the autonomy of the military orders hampered his conduct of the war against Islam. In 1166, a cave-fortress in TransJordan, garrisoned by the Templars and said to be impregnable, was besieged by the forces of Nur ed-Din. It had probably formed part of the bequest made by Philippe of Nablus, the Lord of Oultrejourdain, when he joined the Order in January 1166.

On hearing of the siege, Amalric assembled an army to relieve it but on reaching the River Jordan he met the twelve Templars who had surrendered the stronghold without a fight. Amalric was so angry that he had the knights hanged. This episode, recorded in the history of William of Tyre, could well have been one of the factors that soured relations between the Temple and the King. In 1168, when Amalric decided upon a full-scale invasion of Egypt, he was supported by the Grand Master of the Hospital, Gilbert of Assailly, and most of the lay barons, but the Grand Master of the Temple, Bertrand of Blanquefort, refused point-blank to take part.

Low motives were ascribed to the Templars for this decision: it was said that it was because the plan had been promoted by their rivals, the Hospitallers; or that they had profitable financial dealings with the Italian merchants who traded with Egypt. But the near bankruptcy of the Hospital, which no doubted prompted Gilbert of Assailly to try and recoup its losses on the Nile, was also an object lesson to the Temple which had sustained heavy losses in Antioch and was fully committed to the defence of the Holy Land, both in the north in the Amanus march and in the south around Gaza. There was also Amalric's treaty with Shawar: newcomers from France,

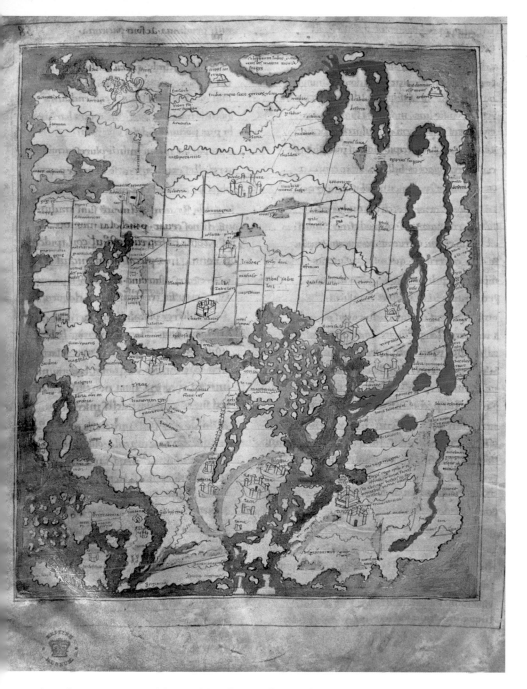

An 11th century map of the world with Jerusalem at the centre and the British Isles in the lower left hand corner from a miscellaneous volume of world knowledge, Winchester or Canterbury. (*British Library / Bridgeman Art Library*)

The assault on Jerusalem during the First Crusade in 1099. An illuminated miniature of the 14th century. (*Bibliothéque Nationale / Bridgeman Art Library*)

The looting of Jerusalem after its capture by the Crusaders in 1099. An illuminated miniature of the 15th century by Jean de Courcy. (*Bibliothéque Nationale / Bridgeman Art Library*)

Bernard, Abbot of Clairvaux preaching the crusade to King Louis VII at Vézelay in Burgundy in 1146. A 15th century illumination by Sebastien Mamerot. (*Bibliothéque Nationale / Bridgeman Art Library*)

Bernard, Abbot of Clairvaux. A 15th century illumination by Jean Fouquet in the Book of Hours of Etienne Chevalier. (*Musée Condé / Giraudon / Bridgeman Art Library*)

Hugh of Vaudemont embraced by his wife upon his return from crusade. A 12th century stone carving from the Priory of Belval in Lorraine. (*Musée des Monuments Français / Lauros-Giraudon / Bridgeman Art Library*)

A Templar knight from a 12th century mural in the Templar chapel at Cressac-sur-Charente in Aquitaine. (*Weidenfeld Archive*)

A crusader kneels at prayer in front of his horse. An illumination from the 12th century Westminster Psalter. (*Weidenfeld Archive*)

The Templar seal showing two knights riding on one horse. (*Weidenfeld Archive*)

Pilgrims escorted by Templar knights coming within sight of Jerusalem. A 19th century engraving of the English school. (*Private Collection / Ken Welsh / Bridgeman Art Library*)

The Dome of the Rock on the Temple Mount in Jerusalem. (*Weidenfeld Archive*)

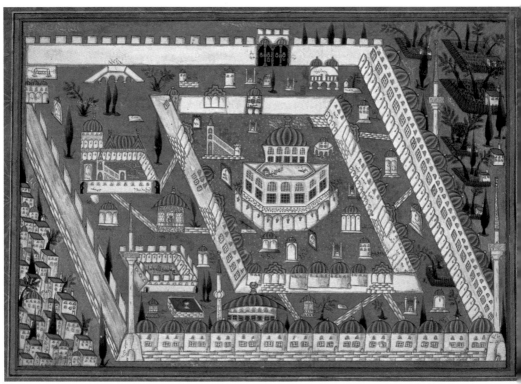

The Al Aqsa Mosque on the Temple Mount in Jerusalem, called the Temple of Solomon by the Crusaders and the Templars' Headquarters until 1187. Gouache on paper from the Muraqqa Album. (*Chester Beatty Library and Gallery of Oriental Art, Dublin / Bridgeman Art Library*)

A contemporaneous portrait of Saladin, Fatimid School.
(*British Library / Bridgeman Art Library*)

PORTRAIT OF SALADIN (?)

FATIMID SCHOOL
About A.D. 1180

Richard the Lionheart tilting at Saladin from a 14th century illuminated manuscript.
(British Library / Bridgeman Art Library)

The bell tower of Cluny Abbey, all that remains following its demolition after the French Revolution of 1789. (*Private Collection / Bulloz / Bridgeman Art Library*)

A reconstruction by Kenneth John Conant of the Monastery and Abbey at Cluny. (*Weidenfeld Archive*)

Pope Innocent III. A 13th century fresco from the church of Sacro Speco (Holy Grotto), Subiaco, Italy. (*Weidenfeld Archive*)

Pope Boniface VIII. A statue attributed to Arnolfo di Cambio from the Cathedral in Florence, now in the Museo dell' Opera del Duomo, Florence. (*Weidenfeld Archive*)

Pope Clement V from The Triumph of Thomas Aquinas by Andrea Buonaiuti, 1365, St Maria Novella, Florence. (*Weidenfeld Archive*)

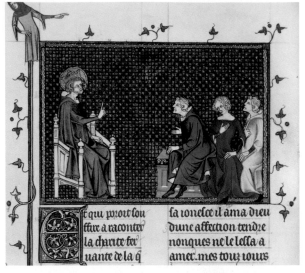

King Louis IX of France giving judgement. A 12th century illumination by G. Ge. de Saint Pathus in the Life and Miracles of St. Louis. (*Bibliothéque Nationale / Bridgeman Art Library*)

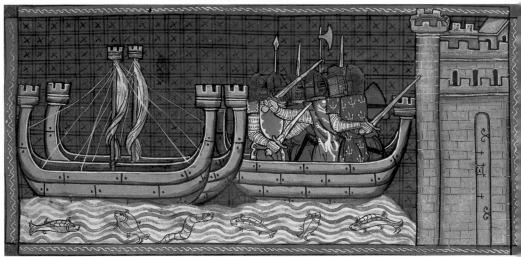

Crusaders under King Louis IX attack Damietta in 1268. A 14th century illumination from the Chronicle of France or of St. Denis. (*British Library / Bridgeman Art Library*)

Crusaders expelling Cathars from Carcassonne. A 14th century illumination by the Boucicaut Master and Workshop. (*British Library / Bridgeman Art Library*)

The Church of the Holy
Sepulchre in Jerusalem.
(Anthony Kersting)

The original design for the rebuilding of the Church of the Holy Sepulchre
after the capture of Jerusalem by the First Crusade. (Weidenfeld Archive)

The fortress of Krak des Chevaliers in Syria, held by the Knights of the Hospital of St. John from 1144–1271. (*Weidenfeld Archive*)

The Templar fortress of Monzon in Aragon. (*Huesca, Aragon / Bridgeman Art Library*)

A 19th century painting by Dominique Louis Papety of William of Clermont
defending Acre in 1291. (*Château de Versailles / Lauros-Giraudon / Bridgeman Art Library*)

King Philip IV of France, Philip the Fair, with his four children and his brother, Charles of Valois. A 14th century illumination. (*Bibiliothéque National / Bridgeman Art Library*)

The burning of the Templars. A 14th century illumination from the Chronicle of France or of St. Denis. (*British Library / Bridgeman Art Library*)

JACQUES DE MOLAY, chef des Templiers
(XIIIᵉ SIÈCLE)

James of Molay, the last
Grand Master of the
Templars. A 19th century
engraving by Ghevauchet.
(*Private Collection / Roger-
Viollet / Bridgeman Art Library*)

An 18th century engraving
of the Templar *donjon* in
Paris where King Louis XVI
was imprisoned prior to his
execution in 1793.
(*Bibliothéque National / Bulloz /
Bridgeman Art Library*)

The Templar fortress of Almourol on the River Tagus in Portugal.

The circular chapel or rotunda of the Templar fortress of Tomar in Portugal, built in 1160 by the Portuguese Master, Gualdim Pais.

The author in front of the cloister and rotunda of the Templar fortress at Tomar.

such as Count William I V of Nevers, who counselled King Amalric, might not understand the value of keeping faith with an infidel, but the Templars already had sufficient appreciation of local conditions to recognise that diplomacy could on occasion be more efficacious than force.

A further example of the Templars' independence, and their willingness to thwart the plans of the King, came in 1173 when Amalric entered into negotiations with the chief of the Assassins in Syria, known to the crusaders as 'The Old Man of the Mountain'. This was Sinan ibn-Salman ibn-Muhammad who came originally from a village near Basra in Iraq. A protégé of Hasan, the Assassin Imam in Alamut, Sinan became the ruler of the Assassins' enclave in Syria and pursued a policy of his own. For thirty years, every ruler in both the Islamic caliphates and every Christian state was at risk from a murderous attack by one of Sinan's Ismaili devotees: exempt were the Grand Masters of the military orders because the Assassins realised that if one was killed there would always be another to take his place.

On the whole, because they were the enemies of their enemies, the Assassins were tolerated by the Franks. The Templars, who might have moved against them from their bases in Tortosa, La Colée and Chastel-Blanc, were paid an annual 'tribute' of 2,000 besants by the Assassins to leave them alone. In the 1160s, the millennial tendencies inherent in Ismaili teaching exploded when Hasan, the leader in Almut, abrogated the Law of Muhammad and proclaimed the Resurrection. Sinan promulgated the new dispensation in Syria and, like the Anabaptists in Münster many centuries later, the elect then gave themselves over to an orgy of debauchery. 'Men and women mingled in drinking sessions, no man abstained from his sister or daughter, the women wore men's clothes, and one of them declared that Sinan was God.'[190]

It was some years after Hasan's abrogation of Islam that Sinan sent word to King Amalric and the Patriarch of Jerusalem that he was interested in conversion to faith in Christ. To this end Hasan sent an envoy, Abdullah, to negotiate a settlement with the King. After a satisfactory conclusion to these preliminary talks, Abdullah started on his journey back from Jerusalem to Massif with a safe-conduct from King Amalric. Shortly after passing Tripoli, his party was attacked by a group of Templars led by a one-eyed knight, Walter of Mesnil.

This outrage infuriated King Amalric who ordered the arrest of the culprits. The Grand Master of the Temple was now Odo of Saint-Amand who had replaced Philip of Nablus in 1168. Odo had been a royal official, holding a number of important posts before joining the Order: he had been a captive of the Muslims between 1157 and 1159. His choice as Grand Master had almost certainly been to further good relations with King Amalric; but now Odo insisted upon the legal rights accorded to the Templars by the papal bull *Omne datum optimum*. His knights were exempt from secular jurisdiction: Walter of Mesnil had been punished by the Order for his transgression and it would now send him for final judgement to Rome. Ignoring these niceties, Amalric rode to Sidon where the Templar chapter was in session, and seized the offending Walter of Mesnil. He was imprisoned in Tyre and Sinan was persuaded by Amalric's profuse apologies that the attack on his ambassador was not of his doing. However, the incident irrevocably alienated the King from the Temple and his plan to petition the Pope and the European monarchs to dissolve the Order was only frustrated by his death in 1174.

What was behind the attack on the Assassin ambassador by Walter of Mesnil? Odo of Saint-Amand never took responsibility for his action; but given the vow of obedience taken by each brother knight it seems improbable that Walter was acting wholly on his own initiative. The motive given by the contemporary chronicler, William of Tyre, is greed: the Templars were unwilling to lose the annual tribute of 2,000 besants which would have lapsed with the Assassin's conversion. A later chronicler, Walter Map, suggests that they were afraid that peace would destroy their *raison d'être*, killing the Assassins' envoy 'lest (it is said) the belief of the infidels should be done away and peace and union reign'.[191]

Modern historians[192] suggest that since the Templars had just received a substantial donation from Henry the Lion, Duke of Saxony, they would not have defied the King for a mere 2,000 besants. More probably, living in proximity to the Assassins, they thought that Amalric was being hoodwinked. Nor were they alone in their mistrust of the Assassins: after Amalric's death, Raymond III, Count of Tripoli, whose father had been killed by the Assassins, was made regent of the Kingdom of Jerusalem. Negotiations with Sinan were not reopened, and there was no further talk of his conversion to the faith of Christ.

eight

Saladin

The year 1174 saw the deaths of both King Amalric of Jerusalem and the powerful ruler of Aleppo, Nur ed-Din. Amalric, who was only thirty-eight years old, had always compared unfavourably with his brother Baldwin III and had dissipated the strength of his kingdom in his fruitless excursions into Egypt. His strategy to ensure the survival of the Latin states in Syria and Palestine had been to enter into an alliance with the Byzantine Empire. This had been secured through the marriage of his cousin, Maria of Antioch, with the Emperor Manuel and his own marriage to the Emperor's daughter, also called Maria, by whom he had only a daughter, Isabella. His esteem for Byzantium was demonstrated when, after returning from a visit to Constantinople, and shortly before his death, he adopted the ceremonial attire in his court in Jerusalem of the Byzantine Emperor.

The hereditary principle was now unquestioned in the Latin kingdoms, and so Amalric was succeeded by his son by his first wife, Agnes of Courtenay, Baldwin IV. Baldwin was thirteen years old and he was a leper – the disease, in the view of some churchmen, being God's punishment of Amalric for marrying his cousin. Until Baldwin came of age, his cousin, Count Raymond III of Tripoli, acted as regent.

Nur ed-Din's legacy was at first sight less sure. His son and heir, Malik as-Salih Ismail, was only eleven and there were rival claims from the governors of Damascus, Aleppo, Mosul and Cairo as to who should act as his regent. However, by establishing his authority over the different emirates that had previously been at one another's throats, Nur ed-Din had demonstrated that it was possible for the Muslims to unite against the Franks. He had, moreover, added a spiritual dimension to this political fact: frugal and austere, 'with regular features and a gentle, sad expression',[193] he was also pious and had elevated his struggle against the Latin Christians to the level of a *jihad* or Holy War.

The man who would take on this combination of spiritual and political ascendancy was not to be one of the progeny of Nur ed-Din but the son of a Kurdish official who had saved the life of Nur ed-Din's father, Zengi, by helping him escape across the River Tigris in 1143 after being defeated in a battle with the forces of the Caliph of Baghdad. This man, Najm ed-Din, together with his brother Shirkuh, were Nur ed-Din's most trusted generals, and it was Shirkuh who had thwarted King Amalric's attempts to establish a Frankish client-state in Egypt. He had done so, however, in tandem with his young and vigorous nephew, Salad ed-Din Yusuf, better known as Saladin. It was Saladin who gave the *coup de grâce* to the Fatimid caliphate in Cairo, switching the Egyptian Muslims' spiritual allegiance to the Caliph in Baghdad. He established a personal rule over Egypt, acting independently from, and sometimes in defiance of, his father's old master, Nur ed-Din.

Both in his lifetime and after his death, Saladin was to be seen as a paragon of courage and magnanimity by both Christian and Muslim alike. The stories of his courtesy and benevolence that were brought back to Europe – how, for example, he gave furs to some of his Christian captives to keep them warm in the dungeons of Damascus; or how, when besieging the castle of Kerak in 1183 during the wedding festivities of Humphrey of Toron and the Princess Isabella, he ordered his mangonels not to fire on the tower where the wedding was being celebrated – had all the more impact because the Christian Europeans had hitherto tended to demonise their infidel enemies.

Pious, frugal, generous and merciful, Saladin was nevertheless a shrewd statesman and able commander. He is described as small in stature with a round face, black hair and dark eyes. Like most members of the Islamic elite, he was literate, cultured and skilled with the lance and the sword. As a young man, he had been more interested in religion than combat; and there is no doubt that his war against the Christian Franks was inspired by a genuine religious zeal, not simply by an appreciation gained from the example of Zengi and Nur ed-Din that the disparate Islam states could only be brought to act in concert in the name of a *jihad*.

To hold the moral high ground in the wider Islamic community was not easy: he had to appear to be loyal not just to his father's master, Nur ed-Din, but also to the Caliph in Baghdad: even after he had proved his commitment to Islam by uniting the disparate Muslim states against the Latins, many continued to regard him as a usurper. It also seems likely, as we shall see, that his famous magnanimity was partly a matter of calculation. When it seemed politic to be cruel, he was cruel: he ordered the crucifixion of Shi'ite opponents in Cairo and at times the mutilation or execution of his captives. Although he came to respect and even admire the chivalrous code of the Frankish knights, and was assiduous in his courtesy to Christian princes and kings, he felt an implacable hatred for the military orders.

In their attempts to frustrate Saladin's rise to absolute power after the death of Nur ed-Din, his rivals made tactical alliances with the Latins. The governor of Aleppo persuaded Count Raymond of Tripoli, acting as regent for King Baldwin IV, to make a diversionary attack on the city of Homs and in return agreed to ransom his Christian captives – among them the parvenu French knight who had married Princess Constance of Antioch, Reginald of Châtillon: his price tag was 120,000 gold dinars.[194]

Had they been able to see into the future, Count Raymond would certainly have decided to leave this rogue elephant in the dungeons of Aleppo. Reginald was now a prince without a principality: his wife had died two years after the capture of her handsome husband, perhaps from a broken heart, and Antioch was now ruled by Bohemond III, Constance's son by her first husband Raymond of Poitiers. However, Reginald could not simply be relegated to the ranks of mercenary knights from which he had come: his daughter Agnes was now the Queen of Hungary and his stepdaughter Maria the Empress of Byzantium. He was therefore married to the richest heiress in the kingdom, Stephanie of Milly, who brought him the lordships of Hebron and Oultrejourdain.

One of the consequences of the death of Nur ed-Din and the confusion that followed was the removal of the restraint he had exercised on the Seljuk Turks. In 1176, their Sultan Kilij Arslan II moved against Byzantium. The Emperor Manuel led an army against him which was annihilated by the Turks at Myriocephalum. This defeat was as catastrophic as that at Manzikert in 1071 that had led to the First Crusade. Anatolia was lost to the Turks for ever, and the ability of Byzantium to influence events in Syria had gone with it. The Franks were now on their own.

Things were made worse by divisions within the Kingdom of Jerusalem.

Although patient and persistent, the young leper King, Baldwin IV, could not be a strong leader. Raymond III of Tripoli who, as his nearest male relative, had acted as regent until Baldwin came of age, was experienced, cautious and, after years as a prisoner of the Muslims, spoke Arabic and knew the psychology of the enemy well. He was supported by the established families in the Kingdom of Jerusalem and the Knights of the Hospital but opposed by the Templars and more recent arrivals in Palestine led by Reginald of Châtillon who were impatient for war and the conquest of new land.

Although there was much talk of help coming from the West in the form of a new crusade led by King Louis VII of France and King Henry II of England, now married to Louis's former wife, Eleanor of Aquitaine, the only prince who appeared in the Holy Land was Philip, Count of Flanders, and he insisted that he had come on a pilgrimage, not on a crusade.

Taking advantage of the Franks' disunity, Saladin led a force across the Sinai Desert towards the Templar fortress of Gaza. The Templars concentrated their forces to defend it but Saladin bypassed Gaza and laid siege to Ascalon. Baldwin IV, who had now come of age, raised an army to defend it. He reached the city before Saladin who, realising that Jerusalem was now undefended, left a minor force to contain Baldwin and marched towards the Holy City. Realising that he had been outflanked, Baldwin summoned the Templar knights from Gaza, broke out of Ascalon, and on 25 November 1177, caught up with the Egyptian army at Montgisard. Saladin was taken by surprise; his army disintegrated, and he fled back to Egypt.

This victory was a triumph for the Franks and may have encouraged them to overestimate their true strength. Although Frankish chronicles state that the army was commanded by Baldwin, Muslim historians insist that it was led by Reginald of Châtillon.[195] It is probable that he fought with great courage and that the victory added to Reginald's prestige.

Lacking the manpower to follow up this victory, King Baldwin IV reinforced his frontier with Damascus by building a castle on the Jordan at a place called Jacob's Ford: it was said to be here that Jacob had wrestled with an angel, as described in the Book of Genesis. Its strategic position on the road from the coast to Damascus, and dominating the fertile plain of Banyas that had hitherto been accessible to both Muslim and Christians, had been recognised by Saladin who felt he had reached an understanding with King Baldwin that it was to remain a demilitarised zone. However,

Baldwin gave in to strong pressure from the Templars and built the fortress at a time when Saladin had been distracted by disaffection among members of his family.

In the summer of 1179, Saladin laid siege to the castle; Baldwin rode to relieve it, calling on Raymond of Tripoli and the Templars under Odo of Saint-Amand to join him. On 10 June, Count Raymond and the Templars made contact with Saladin's army. Impetuously, the Templars attacked but were beaten back. Those that could get across the Litani river took refuge in the great fortress of Beaufort; but among the fatalities suffered by the Franks were a number of Templar knights, and among those taken captive was the Grand Master, Odo of Saint-Amand.

Odo died in captivity the following year, too proud to be exchanged for a Muslim held by the Christians. The chronicler William of Tyre, whose brother was killed in this engagement, condemned Odo for the arrogance that was now seen as a common flaw in the Knights of the Temple: his actions were 'dictated by the spirit of pride, of which he had an excess'; he was 'a worthless man, proud and arrogant having the spirit of wrath in his nostrils, neither fearing God, nor having reverence for man'.[196] Certainly, he was an example of a knight who had made his name in the secular world and subsequently joined the Order not from a sense of religious vocation but as a lateral move in the upper echelons of Christendom's lay administration.

Whether or not the Templar chapter that chose Odo had been interested in the discernment of a sincere vocation, or whether it had seen some advantage in choosing a Grand Master who was already a figure of some stature, it is impossible to tell: but it was perhaps in reaction to Odo of Saint-Amand that the knights now chose as his successor a career Templar, Arnold of Torroja, who had previously been Master in Provence and Spain.

Taking advantage of a two-year truce agreed between Saladin and King Baldwin IV – a truce forced upon them both by a drought and the consequent risk of famine – Arnold of Torroja sailed for Europe with the Grand Master of the Hospital, Roger des Moulins, and Heraclius, the newly elected Patriarch, to seek assistance in Italy, France and England. Heraclius, an almost illiterate priest from the Auvergne, had been the lover of the King's mother, Queen Agnes, whose influence had secured his appointment first as Archbishop of Caesarea and later as Patriarch of Jerusalem. His current mistress, Paschia de Riveri, known as *Madame la Patriarchesse*, was the wife of a draper in Nablus.

When in London, Heraclius dedicated the Templars' new church in their compound west of the City: his scented and bejewelled figure made a poor impression, and led some of those who met him to wonder whether their Christian brethren in the East could be in such dire need. However, the English Temple had already benefited from a momentous event in English history – the murder in 1170 of the Archbishop of Canterbury, Thomas à Becket. The penance imposed on the four Norman knights who killed him was to serve fourteen years with the Templars in the Holy Land. King Henry II, who had incited them, not only did public penance in Canterbury Cathedral but promised to provide the Templars with the money to support two hundred knights for a year. At Avranches, in 1172, as part of his penance, Henry swore to take the Cross; and while events prevented him from fulfilling this vow, his will of 1172 left 20,000 marks for the costs of the crusade – 5,000 to the Temple, 5,000 to the Hospital, 5,000 to them jointly, and a final 5,000 to 'miscellaneous religious houses, lepers, recluses, and hermits in Palestine'.[197]

The Grand Master of the Temple, Arnold of Torroja, fell ill in Verona and died there on 30 September 1184. To succeed him the Templar chapter in Jerusalem chose a knight of Flemish or Anglo-Norman descent, Gérard of Ridefort. Gérard seems to have been a classic case of a knight who joined the order *faute de mieux*. He had come to the Holy Land in the early 1170s and had taken service with Raymond III, Count of Tripoli. According to the chroniclers, he was assured by Raymond that he would receive a fief in his country when one fell vacant. In 1180, William Dorel, Lord of Botron, died leaving his fief to his daughter Lucia. Raymond, possibly pressed by debt, went back on his promise to Gérard and 'sold' Lucia to a Pisan merchant called Plivano for his bride's weight in gold. She brought him 10,000 besants which puts her at around ten stone.[198]

With his prospects dashed in this way, Gérard joined the Temple. It was said that at around this time he suffered from a serious illness, which may have disillusioned him with worldly ambition and concentrated his mind on the world to come. But the onset of piety did not assuage the humiliation he felt as a knight at the preference shown to a merchant, and the incident left him with a deep sense of grievance against Count Raymond of Tripoli.

At the time of the death of Arnold of Torroja he had been the Templars' Seneschal in the Kingdom of Jerusalem.

In March 1185, the young leper King, Baldwin IV, finally died. He was succeeded by his seven-year-old nephew, Baldwin V, the son of his sister Sibylla by her first husband, William of Montferrat. Raymond of Tripoli, who had already been acting as *bailli* (governor or chief minister) for Baldwin IV, now became the regent of Baldwin V. In this capacity he agreed with Saladin to a truce of four years. However, Raymond's authority was undermined when, the very next year, the young King also died leaving no obvious heir.

Under Baldwin IV's will, the succession was to be decided by the Pope, the Emperor and the kings of England and France. Once again, however, the destiny of the Latin Christians in the Holy Land was to be affected by the emotions of a woman. Princess Sibylla, the dead King's mother, was now the wife of a French knight, Guy of Lusignan. Her first husband, William of Montferrat, imported from Europe as a future king, had died of malaria in 1177.

At first a trawl among the royal families of Europe failed to come up with a replacement and for a while Sibylla had considered marriage to a local baron, Baldwin of Ibelin. However, the Constable of the Kingdom, Amalric of Lusignan, who was the lover of Sibylla's mother, Agnes, had a younger brother called Guy. Sibylla was enticed by reports of his attractions to have him brought out from Europe. When he arrived, she liked what she saw and bullied her brother, King Baldwin IV, to consent to their marriage. The King resisted because he could see that this weak and ineffectual younger son of a French count was a poor choice as a future ruler of his kingdom, but his mother and sister worked on him and eventually he gave his consent: they were married at Easter, 1180.

Now, six years later, the two women's plans came to fruition. Sibylla summoned her supporters to Jerusalem and was crowned queen by another of her mother's former lovers, the Patriarch Heraclius. The Grand Master of the Hospital who, with the Grand Master of the Temple, held a key to the strongbox that contained the royal regalia, refused to produce it, preferring to throw it out of the window; but it was retrieved by the holder of the second key, Gérard of Ridefort, a prime supporter of Sybilla and Guy. Once crowned, Sibylla placed a second crown on the head of her husband,

Guy; whereupon 'Gérard de Ridefort cried out aloud that this crown paid back the marriage of Botron'.[199]

Queen Sibylla's *coup* represented the triumph of the hawks over the doves led by Raymond of Tripoli. The doves might have resisted; they represented the entirety of the kingdom's vassals less Reginald of Châtillon. Guy of Lusignan was universally despised. Raymond proposed that they crown the Princess Isabella, the thirteen-year-old daughter of King Amalric I, recently married to the eighteen-year-old Humphrey of Toron. It was at their wedding the year before in the castle of Kerak, while it was being besieged by Saladin, that Saladin had ordered his mangonels not to fire on the tower where the wedding festivities were taking place and had been rewarded by Humphrey's mother with dishes served at the feast which she sent out for the Muslim leader. The siege had been raised by King Baldwin IV in person, riding in a litter, but the experience had possibly unnerved the young Humphrey Toron – 'a youth of extraordinary beauty and great learning, more fitted in his tastes to be a girl than a man'.[200] When Raymond now proposed that he be made king, he slipped away to Jerusalem and paid homage to Guy of Lusignan. The *coup* was a *fait accompli* and all barons apart from Raymond of Tripoli and Baldwin of Ibelin fell into line.

There was nothing now to restrain the aggressive designs of the principal kingmaker, Reginald of Châtillon. The fief of Oultrejourdain which he had acquired through marriage, reaching to the Gulf of Akabah, lay astride the caravan routes between Egypt and Syria and cut Saladin's dominions in two. In 1182 he had used this strategic position to mount a raid whose audacity led to the greatest possible outrage in the Muslim world. He had had galleys built in sections, tested on the Dead Sea, then launched on the Gulf of Akabah. These sailed south to the Red Sea, pillaging the ports on the coasts of Egypt and Arabia, merchant ships and even transports taking pilgrims to Mecca. Landing at the port of ar-Raghib, a raiding party set off for Mecca itself intending to carry off the body of the Prophet Muhammad. They were defeated by a force sent by Saladin's brother, Malik, from Egypt and the survivors were executed in either Mecca or Cairo.

Whether this was an individual act of terrorism on Reginald's part, or 'the most daring part of a concerted campaign in which all the forces of the kingdom joined',[201] it made Reginald a marked man for Saladin whose role as guardian of the Holy Places in Arabia underpinned his authority in the Muslim world. Now, after the accession of King Guy, Reginald compounded this outrage by seizing a large Muslim caravan travelling from Egypt to Syria and killing its escort of Egyptian troops. This was a violation of the truce and Saladin called for reparation, first from Reginald who would not receive his envoys, then from King Guy who, though he ordered Reginald to make amends, did not insist: it was largely to Reginald that he owed his throne.

To Reginald's detractors, his raid on the caravan was a blatant act of brigandage; even his defenders find it 'enigmatic',[202] suggesting that perhaps because of the Egyptian escort Reginald felt that it was Saladin who had broken the truce. Whatever his motive, it made war inevitable at a time when the Latin states were deeply divided. There was both a conflict of interest between the established barons who wanted to hold on to what they had and the newly arrived knights who hoped to make their fortunes from new conquests, combined with an ideological difference between those who sought an accommodation with their Muslim neighbours and those for whom any compromise with the infidel was a betrayal of Christendom. Even at the time, it was sometimes difficult to distinguish between the two: but certainly the knowledge that Raymond of Tripoli was fluent in Arabic and interested in the study of Islamic texts made many suspect that he was not wholly committed to the Christian cause.

As if to prove their suspicions correct, Raymond now approached Saladin for help against Guy of Lusignan. This was going much further than asking for a truce, amounting to outright collaboration. As a favour to his prospective ally, Raymond permitted a force of Egyptian cavalry led by Saladin's son, al-Afdal, to cross his country on a reconnaissance mission into Galilee. It was agreed that it would be non-belligerent and would be gone within the day. Word of this arrangement was sent out to Raymond's subjects and, at the fortress of La Fève, reached a delegation on its way from King Guy to seek reconciliation with Count Raymond that included the Grand Masters of the Temple and the Hospital.

Gérard of Ridefort immediately summoned ninety Templar knights from nearby castles and rode to Nazareth where forty secular knights were added to his force. Beyond Nazareth, they found the Muslim force watering their horses at the springs of Cresson. Seeing its strength, the Master of the Hospital, Roger des Moulins, advised retreat. The Marshal of the Temple, James of Mailly, concurred. This enraged Gérard of Ridefort. He accused his fellow Grand Master of cowardice and scoffed at James of Mailly: 'You love your blond head too well to want to lose it': to which the Templar Marshal replied: 'I shall die in battle like a brave man. It is you who will flee as a traitor.' The combined force of knights then charged at the Egyptians with catastrophic effect. James of Mailly and Roger des Moulins were both killed along with all but three Templars – one of them their Grand Master, Gérard of Ridefort. The secular knights were taken prisoner together with some of the Christian citizens of Nazareth who had left the town in hope of booty.

The only gain for the Latins from this disaster was that it shamed Raymond of Tripoli into breaking his pact with Saladin and making his peace with King Guy. While armies from all over Saladin's dominions – from Aleppo, Mosul, Damascus and Egypt – converged on al-Ashtara on the far side of the Jordan to make up the largest force he had ever had at his command, King Guy proclaimed a *levée en masse*, summoning all the Latin forces to gather at Acre. In Jerusalem, the fund of thirty thousand marks that had been held by the military orders on behalf of King Henry II of England to finance his projected crusade was used to hire mercenaries and equip the Christian forces. By the end of June, King Guy had assembled 20,000 troops including 12,000 cavalry. This was virtually all the fighting men, voluntary and mercenary, available in Outremer: the Latin cities and fortresses were left empty.

On 1 July Saladin crossed the Jordan at Sennabra on the south-western corner of Lake Tiberias with 30,000 soldiers and 12,000 cavalry. Here he split his forces. Half marched west up into the hills, half followed the shore of the lake to Tiberias. The town was taken after a brief assault but Eschiva, the Countess of Tripoli, held out in the citadel, sending word of her predicament to her husband Raymond who was with King Guy in Acre.

There the indecisive King Guy received conflicting counsel from the hawks and the doves. As yet unaware that his wife was in danger, Raymond advised caution, arguing that Saladin could not hold together such a large army for long in arid countryside at the height of summer. Reginald of Châtillon and Gérard of Ridefort favoured an immediate attack to relieve Tiberias, taunting Raymond with cowardice and his earlier pact with Saladin. As before, Guy felt unable to reject the advice of the two men who had won him his throne. He ordered the Christian army to advance towards Tiberias. It camped at Sephoria on the afternoon of 2 July in a strategically advantageous position with plenty of water and fodder for the horses.

Here they were met by the messenger from Tiberias who told them of the plight of Count Raymond's wife. Her sons, who were there with their father, begged Guy to go to her rescue but Raymond argued, as before, that it would be folly to abandon their present position: for the sake of the Christian kingdoms, he was prepared to risk his city and his wife.

The King and his council of barons accepted Raymond's advice; but after they had retired for the night, Gérard of Ridefort returned to the King's tent. How could King Guy, he argued, trust a traitor? What dishonour to abandon a city that was so close. The Templars, he said, would rather 'put aside their white mantles' and sell and pawn all they had than lose this chance to avenge their brothers who had died at the springs of Cresson.

Unable to stand up to Gérard of Ridefort, King Guy ordered the army to march at dawn. Taking the northern route over the arid hills towards Tiberias, constantly harassed by Muslim archers, and soon debilitated by thirst, they reached the village of Lubiya. Here the King received a request from the Templars who brought up the rear, to stop for the night. The King agreed. Count Raymond, leading the vanguard, was aghast: 'Ah, Lord God, the war is over. We are dead men. The kingdom is finished.'

The well at Lubiya was dry. The army camped on the waterless plateau known as the Horns of Hattin, overlooking the village of Hattin where Saladin's army awaited them. As the night progressed, the Muslims edged closer: any soldiers who went in search of water were caught and killed. The Muslims set fire to the scrub that covered the hill: the breeze carried the smoke into the Christian camp.

At dawn, Saladin ordered the attack. Maddened by thirst, the heat and the smoke, the Christian infantry tried to break through the Muslim phalanx to the lake. They were all either killed or taken prisoner. Above them, the armoured knights repelled the repeated assaults of the Muslim cavalry time and time again, but they too were weakened by thirst and each onslaught reduced their numbers. With his knights, Count Raymond charged against the Muslim phalanx which suddenly opened to let them through. Unable to return to the main body of the army, they fled to Tripoli.

Behind them, the remaining knights formed a circle around the King, making numerous sorties against Saladin's men. With them was the Bishop of Acre holding the precious relic of the True Cross. When he fell, the True Cross was taken. The battle was over. King Guy and those knights who remained alive now fell from exhaustion, not from the sword. The most eminent among them were led off captive to the tent of their conqueror, Saladin – among them King Guy, his brother Amalric, Reginald of Châtillon and the young Humphrey of Toron. With the exquisite courtesy for which he was famed, Saladin offered the thirsty King a glass of rose-water, cooled with ice from the peak of Mount Hebron. After drinking from it, the King passed it to Reginald of Châtillon but before Reginald could slake his thirst, the glass was taken from him: according to the rules of Arab hospitality, the life of a captive who is given food or water is assured.

Saladin now berated Reginald for all his iniquities and, again in obedience to Muhammad's teaching, offered him the choice of accepting Islam or death. Reginald laughed in his face, saying that it was rather Saladin who should turn to Christ: 'if you would believe in Him, you could avoid the punishment of eternal damnation which you should not doubt is prepared for you'.[203] On hearing this, Saladin took up his scimitar and cut off Reginald's head.

The lives of King Guy and his secular barons were safe. 'A king does not kill a king,' Saladin said, 'but that man's perfidy and insolence went too far.' They were led off to captivity in Damascus with instructions that they were not to be harmed. The same clemency, however, was not extended to the knights of the military orders. 'I shall purify the land of these impure races,' Saladin said to his chancellor and secretary, 'Imad ad-Din. He rewarded every soldier who had captured a knight brother with fifty dinar and ordered their death. The Koranic scholars, Islamic ascetics and Sufi mystics in his entourage begged Saladin to be allowed to cut off their heads. Only Gérard of Ridefort, the Templar Grand Master, was held captive: the other knights, like Reginald of Châtillon, were given the choice of apostasy or death. All night, to the wild cries of their would-be executioners, they prepared themselves for their fate. None chose to deny Christ. At dawn 230 Knights of the Temple together with their brethren of the Hospital were decapitated by the ecstatic Sufis.

After Hattin, the Christians in the Holy Land seemed doomed. The *levée en masse* had removed the garrisons from all cities and castles in Latin hands and in the wake of Saladin's victory fifty-two either surrendered or were taken. The Countess of Tripoli was permitted to depart from the citadel of Tiberias and Joscelin of Courtenay, formerly one of the hawks, surrendered Acre without a fight on 10 July. At Ascalon, the value of Saladin's eminent captives was tested when Gérard of Ridefort and King Guy were brought to the gates of the city. King Guy ordered the city's defenders to surrender. He was answered with insults, and two of Saladin's emirs were killed in the subsequent siege. However, the ultimate outcome was never in doubt and on 4 September Ascalon surrendered. At Gaza, the Templar garrison, bound by their vows of obedience, surrendered at the command of their Grand Master, Gérard of Ridefort.

Now Saladin turned his attention to the ultimate prize, the city of Jerusalem. There a defence had been organised by Queen Sibylla, the Patriarch Heraclius and Balian of Ibelin. The forces that had been left in the city were wholly inadequate: there were only two knights, and the crisis was so grave that Balian of Ibelin was obliged to bestow the honour of knighthood on thirty bachelors from the bourgeoisie.[204] The city was crammed with refugees, mostly women and children, and the Latins could not count on the loyalty of the Syrian and Orthodox Christians. Again, once the siege had started, the eventual outcome was not in doubt; but threats to raze the Dome of the Rock and burn the city persuaded Saladin to parley. He asked 100,000 dinars as ransom for the population of the city but such a large sum could not be found. A rate was set at ten dinars for a man, five for a woman and one for a child: 30,000 dinars from public funds bought the freedom of 7,000 of those who could not pay. On 2 October 1187, the anniversary of the visit to Heaven of the Prophet from the Temple Mount, Saladin entered the city in triumph. He treated the conquered with great magnanimity; the chroniclers' greatest opprobrium was directed towards the Patriarch Heraclius and the military orders, in particular the Templars, who declined to give up their own treasure, and only reluctantly released what remained of Henry II's funds to save the poorer Christians from slavery.

The Temple was now surrendered to Saladin and the Templars were ousted from their headquarters in the al-Aqsa mosque. It was purified with rose-water and a pulpit installed that had been commissioned in anticipation of this triumph by Nur ed-Din. Though the Church of the Holy Sepulchre was left in the charge of the Orthodox and Jacobite Christians, the Cross was taken down from the Dome of the Rock and was dragged around the city for two days, beaten by the exultant Muslims with clubs.

*

Saladin's generosity towards the Latin Christians in Jerusalem was as much a matter of calculation as the expression of a magnanimous nature. In a military treatise, al-Harawi's *Discussion of the Stratagems of War*, written at the request of Saladin's son, al-Malik, or possibly Saladin himself, the author argues that 'kindness towards non-combatants can be used as a demonstration of power, which may help intimidate the enemy ...' Generously allowing the garrisons of captured cities and castles to retreat to Tyre and other Frankish centres was another demonstration of such power, showing that the Sultan had nothing to fear from his defeated enemies.[205] The Franks were anyway contemptible – 'irresponsible, thoughtless, petty and covetous ... being concerned with rank and status among kings and nobles'. Al-Harawi condemned the Latin clergy for the ease with which they annulled the vows made to Saladin but expressed a grim respect for the military orders, warning Saladin to 'beware of the [Hospitaller and Templar] monks ... for he cannot achieve his goals through them; for they have great fervour in religion, paying no attention to the things of this world'.

Was al-Harawi right in his calculations? There can be no doubt but that the generous terms for the surrender of Jerusalem increased Saladin's prestige and at the same time weakened the will of some of the Latin Christians to resist. However, his treatment of the knights of the military orders stiffened the Templars' and Hospitallers' resolve. The great fortress of Kerak where the royal wedding had been held under Saladin's bombardment in 1183, had to be starved into submission after a siege of more than a year. So too was Montréal. After a month's bombardment, the Templars had surrendered Safed and the Hospitallers their castle at Belvoir. But some of the skittles were left standing. The Hospitallers held on to Krak des Chevaliers and Chastel Blanc. The Templars surrendered Gaston in the Amanus march but held on to la Roche Guillaume and, although the town was taken, held out in the citadel of Tortosa.

This, along with the other coastal cities of Antioch, Tripoli and Tyre, remained in the hands of the Christians. A Sicilian fleet put in to Antioch and reinforced Bohemond's garrison, while the situation at Tyre was transformed by the arrival of a force of crusaders led by a German prince, Conrad of Montferrat, who took charge of the defence of the city. His ships defeated an Egyptian fleet and on 1 January 1188 Saladin abandoned the siege.

In June of the same year, Saladin released King Guy from captivity after he had given his word that he would leave his kingdom. Receiving the Church's assurance that a vow made under duress to an infidel had no validity, Guy assembled a force composed of those knights who had also been ransomed or released and marched to Tyre. Conrad of Montferrat refused to let him in: in his view, Guy's defeat had cost him his crown. After waiting outside the walls for some months, Guy realised that he had either to retire from the Holy Land or do something audacious to re-establish his control.

With unusual resolve, in August 1189, King Guy marched south to Acre, which had surrendered to Saladin's forces after Hattin, and proceeded to besiege it: Gérard of Ridefort and a force of Templars were at his side. Though part of Saladin's army was still in the vicinity, Guy established a fortified encirclement of the city which withstood its assaults, 'the only example in twelfth-century Syrian warfare of a major siege successfully conducted in the presence of a field army able to harass the besiegers and to aid the besieged'.[206] The audacity of the plan makes it seem likely that Gérard was behind it,[207] and it did something to salvage the reputation of the impetuous Grand Master that he died when fighting near the city on 4 October 1189.

nine

Richard the Lionheart

The news of the disasters that had befallen the Holy Land was brought to the Pope, Urban III, who was then in Verona, by knights of the military orders – the Templars carrying a letter from Brother Terence, the Templar Commander in the Holy Land who had been one of the few to escape after Hattin. Urban and the entire Papal Curia were staggered by the news: no one in Europe had imagined that such a setback was possible and they at once assumed that if God had forsaken his people it was because of their sins. The monk, Peter of Blois, who was visiting the Curia at the time, wrote to the English King, Henry II, describing how 'the cardinals, with the assent of the Lord Pope, have firmly promised among themselves that, having renounced all wealth and luxuries, they will preach the Cross of Christ not only by word, but also by deed and example'.[208] Urban III, broken by his sorrow, died shortly after.

When Josias, the Archbishop of Tyre, arrived in Palermo from Tyre in the summer of 1187, sent by the barons of Outremer to solicit help from the West, and told King William II of Sicily of the full extent of the catastrophe, the King threw off his fine silk robes, dressed in sackcloth and went into a penitential retreat for four days. Pope Urban's successor, an elderly Italian, Alberto de Morra, who took the name Gregory VIII, only reigned for the last two months of the year 1187, but in that time he wrote an eloquent appeal for a seven-year truce between the warring European kings to free them for a new crusade. This encyclical, *Audita tremendi*, was 'a moving document and a masterpiece of papal rhetoric',[209] and an immediate response came from King William of Sicily, who dispatched the fleet of fifty galleys that brought relief to the principality of Antioch.

Such penitential reactions, which were consistent with the crusading theology of Bernard of Clairvaux, were now complemented by a more chivalrous idea behind taking the Cross. It is at this time that the word *crucesignata* came into common use, and this not among churchmen but among lay knights and princes. Heraldic devices which had been unknown at the time of the First Crusade were emblazoned on banners and shields; and there was a sense in which the crusade had become in the minds of the European nobility the greatest proof of courage and virtue – the ultimate joust with the forces of evil, the final chivalrous endeavour. Thus Peter of Blois, who had witnessed the penitence of the prelates at the court of Pope Urban III, and wholeheartedly agreed with the penitential sentiments in Pope Gregory VIII's *Audita tremendi*, also wrote in his *Passio Reginaldi* an account of the life and death of the buccaneering Reginald of Châtillon that presents him as not just a martyr but also a saint.[210]

One of the first of the European princes to respond to the Pope's appeal was Richard, Count of Poitou, the son of King Henry II of England and Eleanor of Aquitaine. Eleanor's marriage to King Louis VII of France had been annulled in 1152, three years after their return from the disastrous Second Crusade. Eight weeks later, Eleanor, then aged thirty, had married the nineteen-year-old Count of Anjou who in 1154, on the death of King Stephen, mounted the throne of England as Henry II. This rapid remarriage has been criticised by Eleanor's subsequent biographers: to one, Alfred Richard, she had simply grown tired of Louis's 'almost effeminate grace' and 'wished to be dominated, and as the vulgar crudely put it, she was among those women who enjoy being beaten'.[211] Two chroniclers report that Eleanor had already been seduced, or possibly raped, by Henry's father, Count Geoffrey of Anjou. However, her marriage to Henry was initially a success if measured by the number of their children: having had only two daughters by Louis VII (her failure to produce a male heir inclined the Capetian counsellors to agree to the annulment of the marriage), she bore five sons and three daughters to Henry between 1152 and 1167.

The third of these sons was Richard who, at the age of eleven, was invested with his mother's Duchy of Aquitaine. Immersed from his youth in constant wars with rebellious vassals, Richard established a reputation as a ferocious warrior, a ruthless ruler and, after taking the supposedly impregnable fortress of Taillebourg at the age of twenty-one, a brilliant strategist and general.

In time, the marriage of his mother Eleanor to Henry suffered from

Henry's infidelities, particularly with his English mistress, Rosamund Clifford. In 1173, Eleanor joined her sons in a revolt against Henry II. The rebellion failed: the sons made abject submissions to their father while Eleanor, captured on her way to seek refuge with her first husband, Louis VII, was taken back to England and imprisoned for the next fifteen years.

The death of Richard's elder brother, Henry, in 1183 made him heir to the throne of England as well as the Duchy of Normandy and the County of Anjou. His father, Henry II, at this juncture, had asked Richard to transfer the Duchy of Aquitaine to his youngest son, John. Richard had refused and appealed to his notional suzerain, the successor to Louis VII, King Philip Augustus of France. At one time friends, later rivals and finally implacable enemies, the political and military machinations of both princes were arrested by the news of the defeat of the Latin army at Hattin and the fall of Jerusalem to the forces of Islam.

Impetuously, without his father's consent, Richard took the Cross in the new cathedral of Tours on the same spot from which his great-grandfather, Fulk of Anjou, had set out to marry the Princess Melisende and with her rule the Kingdom of Jerusalem. Philip Augustus protested; Richard was supposed to be marrying his sister Alice: but after hearing an eloquent sermon from the Archbishop of Tyre, he too took the Cross. Henry II, who had long planned to go on crusade and had sent substantial sums of money to the Kingdom of Jerusalem, was forced by the two young princes to join them. They were to set off from Vézelay after Easter in 1190 but Henry II died before he could fulfil his vow, on 6 July 1189.

Now King of England as well as Duke of Normandy and Aquitaine, Richard had enormous resources at his disposal and made meticulous plans for his crusade. There was great popular enthusiasm for the crusade and Cistercians like Baldwin, the Archbishop of Canterbury, promoted the Holy War in the style of Bernard of Clairvaux; but no longer do we find, as at the time of the First Crusade, 'silent and mysterious hermits advising the leaders on military tactics': even the churchmen 'who invoked God's help ... relied on their own resources'.[212] The Pope imposed a ten-per-cent tax on all income and moveable property that came to be known as the 'Saladin tithe'. Although, in the final analysis, the crusade still depended on the individual's willingness to risk his life and property to regain the Holy Places, 'the stirring of the Holy Spirit now moved most obviously in official channels'.[213]

A stream of lesser princes followed the example of King Richard of England and King Philip Augustus of France and, in advance of the two monarchs, joined the Christian army besieging Acre. Many of them were the descendants of earlier crusaders, or the relatives of the nobility of Outremer: Henry, Count of Champagne, a grandson of Eleanor of Aquitaine and so a nephew of the kings of both England and France; Theobald, Count of Blois and Ralph, Count of Clermont; the counts of Bar, Brienne, Fontigny and Dreux; Stephen of Sancerre and Alan of Saint-Valéry. There were also Germans such as Louis, Margrave of Thuringia; powerful fleets from Genoa and Pisa; Italians from Ravenna under their archbishop Gérard; other archbishops from Messina and Pisa, and Baldwin of Canterbury with 3,000 Welshmen; bishops from Besançon, Blois and Toul; the Archdeacon of Colchester, later killed during a sortie against Saladin's camp; knights from Flanders, Hungary, Denmark; and a contingent from London which, like its predecessor during the Second Crusade, stopped off *en route* to help the Portuguese King Sancho take the fortress of Silves from the Moors.

In Germany, in April 1189, the Holy Roman Emperor himself took the Cross. This was Frederick I of Hohenstaufen, knowing as Barbarossa (Redbeard), who had been elected German king in 1152 and crowned emperor by Pope Adrian IV in 1155. His father had been Duke of Swabia and his mother the daughter of the Duke of Bavaria, and as a young man he had accompanied his uncle Conrad on the disastrous Second Crusade. His reign had been marked by an interminable struggle for advantage between Emperor, Pope, King of Sicily, Byzantine Emperor and, a new factor in the equation, the powerful Lombard cities led by Milan.

Now aged around sixty-six, Frederick was a heroic figure with great charm. The plight of the Holy Land not only inspired a private determination to take up his sword once again to fight the infidel, but demanded of him as the lay leader of Christendom a vigorous response. Until now, the Germans had played a secondary role in the crusades: few of them had settled in Outremer. However, Conrad of Montferrat was a kinsman of Barbarossa's, and his valiant defence of Tyre had impressed the Emperor. Now Frederick sent an envoy to Saladin demanding the return of Palestine to Christian rule. Saladin, in response, would go no further than to offer to release all Christian prisoners and return Christian abbeys to their monks.

To Barbarossa, this was not enough. In May 1189, he set out from Regensburg with 'the largest single force ever to leave on a crusade'.[214] Frederick had made arrangements in advance for the passage of this host with the sovereigns over whose territory it would march. It passed through Hungary without incident but ran into trouble when it crossed into the Byzantine Empire.

Relations between the Greek Christians and their Latin co-religionists had been soured by events that had taken place in Constantinople five years before when the people's hatred of the Latin Empress, Maria of Antioch, regent for her son, the young Emperor Alexius, had led to a pogrom of its Latin residents by the Greek population. As many as eighty thousand had been living in the city:[215] men, women and children, the old and the young, the hale and the sick, were all attacked and many slaughtered, their houses and churches burned. Such was the Greek hatred of the Latins that when Saladin captured Jerusalem, the Byzantine Emperor, Isaac Angelus, sent a message to congratulate him.

However, Frederick Barbarossa's army was too strong to be resisted and in the spring he led it across the Bosphorus unmolested and moved into territory controlled by the Seljuk Turks. As with the armies of the Emperor Conrad and the French King Louis VII forty years before, Greek non-co-operation, the harshness of the climate and the aridity of the land through which they progressed led to serious losses in Frederick's forces from thirst and hunger. On 18 May 1190, the German crusaders came upon the army of Saladin's son-in-law, Malik Shah. Battle was joined. The Turks were decisively defeated and swept from the crusader's path. Proceeding unhampered, they now descended through the Taurus Mountains into the plain of Seleucia. While crossing the River Calycadnus, the Emperor Frederick fell into the water and, weighed down by his armour, drowned.

Without his dominating personality, the army he had assembled fell apart. His son, Duke Frederick of Swabia, continued to Antioch with his father's body but many others made for the ports in Cilicia and Syria and returned home. Barbarossa's decomposing corpse was buried in Antioch's cathedral of Saint Peter: some of his bones accompanied the German crusaders in a sarcophagus in the hope that they might reach the Church of the Holy Sepulchre in Jerusalem but were eventually interred in the cathedral of Tyre.

In Palestine, what remained of Barbarossa's army was joined by contingents that had come by sea under Louis of Thuringia and Leopold of

Austria. To cater for their sick and wounded, a group of crusaders from Lübeck and Bremen founded a hospital under the patronage of Saint Mary of the Germans in Jerusalem which, like the Hospital of Saint John, formed an order of knights that adopted the Templar Rule, took the same white habit as the Templars but marked it with a cross that was black rather than red. In 1196 this foundation was approved by Pope Celestine III as the Order of Teutonic Knights.

Just as the Western crusaders converged on the Holy Land in 1190, Guy of Lusignan was ousted as the titular King of Jerusalem by Conrad of Montferrat. Despite his audacious siege of Acre which had become the focal point of the new crusade, he had never been forgiven by the major barons of Outremer for being the consort of Queen Sybilla, heading the party of parvenus and leading them to defeat at Hattin. His two principal champions, Reginald of Châtillon and Gérard of Ridefort, were both dead; and in 1190 his position was further weakened by the death of his wife and their two young daughters from disease.

Since Guy's title to the crown came from Sybilla, it now passed to her niece Isabella, the daughter of King Amalric I. Isabella, as we have seen, was married to the personable young Humphrey of Toron while being besieged by Saladin in the fortress of Kerak, but Humphrey too had alienated the barons by surrendering to Sybilla and Guy. Their solution was to annul her marriage to Humphrey on the grounds that she had been married when below the age of consent and marry Isabella to Conrad of Montferrat. The Princess was perfectly happy with her effete husband but her mother, the dowager Queen Maria Commena, the great-niece of a Byzantine emperor, grasped the political imperatives behind the barons' demand and persuaded her daughter to go along with their plan. The marriage was annulled by the Papal Legate at Acre, the Archbishop of Pisa, and Isabella was married to Conrad by the Bishop of Beauvais.

This dethronement of King Guy was vigorously opposed not just by the Lusignan family but also by the liege lord of the Lusignans in Poitou, Count Richard, now King of England. Baldwin, the Archbishop of Canterbury, present in the camp before Acre, had denounced the arrangement but he had died on 19 November 1190, a few days before the wedding. When Richard eventually reached Acre on 20 April 1191, the deed was done.

*

King Philip II Augustus of France had arrived seven weeks before. The routes taken by the two kings had started in Vézelay in July 1190: Philip and his army had then sailed from Genoa while Richard had met up with his English fleet at Marseilles. Both had stopped off in Italy, then sailed to Messina to stay with King Tancred of Sicily: a dispute between Richard and Tancred led the two guest kings to seize the city of Messina, after which they fell out over the distribution of the booty. Philip was also incensed that Richard now refused to marry Philip's sister Alice, to whom he had been betrothed many years before, on the grounds that she had been seduced by his father, King Henry II, and had borne him a child.

In the spring, Philip Augustus left Messina and after an uneventful voyage reached Tyre. Richard's journey was less straightforward: his fleet was forced to put in at Crete, then was blown north to Rhodes. While one of his ships was wrecked on the coast of Cyprus, another, carrying his betrothed, Berengaria of Navarre, who had been brought to Sicily by Richard's mother, Eleanor of Aquitaine, and was now chaperoned by his sister, the dowager Queen of Sicily, Joan, was forced into the port of Limassol.

The self-appointed ruler of Cyprus, a renegade Byzantine prince, Isaac Ducas Comnenus, had formed an alliance with Saladin and so imprisoned the shipwrecked crusaders. Prudently, Joan and Berengaria declined his offer to land. Richard, when he caught up with them a week later, demanded the release of the captives and, when Isaac Ducas refused, prepared for war. Reinforced by a fleet from Acre carrying Guy of Lusignan, Prince Leo of Cilician Armenia, Bohemond of Antioch and Humphrey of Toron and the senior Templars in Outremer (the Templars, despite the death of Gérard de Ridefort, still backed King Guy), Richard embarked upon a lightning conquest of the island. Unloved by his Greek subjects, Isaac Ducas could put up but a feeble resistance and soon surrendered to the English King on condition that he would not be put in irons: Richard agreed and shackled him with silver fetters instead.

Enormously enriched by this conquest, Richard left a Latin garrison in its fortresses and two English justiciaries in charge of its administration, and sailed for Palestine. He landed near Tyre but by order of King Philip Augustus and Conrad of Montferrat was not allowed in. He therefore sailed south to Acre which he reached on 8 June. There his arrival boosted the morale of the crusaders. Philip Augustus, though intelligent and fascinated by siege-engines, was also sardonic and hypochondriacal, not qualities likely to inspire fighting men. He was also poorer than Richard who, even before the pillage of Cyprus, had emptied the treasuries of England and his French possessions to finance his crusade. With these ample resources and his martial reputation, it was agreed that Richard should take command of the crusade. The Templars admitted his friend and vassal, Robert of Sablé, as a brother and elected him their Grand Master.

One of the first actions of the new Grand Master was to buy Cyprus from Richard for 100,000 besants. News had reached Richard that his judiciaries on the island had been unable to control the Greek population: he wanted to be rid of the problem and must have known that the Templars, for all the recent depredations, had considerable treasure at their disposal. The agreement made, Robert of Sablé dispatched twenty knights with supporting squires and sergeants to take control of the island.

The main Templar force remained with the crusading army besieging Acre. On 12 July 1191, the Muslim garrison surrendered: Saladin had been unable to raise the siege. The price to be paid for the life of its inhabitants was 200,000 besants, the release of 1,500 Christian prisoners and the return of the relic of the True Cross. Conrad of Montferrat led the victorious crusaders into the city. King Richard moved into the royal palace; King Philip into the fortress previously held by the Templars. The Duke of Austria placed his banner on the ramparts next to those of the kings of England and France, thereby staking a claim to a share of the booty: the English, on Richard's orders, tore it down and threw it over the ramparts into the moat. A compromise was reached between King Guy and Conrad of Montferrat: the former would reign until his death; the latter would be his successor. In the meantime the royal revenues would be shared.

With Acre now in Christian hands, a number of crusaders decided that their vows had been fulfilled and returned home. Leopold of Austria departed only days after his humiliation at the hands of King Richard. King Philip Augustus retired to Tyre with Conrad of Montferrat, then took ship for Brindisi: he had suffered from constant sickness and disliked the English King. Though he left most of his army under the command of the Duke of Burgundy, the barons of Outremer who backed Conrad were sad to see him go.

Richard the Lionheart was left as the undisputed commander of the crusading army. He became impatient when there was a hitch in the exchange of prisoners and the payment of the indemnity. According to one source, Saladin asked the Templars to guarantee the terms of an interim arrangement with Richard because, much as he hated them, he knew they would keep their word.[216] The Templars were less sure of Richard and declined to give Saladin the assurance he required. Richard became exasperated at Saladin's procrastination and personally supervised the execution of the Muslim captives: 2,700, among them women and children, were slaughtered by his English soldiers.

To the Muslims, this was a clear breach of Richard's treaty with Saladin; to the Frankish chroniclers, it was a necessary and even praiseworthy action within the accepted conventions of war. Saladin, after all, had massacred the knights of the military orders after his victory at Hattin. Richard would certainly have secured the agreement of the other Christian princes before taking this drastic action: guarding the prisoners would have tied up a large part of the Latin force – something that no doubt entered into Saladin's calculation – and so prevented the further progress of the crusade.

Having disposed of their prisoners and strengthened the fortifications, the crusading army left Acre and marched south on the coast road towards Haifa and Caesarea. Constantly harassed by Saladin's forces, the cavalry rode in tight formation with the Templars in the van and the Hospitallers in the rear. On the landward side they were protected by the Christian infantry, in particular Richard's English archers, and they in turn protected the baggage train which was supplied by the Christian fleet that kept pace with the army. As it emerged from the Forest of Arsuf south of Caesarea, Saladin mounted an all-out assault. It was thrown back and despite light losses on both sides the outcome was a defeat for Saladin, the first in an outright battle since his victory at Hattin.

However, Saladin's army – though weakened and suffering from defections – was not destroyed. Richard proceeded with his forces to Jaffa where he rebuilt the fortifications. It was clear that neither army was strong enough to destroy the other and so the conflict could only be resolved through negotiation. Frequent parleys were held with Saladin's brother, al-Adil. Despite the massacre of the garrison of Acre, Saladin retained his profound regard for the English King. Initial courtesy led on to fraternisation: Richard proposed that al-Adil should marry his sister Joanna and that together they should jointly rule Palestine with the Holy City shared by their two religions, a suggestion that outraged Joanna and was not taken seriously by Saladin.

After spending Christmas at the monastery of Latrun in the Judaean hills, Richard led his army to within twelve miles of Jerusalem. The crusaders who had come from Europe wanted to besiege the Holy City but the barons of Outremer and the Grand Masters of the military orders counselled caution: even if Jerusalem was taken, how could it be held once Richard and the crusaders had departed? Without forward defences between Palestine and Sinai, it would remain permanently vulnerable to attack from Egypt.

Richard therefore returned to the coast and spent the first four months of 1192 fortifying Ascalon prior to a move on Gaza. Time was running out for the English monarch: disquieting news reached him from England about the activities of Philip Augustus and his brother John. Amicable negotiations with Saladin made it seem that a settlement was within his reach. He was also determined to leave the Kingdom of Jerusalem with a clear chain of command. Although his favoured candidate for the crown was Guy of Lusignan, he accepted the unanimous decision of the local barons that it should be Conrad of Montferrat; but even as preparations were made for his coronation, Conrad was murdered in the streets of Acre.

The killers were Assassins, sent by Sinan, the Old Man of the Mountain. His purpose was unclear. Conrad had antagonised the Assassins by seizing a cargo ship that belonged to them and had refused any restitution; however, suspicion also fell on King Richard. Conrad's close friend, the Bishop of Beauvais, whom he had visited just prior to his death, was convinced that the killers had been commissioned by the English King. Others argued that it was not his style to dispose of an enemy in such an underhand way; but the outcome was certainly to his advantage: within two days of Conrad's assassination, his widow, the 21-year-old Queen Isabella, was betrothed to Richard's nephew, Count Henry of Champagne.

For a final settlement of the affairs of Outremer, it only remained to dispose of Guy of Lusignan. With the concurrence of Robert of Sablé it was decided that, to make up for the loss of the Kingdom of Jerusalem, he should have Cyprus. The Templars had been no more successful than Richard's judiciaries in controlling the island. The knights had proved rapacious and unpopular and, on 4 April 1192, the Latin garrison in Nicosia had been besieged by the Greeks. A sortie had dealt with the insurgents, but the incident had made clear that a small garrison could not control the population; 'what was needed, if Cyprus was to be held permanently, was a large number of men with a vested interest in preserving the new regime'.[217] The island was therefore returned to King Richard who promptly resold it to Guy of Lusignan for the balance owed by the Templars of 60,000 besants.

Impatient to return to Europe, Richard put further pressure on Saladin to come to terms. His army took the castle of Daron, south of Ascalon; but then, while Richard was in Acre, Saladin himself attacked Jaffa and after three days took the town. The garrison withdrew to the citadel and were on the point of surrender when fifty Pisan and Genoese galleys reached the city with King Richard on board. Jumping into the water and followed by only eighty knights, four hundred archers and around two thousand Italian marines, Richard fought his way through the streets of the city and put Saladin's forces to flight. Before this small force could be relieved by Richard's main army that was marching up the coast, Saladin counter-attacked. With brilliant improvisation, Richard directed his men to withstand wave after wave of the Muslim assault. 'Saladin was lost in angry admiration at the sight.'[218] When Richard's horse was killed under him, this paragon of Islamic chivalry sent two fresh steeds as a gift for the English King.

By his personal courage and inspired tactics, Richard won the day; but it was now clear to both leaders that they faced stalemate: neither could destroy the other and both had pressing reasons to bring the conflict to an end. It was imperative that Richard should return home to secure his possessions in Europe while Saladin faced the perennial difficulty of maintaining a large army in the field. Although he had established a certain moral ascendancy in his role as the champion of Islam, his troops were often motivated by hope of booty in this world rather than reward in the next. Only this compensated for the dangers and privations of the campaign; and when it was not forthcoming, they found it difficult to resist the pull of home.

The obstacle to agreement in earlier negotiations had always been Ascalon: now Richard backed down. He agreed that Ascalon should be demolished: in return, Saladin guaranteed the Christians' possession of the coastal cities from Antioch to Jaffa. Muslims and Christians were to be free to traverse each other's territory. Christian pilgrims were to be free to visit Jerusalem and the other sites sacred to the Christian religion. Balian of Ibelin, Henry of Champagne and the Masters of the Temple and the Hospital swore on behalf of Richard to keep the peace for the next five years.

Many of Richard's followers now went as unarmed pilgrims to the Holy City. Richard did not. He returned to Acre, settled his affairs and saw his wife and sister off on a ship to France. He himself set sail on 9 October: he had been in the Holy Land for sixteen months. His boat was blown off-course and was forced to put into port on the Byzantine island of Corfu. Fearing to be taken hostage by the Byzantine Emperor, Richard sailed with some pirates heading for Venice: he was disguised as a Templar and travelled with an escort that included four Templar knights.

His choice of route was forced upon him by political developments in his absence, in particular a war between his father-in-law, King Sancho of Navarre, and Raymond, Count of Toulouse. This made it impossible to land in any of the ports of southern France. With winter approaching, the long voyage through the Straits of Gibraltar and around the Iberian Peninsula was too hazardous; to travel through Italy and up the Rhine valley would make him vulnerable to capture by his enemy, the Hohenstaufen Emperor, Henry VI.

Making for Venice, the pirate boat went aground near Aquileia at the northern end of the Adriatic Sea. From here, Richard and his companions made their way north over the Alps disguised as pilgrims, but at an inn in Vienna Richard was recognised, supposedly because of the fabulously valuable ring that he still wore on his finger, and was handed over to his arch-enemy from the siege of Acre, Leopold, Duke of Austria. The man who had bought and sold the island of Cyprus now himself became a commodity: Leopold first imprisoned him in his castle of Dürrenstein, then passed him to his overlord, the Emperor Henry VI, whose terms for Richard's release were that Richard should swear allegiance as the Emperor's vassal and pay a ransom of 150,000 marks.

While Richard was in captivity, his admiring antagonist, Saladin, died. So too did his friend and former vassal, the Templar Grand Master, Robert of Sablé. King Philip Augustus and Richard's brother John lobbied the Emperor to hold on to Richard but Richard – courteous, cheerful, almost nonchalant in his humiliating position – won support among the princes at the court of the German Emperor. In February 1194, he was released: he had made the required vows and, such was the prosperity of England at the time, most of his ransom had been paid. On hearing the news, King Philip Augustus wrote to John: 'Beware, the devil is out.'

After spending only a month in England, Richard returned to Normandy and spent the next five years in intermittent warfare with rebellious vassals and King Philip Augustus of France. In 1199, while besieging the castle of Châlus belonging to one of his vassals, the Viscount of Limoges, he was hit in the shoulder by the bolt from a crossbow and fatally wounded. His mother, Eleanor, was summoned to his side and, after confessing his sins and receiving the last sacraments of the Church, Richard died on 6 April. He was forty-two years old.

In the centuries that followed, Richard the Lionheart was remembered as a paragon of chivalry, the subject of a number of exotic and improbable legends. Each reflects the prejudices of its time. 'If heroism be confined to brutal and ferocious valour,' wrote Gibbon, 'Richard Plantagenet will stand high among the heroes of his age.' The most recent myth, that Richard was homosexual, has been accepted by many historians even though it can be traced back no further than 1948 and is now thought to be false. Contemporary chroniclers rather criticise him for an insatiable appetite for women so 'that even on his deathbed he had them brought to him in defiance of his doctor's advice'.[219]

A more persistent criticism of Richard was that his foreign adventures had an adverse effect on the governance of England. 'No doubt he thought it was a great and good thing to fight for Jerusalem,' wrote H. E. Marshall in his compendium for English schoolchildren, *Our Island Story*, 'but how much better it would have been if he had tried to rule his own land peacefully, and bring happiness to his people.'[220] Again, more recent assessments exonerate Richard: his responsibilities extended far beyond England, the least problematic of his domains. Despite his enthusiasm for fighting, which he shared with other knights of his time, he 'was not a crudely bellicose king, a king bent on war for its own sake and on aggression, but a ruler intelligently concerned to employ his military talents in the widely extended interests of the house of Anjou of which he was the head'.[221] Though, in retrospect, his struggle to preserve his inheritance within the Kingdom of France from the encroachments of the Capetians may appear to have been a lost cause, it did not seem so at the time.

The most telling criticism made of Richard by his contemporaries was that he recklessly endangered his own person by throwing himself into the fray. Even his enemies, the Saracens, thought it folly for a such an inspired commander to risk his life in combat; for alongside his daring and impetuosity, there was a genius for planning and logistics. It was this daring that brought his life to a premature end. But this does not detract from his overall achievements. The conclusion of the contemporary historian, John Gillingham, that 'as a politician, administrator and warlord – in short, as a king – he was one of the most outstanding rulers of European history', echoes the verdict of the Muslim chronicler, Ibn Athir, that Richard's 'courage, shrewdness, energy and patience made him the most remarkable ruler of his times'.[222]

ten

The Enemies Within

One of the stories later told about Richard the Lionheart was that, as he lay dying, he humorously shed his principal vices, leaving his avarice to the Cistercians, his love of luxury to the mendicant friars, and his pride to the Templar Knights.[223] This same sin of pride was also ascribed to the Templars by Richard's contemporary, Pope Innocent III, one of the most outstanding men to wear the papal tiara in the two-thousand-year history of the Catholic Church.

Elected in 1198 at the young age of thirty-seven, Innocent was the son of the Count of Segni and so a member of the patrician Roman family of Scotti who provided a number of popes in the eleventh and twelfth centuries: Innocent's uncle, Pope Clement III, had made him a cardinal in 1190, and both a nephew and a great-nephew were to become popes. However, if an element of nepotism had entered into his advancement, it did not mean that Innocent was not the best man for the job. He was exceptionally intelligent, of great integrity, witty, magnanimous, 'keenly alert to the absurd in the events and people around him',[224] yet utterly convinced that, as supreme pontiff and the 'Vicar of Christ' – a term he was the first to use – he had authority over the whole world, 'lower than God but higher than man: one who judges all, and is judged by no one'.

By training, Innocent was a canon lawyer, the first of a number of lawyer-popes, but his approach was never narrow or pedantic. With extraordinary energy, he promoted the pastoral reform of the Catholic Church and the clarification of its teaching that was codified in the decrees of the Fourth Lateran Council that met in 1215. He insisted upon orthodoxy: it was a time when, beneath the superficial uniformity of the Catholic faith, there were many undercurrents of religious enthusiasm and variant belief. The affluence and worldliness of many of the clergy provoked challenges to the

Church. Innocent was sufficiently open-minded to recognise the value of an idealistic innovator like Francis of Assisi but he condemned and set out to extirpate the heretical teaching of the Cathars in Languedoc.

Like all popes since Urban II, Innocent III was an enthusiastic supporter of the war against Islam. In 1198, soon after his accession, he called for a new crusade and in 1199 wrote to the bishops and barons of Outremer to complain that treaties with the Saracens undermined his attempts to persuade Christians in Europe to take the Cross. To finance the crusade he imposed a two-and-a-half-per-cent tax on Church income. He granted a plenary indulgence, the forgiveness of all confessed sins, not just for those who went to Palestine but also those who sent proxies in their place. The waging of a Holy War in the Holy Land now became accepted 'as an ideal in the daily lives of Western Europeans';[225] but 'the presence of the crusade in late medieval Europe was perhaps more than anything else that of the armies of collectors, bankers, bureaucrats who busied themselves assembling and distributing money without which nothing could be done'.[226]

Like Richard the Lionheart, Innocent III had an ambivalent attitude towards the Order of the Temple. He was aware of its failings. The popes, as the overall sovereigns of the military orders, were constantly assailed by complaints against the knights, either from secular leaders such as King Amalric of Jerusalem in the case of the killing of the Assassin envoys by the Templars; or more often from the clergy who felt that their rights had been transgressed. Since most of the chroniclers of the period were clerics, such as William of Tyre, they probably give an exaggerated impression of the opprobrium felt for the Temple by the public at large.

Some of the charges are quite trivial – for example, that the ringing of bells in the Hospitaller compound in Jerusalem disturbed the Patriarch of Jerusalem and confused the canons of the Church of the Holy Sepulchre. Others stem directly from the privileges that the popes had given to the military orders, in particular exemption from the payment of tithes. At the Third Lateran Council in 1179, a number of decrees were passed curtailing the privileges of the military orders which had later to be annulled by the Pope. In 1196 Pope Celestine III rebuked the Templars for breaking an agreement they had made with the same canons of the Holy Sepulchre over the division of tithes; and in 1207 Pope Innocent III chided them for disobeying his legates, exploiting the privilege of saying Mass in churches placed under interdict, and admitting anyone 'willing to pay two or three pence to join a Templar confraternity ... even if he is excommunicate' with the result that adulterers and usurers could be assured of a Christian burial. They were, he said, 'exhaling their greed for money'.[227]

Few questioned the very existence of the military orders. The Cistercian Abbot of l'Etoile near Poitiers, an Englishman called Isaac, in the mid-twelfth century preached against the 'new monstrosity' of the *nova militia*, a term which echoed Bernard of Clairvaux's tract in favour of the Templars, *De laude novae militiae*: he denounced those who used force to convert Muslims and regarded as martyrs those who died while despoiling non-Christians. Later in the twelfth century, two other Englishmen, the chroniclers Walter Map and Ralph Niger, also questioned the use of force to spread the Christian religion. Walter Map, an enemy of the Cistercians, criticised the Templars for their avarice and extravagance, contrasting those vices with the poverty and charity of their founder, Hugh of Payns.

Resentment against the Templars was exacerbated by their culture of secrecy. In the Holy Land there were good military reasons why their deliberations should not be disclosed, but in Europe it was rather that they did not want their failings to become known. It was in chapter that the transgressions of the brothers were confessed and penances imposed; like most institutions, the Templars preferred to hide their shortcomings, and by the middle of the thirteenth century 'all three [military] orders contained regulations forbidding the brothers to make public the chapter proceedings of the order, or to allow outsiders to see copies of the rule'.[228] Great secrecy also surrounded the ceremony of reception into the Order.

A source of envy was the apparent wealth of the Order of the Temple which, given the bad news that came from the Holy Land, made many wonder if they were giving value for money. Unlike the monastic orders, they made only a minor contribution to the medieval welfare state: one of the first critics of the Order, John of Würzburg, conceded that they did give alms to the poor but not as generously as the Knights of the Hospital. As with the Benedictines and the Cistercians, past endowments and successful estate management had made both the Temple and Hospital among the richest corporate bodies in the kingdoms of western Europe. Among the spiritual descendants of Benedict of Nursia and Bernard of Clairvaux, this wealth had led to considerable compromises with their original ideals, with the charism of apostolic poverty passing to the orders of friars such as the Franciscans until they in turn were corrupted by their success.

Despite this trend among the religious, the Templars lived in a state of rough frugality. Outside the capital cities, or the territories where they were at war, they did not spend large sums on great castles or magnificent churches: the extant commanderies such as Richerenches appear quite modest, particularly when compared to the splendour of the monastic foundations. The buildings of their commanderies and preceptories were wholly practical: barns to store their corn, stables for the horses, dormitories to house the half-a-dozen or so brothers who staffed them, and modest fortifications to keep out thieves. Their churches were also modest and were built as symbols of their mission: the salient feature of both Templar and Hospitaller churches was the rotunda copied from the Church of the Holy Sepulchre in Jerusalem. Both orders 'vied to associate themselves in the public eye with the defence of the site of the Resurrection'.[229]

The public perception of the military orders was that they were wealthy, but 'the orders themselves were at pains to point out to new recruits that life in the orders was not as comfortable as their image might have led them to believe'. Direct accusations of *luxure* 'were reserved for Cluniacs and bishops'.[230] A more telling charge against the Templars in Europe was that, while all claimed the exemptions that had been given to the Order, only a small proportion actually took up arms against the infidel. The great majority were administrators of the more than 9,000 manors that had been given to the Order by pious benefactors over the years or the labourers who worked on them, the Templars' 'men'. The exemptions from feudal justice and obligations enjoyed by even these subordinate members of the Order were inevitably resented by the feudal lords. By and large, since it was the royal courts who upheld their privileged status, relations with royal officials were cordial; but there were instances, for example in the Bulmer Hundred in Yorkshire, when the Templars abused their privileges by enrolling felons and robbers into the Order and preventing royal justices from making arrests.

Like the Cistercians, the Templars managed their own estates. In England, they had holdings as far west as Penzance or in such remote places as the island of Lundy. In Lincolnshire and Yorkshire they contributed significantly to the development of agriculture, and drew recruits from the families who had bequeathed the land. Criticism of the Order was often counterbalanced by praise, particularly from barons returning from the crusades. A great magnate in the north of England, Roger of Mowbray, Earl

Templar Preceptories and Castles in the West in the Mid-Twelfth Century

N

North Sea

Atlantic Ocean

Willoughton

Temple Cowley
Temple Guiting
Temple Dinsley
Cressing
London
Shipley

Sommereux
Laon
Beauvais

Paris
Coulours
R. Seine
La Neuville

Nantes
Orléans
R. Loire
Marmoutier
La Rochelle

R. Rhine

R. Rhône

R. Po

Rodez
Richerenches
La Selve
Roaix
Saint-Gilles
Avignon
Pézenas
Arles
Albenga

Montsaunès
Monzón
Doûzens
Siena

Chalamera
Grañera
Mas-Deu
Rome

Novillas
Palau
Ambel
Barbará
Remolins
Corbins

R. Ebro

R. Garonne

Braga

Soure
Tomar
R. Tagus
Almourol
Santarém

Mediterranean Sea

0	250	500 km
0	150	300 miles

of Northumberland, after being captured by Saladin at Hattin, had his ransom paid by the Temple and, on his return, expressed his gratitude in a number of benefactions.

The Templars' reputation for probity meant that they were trusted both to hold the money of others and to transfer it to different locations. It was through the Temple in London that King Henry II built up a crusading fund in Jerusalem that proved so useful at the time of Hattin. The Templars also lent money to individuals and institutions, including the Jews, but their principal clients were kings and their loans frequently staved off the collapse of royal finances. Fortuitously, the Templars thus became the bankers of Christendom and held in their vaults not just the wealth of the Order but the treasure of kings. The Paris Temple became 'one of the key financial centres of north-west Europe'.[231] Its great keep, or *donjon*, a turreted tower that was to serve as a prison for King Louis XVI and Queen Marie Antoinette at the time of the Revolution of 1789, would have had its equivalent in the London Temple where today only the church is extant. In Paris it is estimated that around four thousand men marked with the cross of the Order resided in the Temple, though few of these would be in the white habit of a fully fledged knight.

In the Kingdom of Aragon, the kings were constantly borrowing money from the Temple and in France the order often had difficulty in meeting the royal demands.[232] Church institutions were readier to lend money to the Crown if the Temple secured the loan. In Aragon, loans were made on the security of an income from land or a benefice, and 'it was often agreed that the Order could deduct part of the sum collected to cover its expenses, as was permitted in canon law'. On some loans they charged interest of ten per cent which was 'two per cent less than the maximum allowed to Christian moneylenders in Aragon and half of the Jewish rate' and while 'in a few instances the Templars definitely obtained a direct monetary gain from moneylending, on some other occasions they appear not to have done so'.[233]

Among the financial services provided by the Templars were the provision of annuities and pensions. Frequently a donation of land or money would stipulate that it should provide for a man and his wife until they died: 'there were few ways of providing for one's old age or the welfare of one's dependants except by making a gift to an ecclesiastical institution'.[234] Payment was also made for a package of spiritual and temporal benefits: for the salvation of the donor's soul and protection by the Temple in a society where violence was endemic, there was much to be said for having a Templar cross on one's property whether or not one was also under the nominal protection of a liege lord.

This function of the Templars as a form of police force had, of course, been envisaged by their founder, Hugh of Payns: now it was extended from escorting pilgrims in Palestine to safeguarding the transfer of cash. In July 1220, Pope Honorius III told his legate, Pelagius, that he could find no one whom he trusted more to transport a large sum of money.[235] Templars also worked as civil servants: brothers of the Temple and Hospital are frequently found serving both popes and kings. As monks, they had the habit of obedience and, as celibates, no dynastic ambitions. Their status as knights gave them authority and qualified them to take on military duties: for example, Pope Urban IV appointed three Templar brothers to take charge of castles in the Papal States, and at Acre the Temple and Hospital were the only bodies trusted by both Richard the Lionheart and Philip Augustus. With their financial acumen, Templars were often made royal almoners by the European kings.

Despite the unitary structure of the military orders, the knights' vow of obedience to their Grand Master, and their fealty to the Pope, it seems to have been accepted that brothers in the same Order should work for monarchs whose interests diverged from one another, or from those of the Pope. In almost every European kingdom, Templars and Hospitallers were a source of dependable public servants, and as such were in a position to exert influence in favour of their Orders. King John of England, who succeeded his brother Richard, was excommunicated by the Pope and yet was advised by the Templar Master in England, Aimery of Saint Maur: he was almost the only man John trusted. In the same way, the Emperor Frederick II, in his constant conflicts with the Papacy, was counselled and supported by the Hermann of Salza, the Grand Master of the Teutonic Knights.

The presence of Templars in the councils of popes and kings puts Innocent III's criticisms of the Order in perspective. Despite their pride, and the occasional abuse of their privileges, the military orders had become indispensable to the papal governance of Christendom and so received full papal support. Thus, when the Patriarch Fulcher of Jerusalem went to Rome to persuade the Pope to revoke some of the privileges of the Hospital he got nowhere. The chronicler, William of Tyre, put this down to bribery but it seems more likely that the Curia's attitude reflected the growing disenchantment in Europe with the Latins in Outremer and that it saw in the military orders the most effective means of achieving the Church's objectives. In the same way, the decrees passed by the third Lateran Council curtailing the privileges of the military orders were reversed by later popes.[236]

Innocent III was even more emphatic in his defence of the Templars' privileges and exemptions, insisting upon the Order's right to build churches, to have their own cemeteries, to collect their own tithes; and he warned the clergy not to interfere with the Templars' rights by taking tithes from their estates or putting their churches under interdict. He denounced bishops who had imprisoned Templars and insisted that they punish anyone who robbed Templar houses. He suspended the Bishop of Sidon for excommunicating the Grand Master of the Temple in a dispute over the revenues of the diocese of Tiberias; renewed all the privileges given to the Temple by Pope Innocent II's bull of 1139, *Omne datum optimum*; and, giving us an insight into the way popular resentment against the Templars found expression, condemned anyone who attacked a Templar knight and dragged him from his horse.

Given that the popes had supreme authority over the military orders, it shows some restraint that there is only one instance where they involved them in their own wars: in 1267, Pope Clement IV asked for Hospitaller help against the Germans in Sicily.[237] Clearly, where they were in the service of popes or kings, individual knights belonging to the military orders were expected to take up arms to protect their masters' interest, and there were instances where the kings of Aragon summoned the Templars' men, and even the knights themselves, to fight against the Castilians and the French. However, this was the exception, not the rule. 'The Crown was clearly wary of using the Templars themselves against its Christian enemies' and the Templars were reluctant so to be used: the kings had to threaten strong measures to ensure that their summons would be obeyed.[238]

Two other areas where the Templars came into armed conflict with their fellow Christians were Cyprus and Armenian Cilicia. The uprising against the Templars in Nicosia in 1192 had been forcefully put down and, even after the island had been resold to Guy of Lusignan, the Templars held on to the stronghold of Gastria, north of Famagusta, and had fortified estates at Yermasoyia and Khirokitia, and a fortified house in Limassol. In Cilicia, the order came to blows with Leo, the Prince of Lesser Armenia, over the fortress of Gaston overlooking Antioch in the Amanaus Mountains.

In the two most significant conflicts between Christians in this period, the Templars were only marginally involved. The first was the Fourth Crusade that set out in response to Pope Innocent III's first appeal on his accession for aid to the Holy Land and, like the First Crusade, was led by a group of secondary rulers with a crusading pedigree such as Count Louis of Blois, Count Baldwin of Flanders and Count Theobald of Champagne.

Since the death of the Emperor Barbarossa in Anatolia, the land route to the East was considered impassable and so envoys of these magnates went to Venice to arrange for passage by sea. The Doge of Venice, Enrico Dandolo, though an old man, was far from senile: he agreed that for the sum of 85,000 silver marks the republic would provide a fleet of fifty galleys and transport for 4,500 knights, 9,000 squires and 20,000 foot-soldiers with sustenance for a year. The date of departure was set for twelve months' time.

The ostensible aim of this expedition was to liberate Jerusalem because now, as at the time of the First Crusade, Western Christians were only prepared to risk their lives for the Holy City: but in a secret clause to the treaty, it was agreed that the crusade would attack Egypt. Since the Third Crusade a consensus had grown up among the leaders of the Latins, both in Europe and in Outremer, that Jerusalem could never be secure while menaced from Cairo. However, the Venetians, who had profitable trading links with the Ayyubids (sultans descended from Saladin's father, Ayyub) in Egypt, almost certainly had no intention of aiding an assault on the Nile.

Count Theobald of Champagne died early in 1201 and the high command of this new expedition chose as their new leader Marquis Boniface of Montferrat. However, on the date set for their departure only around 10,000 men had assembled in Venice and there was a deficit of 35,000 marks in the sum that had been promised to the Venetians. The Venetians refused to lower their price but agreed to accept in lieu the help of the crusading army in taking the city of Zara on the Dalmatian coast *en route* to the East. This was held by the Christian King of Hungary and many of the crusaders objected, among them the Cistercian Abbot of Les-Faux-de-Cernay and a French baron, Simon of Montfort. They were overruled; Zara was taken. Innocent III was so outraged at this attack on a Christian king that he excommunicated the whole army; but, faced with the collapse of the crusade, the sentence was rescinded.

While wintering in Zara, intending to continue east in the spring, the crusading army was approached by a Greek prince, Alexius IV Angelus, who had a claim to the Byzantine throne. He proposed that, if the Western army would return his father to the throne, he could guarantee a reunion of the Orthodox with the Catholic Church, large subventions and ten thousand Byzantine soldiers to join the crusade. The idea appealed to the Doge, Enrico Dandolo, and to Boniface of Montferrat but was opposed by the same parties who had objected to the attack on Zara: Simon of Montfort and the Abbot of Les-Faux-de-Cernay. Again, they were overruled and as a result abandoned the crusade.

The restoration of a legitimate ruler was a just cause in the canon of feudal law, and the bishops accompanying the crusade were persuaded to support it; but when the fleet arrived off Chalcedon opposite Constantinople in June 1203, there were other less creditable emotions in the minds of the Latin warriors. The French remembered the ordeal of King Louis VII and the knights on the Second Crusade as they had marched across Anatolia in 1148, which the King had blamed on the perfidy of the Greeks; and Enrico Dandolo had his own reasons for loathing the Greeks: he had lost his sight during the pogroms against the Latins in Constantinople in 1182.

The memory of this atrocity was still vivid in the minds of the Latins: we can see its effect on the history of William, Archbishop of Tyre. At first his only criticism of the Byzantines is that they are too weak to defend the Holy Places, but he considers them worthwhile as allies against the Saracens. After the pogroms of 1182, his illusions are shattered; he decides that he has been wrong about 'the deceitful and treacherous Greeks' whose 'pseudo-monks and sacrilegious priests' are not just schismatics but heretics[239] – the most damning epithet that a medieval churchman could devise.

Acting on this latent hatred was 'the medieval soldier's notorious greed for booty',[240] something which to those living in an age of well-paid and even cosseted armies seems more reprehensible than it did at the time. It was not just that the barbarian passion for plunder was still strong in the Frankish psyche, but also that all military campaigns had to some extent to pay for themselves. What Innocent III had failed to appreciate was that, despite his tax on the clergy, the costs of crusading were beyond the resources of all but the richest kings. By giving the go-ahead to the minor magnates like the counts of Blois, Flanders and Champagne, he may have hoped to keep a greater measure of papal control over the expedition than if he had waited on the kings of England and France; but, as the taking of Zara had demonstrated, his control was tenuous; and the crusade was inadequately funded.

It is also clear that in this, as in all other crusades, the penitential motivation was combined with the hope in the minds of many of the participants that they would both save their souls and make their fortunes: it was wholly accepted among all parties to these incessant conflicts that risk should have its reward. Despite this, however, there can be no doubt that what now followed was 'a scandalous undertaking',[241] even if it remains unclear who was to blame. In June 1203, soon after their arrival, the crusaders attacked the outskirts of Constantinople, captured the suburb of Galeta and broke the chain that protected the entrance to the city's harbour, the Golden Horn. On 17 July they mounted an assault on Constantinople itself but were beaten back by the Emperor's Varangian Guard. This was enough, however, to frighten the Emperor Alexius III into flight and put the crusaders' candidate Isaac Angelus on the throne.

Despised by his Greek subjects as a stooge of the Latins, the new Emperor was unable to raise the money that had been promised to the crusaders and in January 1204 he was deposed and murdered by the angry populace together with his son. The Emperor who replaced him, Alexius V Ducas, was more to the Greeks' liking but he antagonised the crusaders. On 12 April 1204 they attacked the city and within a day it was taken. The ancient and as yet unconquered capital of the eastern Roman Empire was subjected to the slaughter of its inhabitants and the pillage of its treasures. Most prized were the repositories of relics that, as magnets to attract pilgrims to churches in Europe, were worth very much more than their weight in gold. One of the chroniclers of the sack of the city, Gunther of Pairis, described how a Latin abbot, finding the store of relics in the Church of Christ the Pantocrator after threatening to kill a Greek priest if he did not tell him where they were hidden, 'filled the folds of his gown with the holy booty of the Church which, laughing happily, he then carried back to the ship'.[242]

Not only the treasures of Constantinople but those of the Byzantine Empire itself were shared out among the Latin conquerors. On 16 May Baldwin of Flanders was crowned emperor in the cathedral of Hagia Sofia and was given lands in Thrace, parts of Asia Minor and some of the Cycladic islands. Boniface of Montferrat founded a kingdom in Thessalonika while the Venetians took over the Byzantine possessions on the Adriatic coast, cities on the coast of the Peloponnese, Euboea, some the Ionian islands and Crete. Constantinople was also subdivided into quarters with the Venetians taking almost half the city. Not only had Enrico Dandolo taken his revenge; he had also established Venetian control over the trade routes from the Adriatic to the Black Sea.

None of those who had set out under Boniface of Montferrat went on to the Holy Land. All stayed to stake their claim to fiefs on the carcass of the Byzantine Empire. From now on, potential recruits among the landless knights of western Europe who might have sought their fortunes in Syria and Palestine were diverted by the easier opportunities offered by fiefdoms in Greece. It was therefore not just the Byzantine Greeks who suffered from the conquest of their empire but the beleaguered Christians in the Holy Land whom the crusaders had set out to assist. Even the Templars, though they had played a negligible role in the Fourth Crusade, took part in the conquest of central Greece between 1205 and 1210.[243] Together with the Hospitallers and the Teutonic Knights, they acquired lands in the Peloponnese and, 'although the military service they owed was nominal',[244] did contribute 'to the defence of the Latin empire of Constantinople'.[245]

The second major conflict between Christians which followed soon after the conquest of Byzantium was the Albigensian Crusade, named after the city of Albi in south-west France. This was a centre for the Cathars, a heretical sect that had established itself in the rich territories stretching from the River Rhône to the Pyrenees, known because of its distinctive French dialect as the *langue d'oc.* The origins of Catharism are found in the ancient Zoroastrian religion of Persia. This held that there were two Gods, a benevolent deity whose realm was pure spirit and a malevolent one who had created the material world. Everything material was therefore intrinsically evil and salvation lay in emancipating oneself from the flesh. Buddhism, Stoicism and Neoplatonism showed a certain affinity with this condemnation of matter, while Christianity, despite its esteem for self-denial, held that God not only approved his material creation but, in Jesus, became part of that material creation as the Word made flesh.

Dualistic concepts affected the belief of Christians from the earliest days of the Church. Part of their appeal lay in the solution they posited to the eternal conundrum: why, if the Devil was God's creation, did God continue to permit him to exist? Condemnation of the flesh, and all the bestial and selfish passions that it engendered, seemed to accord with the teaching of Christ. To the dualists, celibacy was not a matter of choice. All carnal intercourse was evil and to have children was to co-operate with the Demiurge or Devil in the perpetuation of matter. Marcion, for example, a Christian heretic in the second century, forbade marriage and made celibacy a condition of baptism.

In the third century, a Persian, Mani, taught that to avoid contact with the evil of the material world one should neither work, fight nor marry. After he was martyred for his beliefs by the Zoroastrian hierarchy in 276, Mani's ideas spread from Persia to the Roman Empire and made converts such as the young Augustine of Hippo. In the fifth century, a vigorous community of Manicheans, the Paulicians, was established in Armenia. They became sufficiently powerful to provoke the Byzantine emperors to send military expeditions against them and, in the tenth century, to deport them *en masse* to Thrace in northern Greece. From here, their ideas spread into Bulgaria and were adopted by the followers of a Slav priest called Bogomil who founded a dualist church in the Balkans. Like the Paulicians, the Bogomils rejected the Old Testament, Baptism, the Eucharist, the Cross, the sacraments, and the whole structure of the visible church. They too thought that to have children was to collaborate with the Devil in the perpetuation of matter and some avoided it through anal intercourse: the word 'bugger' comes from Bulgar.

Despite persecution by the Orthodox emperors, the Bogomil Church survived until the conquest of the Balkans by the Ottoman Turks when many of the Bosnian Bogomils became Muslims. Some pockets of Paulicians were encountered by the forces of the First Crusade in the neighbourhood of Antioch and Tripoli; and it is possible that returning crusaders brought dualist ideas back to western Europe. They were found in the crusaders' home territories such as Flanders, the Rhineland and Champagne and were vigorously and effectively suppressed.

In southern Europe dualist theories had to compete with other unorthodox ideas, in particular those of a merchant from Lyons called Peter Valdes who, though not a dualist, rejected the idea that sacramental grace was necessary for salvation. He condemned the gross wealth of the clergy and left his wife and possessions to live as a hermit. His view of poverty as a paramount virtue was not so different from that of Francis of Assisi, and it has been said that whether the holy men of the period 'were revered as saints or excommunicated as heretics seemed to be largely a matter of accident'.[246] Clearly, it was not always easy to distinguish between zeal for reform, anticlericalism and the promotion of ideas inimical to Christian teaching: but the success of Islam had shown what could result when heretical ideas went unchecked and were exploited by an emerging social class. The greatest support for those who attacked the wealth of the Church came from the rising class of merchants in the cities of Lombardy, Langue-doc and Provence.

In Languedoc there were other factors that favoured the spread of the Cathar religion. As Bernard of Clairvaux had seen when he had preached against Henry of Lausanne, the Church was in a deplorable condition, with negligent, greedy, ignorant priests and bishops more intent on fleecing than guarding their flocks. At the same time, contact with Islamic ideas that came with trade with Moorish Spain, and the prominent role played by the Jews in the economy of the region, created a climate of tolerance towards other beliefs. There was less centralised control because many of the minor principalities were held as freeholds, not fiefs. Even those barons that held fiefs had no single feudal lord: some held them from the Count of Toulouse, others from the kings of Aragon and even, notionally, the German Emperor. Anticlericalism was rife. Much of the wealth enjoyed by the corrupt clergy had been given by the ancestors of the landed nobility who, seeing them now in apparently unworthy hands, did what they could to claw them back. This brought them into constant conflict with both the local bishops and the Pope. It was therefore hardly surprising that a religion that thought the clergy superfluous should have considerable appeal.

What at first sight seems incongruous is that 'a turbulent, restless, ego-tistical society',[247] perhaps the most educated, cultured and hedonistic in Europe – a haven for *jongleurs* and *troubadours*, the poets of courtly love – should have proved so receptive to the bleak dualism of the Cathars. But it should be remembered that only a few of their number, known as the *parfaits*, led lives of superhuman self-denial: for the mass of *credentes*, the mere believers, the Cathar doctrine was that only one sacrament was necessary for salvation, and that the last one, the *consolamentum* which washed away all sins, made it unnecessary to strive to be virtuous until faced with death. Catharism was also a religion that appealed to women: female *parfaits* were accorded the same reverence as those who were men. As a French priest was to put it, '*Les hommes font les hérésies, les femmes leur donnent cours et les rendent immortelles*': men may invent heresies but it is women who spread them and make them immortal.[248]

In 1167, the Greek 'pope' of the Cathars from Constantinople, Niquinta, presided over a council of the faithful outside a town near Castelnaudary in Languedoc, Saint-Félix-de-Caraman. Already, by this time, there was a Cathar bishop of Albi and now further bishops were appointed to Toulouse, Carcassonne and Agen. The Catholic bishops in Languedoc, horrified by the spread of this heretical sect, tried to counter it with public disputations but to no avail. Reports of its growth and entrenchment reached Rome. When a zealous Castilian, Dominic Guzman, the prior of the canons of the cathedral of Osma, called on Pope Innocent III in 1205 to ask for his permission to preach the Gospel to the pagans on the Vistula, Innocent accepted his mission but redirected it to the south of France. Two years earlier he had appealed to the Cistercians to reconvert the Cathars and, despite their best efforts, they had failed.

Dominic, playing the *parfaits* at their own game, adopted a lifestyle of abject poverty and rigorous mortification. He joined the Cistercians in preaching the orthodox Catholic faith and debating with the Cathar divines. Again, persuasion failed. Innocent, who recognised perfectly well the grave shortcomings of the Catholic clergy in Languedoc, deposed seven bishops in the region and replaced them with incorruptible Cistercians and repeatedly appealed to the counts of Toulouse to take action; but the counts were unwilling and probably unable to do so because the roots of Catharism had grown too deep. Too many Catholics had Cathar brothers, sisters or cousins who were seen to lead exemplary lives.

The Catholic hierarchy regarded the triumph of this heretical religion with dismay. It was not simply that Catharism removed their *raison d'être*, though that may well have been a factor among the prelates of Languedoc. It was rather that souls placed by God in their care were being lured to eternal damnation. The Cathars had an especial hatred both for the Cross which they thought blasphemous for its depiction of the suffering divinity, and for the Mass which they thought sacrilegious because it claimed that at the consecration the bread became the flesh of Christ. Rather than live peaceably side by side with Christians, they made no bones about their ambition to destroy the Church: in 1207 the Cathars of Carcassonne ejected the Catholic bishop from the city.

In medieval Europe, however Church and society were coterminous; the year was punctuated with the fasts and feasts of the Christian calendar and life mediated through the sacraments. Vows, which the Cathars condemned, were the basis upon which the whole structure of feudal society was based. Apostasy would lead to anarchy and undermine the most fundamental human institutions. That this was not an extravagant fantasy was confirmed by the Cathar teaching that marriage, in the words of an apostate heretic, Rainier Sacchoni, was 'a mortal sin ... as severely punished by God as adultery or incest'.[249]

After the failure of repeated campaigns of persuasion, Pope Innocent called upon the principal ruler of the region, Raymond VI, Count of Toulouse, to extirpate the heresy by force. In 1205 Raymond promised to do so but did nothing. In 1207, after a meeting with Raymond at Saint-Gilles in Provence, the Papal Legate, Peter of Castelnau, was killed by a man from Raymond's entourage. This outrage prompted Innocent III to proclaim a crusade. There followed twenty years of warfare with indiscriminate massacres on both sides that only ended with the annexation of Languedoc by the King of France. The Cathars were hunted down and burned, some happily consigning their corrupt bodies to the flames. The heresy was eventually destroyed but with it went what some historians see as a uniquely refined and cultivated civilisation and others 'a society in an advanced stage of disintegration which still clung to the husk of a civilisation that had all but disappeared'.[250]

The first leader of the Albigensian Crusade was Simon of Montfort, the same knight from northern France who had abandoned Boniface of Montferrat and the Venetians at Zara. At one point the whole of Languedoc was within his grasp and, like the Franks in Palestine or the Normans in Antioch, he might have founded a dynasty while in the service of the Church; but with the changing fortunes of the war this prize eluded him and he was eventually killed while besieging Toulouse.

To the native nobility, whether Catholic or Cathar, the crusade was an invasion of their homeland by an enemy from the north; and despite a constant flux of loyalties they fought to defend it. Feudal loyalties and political interests became inextricably entangled with religious zeal leading to paradoxical alliances: King Peter II of Aragon, who had won a major victory against the Muslims in Spain at Las Navas de Tolosa in 1212, was killed in the following year fighting Simon of Montfort outside the walls of Muret.

What was the role of the military orders in this internecine warfare and fratricidal strife? Both the Temple and the Hospital had considerable holdings in the region. Raymond of Saint-Gilles, Count of Toulouse, had been among the leaders of the First Crusade, and both his descendants and those of his vassals had settled substantial benefices on the military orders, particularly the Hospital. However, the preceptory of Mas-Deu in Roussillon was one of the most important strongholds of the Temple. Both orders were also heavily engaged in the Kingdom of Aragon and committed to the war against Islam in Spain.

As a result, a war between Simon of Montfort on behalf of the Pope, and Count Raymond VI and King Peter II of Aragon together with most of the nobility of Languedoc, led to divided loyalties among the military orders. By and large, both attempted to remain neutral and were recognised as such by the Treaty of Paris that eventually brought the conflict to an end. Where the orders were drawn into the conflict, it seems that the Hospital sided with Raymond VI and Pedro II, and the Temple with the crusaders. Templars had fought with Pedro II at Las Navas de Tolosa, but 'all respected unreservedly their duty towards the pope and the Church ... The fidelity of the Knights Templar to Simon of Montfort and the crusades never diminished':[251] in 1215 we find Simon staying in the Templar house outside Montpellier.

However, it seems to have been accepted that the Templars' primary commitment was to the war against Islam in the East; certainly Pope Innocent III made no attempt to enlist them against the Cathars and the foundation of an order modelled on the Temple by Conrad of Urach in 1221, the Militia of the Faith of Jesus Christ, would seem to confirm this. It was possibly as vassals of the King of France that they are found with Prince Louis at the taking of Marmande in the spring of 1219, witnesses to, if not participants in, the slaughter of the inhabitants of the city. In 1226, King Louis VIII of France, when besieging Avignon, vested full powers in his absence to a Templar knight, Brother Everard, dispatching him to Saint-Antonin to accept the city's surrender.[252]

The charge of Templar support for the Cathars, which was to inspire a number of fabulous theories in modern times, is more credible if levelled at the Hospitallers but here again there is no evidence that they showed any sympathy for the heretical religion. From the time of its evolution into a military order, the Hospital had had close links with the counts of Toulouse both in Europe and in Outremer. There were numerous foundations in Languedoc, while in Syria the great fortress of Krak des Chevaliers had been given to the Hospital by Raymond II of Tripoli, a great-grandson of Raymond IV of Toulouse. During the Albigensian Crusade, therefore, their sympathy tended to be for the descendants of their benefactors to whom the knights themselves, unlike the knights of the Temple, were frequently related. Thus we find that some of the most courageous defenders of the Cathars who asked to receive the *consolamentum* from their *parfaits* also endowed the Hospital and asked to be admitted as *confrères*, suggesting that they either had little understanding of theology or that they were hedging their bets.

The Hospital benefited from its links with the enemies of the crusade. After the death of Simon of Montfort at the siege of Toulouse, and the retreat of the crusaders, the Catholic bishops and the Cistercians withdrew from the area and the Templars abandoned their preceptory at Champagne but the Hospitallers and the Benedictines remained: the Benedictines at Alet were later evicted from their abbey for complicity with the Cathars.[253] Probably the most overt demonstration of their loyalties came with the death of King Pedro II of Aragon at the Battle of Muret: the Hospitallers asked for and were given permission to retrieve his dead body from the field. Similarly, they admitted Raymond VI as a *confrère* and after his death in 1222 were given charge of his body which, as that of an excommunicate, could not be buried in hallowed ground. His body stayed outside the priory of the Hospitallers while Raymond VII petitioned successive popes to permit it to be buried in the chapel. It was still there in the fourteenth century, but by the sixteenth, 'rats had destroyed the wooden coffin and Raymond's bones had disappeared'.[254]

eleven

Frederick of Hohenstaufen

In 1213 Pope Innocent III published a bull, *Quia maior*, calling for a new crusade against the Saracens in the East. A number of factors suggested that the moment was propitious: Simon of Montfort was at the height of his fortunes in Languedoc; a Muslim army had been defeated in Spain at Las Navas de Tolosa; and the extraordinary phenomenon of the children's crusade in which seven thousand young people from France and the Rhineland had set off to deliver the Holy Sepulchre, while ill conceived, ill fated and discouraged by the Church, had demonstrated the strength of popular enthusiasm for the pursuit of a Holy War.

Even the scandalous diversion of the Fourth Crusade to Constantinople seemed to the Pope to be a cloud with a silver lining: all the powers of Christendom were now united under his command. Even the disadvantages, such as the continuing conflicts between the Capetians and Plantagenets in France and the Welfs and the Hohenstaufen in Germany served Innocent's purpose by removing any rivals for the command of the crusade. His call was repeated by the 1,300 bishops who assembled in Rome for the Fourth Lateran Council in 1215 and extensive legal and administrative measures were put in place to raise the money to finance the project, including the extension of the crusade indulgence from those who fought to those who paid. This enabled women to take the Cross through donations and legacies.[255] Women were also used to persuade their husbands to go on crusade: James of Vitry, whose horses were requisitioned by some Genoese for a military excursion, preached instead to their wives. 'The burghers took my horses and I made their wives crusaders.'[256] The sums raised were banked with Brother Haimard, the treasurer of the Temple in Paris.

Innocent died in 1216 before his plans had been put into effect. They were taken over with equal enthusiasm by his successor, Cardinal Savelli, who chose the title of Honorius III. Already an old man at the time of his elevation, Honorius lacked Innocent's qualities of leadership and drive. However, the new crusade now had its own momentum: the knighthood of France and England might be distracted by the wars of their kings and the suppression of heretics, but further east Austrian and Hungarian contingents assembled at Spoleto to be transported to Palestine by the Venetians.

The King of Jerusalem was now an elderly knight from Champagne, John of Brienne. It was a sign of the low standing of Outremer among the European nobility that he was the best bridegroom that could be found for the Princess Maria, the heiress to the Kingdom. When they were married in 1210, he had been aged sixty, she seventeen. Two years later, Maria died after giving birth to a daughter, Isabella, known as Yolanda. John now reigned as regent for his daughter, pursuing a cautious policy towards Saladin's brother and successor, al-Adil. It was in the interests of both to renew the truce in 1212. When King Andrew arrived with his contingent of Hungarians in 1217, a number of minor forays were made into Muslim territory with no significant results. Having fulfilled their vows, the Hungarians returned home through Anatolia with a horde of relics, among them the head of Saint Stephen and one of the jugs from the Marriage Feast at Cana.

While in the Holy Land, the Austrian and Hungarian pilgrims had helped the Templars and the Teutonic knights build a new fortress at 'Atlit which, to honour their contribution, was called Castle Pilgrim. Built on a promontory on the coast south of Haifa to protect the road, and also the vines, orchards and cultivated fields in the locality that were vulnerable to Muslim raids, it was a formidable stronghold with a moat and double wall on the landward side. The German Dominican, Burchard of Mount Sion, judged 'the walls and ramparts and barbicans so strong and castellated, that the whole world should not be able to conquer it'.[257] Within the ramparts were three great halls and a Templar church with its rotunda. According to the chronicler, Oliver of Paderborn, it was stocked with sufficient supplies to feed 4,000 fighting men.

In April 1218, a fleet from Frisia arrived at Acre providing King John of Jerusalem with the means to launch an invasion of Egypt. On 24 May the fleet set sail and on 27 May disembarked on the banks of the Nile opposite the city of Damietta. Here they pitched camp and on 24 August mounted a successful attack on the fort that guarded the entrance to the river. The Templar Grand Master, William of Chartres, commanding a major Templar contingent, died of fever two days later. He was succeed by an experienced 'career' Templar, Peter of Montaigu who had been Templar Master in Provence and Spain and had fought in the Battle of Las Navas de Tolosa.

Having established this bridgehead opposite Damietta, the crusaders were joined by further contingents from Europe, among them the French counts of Nevers and la Marche, the English earls of Chester, Arundel, Derby and Winchester, the bishops of Paris, Laon and Angers, and the Archbishop of Bordeaux; and finally a force of Italians led by Pope Honorius's Legate, the Spaniard Cardinal Pelagius of Saint Lucia.

Pelagius, as Papal Legate, was now in command. He was determined and energetic but smug, tactless and autocratic. The siege of Damietta continued through to the summer of 1219 with disease taking its toll on the crusaders. Unable to dislodge them, the Sultan al-Kamil, Saladin's brother, sought to make peace and, as evidence of his pacific intentions, he permitted Francis of Assisi, who was visiting the crusaders, to pass through the lines and preach to him at his camp at Fariskur. The two men had an exchange of exquisite politeness but neither was persuaded to accept the other's belief. Although unwilling to become a Christian, however, al-Kamil was ready to sacrifice Jerusalem if the crusaders would raise the siege of Damietta.

This offer caused a rift in the camp of the crusaders: Pelagius and the Patriarch of Jerusalem were against any pact with the infidel while King John, supported by the barons from Palestine and Europe, wanted to accept it. The Grand Masters of the military orders took the view that Jerusalem could not be held unless Oultrejourdain was ceded as well. This was unacceptable to al-Kamil. His terms were therefore rejected and on 5 November the crusaders mounted a successful assault on Damietta: its garrison and citizens were too debilitated to oppose them.

Established in Damietta, the Christians now awaited the arrival of an army led by the German Emperor, Frederick II of Hohenstaufen, before continuing up the Nile. In 1221 Duke Louis of Bavaria arrived with 500 knights, supposedly the vanguard of Frederick's army. Realising that no further reinforcements were forthcoming, Pelagius ordered an advance into Egypt despite the misgivings of John of Brienne and those Templars who took the view that the crusaders' resources were over-stretched and the conquest of Egypt beyond them. Their objections were overruled. The crusading army marched up the bank of the Nile towards Mansurah which they reached a week later. While they established themselves outside the city, contingents of al-Kamil's army moved in behind them and Egyptian ships sailed in from Lake Manzalah to cut off the Christians' retreat. The crusaders might have fought their way out of this encirclement had not the Egyptians opened the sluice-gates and flooded the ground that they had to cover. They were, as the Templar Grand Master later wrote to the Templar Preceptor in England, 'trapped like a fish in a net'.[258]

Literally bogged down in the swamps of the Delta, Pelagius had no choice but to sue for peace. Damietta was abandoned and the Latin army sailed for Acre with nothing achieved. The only concession that al-Kamil had been prepared to grant Pelagius was the return of the relic of the True Cross taken by his brother Saladin at Hattin; but, when he called for it to be handed over, this most precious of all Christian relics could not be found.

Responsibility for the failure of this, the Fifth Crusade, is invariably ascribed to the tactless and wilful Cardinal Pelagius, and there is no doubt that his abrasive nature made him an unsatisfactory commander just as his strategic calculations were distorted by religious zeal. However, the crusading armies were always weak when they lacked an undisputed military leader. Richard the Lionheart had stood up to Saladin not just because of his courage and charisma but because he was a king. John of Brienne was also a king, but his claim to the title of King of Jerusalem was too remote to inspire the loyalty of the barons of Europe or even those of Outremer; while Pelagius's clerical status was considered by many to make him ineligible to command. The one undisputed leader whom the popes, their legates and all the feudal princes awaited throughout the campaign was the grandson of Frederick Barbarossa, the Hohenstaufen emperor, Frederick II.

On 7 September 1228, Frederick II of Hohenstaufen landed at Acre to assume the leadership of the crusade fifteen years after he had first taken the Cross. He was now thirty-six years old and had already established the extraordinary reputation that was to earn him the title, *stupor mundi et immutator mirabilis*. His father, the Emperor Henry VI, had died when he was three years old. His mother, the Empress Constance, the heiress to the Norman Kingdom of Sicily, had then taken him to Palermo where she died only a year later. Frederick was raised by tutors selected by Pope Innocent III, the guardian appointed by Constance. The lack of any parental affection, together with the mix of Norman, Greek and Muslim influences that made up the culture of the Sicilian court, created an idiosyncratic character in an exceptionally cultivated mind. 'He was an adroit man,' wrote a contemporary, Salimbene, 'cunning, greedy, wanton, malicious, bad-tempered. But at times, when he wished to reveal his good and courtly qualities, consoling, witty, delightful, hard-working.'[259] He could sing and compose music, speak German, Italian, Latin, Greek, French and Arabic. He was an excellent rider and skilled falconer. Salimbene describes him as 'a handsome man, well built but of medium stature'; but the receding red hair inherited from his grandfather, Frederick Barbarossa, and his slightly bulbous eyes, made him seem unappealing to one Muslim observer who thought that 'had he been a slave, he would not have fetched 200 dirhams'.[260]

At his coronation as King of Germany at Frankfurt in 1212, Frederick had impetuously vowed to go on crusade. This was not part of the plan of his guardian, Pope Innocent III, and so, for the time being, was ignored. The following year, Innocent was succeeded as pope by Frederick's tutor, Cencio Savelli, as Honorius III, and in his early years Frederick appeared to be a dutiful son of the Church. His chamberlain was a Templar knight, Brother Richard, who had previously served the Pope in the same capacity. However, the inherent rivalry between the spiritual and lay leaders of Christendom was exacerbated by the fact that Frederick was King of both Germany and Sicily. Hitherto, the security of the Papal States, and therefore the Papacy, had been secured by exploiting the rivalry of the two kingdoms to maintain a balance of power. Now, with the union of the two states in the person of Frederick, Rome was threatened with encirclement.

Equally threatening was the scepticism which developed in the young King's mind. Unlike the monarchs of northern Europe whose learning was limited by the curriculum set by the Catholic Church, Frederick's education in Palermo had made him familiar with Arabic and Byzantine ideas. Both were more developed than their Latin counterparts and led to a tolerance towards those who held them that contrasted sharply with the partisan sentiments of other Christian kings. Frederick's lenient treatment of Muslims within his kingdom shocked some of his Catholic contemporaries but it almost certainly sprang from practical as well as ideological considerations: the Templars in Spain, for example, allowed Muslims to practise their religion on the Templar estates as an inducement to keep them on the land.

The dependence on his favour of his Muslim subjects also made them more trustworthy in Frederick's eyes: he had a Saracen bodyguard. But his tolerance was not a matter of mere calculation: to an admiring biographer, 'he possessed the qualities inherent in the truly cultivated man of any era: a sincere and deep appreciation of the cultural potentialities of mankind, regardless of race or nationality'.[261] But equally, as in any era, there was a natural progression from tolerance to indifferentism and from indifferentism to outright scepticism, and some of Frederick's contemporaries wondered whether or not he believed in God.

Because of the black propaganda that came to be directed against him by his enemies, it is difficult to distinguish fact from fiction: but it is significant that even his Muslim contemporaries, such as the Damascene chronicler Sibt Ibn al-Jawzi, thought that he was 'most certainly an atheist'.[262] The Catholic Salimbene, too, wrote that 'as to faith in God, he had none' and that 'if he had been a good catholic, and loved God and His Church, and his own soul, he would have had few equals among the emperors of the world'. Frederick was said to have scoffed at the Eucharist – 'How long will this hocus-pocus continue?' – and the Virgin Birth of Jesus: 'They are complete fools who believe God could be born of a Virgin ... no one can be born whose conception was not preceded by coitus between a man and a woman.' The Virgin Birth of Jesus, however, is also a tenet of Islamic belief; and, despite his friendship with Muslims, Frederick showed no greater respect for Muhammad than he did for Christ, listing him along with Moses as one of the 'three impostors or deceivers in the world'.[263]

Though these remarks may have been exaggerated by his papalist enemies, they are consistent with the perception of his Muslim friends. In other ways, Frederick was out of tune with his times. He displayed a scientific spirit that is more modern than medieval: in the preface to a treatise on falconry, De arte Venandi, he wrote that 'our intention in this book is to set forth ... those things that are as they are'; and again, in another context, 'one ought not to believe anything, save that which can be proven by nature and the force of reason'. The result was a combination of King Solomon, Isaac Newton and – if his contemporaries are to be believed – a Dr Mengele.

The first was demonstrated in the way he dealt with a charge made against Jews in Germany in 1235–6 of the ritual murder of a Christian child: the exhaustive investigation that he initiated resulted not just in their acquittal but in a decree '*in Favorem Judaeorum*'. He also abolished the trial by ordeal of fire which Francis of Assisi had offered to undertake before the Sultan al-Adil to prove the truth of the Christian religion: how could a red-hot iron become lukewarm or cold, Frederick asked, 'without the intervention of a natural cause'?

We find the Dr Mengele in the experiments he supposedly initiated to test certain hypotheses. A man was imprisoned in a wine barrel to see if a soul could be seen leaving his body when he died. Two men were killed and then disembowelled to study the relative effects of sleep and exercise. Children were raised in complete silence to discover whether humanity's mother tongue was Hebrew, Greek, Arabic or Latin: 'but he laboured in vain', wrote Salimbene, 'for the children all died'.[264]

His sexual morals were undoubtedly at variance with Christian teaching, though here again it is not easy to distinguish between truth, exaggeration and fabrication. The papal apologist, Nicholas of Carbio, 'skilled in the art of character assassination',[265] accused him of turning churches into brothels and using an altar as a lavatory. He wrote that Frederick prostituted not only young women but also young men, indulging 'a vice disgraceful even to think about or to mention, and most evil to practise'. According to Nicholas, Frederick 'broadcast his crime, that of Sodom, openly, not attempting to conceal it'. Some scholars have, perhaps somewhat naively, held that the two passions are usually mutually exclusive. What is undisputed, is that Frederick kept a harem containing both Muslim and Christian *houris* and fathered a number of illegitimate children, among them Manfred, later King of Sicily, and Violante, the Countess of Caserta.

Once he had shaken off the tutelage of the popes, Frederick applied his rational and secular beliefs to the government of his domains. After his coronation as Emperor by Pope Honorius III in 1220, he replaced the clergy and feudal retainers in his Sicilian administration with lawyers, and founded a university in Naples to train his officials in legislative and judicial processes of the ancient Roman administration. The old Pope had bestowed the imperial crown on his wayward pupil as a way to commit him to the crusade and there is no doubt that Frederick took this duty seriously, not because he cared whether or not Jerusalem was in the hands of Christians, but because leading a crusade would confirm his status as the supreme sovereign of Christendom. Both a throwback to the despots of antiquity, and at the same time a precursor of the dictators of the modern age, Frederick eschewed the Christian virtue of humility and came to believe in his own God-given right as Emperor to a supreme authority exercised by the Roman emperors of old. 'From our earliest days,' he wrote, 'our heart has never ceased to burn with the desire to re-establish in the position of their ancient dignity the founder of the Roman Empire and its founderess, Rome herself.'[266]

This inevitably brought him into conflict with the Papacy which claimed the same if not a greater authority, and also with the cities of the Lombard League led by Milan which valued their independence: but in 1221, it was in the interest of both Frederick II and Honorius III that the Emperor should fulfil his vow and go on crusade. Time and again, Frederick put off his departure. In 1223 his wife, Constance of Aragon, died. She had been considerably older than him but had brought invaluable assistance when they had married in 1209. Now that he was free to remarry, the Princess Yolanda of Jerusalem was proposed as a bride. Her father, John of Brienne, had come to Europe to find her a husband and the match was promoted by the Grand Master of the Teutonic Knights, Hermann of Salza.

After an initial reluctance, Frederick agreed. The sixteen-year-old was crowned Queen of Jerusalem at Acre and then brought to Europe where she was married to Frederick in the cathedral of Brindisi on 9 November 1225. Despite his faith in reason, Frederick was governed by astrological predictions and so postponed the enjoyment of his young bride until the morning after their wedding, a propitious moment for engendering a son according to the stars. He subsequently seduced Queen Yolanda's cousin and broke his promise to her father that he could continue as her regent, claiming his own right as Yolanda's husband to be king. When it was established that Yolanda was pregnant, Frederick dispatched her to his harem in Palermo where she gave birth to a boy, Conrad, and a few days later died.

In March 1227, it was the turn of Pope Honorius III to die. He was succeeded by another member of the Segni family, Ugo, who took the name Gregory IX. Like his uncle, Pope Innocent III, Gregory IX was a canon lawyer and, as Papal Legate, had given the Cross to Frederick II at his coronation in 1220. Profoundly spiritual, the friend and champion of both Dominic Guzman and Francis of Assisi, he was also, in contrast to the easy-going Honorius III, determined, uncompromising, unusually energetic and politically skilled. At one time close to Frederick II, he was suspicious of his intentions and when Frederick, after setting sail for the Holy Land as promised in August 1227, put in at Otranto because he was ill, Gregory excommunicated him for failing to fulfil his vow.

In fact, Frederick's companion, Ludwig IV, Landgrave of Thuringia, had died from a fever and it is likely that Frederick suffered from the same disease. Having recovered the following year, he continued his journey without bothering to wait for the Pope to lift the ban. This incurred a second excommunication. The apparently facile use of the Church's ultimate sanction was considered necessary by a pope who believed it his duty to uphold his authority: Gregory IX accepted unequivocally the view of Bernard of Clairvaux that, while the Emperor wielded the temporal sword, it might only be drawn from its sheath at the Pope's command.

As a result of this second excommunication, Frederick encountered a measure of hostility among the Latin clergy when he arrived in Acre in 1228. At first it was assumed that now that he had finally fulfilled his crusading vow, he would soon be reconciled with the Church; but Frederick had shown no sign of contrition and, since his departure, war had broken out in southern Italy between imperial forces under Reginald of Spoleto and a papal army led by Frederick's humiliated former father-in-law, the ex-King of Jerusalem, John of Brienne.

Letters from Pope Gregory IX now reached the Patriarch in Acre confirming the sentence of excommunication. This removed the Emperor's authority to command the crusade and, in the eyes of the Church, annulled the oaths of fealty of his vassals. The Christian forces were anyway not large – the barons of Outremer, around 800 pilgrim knights and 10,000 foot-soldiers. These now divided into two factions – one loyal to the Emperor, the other to the Church under the Patriarch Gerold. The Grand Master of the Teutonic Knights, Hermann of Salza, supported his friend Frederick, but the Temple and the Hospital refused to take orders from the excommunicate.

From Frederick's perspective, this split in Latin loyalties would only have mattered if he had contemplated a war. In fact, the weakness of the forces at his disposal reinforced his inclination to attain by diplomacy what could not be seized by force. The auguries were good. Even before he had left Sicily, Frederick had received at his court in Palermo the Emir Fakhr ad-

Din ibn as-Shaikh, an emissary of the Sultan of Egypt, Saladin's nephew, al-Kamil: al-Kamil offered to return Jerusalem to the Christians in return for military help against his enemies further east. Frederick in turn sent the Bishop of Palermo and Thomas of Accrra to Cairo with valuable gifts and protestations of friendship; Fakhr ad-Din returned once again to Palermo where he and Frederick became close friends.

By the time Frederick arrived in Palestine, circumstances had changed within the Ayyubid empire and al-Kamil had become fully aware of the damage that would be done to his standing in the Islamic world if he should return Jerusalem to the Franks. Frederick sent emissaries to al-Kamil, now in Nablus, to remind him of his promise to surrender Jerusalem. While al-Kamil prevaricated, Frederick made sporadic and mostly unsuccessful attempts to assert his authority. At one point he tried to take possession of Pilgrim Castle but the Templars closed the gates against him. The Order's animus against the Emperor was possibly exacerbated by the favour he had shown to the Teutonic Knights; and by the presence among the Templars of a number of knights from Apulia who had rebelled against Frederick and had subsequently sought refuge by taking the white habit of the Temple.

In November 1228, Frederick decided to coax his friend al-Kamil by a show of force. He set out from Acre and marched south. The knights of the Temple and the Hospital refused to place themselves under his command but followed a day behind. When the army reached Arsuf, Frederick agreed to delegate his command to leaders who were not under the ban of the Church and the military orders therefore joined the main force.

Neither Frederick nor al-Kamil wanted a war, not just because Frederick had insufficient forces and al-Kamil was besieging Damascus, but because they were men of like mind. Throughout the long months of negotiations, Fakhr ad-Din had been the conduit of frequent exchanges between the Emperor and the Sultan which had nothing to do with matters at hand. Through Fakhr ad-Din, Frederick asked the Sultan to consult his scholars on profound philosophical questions such as the origin of the universe, the immortality of the soul and the logic of Aristotle. Less zealous as a Muslim than his brother, Saladin, al-Kamil warmed to this sceptical intellectual, and sent him gifts that would make his sojourn in Palestine more agreeable. 'It is with the greatest shame and disgrace', wrote the Patriarch Gerold to Pope Gregory IX, 'that we report to you that it is said the sultan, hearing of the Emperor's enjoyment of living in the manner of the Saracens, sent to him singing girls and jugglers, persons who were not only of ill repute but unworthy even to be mentioned among Christians.'[267]

In what was probably the high point in irony in the history of the crusades, two essentially irreligious men bickered about a city about which neither cared as such, but both aware of what it meant in terms of their prestige. 'It was you who urged me to make this trip,' Frederick wrote to al-Kamil, according to Arab chroniclers. 'The Pope and all the kings of the West now know of my mission. If I return empty-handed, I will lose much prestige. For pity's sake, give me Jerusalem that I may hold my head high.' To which al-Kamil replied: 'If I deliver Jerusalem to you, it could lead not only to a condemnation of my actions by the caliph, but also to a religious insurrection that would threaten my throne.'[268] In the end, al-Kamil's sense of honour prevailed. Frederick had come east at his invitation and must be given something in return. On 18 February 1229, a treaty was signed that returned Jerusalem to Christian rule. Also ceded was Bethlehem, a corridor of land from the coast at Jaffa, Nazareth and parts of Galilee including the castles of Montfort and Toron. In Jerusalem itself, the Temple Mount with the Dome the Rock and the al-Aqsa mosque were to remain in Muslim hands with free access accorded to Muslims who wished to go there to pray. All prisoners were to be released and a truce was agreed for the next ten years.

For reaching this historic agreement, neither ruler received any thanks. Al-Kamil was execrated by his imams for his betrayal of Islam, while in the Christian camp only Frederick's partisans, mainly the Sicilians and Germans, praised the treaty. 'What more can sinners desire', asked the German poet and crusader, Friedank, 'than the sepulchre and the glorious cross?' The answer, in the mind of the Patriarch, the crusading pilgrims and the two major military orders, was a military triumph. It seemed to demean the penitential value of the crusading vow that it should be fulfilled without the shedding of blood. No mention was made in the treaty of Christ or the Church; nor was the city to be cleansed of infidels. It particularly enraged the Templars that their headquarters on the Temple Mount was to remain a mosque.

There were also the same strategic objections to the settlement that had been made when it had been proposed by al-Kamil to Cardinal Pelagius during the Fifth Crusade. Jerusalem and Bethlehem would remain isolated from the coastal cities, linked only by a narrow corridor of land. Nor did they want to acknowledge an accomplishment that would augment Frederick's power by adding to his prestige. Thus, on 17 March 1229, when Frederick made a ceremonial entry into the Holy City, the native barons stayed away. So too did the knights of the Temple and the Hospital and the whole Latin clergy, obedient to the interdict that had been placed on Jerusalem by the Patriarch Gerold should the Emperor Frederick pass through its gates. Only the loyal Hermann of Salza and his Teutonic Knights, and the English bishops of Winchester and Exeter accompanied him, but they did not dare defy the interdict. When Frederick entered the Church of the Holy Sepulchre, there was not a bishop or priest to be found. He therefore took up the crown of the Kingdom of Jerusalem and placed it on his own head. Hermann of Salza then read an address in both Latin and German – an apologia for the Emperor that forgave the Pope for opposing him, and promised to do everything in his power as God's 'Vicar on earth' that would rebound 'to the honour of God, the Christian Church, and the Empire'.

After this, the Western Emperor went on a tour of the Holy City, visiting Muslim as well as Christian shrines. Al-Kamil had ordered the mullahs at the al-Aqsa mosque to refrain from calling the faithful to prayer. Frederick rebuked them, saying that it was precisely to hear the call to prayer that he had come to Jerusalem. When a Catholic priest tried to follow him into the Dome of the Rock, Frederick threw him out. 'By God, if one of you dares step in here again without permission, I will pluck out your eyes.' When told that the wooden lattice at the entrance to the Dome was to prevent birds from entering, he said, using the abusive term used by the Muslims for the Franks: 'God has now sent you the pigs.'

Frederick did not tarry in Jerusalem. News of setbacks in Italy made it imperative that he return to Europe. Leaving a number of knights of the Teutonic Order to garrison the city, and instructions for the rebuilding of its towers and walls, Frederick returned to Acre. There the Patriarch Gerold, together with the Templars, was raising an army to take possession of Jerusalem in the name of the Pope, and to proceed against the Sultan of Damascus who had not agreed to the truce. Frederick objected. Gerold refused to listen to the excommunicate Emperor. Acre itself was in turmoil. The indigenous nobility were furious that they had not been consulted about the settlement; the Venetians and Genoese were resentful of the preference shown by Frederick towards the Pisans, his allies in Italy; and there were riots among the populace against the imperial garrison.

To assert his authority, Frederick summoned all the citizens, prelates, barons and pilgrims to justify his own actions and complain about the enmity of the Patriarch and the Templars. The assembly was not won round. Frederick turned to coercion. He ordered his troops to close the gates of the city to his enemies, including the Templars, and surround the Patriarch's palace and the Templars' fortress. He had plans to kidnap Peter of Montaigu, the Templar Grand Master, and John of Ibelin, the Lord of Beirut, but both were too well protected for them to be put into effect. Appointing *baillis* to represent his interests, whose good standing with his opponents exposed the reality of his defeat, and destroying all arms that might have fallen into the hands of his enemies, Frederick set the date for his departure for 1 May. At dawn, as he proceeded down the Butchers' street from his palace to the port, the jeering citizens of Acre pelted him with offal.

twelve

The Kingdom of Acre

On his return to Italy, Frederick met with greater success in confounding the plans of the Pope than he had in overcoming the opposition of the Pope's allies in Outremer. The papal army besieging Capua under the two old-timers, John of Brienne and Cardinal Pelagius, retreated and then disintegrated as Frederick marched to relieve the city. John of Brienne was obliged to flee to his native Champagne. The Templars paid a price for their defiance: their houses in Sicily were seized by imperial forces and a hundred Muslim slaves belonging to the Templars and Hospitallers were returned to the Saracens without any compensation being paid to the orders.[269]

Frederick's bequest to the Holy Land was a liberated Jerusalem, but a Jerusalem so strategically vulnerable that 'it remained an open city';[270] and an imperial administration under the Marshal, Richard Filangieri, that was constantly at war with the native barons under John of Ibelin both in Palestine and on Cyprus. The titular King of Jerusalem was Conrad, Queen Yolanda's son by Frederick II, but even when of age, Conrad did not come east to claim his crown which led the barons to declare it forfeit and oust Filangieri from Tyre. Alice of Cyprus was chosen as regent by the High Court of Jerusalem but the kingdom was in fact ruled by an oligarchy of the Frankish nobility which developed 'a passionate and even fanatic interest in law and legality. In no contemporary Christian nobility was knowledge of customary law and procedure, and mastery over the intricacies of constitutional law, so cultivated and cherished as in the Latin kingdom.' There was no university in Outremer and there were no scholars or men of letters apart from William of Tyre. 'All its intellectual energies appear to have been concentrated in the study of law.'[271]

In this state of pedantic anarchy, the military orders acted with the autonomy of sovereign states. In the north, in the 1220s and 1230s, the

Templars tried to expand into the territory of Aleppo from their base at Gaston in the Amanus Mountains, making it 'a semi-independent territory in which the Templars went their own way, with little reference to their nominal lords in Cilicia'.[272] In Syria and Palestine, too, the Templars' wealth and power increased because the nobility of Outremer, whose fiefs were now confined to the enclaves around the coastal cities, could not afford to garrison their castles and so handed them over to the military orders: in 1186, for example, Marqab, one of the largest and most powerful fortresses in Syria, was sold to the Hospital because its lord could no longer afford to run it.[273]

Some members of the indigenous nobility flourished, notably the Ibelins, whose luxurious palace in Beirut amazed an envoy from the imperial German court; but the resources that afforded such luxury now came less from the land than from the profits that could be siphoned off from trade. Acre had become a commercial centre on a par with Constantinople and Alexandria: the annual revenue of the kings of Jerusalem from Acre was estimated at 50,000 pounds of silver which was more than that of the King of England at the time. Merchants flocked there from Damascus to deal in sugar, dyes and spices. Much of the sugar consumed in Europe was exported from Acre together with a multiplicity of exotic products which not only supplied but created a market for luxuries in the West.[274] In turn, the 250,000 inhabitants of Outremer provided a market for European exports such as capes and berets from Champagne, and the Muslim hinterland for iron, timber, textiles and fur.

There was also an active market in slaves, either Muslim captives or Greeks, Bulgarians, Ruthenians and Wlachs imported by merchants of the Italian republics. These were sold as Muslims because by law no Christian could be enslaved; but slave traders would disregard this statute and the owners forbid their slaves' conversion. In the early thirteenth century, a Latin bishop complained that 'the Christians continually refused their Muslim slaves baptism, although these sought it earnestly and tearfully';[275] and in 1237 Pope Gregory IX complained of the same abuse to the bishops of Syria and the Grand Masters of the military orders.

Individual conversion of free Muslims did take place, leading to assimilation into the Syrian Christian population. There was a wide choice of Christian churches – Catholic, Greek Orthodox, Maronite, Armenian, Jacobite and Nestorian – but the occasional attempts in Rome and Constantinople to unite them met with success only with the Maronites in Lebanon. Whatever the intentions of the popes, the Latin clergy were only interested in a union with other churches that would ensure their pre-eminence. Not only did the churches fail to unite, but there was no inte-gration of the different Christian communities. The Latins' treatment of native Christians was little better than that of Muslims, Jews or Samar-itans.[276]

Given the great missionary endeavour of the Catholic Church in the ninth and tenth centuries, it seems puzzling that almost no effort was made by the victorious crusaders to convert the Muslims under their rule. Certainly, conversion was never a crusading objective as such. Although Pope Urban II no doubt wanted to aid the Byzantine Emperor, and perhaps divert the destructive aggression of the Frankish warriors to a noble cause, his principle intentions were, like those of Bernard of Clairvaux, Christian recovery of the Holy Places and the salvation of the crusader's soul.

It was only at the beginning of the thirteenth century that we find the genesis of a missionary endeavour, not surprisingly in Spain where the success of the *Reconquista* had brought large numbers of Muslims under Christian control. Significantly, the Spanish Bishop Diego of Osma, and his companion Dominic Guzman, asked Pope Innocent III to let them preach the Gospel not to the Saracens but to the pagans on the Vistula. However, by 1255, Humbert of Romans, the Master General of the Domin-icans, called on the friars to study Arabic and commit themselves to the conversion of the Saracens.

Francis of Assisi, in crossing the lines between Christian and Muslim forces at the siege of Damietta to preach to the Sultan al-Kamil in Cairo, set an example which his mendicant friars were to follow, their pacific bearing earning them the privilege of acting as the guardian of the Holy Places when these returned to Muslim control. However, Francis did not disapprove of crusading. He admired the heroes of Roncesvalles as depicted in the *Song of Roland*, regarded as martyrs those who died fighting the infidel, accepted the Christians' right to the Holy Land, and felt that it could be deduced from the Gospel that the crusade was a legitimate act of retribution for the Saracens' forcible conquest of Christian territory and their blasphemies against Christ.[277]

Almost the only Latin bishop to make any attempt to convert the Muslims in the Holy Land was the French prelate, James of Vitry, who was appointed

Bishop of Acre. He had a low opinion of his co-religionists in the Holy Land: he wrote to the Pope that the indigenous Christians so loathed the Latins that they would rather be ruled by the Muslims; and that the Latins had gone native, leading indolent, luxurious and immoral lives. The local clergy were greedy and corrupt while the Italian merchants were always at one another's throats. The only institutions he felt he could respect were the military orders.

Although James of Vitry was unusual in preaching the Catholic faith to the Muslims in Outremer, he did not see this as an alternative to extending the Christian domain by force. He was an enthusiastic crusader, accompanying Cardinal Pelagius to the Nile Delta. He also defended the military orders, in particular the Templars, from the charge that they were disobeying Jesus's injunction to Peter in the Gospel of Matthew to put up his sword – an argument advanced in Europe not just by heretical Cathars and Waldensians, but also by churchmen like the monk of Saint Alban's, Walter Map: in one of his extant sermons preached to the Knights of the Temple, James of Vitry tells them not to listen to such reasoning of 'false Christians, Saracens and Bedouins'.[278]

The very fact that James of Vitry felt it necessary to reassure the Templars in this way suggests that they still felt they were following a religious calling. Although they chiefly appear in the historical records through their role in warfare, or through the political stance taken by their leaders, the ordinary knight seems to have kept to the severe Rule laid down by the Council of Troyes. At a time when the monastic orders are frequently accused of laxity and corruption, no such charge appears to have been made against the individual knights. Living with the odour not of incense, but of horse dung, leather and sweat, they must have been aware of the rate of attrition among those who served in Palestine and have acknowledged that sooner or later they would suffer death at the hands of the enemies of their faith.

If we look once again at the Rule and the penitentiary that came to be written in the mid-twelfth century, we get the impression of an austere life with strict discipline and severe punishment for any breach of the regulations. Their principal human consolation was probably the companionship of the other knights who came from a similar background. Friendship, as we have seen, was highly esteemed in the Cistercian Order and it would appear from the Rule that, despite the rivalry of the two orders that on occasion broke out into open conflict, the camaraderie of the

Templar knights and sergeants was felt for the brothers of the Hospital too. Templars had to get permission from their superiors to eat, drink or visit the lodgings of other religious unless they were Hospitallers: in battle, it was to the Hospital's banner that a Templar was to rally if he lost sight of his order's piebald standard; and in 1260, when a Templar contingent were ordered to withdraw from Jerusalem by their superior, their commander would not do so without the Hospitallers who had joined them.

Homosexual relations between knights were regarded as a major breach of the Rule, a crime 'against nature and against the law of Our Lord'. It is placed in the penitentiary between losing faith in Christ and desertion on the field of battle, all punished by expulsion from the Order. A case study given in clause 573 of the penitentiary describes how, when a case of three brothers at Castle Pilgrim 'who practised wicked sin and caressed each other in their chambers at night' was brought to the attention of the Grand Master, he wanted to avoid bringing it before the Temple chapter 'because the deed was so offensive'. Instead, they were summoned to Acre, made to remove their habits, and put in irons. One of them, called Lucas, escaped and defected to the Muslims; the second tried to escape but died in the attempt; while the third 'remained in prison for a long time'.[279]

Among the principal vices ascribed to the Templars was their avarice. The wealth generated by the Temple's holdings where the munificence of pious donors had been exploited by efficient administration, inspired envy and resentment by those in Europe who were unaware of the enormous costs borne by the Order, not just in the Holy Land but throughout Christendom. The Temple, like the Hospital, was a multinational force funded by a multinational corporation fighting the enemies of the Church on a number of fronts. Six Templar knights died fighting the Mongols at the Battle of Legnica in eastern Europe in 1241. The Temple remained a considerable power in Portugal and Spain, though its relative contribution to the *Reconquista* had declined: when the Christians attacked Mallorca in 1229, the Templars contributed only about four per cent of the force. Even in Aragon it was accepted that the Templars' principal mission was in the Holy Land: recruits to the Order, horses and between one-third and one-tenth of their revenue, were sent to the East.[280]

In the same way that modern charities build up investments, the Templars used their funds not just to pursue the war against the Saracens but also to expand their estates in the East: when John of Ibelin was desperate to raise funds to fight Frederick II, he did so by selling lands to both the Temple and the Hospital. This reinvestment of the Templars' income attracted criticism from Pope Gregory IX: 'many people have been forced to the conclusion', he wrote to the Grand Master, 'that your chief aim is to increase your holdings in the lands of the faithful, when it should be to prise from the hands of the infidel the lands consecrated to the blood of Christ'.[281] They were also accused of being soft on the Muslims, entertaining them in their houses and allowing them to pray to Allah in Templar houses: ironically, this charge was made by Frederick II in a letter to Richard, Earl of Cornwall, in 1245.

The Order also spent lavishly on their corporate headquarters in the city of Acre which, repudiating the administration of Frederick's governor, Richard Filangieri, was ruled by a commune. The different quarters of the city were 'miniature republics surrounded by walls and towers',[282] its streets, as described by the Muslim writer Ibn Jubayr, 'choked by the press of men, so that it is hard to put foot to the ground. It stinks and it is filthy, being full of refuse and excrement.'[283] The Temple compound was on the seaward spur of the city and formed a pivotal stretch of the city's defences. 'At its entrance', wrote the Templar of Tyre,

> was a stronghold very high and strong and its walls were very thick, a block of 28 feet. On each side of the fortress was a small tower and on each a lion passant as big as a fattened oxen, all covered with gold. The price of the four lions, in material and work, was 1,500 Saracen besants. It was marvellous to behold. On the other side, towards the Pisan quarter, was a tower. Nearby, above the monastery of the nuns of Saint Anne, was another huge tower with bells and a marvellous and very high church. In addition there was a tower on the beach. This was an ancient tower, a hundred years old, built by command of Saladin. Here the Templars guarded their treasury. This tower was so near the beach that the sea waves washed it. And many other beautiful abodes were in the Temple, which I will forgo mentioning.[284]

However, many of the charges made against the Templars were contradicted by others. When King James I of Aragon, at the Second Council of Lyons, accused the Templars of dragging their feet over a new crusade against the Moors, the charge was not supported by the other members of the Spanish delegation;[285] and the English Franciscan, Roger Bacon, attacked not the pusillanimity but the aggressiveness of the Templars which he thought prevented the conversion of Muslims to Christianity. Moreover, all the religious orders in this period with the exception of the Carthusians were criticised for their extravagance, and the betrayal of their original charism – the Temple, on the whole, less than the orders of monks and friars. The golden lions were no doubt unnecessary, and Hugh of Payns cannot have envisaged the Master of his Poor Fellow-Soldiers of Jesus Christ living in a palace; but the proportion of resources devoted by the Temple to the purposes of their original foundation would have compared favourably to that of other religious foundations, and even to some charities today. Certainly the popes, though they occasionally chided the Temple, were fulsome in their praise of the military orders in their bulls and continued to defend them by the granting of privileges and exemptions.

It was also clear that the finances of the military orders suffered as a result of inexorably rising costs. The land required to equip and maintain a Burgundian knight in 1180 amounted to around 750 acres; by the mid-thirteenth century this had risen fivefold to almost 4,000 acres:[286] the cost, as well as the military value, made a fully armed knight with his entourage of squires and sergeants the equivalent of today's heavy tank. Despite the evidence that the Temple often had cash in hand, their running costs were considerable: in the Latin states of Outremer they garrisoned and maintained at least fifty-three castles or fortified staging posts ranging from great fortresses like Castle Pilgrim to small watch-towers on pilgrim routes. At the height of the Order's fortunes, there were almost a thousand Templar houses in Europe and in the East, and around 7,000 members. The number of non-professed auxiliaries and dependants is estimated to have been seven or eight times that number. The ratio of support personnel to combatants was around 3:2.[287] By the mid-twelfth century the Order had built its own fleet of galleys which transported horses, grain, arms, pilgrims and military personnel. The traditional carriers suffered from this competition for the lucrative pilgrim traffic and in 1234 the city of Marseilles limited the Templars to one shipment of pilgrims per year.[288]

Despite their involvement with the financial, logistical and military aspects of war, the Templars do not appear to have lost sight of their commitment to the defence of the Holy Land and recovery of Jerusalem. One of the earliest translations of scripture from Latin into the vernacular was that of the Book of Judges commissioned by the Temple so that, in the words of its introduction, they could learn of the 'chivalry' of the period and see 'what honour it is thus to serve God and how He rewards his own'.[289] Since most of the knights, squires and sergeants were illiterate, such readings were not just for their enlightenment but to sustain their morale. The Book of Judges was well chosen. While the Book of Joshua describes the Jews' conquest of the Promised Land in a series of efficient military campaigns, 'the book of Judges sees it as a more complex and gradual phenomenon, punctuated by partial success and failure'. There was a close and unquestioning identification by the Christians in Palestine with the Israelites of old. The narratives of the Old Testament, unlike the sayings of Jesus in the New, accept that systematic pillage of the enemy is part of war and indeed that it is not only permitted but actually ordered by God.[290]

In 1239, Frederick II's treaty with the Egyptian Sultan, al-Kamil, was due to expire. Aware of this, Pope Gregory IX preached yet another crusade. This was encouraged by the kings of France and England but neither took the Cross. Instead, as in the days of the First Crusade, lesser Frankish nobles set out for the Holy Land, led by Theobold, Count of Champagne. He was a cousin of the kings of England, France and Cyprus, and saw the crusade as the apogee of chivalrous knighthood: 'blind is he', he said, 'who has not once in his life crossed the sea to succour God'.[291]

The complexity of the political situation in the Holy Land baffled the new crusaders, and the advice they received was contradictory. The Ayyubids were at war with one another and Ismail, the Sultan of Damascus, proposed a pact with the Franks against his nephew, al-Kamil's son Ayyub, now Sultan in Cairo. In exchange for defending the frontier facing the Sinai Desert, he would give them the fortresses of Beaufort and Safed. Before Hattin, Safed had belonged to the Templars and they were now eager for its return.

The deal was done and as a result the Latin possessions in Palestine were now greater than at any time since Hattin; but the cost was considerable to both parties. Many zealous Muslims among the Damascenes defected to the Egyptians, while in the Christian camp it led to outright enmity between the Templars and Hospitallers who until then had formed a common front against the minions of Frederick II. Ignoring the agreement made with Ismail in Damascus, the Hospitallers signed a treaty with Ayyub in Cairo.

This was the confused situation found upon his arrival in the Holy Land by Richard, Earl of Cornwall, the nephew of Richard the Lionheart, brother of King Henry III and brother-in-law of the Emperor Frederick II. Aged only thirty-one, he had already established a reputation for courage and competence. He came with considerable resources and also the full authority of the Emperor who, after the death of the wretched Queen Yolanda of Jerusalem, had married Princess Isabella of England.

Richard found the Kingdom of Jerusalem in a state of chaos, but with tact and energy reached an agreement with both Damascus and Egypt which resulted in the release of all the Christian prisoners held in Cairo and confirmation of the Latin possession of the recently ceded lands. But no sooner had he set sail for England than this settlement fell apart. The Templar Grand Master, Armand of Périgord, ignored the treaty with Egypt and in 1242 attacked the city of Hebron which had remained in Muslim hands. Subsequently, after a feeble response by the Egyptians, the Templars took Nablus, burned its mosque and killed many of its inhabitants, Muslim and Christian alike.[292]

At around the same time, the imperial *bailli*, Richard Filangieri, attempted to reimpose Frederick II's authority on Acre with the help of the Hospitallers. The coup failed, leading to a six-month siege of the Hospital compound by the forces of the leader of Latin barons, Balian of Ibelin, assisted by the Templars. This open conflict between the two military orders scandalised public opinion in Europe, and was blamed on the Templars by chroniclers who favoured the imperial party such as the monk of Saint Alban's Abbey, Matthew Paris. The Templars, he wrote, would not permit food to be sent into the Hospital compound, or the Hospitallers to bring out their dead. They also ejected the Teutonic knights from some of their holdings: how scandalous that 'those who had stuffed themselves with so many revenues in order to be able powerfully to attack the Saracens, were impiously turning violence and venom against the Christians, indeed against their own brothers, thus most gravely bringing God's anger down upon them'.[293]

There can be no doubt that the Temple, under Armand of Périgord, was in the anti-imperial camp, supporting Alice, the Queen of Cyprus, as regent of the Kingdom of Jerusalem and accepting the legality of excluding Conrad, Queen Yolanda's son by Frederick II, when he came of age in April 1243, on the grounds that he had not visited the Holy Land to claim his crown. In this, they were not alone. The Venetians and the Genoese were of a like mind and in the summer of 1243 joined the barons of Outremer in ejecting Filangieri and the imperialists from Tyre. But this was not necessarily an expression of envy, or of the Order's pursuit of its own interests. In a letter to Robert of Sandford written in 1243, Armand of Périgord explained the basis of his policy. Templar envoys that had been sent to Cairo were being kept in virtual captivity. The Egyptians could not be trusted and were only buying time. By contrast, the alliance with Damascus had secured not only the return of a number of fortresses and extensive territory, but the eviction of the remaining Muslims in Jerusalem.

To cement the Damascene alliance, the Muslim Prince of Homs, al-Mansur Ibrahim, was invited to Acre and there lavishly entertained in the Temple. The celebrations were premature. To counter the forces ranged against him, the Egyptian Sultan Ayyub called on a wild tribe of mercenary nomads who had settled near Edessa, the Khorezmian Turks. In June 1244, a force of ten thousand Khorezmian cavalry invaded Damascene territory and, bypassing Damascus itself, rode on into Galilee and captured Tiberias. On 11 July, the Khorezmians reached Jerusalem and breached its feeble defences. For a time its garrison held out but on 23 August, on a safe-conduct secured by the Muslim Lord of Kerak, the garrison and the entire Christian population left the city for Jaffa and then, seeing Frankish flags on the ramparts of Jerusalem and imagining that the city had been relieved, turned back, only to be massacred by the waiting Khorezmians. Only three hundred of their number reached Jaffa.

The Khorezmians now sacked the city, disinterring the bones of Godfrey of Bouillon and the other kings of Jerusalem buried in the Church of the Holy Sepulchre, and killing the few priests who had remained there before setting the church on fire. Then, evacuating the empty city, they rode down to the coast, joining the Egyptian army of the Sultan Ayyub at Gaza under the command of a young Mameluk officer, Rukn ad-Din Baybars.

On 17 October 1244, on a sandy plain by the village of Herbiya known to the Franks as La Forbie, this Egyptian host was confronted by the joint armies of Damascus and Acre. The Damescene forces were led by the Prince of Homs, al-Mansur Ibrahim, and included a contingent of Bedouin cavalry under the Lord of Kerak, an-Nasir. The Christian army was the most considerable that had been assembled since Hattin. There were six hundred secular knights under Philip of Montfort and Walter of Brienne, and six hundred from the Temple and Hospital led by their Grand Masters, Armand of Périgord and William of Châteauneuf. There were also a number of Teutonic Knights and a contingent from Antioch.

As at Hattin, there was a debate among the allies about whether to attack or remain on the defensive: al-Mansur Ibrahim favoured the latter, Walter of Brienne the former, and it was the view of Walter of Brienne that prevailed. The superior allied army advanced on the Egyptians but the Egyptians held them and the Khorezmian cavalry attacked their flank. The Damascene troops took flight and with them went an Nasir, the Lord of Kerak. In a matter of hours, the Latin army was destroyed. At least 5,000 were killed and 800 prisoners taken to Egypt, among them the Grand Master of the Temple, Armand of Périgord. The total loss to the Temple was between 260 and 300 knights. Of the knights of the military orders, only thirty-three Templars, twenty-six Hospitallers and three Teutonic Knights survived.

thirteen

Louis of France

Who now could save the Holy Land? In western Europe, the bitter rivalry between the Papacy and the Emperor Frederick excluded the lay leader of Christendom from resuming the role. In any case, Frederick felt that his enemies in Palestine, in particular the Templars, had brought their fate upon themselves by breaking his carefully constructed truce with the Ayyubids in Egypt.

Only one European monarch was in a position to lead a new crusade, and that was King Louis IX of France. Providentially, or coincidentally, in the same year as the catastrophic defeat at La Forbie, Louis, having fallen ill with a fever, probably malaria, felt close enough to death and judgement to resolve, if he recovered, to take the Cross.

The son of a formidable mother, Blanche of Castile, and married to Margaret of Provence, both from families with a long tradition of service in the war against Islam, Louis had inherited the throne of France in his infancy and held it thanks to the vigorous regency of his mother. At the age of fifteen, Louis had commanded an army campaigning against the King of England, Henry III. Handsome, good-humoured, boisterous, occasionally ill-tempered, Louis, in contrast to Frederick II, was also profoundly pious and untroubled by doubts about the Catholic faith. Early in his reign, under the Treaty of Paris, he established French rule over Languedoc and finally brought the Cathar heresy to an end. He had no qualms about using force to defend the Christian religion: a knight, he told his friend John of Joinville, 'whenever he hears the Christian religion abused, should not attempt to defend its tenets, except with his sword, and that he should thrust into the scoundrel's belly, as far as it will enter'.[294] Even if Louis's words may not have been as brutal as Joinville remembered them in his old age, they are in marked contrast to the sceptical views of the Emperor, Frederick II.

Unlike Frederick, Louis was happily married to a single wife. His affection for Margaret of Provence provoked the jealousy of his mother: when they were newly married they had separate quarters and only dared meet on the stairs, returning to their rooms when alerted by their servants of the approach of the Queen Mother. During the crusade, Joinville reproached Louis for waiting for Mass to end before rising to greet Margaret who had just arrived with their newlyborn child: but this was probably a sign of his piety, not of his indifference to his wife. There is no evidence of any estrangement: Margaret bore the King eleven children.

Louis IX had a passion for relics. He bought the Crown of Thorns from Baldwin, the Latin Emperor of Byzantium, and carried it barefoot through the streets of Paris to the exquisite chapel he built to house it, the Sainte-Chapelle on the Ile de la Cité. He also endowed a number of religious foundations, among them the Abbey of Royaumont, but he would not allow himself to be brow-beaten by the French bishops and mediated in the conflict between the Emperor and the Pope. Louis's zeal for justice, and his scrupulous attention to the needs of the poor, established his saintly reputation and an unparalleled prestige, but it was taking the Cross that set the seal on his kingship: 'crusading still held its place as the highest expression of the chivalrous ideas of the aristocracy in the west'.[295]

Once the vow had been made, Louis prepared for the crusade with the same efficiency that he had shown in subduing his rebellious vassals and reorganising the administration of France. His first objective was to raise the money to fund his expedition overseas. This he did with a twentieth tax on the resources of the Church and subventions from the cities. Because the port of Marseilles at that time came under the sovereignty of the Emperor, Louis built a new outlet to the Mediterranean on his own territory, the port of Aigues Mortes. It was from here that he embarked for the Holy Land on 25 August 1248. Reluctantly, his brothers and many of his vassals went with him. So too did his wife Queen Margaret and their children: France was left in the charge of his mother, Blanche of Castile.

Louis was joined by crusaders from outside France such as John of Joinville, the Seneschal of Champagne. The point of assembly for the crusading army was Cyprus where, as a result of careful planning, supplies had been assembled for Louis's army of around 25,000 men, among them

5,000 crossbowmen and 2,500 knights. King Louis remained there through-out the winter. In January 1249, he sent two Dominican preachers as envoys to the Mongol Khan, hoping that this rising power in Asia, rumoured to be sympathetic to Christianity, might join forces against Islam.

Accepting the same strategic view as Cardinal Pelagius that it was only by subduing Egypt that the Holy Land could be secured, and undeterred by the failure of the earlier crusade, Louis and his army set sail at the end of May for the Nile Delta. At dawn on 5 June, the Latin fleet anchored before Damietta. The Muslim army, commanded by the Emperor Fred-erick's friend, Fakhr ad-Din, were waiting on the shore. 'It was a sight to enchant the eye,' Joinville remembered in his old age, 'for the sultan's arms were all of gold and where the sun caught them they shone resplendent. The din this army made with its kettledrums and Saracen horns was ter-rifying to hear.' The Latin forces were equally flamboyant: the Count of Jaffa's galley 'was covered, both under and above the water, with painted escutcheons bearing his arms ... He had at least three hundred rowers in his galley; beside each rower was a small shield with the count's arms upon it, and to each shield was attached a pennon with the same arms worked in gold.'[296]

Although advised to wait for part of his fleet that had been scattered in the storm, Louis ordered a landing and, once the *oriflamme* was staked on the beach, led his knights against the Saracens who, unable to withstand the impact of the Frankish assault, withdrew to Damietta and then aban-doned the city, burning the bazaar. It was a quick and easy victory for which King Louis gave thanks to God; but, remembering the fate of the Fifth Crusade under Cardinal Pelagius, he did not pursue the Egyptians up the Nile. Instead, he established Damietta as his temporary capital in Outremer, sending for Queen Margaret from Acre, and awaited reinforcements from France led by his brother, Alfonso, Count of Poitou, and for the waters of the Nile to subside.

On 20 November Louis felt ready to move further into Egypt. Rejecting the advice of the barons of Outremer to move against the port of Alexandria, he was persuaded by his brother Robert, Count of Artois, to march south along the east bank of the Nile towards Mansurah. In the vanguard of his army were the Knights Templar under their Grand Master, William of Sonnac, chosen after the death of Armand of Périgord in an Egyptian prison. Behind them came the Count of Artois and an English contingent under the Earl of Salisbury. Guided to a ford by a turncoat Bedouin, this force, without waiting as instructed by King Louis for the rest of the army, attacked the Saracen camp where the commander, Fakr ad-Din, was taking a bath. Without waiting to put on his armour, ad-Din rode into battle and was killed by the Templar knights.

Robert of Artois now prepared to pursue the retreating Saracens into Mansurah. The Templar Grand Master, William of Sonnac, tried to stop him. He was already angry that the King's brother had usurped the Templars' position in the van. Chroniclers differ as to what happened next. John of Joinville, still with the main body of the army on the south bank of the river, later wrote that William of Sonnac insisted that the Count of Artois should wait for the Templars to lead the attack but because the knight holding the Count's bridle was deaf, he failed to pass on the message. According to the chronicler, Matthew Paris, Robert of Artois heard the Grand Master only too well, but answered him with insults, repeating the calumny of Frederick II that the Templars had no interest in an outright victory because the Order profited from the continuing war. When the Earl of Salisbury suggested that perhaps the Templar Grand Master had the benefit of experience in fighting the Saracens, Robert of Artois said that he too was a coward, dug his spurs into the flanks of his charger and galloped off at the head of his French knights.

Feeling that they had no choice, the Templars and the English knights followed the Count of Artois in pursuit of the retreating Saracens right into the city of Mansurah. Here all was not as chaotic as it seemed. Although Fakr ad-Din was now dead, the commanding officer of the elite Mameluk guard, Rukn ad-Din Baybars Bundukdari, had taken charge. Putting up little initial resistance to the Latin knights, he waited until they had penetrated into the city and reached the gates of the citadel before ordering his men, waiting in the side streets, to attack the crusaders. Unable to manoeuvre in the narrow streets, and trapped by beams thrown from the roofs, the knights were slaughtered. Three hundred knights died, among them the Earl of Salisbury and the Count of Artois. The Templars lost 280; only two returned alive, one of them the Grand Master, William of Sonnac, who had withdrawn from the mêlée after losing an eye.

Although this setback had been caused by the vainglory and impetuosity of Robert of Artois, it was a foretaste of what was to come. Once the main army had crossed the branch of the Nile, it joined battle with the Muslim forces. Joinville, already wounded, saw King Louis on a raised causeway at the head of his host, the very image of chivalry and honour. 'Never have I seen a finer or more handsome knight! He seemed to tower head and shoulders above all his people; on his head was a gilded helmet, and a sword of German steel was in his hand.'[297] After a day of fierce fighting, the Egyptians were forced back into Mansurah. When the Provost of the Hospitallers told Louis that his brother Robert of Artois 'was now in paradise ... big tears began to fall from his eyes'.

That night, the Egyptians made a sortie from Mansurah and again were beaten back. On 11 February they attacked again and in this engagement William of Sonnac, at the head of the few remaining Templars, lost his second eye and subsequently died. Louis's army was almost broken but the centre held and eventually the Egyptians withdrew once again into Mansurah. Now it was clear that, while the crusaders could not be beaten, neither could the city be taken. Louis's best hope lay in the outcome of the political upheaval in Cairo that had followed the death of the Sultan Ayyub and his commander, Fakr ad-Din. For eight weeks he waited, encamped before the walls of Mansurah. But chaos in the Ayyubid court had been averted by the widowed Sultana and at the end of February Ayyub's son Turanshah returned from Syria to take command.

Transporting a fleet of light vessels on the backs of camels to the Nile down-river from the crusading army, the Muslims severed its link with Damietta and stopped the supply of fresh food. Disease spread in their camp. Louis himself suffered from chronic dysentery: his servants, Joinville tells us, because he was 'continually obliged to visit the privy, had to cut away the lower part of his drawers'. He ordered a retreat to Damietta but despite his sickness refused to abandon his men and escape on a galley. Pursued by the Egyptians, Louis was finally made captive and obliged to surrender. Joinville was saved from death when it was discovered that his wife was a cousin of the Emperor Frederick. Prisoners of any standing were held for ransom; the less eminent were killed. In the city of Damietta, the Pisan and Genoese garrison was dissuaded from desertion by Queen Margaret: the city was a valuable counter in the bargaining which followed and, together with a ransom of a million besants or half-a-million *livres tournois*, bought liberty for the King and his army.

Raising this ransom gave rise to an incident that reveals the scrupulosity, or obduracy, of the Templars. In the course of counting out the money to pay the agreed deposit, it was found that the King was thirty thousand *livres* short: on it depended the release of his brother, the Count of Poitiers. John of Joinville suggested that the sum should be borrowed from the Templars and with the King's authority went to ask for the loan. The request was refused by the Commander of the Temple, Stephen of Otricourt, on the grounds that he had sworn on oath never to release money except to those who put it in his charge.

This led to a bitter altercation between Joinville and Otricourt until the Marshal of the Temple, Reginald of Vichiers, proposed a solution. The Templars could not break their vow but there was nothing to stop the King taking their funds by force, particularly since the Temple held his deposits in Acre and could recoup this forced loan when he returned. Therefore Joinville went to the Templar galley, broke open a strongbox with an axe, and returned to King Louis with the money.

With his brother's release secured, King Louis and his entourage sailed for Acre. Here he found letters from his mother, Blanche of Castile, urging him to return to France. The same advice was given by his brothers and his barons, but it was not just a French army that had been defeated on the Nile: the forces of the Christians of Outremer had been seriously weakened by the disaster. Louis was reluctant to leave the Holy Land in such a perilous condition or abandon the Frankish prisoners still held in Egypt; and so, while most of his French vassals, among them his brothers, now returned to France with his blessing, he himself remained in Acre with his wife and children. The legitimate King of Jerusalem may have been Conrad, the son of Frederick II by the Queen Yolanda, but Louis was accepted as *de facto* ruler and he now attempted to achieve through diplomacy what he had failed to gain by force.

In Cairo, power had been seized by the elite regiment of slave warriors, the Mameluks. Captured as boys from the nomadic tribes of Kipchak Turks living on the steppes of southern Russia, they were sold by slave-traders to the Ayyubid Sultans who raised them as a military force with no links and therefore no loyalties to any class or faction. Described by the Arabic chronicler, Ibn Wasil, as 'the Templars of Islam',[98] they had gained an ascendancy under the Ayyubid sultans that seemed to be threatened when Ayyub's son, Turanshah, came to power. On 2 May 1250, in the midst of the negotiations with King Louis, the Mameluks murdered Turanshah and brought the rule of Saladin's descendants in Egypt to an end. However, the Ayyubids remained in power in Syria and, on hearing the news of the Mameluk coup, Saladin's grandson, an-Nasir Yusuf, the Sultan of Aleppo, occupied Damascus and at once dispatched an embassy to King Louis to ask for his help.

King Louis used this approach to put pressure on the Mameluks to come to terms, sending an emissary, John of Valenciennes, to Cairo. Unknown to the King, the Templars were pursuing a diplomatic initiative of their own. The former Marshal of the Order, Reginald of Vichiers, had been elected Grand Master in succession to William of Sonnac. Reginald had undoubtedly been the favoured candidate of King Louis: he had been the Templar Preceptor in France while Louis had been preparing his crusade, had arranged transport for his troops from Marseilles, had been Louis's Marshal in Cyprus, his comrade-in-arms on the Nile, and was godfather to the son born to Queen Margaret at Castle Pilgrim, the Count of Alençon.

Once Grand Master, however, the pretensions of the post seem to have gone to his head. Without consulting King Louis, he had sent the Templar Marshal, Hugh of Jouey, to Damascus to negotiate with the Sultan over a disputed tract of land. Having reached an agreement, Hugh returned with a Damascene emir to have it ratified at Acre. Upon discovering what had been going on behind his back, King Louis flew into a rage and insisted not only that the treaty be annulled, but that the Templar Grand Master and all his knights should humble themselves before the whole army, walking barefoot through the camp and kneeling in submission before the King. The scapegoat was Hugh of Jouey whom Louis banished from the Kingdom of Jerusalem – a sentence he would not rescind despite the pleas of the Grand Master and the Queen. No doubt, this gesture was not so much to establish his authority among the Latins as to impress upon the Mameluks that he was in command. His policy paid off. In March 1252, all Christian prisoners still held by the Mameluks were set free.

There were two others powers in the region with whom Louis treated while in Acre. The first was the Old Man of the Mountain, the leader of the Assassins, who sent envoys soon after Louis's return from Damietta to demand the tribute, or protection money, that they claimed had been paid by the Emperor Frederick, the King of Hungary and the Sultan of Cairo.

As an alternative to tribute the Emir suggested that the King exempt the Assassins from the tribute that they paid to the Temple and the Hospital. As Joinville observed in describing this parley, the Assassins knew that there was no point in killing either of the Grand Masters because another knight, 'equally good, would be put in their place'.[299]

The Grand Masters, whom the King invited to this parley, were outraged at the Assassins' insolence: they sent the envoys back to the Old Man of the Mountain with the advice that he approach King Louis in a different vein. Within a fortnight they had returned to Acre with lavish gifts. King Louis reciprocated, returning equally valuable trinkets and an Arabic-speaking friar, Yves le Breton, to preach the Christian faith.

The second set of envoys came from the Mongols, the power that within twenty years was to defeat the Old Man of the Mountain, taking the hitherto impregnable Assassin fortress of Almut in 1256. Their ambassadors reached Acre with the two Dominican friars that Louis had sent to the Mongol Khan suggesting an alliance against Islam. The Khan's answer was a demand that the French King become his vassal, and send 'a sufficient amount of money in yearly contributions for us to remain your friends. If you refuse to do this we will destroy you ...' It was not the response that the King had hoped for and, according to Joinville, Louis 'bitterly regretted that he had ever sent envoys to the great King of the Tartars'.[300]

The defeat of King Louis's army in the Nile Delta saw the end of the Latins' ambition to retake Jerusalem by attacking the source of Muslim power. Now the imperative was to gain maximum advantage by exploiting the rivalries of the Islamic powers and improving the defences of the territory they still held. Louis therefore ordered the refortification of the coastal cities of Acre, Caesarea, Jaffa and Sidon whose garrisons were strengthened with permanent contingents of French troops.

The inland fortresses were now too costly to be held by the feudal barons of Outremer and were therefore sustained by the military orders: the Teutonic Knights held Montfort, the Hospitallers Belvoir and the Templars Chastel Blanc and Saphet. Saphet had been rebuilt in the 1240s at enormous expense and was now the largest castle in the Kingdom of Jerusalem, dominating Galilee and the route between Damascus and Acre. It had a peacetime garrison of 1,700 men to which a further 500 were added in time of war. Of these, 50 were Templar knights and 30 Templar sergeants, 50 turcopoles and 300 crossbowmen. The cost of its construction was put at 1,100,000 Saracen besants, and 400 slaves were employed to assist the skilled masons. Twelve thousand mule loads of barley and grain were required to provision the castle every year, some of it now imported from the Templar preceptories in Europe.[301]

After completing the refortification of Sidon, King Louis decided to return to France. His presence was urgently required in his kingdom and he was told by the Patriarch of Jerusalem and the local barons that he had done what he could and should now go home. On 24 April 1254, Louis set sail from Acre on a Templar ship. He had fulfilled his vow as best he could; he had risked his life, come near to death, and remained for four years in the Holy Land after his brothers and barons had departed. He had spent a phenomenal amount of money, estimated by his royal treasury at 1.3 million *livres tournois,* eleven or twelve times the annual income of his kingdom.[302] There was peace in Outremer at the time of his departure but the position of the Christians in the Holy Land was precarious and he was leaving Jerusalem in infidel hands.

Remaining in Acre to represent King Louis was Geoffrey of Sargines who became Seneschal of the Kingdom. However, following the death of the Emperor Frederick II in 1250, and of his son Conrad in 1254, the legitimate King of Jerusalem was now Conrad's son Conradin, not Louis IX; and though there was a French garrison at Geoffrey's command, it was insufficient to impose order on the rival factions, particularly the Italian maritime cities. In early 1256, a dispute between the Venetians and Genoese over the monastery of Saint Sabas in Acre led to armed conflict: the Templars and Teutonic Knights supported the Venetians, the Hospitallers the Genoese. The same year saw the death of the Templar Grand Master, Reginald of Vichiers, who was succeeded by Thomas Bérard.

In 1258 the Mongols captured Baghdad, murdered the Caliph and massacred the population. The approach of this Asiatic horde created panic among the Latins in Syria and Palestine. Realising the folly of internal dissension at such a time, Thomas Bérard made a pact to keep the peace with the other Grand Masters – Hugh of Revel of the Hospital, and Anno of Sangerhausen of the Teutonic Knights. Aleppo fell in January 1260, and Damascus capitulated in March. Thomas Bérard wrote to the officials of the Temple in Europe, telling of the devastation brought about by the

Mongols and asking for help: such was the urgency that the Templar courier, Brother Amadeus, reached London in only thirteen weeks, travelling from Dover to London in a single day. He described how the Mongols used Christian captives, including women, as a human shield against their enemies. Unless help was given, 'a horrible annihilation will swiftly be visited upon the world'.[303]

The Mongols' intentions towards the Christians were as yet unclear: in Baghdad, while the Muslims had been massacred, the Christians had been spared. It was therefore the Mameluks in Egypt who prepared to oppose them, requesting both unimpeded passage for their army and assistance from the Franks. The first was agreed by the Council of the Kingdom but an actual alliance was vetoed by the Master of the Teutonic Knights, Anno of Sangerhausen. The Mameluk army marched into Palestine and, on 3 September 1260, under their sultan Kutuz, defeated the Mongol army led by Kitbogha south of Nazareth at Ain Jalut. Kitbogha was killed and a month later Kutuz himself was assassinated by the hero of Mansurah, Baybars.

Al-Malik az-Zahir Rukn ad-Din Baybars was a Kipchak Turk from the north shore of the Black Sea who had been sold as a slave by the Mongols to the Ayyubid Sultan in Cairo. Trained as a member of the Sultan's body-guard on an island in the Nile, Baybars had risen to become its commander and one of the ablest officers in the Egyptian army. It was Baybars who had commanded the Egyptian cavalry at the Battle of La Forbie in 1244. It was Baybars who, as commander in Mansurah during King Louis's crusade, had trapped and slaughtered Count Robert of Artois and his force of French, English and Templar knights. It was Baybars who, together with other Mameluk officers, had murdered the Ayyubid Sultan, Saladin's nephew, Turanshah. It was Baybars who had led the vanguard of the Egyptian army against the Mongols at the Battle of Ain Jalut.

Angry at the refusal of the Sultan Kutuz to reward him with the city of Aleppo, Baybars murdered his master and seized the throne. He immediately proved himself to be as able a ruler as he was a soldier, refortifying the citadels destroyed by the Mongols, rebuilding the Egyptian fleet and, in time, expelling the Assassins from their strongholds and the last of Saladin's successors from their principalities in Syria, uniting, as had Saladin, Syria and Egypt under his rule.

At first the Latins in Outremer failed to appreciate the significance of the

Mameluk victory at Ain Jalut on the region's balance of power. In February 1261, John of Ibelin and John of Giubelet, Marshal of the Kingdom, led 900 knights, 1,500 turcopoles and 3,000 foot-soldiers, among them strong contingents of Templars from Acre, Safed, Beaufort and Castle Pilgrim, against a marauding army of Turcoman tribesmen. The Latin army was defeated; the Templar Marshal, Stephen of Sissey, was one of the few to escape alive. Subsequent negotiations with Baybars for the release of the Christian prisoners were scuppered by the Templars' and Hospitallers' refusal to surrender some of their Muslim captives because they valued their skills.

Infuriated by what he took to be a manifestation of gross greed, Baybars sacked Nazareth and descended on Acre, wounding the Seneschal, Geoffrey of Sargines, in fighting outside the city walls. With the Mongols in northern Syria still a threat in his rear, Baybars was not in a position to besiege Acre but the Franks could put up no force to prevent his troops moving at will from Egypt into Palestine, and what concentrations they could muster were made known to the Muslims thanks to their use of homing pigeons. In 1265, Baybars suddenly appeared with a large army before Caesarea, the city so recently refortified by King Louis IX. The town capitulated on 27 February; the citadel a week later. Some days after this, it was the turn of Haifa where those inhabitants who had not fled were killed.

Baybars' next target was the Templar fortress, Castle Pilgrim, but while the town outside the walls was taken and burned, the castle itself proved impregnable and so Baybars moved on to the Hospitaller castle of Arsuf. There, after the Egyptians' siege-engines had made a breach in the wall and a third of the 270 Hospitaller knights had fallen, terms of surrender were agreed with the commander that guaranteed the liberty of the survivors – an agreement that Baybars then broke, making prisoners of the surviving knights.

In June of 1266, Baybars besieged the great Templar fortress of Safed. Its massive fortifications, so recently rebuilt, withstood the first assault but the very size of the castle meant that a large part of the garrison was composed of Syrian Christians whom Baybars' emissaries promised to spare should they surrender. Knowing that they would not be relieved, and seeing that the turcopole soldiers were starting to desert, the Templar commander sent a native Syrian sergeant called Leon Cazelier to negotiate a surrender. Cazelier returned with Baybars' assurance of safe-conduct to Acre; but the only skin to be saved was Cazelier's. Once the Egyptians had taken control of the castle, the women and children were taken captive and sold as slaves in Cairo while the Templars were beheaded.

The loss of Safed after a siege of only sixteen days was a catastrophe for the Franks in Outremer and a humiliation for the Temple. The stronghold was refortified by Baybars, giving the Mameluks control of Galilee and the approaches to the coastal cities of Acre, Tyre and Sidon. To impress upon the Franks the fate that awaited them, the heads of the decapitated Templars were placed in a circle around the castle.

The next fortress to fall, after token resistance, was Toron. Marching unimpeded down the Mediterranean coast, Baybars' soldiers killed every Christian that they captured. In the spring of 1268, Jaffa surrendered to a Mameluk army in less than a day. The garrison was allowed to withdraw to Acre but the city was demolished and its Christian inhabitants killed. It was then the turn of the fortress of Beaufort, recently garrisoned by the Templars; this fell, after ten days' bombardment, on 18 April.

By 14 May, Baybars had arrived at Antioch which, despite its decline as a trading centre, remained the largest Christian city in Outremer. Its ruler, Prince Bohemond, was in Tripoli and the garrison was commanded by his constable, Simon Mansel; but it was too small to man the long walls that had thwarted for so long the soldiers of the First Crusade. On 18 May the Mameluks poured through a breach to take the city. The gates were closed and the inhabitants either massacred or enslaved. The souks and gracious houses were plundered and later abandoned. This once great metropolis of the Roman Empire which had been the first prize of the Latin crusaders was never to recover from this devastation, decaying until it was finally erased from the map of the world.

With the capture of Antioch by the Mameluks and earlier of Sis, the capital of Cilician Armenia, the Templar fortresses in the Amanus Mountains became exposed. The Templar garrison at Gaston (Baghras), the impregnable castle guarding the Syrian gates, on learning that Antioch had fallen after only a few days, decided that it would be impossible to hold out. However, surrendering a fortress in border territory without the Grand Master's permission was a serious breach of the Order's rules and the commander therefore determined to withstand the Mameluk army as best he could. However, while the community was eating, one of the brothers, Guis of Belin, left the fortress with the keys to the gate and took them to

Baybars saying that the Templar garrison wanted to surrender.

The commander and the Templar knights were ready to repudiate this unauthorised surrender but the Templar sergeants were less resolute. Faced with the prospect of their desertion, and realising that by now Baybars would have been told of their weak position by Guis of Belin, the commander ordered the evacuation of Gaston. In this he anticipated, correctly, the orders of the Grand Master who had dispatched a Brother Pelestort to tell the garrison of Gaston to fall back on La Roche Guillaume, but none the less, on reaching Acre, the knights from Gaston were charged with the unauthorised surrender of the castle. Given the circumstances, the prescribed punishment of expulsion from the Temple was reduced to the loss of their habits for a year; and might have been lighter still had they destroyed the arms and supplies held in Gaston before they left.[304]

On learning of the fall of Safed in 1267, King Louis IX once again took the Cross. However, the purity of the King's intentions was now contaminated by the ambitions of his brother, Charles, Count of Anjou, who had wrested the crown of Sicily from the Hohenstaufens with the blessing of the Pope. In 1268, the young grandson of Frederick II, Conradin, attempting to recover his patrimony, was defeated at the Battle of Tagliacozzo and subsequently executed. Charles, with ambitions to establish an empire in the eastern Mediterranean, persuaded his brother Louis that he should take Tunis as a prelude to an invasion of Egypt. As in the Nile Delta twenty years before, Louis met with some initial success, capturing Carthage, but once again fell ill and this time he did not recover. He died on 25 August 1270. His body was brought back to France by way of Lyons and the Abbey of Cluny with crowds gathering along the route to pay their last respects to the saintly monarch, and in Paris his body was interred in Suger's Abbey of Saint-Denis, now the mausoleum of the Capetian kings.

Louis's crusade disintegrated on his death and Baybars, who had withdrawn to Egypt to prepare for a possible invasion by the French, could now continue his inexorable reduction of the Latin fortresses in the East. In February 1271, the Templar castle of Chastel Blanc surrendered on the advice of the Grand Master, its garrison being then permitted to withdraw to Tortosa. In March it was the turn of Krak des Chevaliers, the magnificent fortress of the Hospitallers. It was fiercely defended but eventually surrendered on 8 April. Another Hospitaller castle, Akkar, fell on 1 May after a two-week siege. Baybars then marched on to Montfort, held by the Teutonic Knights, which surrendered on 12 June after a siege of seven days. It had been the last inland fortress to be held by the Franks.

The coastal cities that remained in the hands of the Franks were reinforced by contingents of crusaders from Europe led by Theobald Visconti, the Archdeacon of Liège who, serving as the Papal Legate in London, had taken the Cross at Saint Paul's; and, most significantly, by Prince Edward of England, the nephew of Richard of Cornwall, and son and heir of King Henry III. Aged in his early thirties, able and energetic, Edward had been encouraged by his father to fulfil the vows that Henry had frequently taken but had never felt able to fulfil. Sailing first to Tunis to join King Louis, he had arrived to find that he was dead. He had therefore sailed on to Sicily to stay with his uncle, Charles of Anjou, then to Cyprus and finally to Acre which he reached in May of 1271, shortly after the fall of Krak des Chevaliers.

Edward was appalled by the state of affairs that he found in Outremer – not simply the inability of the indigenous forces to hold the inland fortresses, but the zeal with which the Italian maritime republics traded with the enemy: the Venetians supplied Baybars with the metal and timber that he required for his arms and siege-engines, and the Genoese the slaves for his Mameluk regiments, both under licence from the High Court at Acre. He found that the knights of Cyprus were unwilling to fight on the Syrian mainland, and that the Mongols, to whom he sent an embassy of three Englishmen, were in no position to give him substantive help. Having been unable to persuade the English barons to join him on crusade, Edward's own forces were limited to around a thousand men – sufficient for a few raids into Muslim territory but wholly inadequate to affect the underlying balance of power.

Baybars knew this but, with the Mongols still able to threaten his rear, was in no position to move on the Christians' coastal domains. The arrival of Edward in May 1271 had prompted him to offer a truce to Bohemond of Tripoli which Bohemond had accepted with relief. Now, a year later, a similar agreement was reached with the Kingdom of Acre: the integrity of its territory was to be guaranteed for the next ten years and ten months. Neither side regarded this as a permanent settlement: Edward built a tower at Acre which he put in the charge of the chivalrous Order of Saint Edward that he founded. He then embarked for England, meaning to return with more substantial forces, but found when he reached home that his father had died and he was now king, ascending the throne as Edward I.

fourteen

The Fall of Acre

Another crusader elevated in his absence from Europe was Edward's com-panion-in-arms, Theobald Visconti, the Archdeacon of Liège: while he was in Acre two emissaries arrived from Europe to tell him that he had been chosen as the new Pope. After years of wrangling, the Catholic cardinals meeting in Viterbo had been locked in the Papal Palace by the prefects of the city to oblige them to reach a decision, then exposed to the elements with the removal of its roof, and finally denied any provisions until they made a choice.

Taking the title of Gregory X, the Pope-elect returned first to Viterbo and then to Rome, which his two predecessors had avoided, and there was crowned with the papal tiara on 27 March 1272. In spirit, however, he remained in Palestine: he 'preserved a vivid recollection of Jerusalem and worked for its recovery. His genuine devotion to the cause of the Holy Land became the basis of his policy.'[305] Less than a month after his accession, he summoned a general Council of the Church to meet at Lyons. At the top of its agenda was a new crusade, and he asked for proposals to be put forward in the light of the failure of Louis IX's expedition to Tunis two years earlier.

As a prerequisite to a successful crusade, Gregory X did what he could to reconcile the warring factions in Europe, and he also made approaches to the Greek Emperor in Constantinople, Michael VIII Palaeologus, invit-ing him to send delegates to Lyons with a view to reuniting the two churches. In the wake of so many setbacks, the preaching of a crusade was no longer straightforward: Humbert of Romans, the fifth Master General of Dominic Guzman's Order of Preachers, had warned his friars in his manual *De predictatione sancte crucis* that they must be ready to answer blunt and hostile critics, and that their sermons would often be met 'with mockery and derision'.[306] Humbert listed the arguments used by their antagonists – for example, that it was incompatible with Christ's teaching to kill in the name of the Church: 'the supporters of peaceful missions to the infidels were quite numerous at the time of the Second Council of Lyons'.[307] Even among those who backed a new crusade, there was widespread agreement that it should not be the kind of popular levy seen during the First Crusade – the *passagium generale* – but, as proposed by Gilbert of Tournai, an expeditionary force of professional soldiers – the *passagium particulare.*

Only one European monarch, King James I of Aragon, came to Gregory X's Council at Lyons which convened on 7 May 1274. The absence of the Pope's former comrade-in-arms, Edward I of England, was a particular disappointment because he would have been able to give the Council fathers the benefit of his experience. Without King Edward and King Philip III of France, Gregory fell back on the advice of the Grand Masters of the military orders – Hugh Revel of the Hospital and William of Beaujeu, elected Grand Master of the Temple after the death of Thomas Bérard the year before.

William was a career Templar with considerable experience of fighting in Palestine and administering the Order. In 1261 he had been captured in a raid and subsequently ransomed; he had been the Templar Preceptor in the County of Tripoli in 1271 and was Preceptor of the Kingdom of Sicily at the time of his election. However, his elevation almost certainly came about because of his links with the French Crown. His uncle had fought with Louis IX on the Nile, and through his paternal grandmother, Sybil of Hainault, he was related to the Capetian royal family. Not only had the French kings been the most reliable European source of help to the Holy Land, paying for a permanent force of knights and crossbowmen at Acre, but, with the triumph of Charles of Anjou over his Hohenstaufen rival at the Battle of Tagliacozzo, French power now reached throughout the Mediterranean. As a result, William of Beaujeu, at the Council of Lyons, spoke against a proposal put forward by King James I of Aragon to send a force of 500 knights and 2,000 infantry as the vanguard of a *passagium generale*, arguing that hordes of enthusiastic but ill-disciplined and transient crusaders would be ineffective. What was required was first a permanent garrison in the Holy Land, periodically reinforced by small contingents of professional soldiers; and second, an economic blockade of Egypt to undermine its economy.

As a prerequisite to such a blockade, William of Beaujeu argued, the

Christians would have to establish a naval ascendancy in the eastern Mediterranean that did not depend upon the Italian maritime republics – Venice, Genoa and Pisa: their trade with Egypt was simply 'too profitable to be abandoned',[308] the Venetians even using Acre for their trade with Egypt in prohibited war materials originating in Europe. Following this advice, the Council of Lyons ordered the Grand Masters of the Temple and the Hospital to build a fleet of warships.

There was a further reason for the Templars to support Charles of Anjou: he had bought the rights to the throne of Jerusalem from a credible pretender, Mary of Jerusalem, for a thousand pounds of gold and an annual pension of 4,000 *livres tournois*. To the Templars, and no doubt to the Pope, a single sovereign from the French royal house reigning over a joint kingdom of Sicily and Jerusalem was by far the best political basis for the preservation of a Latin presence in the Holy Land; but it brought the Order into conflict with the indigenous nobility of the Kingdom of Acre who supported the claim of King Hugh of Cyprus. When William of Beaujeu returned to Acre in September 1275, he refused to acknowledge the authority of King Hugh who in consequence returned to Cyprus in high dudgeon and wrote to the Pope complaining that the military orders made the Holy Land ungovernable.

Charles of Anjou, who also had the support of Pope Gregory X, sent a *bailli* to Acre to govern in his name, Roger of San Severino. The indigenous nobility saw no alternative but to accept Roger's authority, which he exercised in tandem with William of Beaujeu. Two attempts by King Hugh to recover his position with expeditionary forces to Tyre in 1289 and Beirut in 1284 were frustrated, largely by the Templars. The price paid by the Order was the sequestration or destruction of their properties in Cyprus which in turn led to protests from the Pope.[309]

More arbitrarily, William of Beaujeu also involved the Temple in a protracted dispute over the hand of an heiress between Bohemond VII of Tripoli and his principal vassal, which led to a minor civil war. Such internecine conflict among the Latin Christians at a time when their kingdom was already in a perilous position scandalised European opinion and undermined the moral authority of the Templar Grand Master, creating 'an image of him as untrustworthy and partisan, an image which in turn came to be reflected in some of the later judgements of him and of the last years of the Templars in Palestine'.[310]

At the end of March 1282, the whole basis of William's policy was under-mined with the revolt of the Sicilians against Charles of Anjou. This started with a fracas outside the cathedral in Palermo during the singing of Vespers that led to an attack on the French garrison. Charles, an arrogant and cold-hearted man with none of the judicious qualities of his saintly brother, Louis IX, had already antagonised the Sicilians in general with his oppressive rule, and the people of Palermo in particular by moving his capital to Naples, thereby accelerating the city's economic decline. Incited by the rival claim-ant to the Sicilian throne, Peter III of Aragon, the people of Palermo followed the attack on French soldiers outside the cathedral with the mas-sacre of the 2,000 French living in the city.

The landing of an Aragonese army at Trapani some months later started a war which ended any hope of help for the Latins in the Holy Land. A crusade was proclaimed by the Pope, Martin IV, not against the Saracens but against the Aragonese. Like a number of other crusades preached against the enemies of the Papacy in the fourteenth century, it debased the whole concept of Holy War. It was not simply that Europe was scandalised by a war against the Pope's Christian enemies but there was also an explicit diversion of resources. On 13 December 1282, Pope Martin IV, a Frenchman, Simon of Brie, authorised King Philip III of France to withdraw 100,000 *livres tournois* from the Paris Temple raised by the crusading tax to finance the war against the Sicilians and the Aragonese. The ten-per-cent tax on the Church that had been collected in Hungary, Sicily, Sardinia, Corsica, Provence and Aragon, amounting to 15,000 ounces of gold, was made over to Charles of Salerno, the son and heir of Charles of Anjou. The consequences for the Holy Land were clear at the time, at any rate to the anti-papal propagandists. Bartholomew of Neocastro describes a Templar knight rebuking Pope Nicholas IV: 'You could have relieved the Holy Land with the power of kings and the strength of the other faithful of Christ ... but you preferred to attack a Christian king and the Christian Sicilians, arming kings against a king to recover the island of Sicily.'[31]

In the Holy Land itself, the Sicilian Vespers had made the position of Charles of Anjou's new *bailli*, Odo Poilechien, untenable and the Templars shifted their support to King Henry II of Cyprus, the son and heir of King Hugh. Demonstrating a rare concord, the Grand Masters of the Templars, Hospitallers and Teutonic Knights persuaded Odo Poilechien to surrender the citadel at Acre to them, and then themselves gave it to the King. Six weeks later, after the young King's coronation at Tyre, the court returned to Acre where his accession was celebrated with games, pageants and tournaments hosted by the Hospitallers. The young nobility of Outremer enacted scenes of chivalry from *The Knights of the Round Table*, and from *The Queen of Femenie* where knights dressed as women performed mock jousts. These celebrations continued for two weeks.

One factor which had hitherto worked to the advantage of the Latins in Palestine had been the chaos that had followed the death of a Muslim ruler – for example, after the death of Saladin in 1193. However, when Baybars had died in 1177, his ineffectual sons were replaced within three years by Baybars's most competent commander, Qalawun. The chief factor that had inhibited the new Sultan from moving against the Franks in force had been a residual fear of Charles of Anjou: once that had been removed by the Sicilian Vespers of 1282, nothing remained to prevent him from pursuing Baybars's ambition to drive the Franks into the sea.

In 1287 Qalawun sent one of his emirs to attack Latakia, the last port in the principality of Antioch that remained in the hands of the Christians. No attempt was made to relieve it and Latakia fell after token resistance. In 1288, taking advantage of a dispute over the government of Tripoli after the death of Bohemond VII, Qalawun secretly prepared an assault on the city. His plan was betrayed by a spy in the pay of the Temple, the Emir al-Fakhri, and William of Beaujeu wrote to warn the citizens of Tripoli but, because of his record of self-interested duplicity, they would not believe him and so Qalawun's army found them unprepared. When the Mameluk troops broke into the city, the Templar commander, Peter of Moncada, remained and was killed along with all the male captives: the women and children were taken as slaves. After the city was in his hands, Qalawun ordered it to be razed to the ground to prevent any return by the Franks.

Notionally, the Kingdom of Acre was still protected by a truce but Qalawun soon found a pretext for breaking it. An enthusiastic but undisciplined group of crusaders, newly arrived from northern Italy, responded to a rumour that a Christian woman had been seduced by a Saracen by attacking all the Muslims in the city of Acre. The Latin barons and the military orders did what they could to stop this pogrom but a number of Muslims were killed. When Qalawun heard of the massacre, he demanded that the miscreants be handed over to him for execution. The authorities in Acre balked at surrendering Christian crusaders to the infidel. William of Beaujeu proposed sending all the condemned prisoners held in the city's gaols in their place but this was rejected. Instead, emissaries were sent to Qalawun by King Henry to explain that the Lombards were newcomers and so had not understood the law; and that, anyway, the riot had been started by the Muslim merchants.

This was not good enough for Qalawun. Advised by his councillors that he had just cause for breaking the truce, he ordered his army to prepare in secret for an assault on Acre. Once again, the Emir al-Fakhri sent word to William of Beaujeu but again the Templar Grand Master was disbelieved. In desperation, William of Beaujeu sent his own envoy to Cairo to treat with Qalawun, who offered peace in return for one sequin for each inhabitant of Acre. William recommended this offer to the High Court in Acre but it was contemptuously rejected. William himself was accused of treachery and abused by the crowd as he left the hall.

On 4 November 1290, Qalawun set out for Acre at the head of his army but fell ill and within a week he was dead. He was succeeded by his son al-Ashraf who, as his father lay dying, promised that he would continue the war against the Franks. New emissaries from Acre, among them a Templar knight, Bartholomew Pizan, were thrown into prison; and in March 1291, al-Ashraf's armies from Syria and Egypt began to converge on Acre with over a hundred siege-engines, giant catapults and mangonels. On 5 April al-Ashraf himself arrived before the walls of Acre and the siege began.

Christendom had had a good six months' notice of the Muslims' designs on Acre but little had been done to strengthen its forces in the Holy Land. The military orders had summoned knights from Europe; King Edward I had sent some knights under Otto of Grandson; and King Henry a contingent of troops from Cyprus. At most, the combined Christian forces consisted of around a thousand knights and fourteen thousand infantry, among them the undisciplined Lombards. The population of the city was put at around forty thousand, and every able-bodied man took his place on the ramparts. To the north was the suburb of Montmusard, protected by a double wall and moat; and between Montmusard and Acre itself there was a further moat and wall linking fortified towers built by prominent crusaders such as Prince Edward of England.

Each contingent of the defending forces was assigned a section of the walls. The Templars under William of Beaujeu manned the northernmost section from where the ramparts of Montmusard met the sea. Next to them were the Hospitallers and, at the juncture with the walls of Acre, the royal knights commanded by the King's brother Amalric reinforced by the Teutonic Knights; then the French, the English, the Venetians, the Pisans, and finally the troops of the Commune of Acre.

On 6 April the siege began with a bombardment by the Sultan's catapults and mangonels. Covered by a hail-storm of arrows aimed at the defenders, Mameluk engineers moved forward to undermine the towers and walls. Although adequately supplied with food from the sea, the Christians were short of arms and soldiers to man the ramparts. On the night of 15 April, William of Beaujeu led a sortie to attack the Muslims' camp but after an initial success the knights became entangled in the guy ropes of the tents and were forced back into the city, leaving eighteen dead. On 8 May the first of the towers undermined by the Muslim engineers was on the point of collapse, obliging its garrison to set in on fire and then withdraw.

During the week which followed, other towers started to crumble and on 16 May the Mameluks made a determined assault on Saint Anthony's Gate, which was repulsed by the Templars and Hospitallers. On 15 May, while he was resting, William of Beaujeu learned that the Mameluks had captured the Accursed Tower. Without waiting to put on all his armour, he rushed out to lead a counter-attack but was repulsed and wounded. His Templar brethren carried him back to the Templar fortress on the south-western extremity of the city. He died that night.

The Hospitaller Marshal, Matthew of Clermont, who had been with William of Beaujeu, returned to the battle and was killed. The Grand Master of the Hospital, John of Villiers, was also wounded but not fatally and was taken by his brethren to a galley in the harbour. On the quays, all was confusion as those who could tried to abandon the doomed city. King Henry and his brother Amalric sailed for Cyprus. Otto of Grandson and John of Grailly commandeered a ship. Desperate fugitives plunged into the sea to swim to the galleys lying offshore. The Patriarch, Nicholas of Hanape, welcomed so many on to the dinghy that was taking him to a galley that the small boat capsized and the Patriarch drowned.

Roger de Flor, the commander of a Templar galley, founded his subsequent career as a pirate by extorting large sums from the rich matrons of Acre for a place on his boat. But eventually the harbour was cut off by the Mameluk forces fighting their way through the streets, killing without distinction men, women and children. Those who hid in their houses until the rage of battle had subsided were made captive and enslaved: so many were taken that the price of a girl in the slave-market of Damascus dropped to a drachma, and 'many women and children disappeared for ever into the harems of the Mameluk emirs'.[312]

By nightfall on 18 May, all of Acre was in the hands of the Muslims except for the Templar fortress at the seaward extremity of the city. There the remaining Templars, under the command of their marshal, Peter of Sevrey, held out with civilians who had taken refuge behind its massive walls. Galleys returned from Cyprus to keep them supplied and their residual strength was sufficient to induce the Sultan al-Ashraf to offer terms. It was agreed that the Templars would surrender the fortress in return for an unimpeded embarkation of all those within the compound, together with their possessions. But the Emir, with a hundred Mameluks who were admitted to supervise this truce, immediately seized the property of the civilians, and began to manhandle the Christian women and children. Enraged, the Templars killed the Mameluks and tore down the Sultan's standard which they had raised over the tower.

That night, under cover of darkness, the Templar commander, Theobald Gaudin, was ordered by the Marshal, Peter of Sevrey, to take ship with the Order's treasure and some of the civilians and sail to the Templars' stronghold at Sidon. The next morning, the Sultan al-Ashraf asked to reopen negotiations for the Templars' surrender. The Marshal, Peter of Sevrey, with a small group of Templar knights, left the fortress under a safe-conduct to parley. When they reached the Sultan's camp, they were seized and beheaded. Those remaining behind the Temple's ramparts closed the gates and awaited the Muslims' final assault. On 28 May, part of the land-ward wall was undermined and the Mameluks poured through the breach. The last defenders were overwhelmed and slaughtered. Acre was finally taken.

In Sidon, Theobald Gaudin was elected Grand Master in succession to William of Beaujeu; he was an experienced soldier who had served in the Holy Land, first as the Order's Turcopolier, then as commander at Acre, for thirty years. He remained at Sidon for a month after the fall of Acre and, when a Mameluk army appeared before the walls of the city, withdrew with the Templar garrison to the offshore citadel. Already, Tyre had surrendered

to the Mameluks; while Acre, on the orders of the Sultan, had been sys-
tematically demolished, with the portal to the Church of Saint Andrew
taken to Cairo as a memorial to the glorious victory of al-Ashraf.

Still intending to resist, Theobald Gaudin sailed to Cyprus for reinforcements, taking the Order's treasure with him. He did not return. Advised by
their brethren in Cyprus to leave Sidon, and seeing that the Mameluks had
started to build a causeway, the Templars abandoned the castle and sailed
up the coast to Tortosa. Haifa fell on 30 July; Beirut a day later, its ramparts
demolished, its cathedral made into a mosque. Tortosa was evacuated on 3
August and eleven days later the Templars withdrew from their greatest
fortress, the impregnable Castle Pilgrim. All that remained was their garrison on the island of Ruad, two miles off the coast by Tortosa.

Here, the Templars maintained a garrison for the next twelve years. In
that period, the Muslims demolished the cities and laid waste the land on
the Mediterranean littoral. In a short time. The Frankish presence on the
mainland of Asia were ruins amid the sand.

part three

THE FALL OF THE TEMPLARS

fifteen

The Temple in Exile

The fall of Acre, though it was foreseen, came as a shock to Latin Christendom and gave a sense of urgency to Pope Nicholas IV's plans for a new crusade. This had been proclaimed some two months before the news reached Europe, on 29 March 1291, and had been made possible by a settlement of the Sicilian imbroglio by the Treaty of Brignoles the month before. It was to be led by the English King Edward I who, having dealt with the Welsh, felt able to fulfil his long-time aspiration to return to the Holy Land at the head of an army: the date for his departure was fixed for the Feast of Saint John the Baptist, 24 June 1293.

The fall of Acre was not seen at that time as the end of the Latin presence in the Holy Land. There was a widespread view that the Mongols would prove to be the Christians' salvation. The conversion to Christianity of some of the Mongol delegates to the Second Council of Lyons led to the hope that others might follow their example, and wishful thinking made the hope into an expectation. Pope Nicholas IV, the first Franciscan friar to occupy the See of Saint Peter, had sent a Franciscan missionary, Giovanni di Monte Corvino, to the court of the Great Kubla Khan. Moreover, there was still a Christian presence on the mainland of Asia in Cilician Armenia, and Cyprus remained in the hands of the Franks. The Pope's strategy was to reinforce these Christian outposts and weaken Egypt with a naval blockade prior to King Edward's crusade.

Recriminations were muted, especially when contrasted to those which had followed the failure of the Second Crusade. The Lombards who had given Qalawun an excuse to break the truce; the sinful decadence of the inhabitants of Outremer; and, among the lower classes, the procrastinating leaders of Christendom, were all blamed. 'Cry the daughter of Zion,' wrote the author of a tract *De Exidio Urbis Acconis*,

Cry over your chiefs, who abandoned you. Cry over your pope, cardinals, prelates and the clergy of the Church. Cry over the kings, the princes, the barons, the Christian knights, who call themselves great fighters, but ... left this city full of Christians without defence and abandoned it, leaving it alone like a lamb among wolves.[313]

The moral laxity of the Christians was contrasted with the religious fervour of the Muslims. However, the Lord had been prepared to spare Sodom for the sake of ten righteous men, and within Acre, for all its decadence, there had been many more than ten. Thirty Dominican friars in the city had been massacred by the Mameluks after its fall; and one of their brethren, the missionary Ricoldo of Monte Croce, who was in Baghdad at the time, suffered grievously from Muslim taunts that the failure of Christ to save the Christians proved that he was a mere man. 'Jews and Mongols, too, mocked the Christians ... Many Christians drew extreme conclusions and converted to Islam.'[314]

Finding in the kasbah the contents of a church plundered in Acre, Ricoldo bought a missal and a copy of Pope Gregory the Great's *Morals of Job*. Ricoldo was driven to the edge of despair. Muhammad had triumphed in Christ's homeland. All around him was apostasy and subjection. Priests had been slaughtered, nuns made concubines, and 'if the Saracens continue to do as they did in two years to Tripoli and Acre, in several years there will be no Christians left in the whole world'.[315]

In Europe, far from the taunts of the Muslims, and with the fate of the Christians in Asia witnessed only at second hand, no one had the temerity to make Christ the scapegoat but there was retrospective criticism of the Italian maritime republics and the military orders. John of Villiers, the Master of the Hospital, who had been wounded and carried to safety in Cyprus, wrote subsequently to William of Villaret, the Hospitaller Prior of Saint-Gilles, in a tone which suggests he was well aware that it was thought he should have died at his post.[316] The heroic death of William of Beaujeu did not altogether expunge his reputation as a prime source of disunity in the Latin kingdom. Pope Nicholas IV stated publicly that the disputes between the Temple and the Hospital had contributed to the downfall of Acre and proposed that the two orders should therefore be merged. This was endorsed by almost all the Church councils after 1291 and was coupled with demands, such as that of the Council of Canterbury that met at the

Temple in London in February 1292, that a new crusade should be paid for from the funds of the two orders. However, when Nicholas IV died in 1293 the firm plans for a new crusade died with him.

The proposed merger of the Temple and the Hospital was ill-received by the two military orders themselves. Neither wanted to give up their autonomy and both felt that they were being made the scapegoats for the failure of others to organise aid for Acre. Both were confident not just that they were too powerful to be coerced into a union but that they were indispensable to any future crusade. None the less, the defence of the Holy Land had been their *raison d'être*, and though their courage in the defence of Acre had done them credit, the surrender of Sidon and Castle Pilgrim without a fight, while undoubtedly justified by strategic considerations, had not added to their prestige.

With some prescience, the Teutonic Order had, after the fall of Acre, moved its headquarters first to Venice and then in 1309 to Marienburg in Prussia: from now on it fought exclusively against the pagan Prussians and Lithuanians. The Hospital, like the Temple, took refuge in Cyprus where it had extensive holdings, establishing its convent at Limassol in 1292. But having expanded its fleet of galleys to enforce the blockade on Egypt as instructed by the Second Council of Lyons, the Hospitallers now looked for a base free from the jurisdiction of the King of Cyprus. The eye of the Grand Master, Fulk of Villaret, elected in 1305, fell on the island of Rhodes.

Nominally still part of the Byzantine Empire, Rhodes had for the past thirty years been ruled by freebooting Genoese. There was no sovereign power in the Aegean region: southern Greece was still ruled by Latin princes, Crete and some of the Ionian islands by Venice, and little distinction was made between traders and pirates, or between mercenaries and buccaneers. In March 1302, the Temple in Cyprus paid a ransom of 45,000 silver pieces to secure the release of Guy of Ibelin and his family who had been kidnapped by pirates from their castle on Cyprus.

A good idea of the chaos that prevailed in the Mediterranean at this time is given by the career of Roger of Flor, the Templar who had extorted the treasure of the matrons of Acre in exchange for a place on his galley. Said to be the son of the falconer of the Emperor Frederick II, Richard von der Blume, he had, after the fall of the Hohenstaufens, been taken on, aged eight, as a cabin-boy on a Templar galley at the port of Brindisi. Latinising his name to Roger of Flor, he had joined the Templars and risen to command the galley *Falcon*.

Expelled from the Order for his behaviour at Acre, he had sailed to Marseilles, then moved on to Genoa where he was put in command of a new galley, the *Olivetta*. Enormously enriched first through piracy and then as the leader of a band of Catalan mercenaries fighting in Sicily, he was by 1302 in command of a fleet of thirty-two galleys and transports and a force of 2,500 men. These he put at the disposal of the Byzantine Emperor Andronicus Palaeologus in exchange for the hand of his niece Maria, the title of *megas dux*, and, for his Catalan Company, double the usual rates of pay. After a triumphant campaign against the Turks in Anatolia, Roger was assassinated. His Catalan Company, under a new commander, took over the Duchy of Athens in 1311 where they remained for seventy-seven years.[317]

One of only a very few recorded renegade Templars, Roger of Flor's rapid rise and sudden fall shows the relative ease with which a well-organised body of fighting men could carve out a domain of their choosing. Taking advantage of this anarchy, a force of Hospitallers landed on Rhodes in June 1306, and by the end of the year had captured the capital, Filermo. In 1307 the Pope, Clement V, endorsed their conquest and, although it took three more years to subdue the whole island, the Hospital had possession of a well-fortified and self-sufficient principality that ensured its independence of extraneous control.

The Templars were not so shrewd. They had substantial possessions on the island of Cyprus, among them a fortress to the north of Famagusta and fortified towers at Limassol, Yermasoyia and Khirokitia, but they were in no position to rule or even dominate the island. Moreover, they had been punished by King Hugh of Cyprus for backing Charles of Anjou for the crown of Jerusalem: their house in Limassol, seized by King Hugh, was only returned to them after the intervention in the 1280s of Pope Martin IV.

Relations remained sour after the fall of Acre when the headquarters of the Temple moved to Cyprus: King Henry II can hardly have welcomed an influx of Templar knights, sergeants and auxiliary troops. The Chapter General held in Nicosia in the wake of the disaster was attended by 400 Templar brothers; and in 1300 the Order was able to send 120 knights, 500 archers and 400 servants to reinforce the garrison on the island of Ruad. As always, the Templars were resented for their privileges and exemptions.

In 1298, King Henry II sent an embassy to complain to the Pope about the behaviour of the Order; and, when he was forced to abdicate by the Cypriot barons in favour of his brother Amaury in 1306, the Templars belonged to the group ranged against him.[318]

The direction of the Order had by this time passed from the hands of Theobald Gaudin, who had died in April 1293, into those of a new Grand Master, James of Molay. Coming from the lesser nobility of the Franche-Comté, part of the post-Carolingian middle kingdom of Lotharingen that had given many knights to the Order, he was the son of John of Longwy and related to the distinguished Rohan family through his mother. He took the name of Molay from an estate in the diocese of Besançon and had been received into the Order in Beaune in Burgundy in 1265 by two high officials, Humbert of Pairaud, Master in England, and Amaury of La Roche, Master in France. Much of his career had been spent in Outremer but whether or not he was at the siege of Acre is not known.

Undoubtedly experienced after thirty years in the Order, and most certainly able in many ways, James of Molay was also unimaginative, inflexible and lacked the cunning of the Hospitaller Grand Master, Fulk of Villaret. The only role he could envisage for the Temple was that of the vanguard in a reconquest of the Holy Land. To that end, he maintained the garrison on the island of Ruad, and summoned knights and sergeants from Europe to make up the losses the Order had suffered at Acre.

In 1294, James of Molay travelled to Europe to drum up support for his Order. He was in Rome in December at a unique moment in the history of the Roman Catholic Church when for the first and last time a pope, Celestine V, abdicated, to be succeeded by one of his cardinals as Boniface VIII. From Rome, Molay travelled to central Italy, then on to Paris and London. Either in person, or through correspondence, he was in contact with all the monarchs of western Europe: he had particularly cordial relations with King Edward I in England, who wrote to him in 1302 that only wars in France and Scotland had prevented him from 'going to Jerusalem as he had vowed ... upon which journey he had fixed his whole heart'.[319] Edward exempted the Order from a general prohibition on the export of treasure so that the funds collected by the London Temple could be sent to Cyprus.

James de Molay's lobbying in Rome also proved fruitful: the new Pope, Boniface VIII, issued a bull stating that the Temple was to enjoy the same privileges and exemptions in Cyprus as it had done in the Holy Land; and

Charles II in Naples ruled that Templar exports of food from south Italian ports should be exempt from taxes so long as they were for the use of the Order. Cargo ships were built to carry the Temple's cargoes and in 1293 six galleys were purchased from Venice. These formed part of a fleet that in July 1300 made a number of raids on the coast of Egypt and Syria, and in November transported a force of 600 knights to Ruad as a base for an assault on Tortosa.

This return to the Holy Land was planned as a combined operation with the Mongols under the Il-khan Ghazan and the Armenians under King Hetoum, but by the time their armies reached Tortosa in February 1301, the Latin forces had given up waiting and returned to Cyprus. The Temple continued to fortify and supply Ruad but the Mameluks in Egypt, seeing how it might have been used as a base for a reconquest of Palestine, sent a fleet of sixteen galleys to besiege it. The garrison resisted until it faced starvation. Its commander, Brother Hugh of Dampierre, then arranged a safe-conduct contingent upon their surrender; but once again the Mameluks went back on their word and the Templars were either killed or made captive: travellers later reported Templar knights living in poverty in Cairo and, as late as 1340, working as woodcutters by the Dead Sea.

The attack on Tortosa came at the crest of the wave of enthusiasm for a new crusade in western Europe which envisaged a leading role for the military orders, seeing them as 'the most important single source of crusading schemes'.[320] For most of the year 1300, a heady optimism had prevailed in the Papal Curia where it was believed that Jerusalem had been conquered by the Mongol Il-khan Ghazan and was to be handed back to the Christians. This was not just the result of wishful thinking for throughout the first half of 1300 there were no Mameluk forces left in Syria and the Mongols did control the Holy Land; but the optimism was premature because in the following year the Mameluks returned.

With the fall of Ruad, the best hope for a successful crusade appeared to lie once again with the King of France. Philip IV, had ascended the throne in 1285 when his father, Philip III, had died of fever while campaigning in Pope Martin IV's 'crusade' against the Aragonese. Unenthusiastic about this war against his late mother's brother, Philip IV, on his accession, made peace with Aragon and concentrated his energies on modernising the royal administration of France. In this early phase of his reign, he showed little interest in a crusade and in December 1290 asked the Pope, Nicholas IV, to relieve him of the responsibility for the custody of the Holy Land that he had inherited from his father.

Like the Emperor Frederick II, Philip IV had suffered in his infancy from his mother's early death. He had seen little of his father, and the advent of a scheming stepmother, Mary of Brabant, when Philip was aged six, only made him feel less secure; for when his brother Louis died two years later, it was rumoured that he had been poisoned by Mary of Brabant, and that she intended to get rid of her other stepsons in a similar way. Increasingly, Philip took refuge in a mistrustful piety, turning for a role-model to his pious grandfather, Louis IX.

Married at the age of sixteen to his childhood companion, Joan of Navarre, who brought not only Navarre but also Champagne as her dowry, Louis became king only a year later. He was the eleventh member of the dynasty founded by Hugh Capet in 987 and, fully imbued with his family's elevated concept of kingship, promoted by courtiers and churchmen alike: to the Council of Sens he was the 'most Christian' King of France, and to Giles of Rome, 'more than man, wholly divine'.[321]

Philip's piety was sincere: he undertook different penances to mortify his flesh, among them the wearing of a hair shirt. A tall, handsome, aloof man with fair hair and a pallid complexion that led to his being called Philip the Fair, the French King was a skilled hunter and was considered an accomplished knight. Bernard Saisset, Bishop of Pamiers, acknowledged that Philip was 'more handsome than any man in the world', but thought that his distant manner was a cover for an empty head: he 'knew nothing, except to stare at men like an owl which, though beautiful to look at, is an otherwise useless bird'. These remarks led to the bishop's arrest in 1301 on charges of blasphemy, sorcery, heresy, treason, simony and fornication. A modern historian sees in Philip a more complex but equally unattractive personality – 'a captious, sternly moralistic, literalistically scrupulous, humourless, stubborn, aggressive, and vindictive individual, who feared the eternal consequences of his temporal deeds'.[322]

Philip's marriage to Joan of Navarre was a happy one: Joan was a strong-willed, studious woman who had a profound devotion to her husband's grandfather, Louis IX. She and her mother became the enemies of Guich-ard, Bishop of Troyes, who, when Joan died in April 1305, was accused of murdering her by sorcery and black magic. Philip was deeply affected by her death and never remarried.

Philip was the heir not just to a tradition of piety but to the Capetian monarchs' policy of inexorable aggrandizement at the expense of surrounding principalities such as Toulouse; and within their realm, through the extension of royal rights at the expense of the nobility, the cities and the Church. To later historians, but also to his contemporaries, it was difficult to measure the influence exercised by the ministers who enforced this policy, promoting the absolutist ideology that marked Philip's reign. These came from a rising class of lawyers, the *légistes*, who owed nothing to either the Church or the nobility but derived their power exclusively from the favour of the King. In the 1290s, the most prominent of these ministers was Peter Flote, Keeper of the Seals and head of the Chancery; but after his death in 1302, the Seals were passed to William of Nogaret, a lawyer from near Saint-Félix-de-Caraman in the county of Toulouse.

Little is known about the origins and early life of William of Nogaret which has led some historians to suppose that he had something to hide, possibly descent from Cathars. 'Different chroniclers have suggested that William's father, his mother and several of his relatives had been burned for heresy':[323] his home town, Saint-Félix-de-Caraman, was where the Cathar 'pope' Niquinta had held a council in 1167. Whether or not Nogaret came from a heretical family, and whether, if he did, his residual sympathy with the defeated Cathars led to an animus against the Catholic Church, is a matter of conjecture. It would clearly have been impolitic for him to reveal any sympathy for heresy; and indeed more effective, given King Philip's piety, to express a particular repugnance for it, and promote his sovereign as a 'most Catholic' king descended from 'fervent champions of the faith, and strong defenders of the Holy Mother Church'.[324]

Nor does the consensus among modern historians accept that Philip was manipulated by his ministers, but sees him rather as 'the controlling power in the reign'.[325] Philip's belief that he was God's elect did not raise him above practical politics but rather made him all the more determined to acquire the means to fulfil his divinely appointed role. The main obstacle was the obduracy of his chief vassal, the Duke of Gascony, who was at the same time the King of England, Edward I. First of all, as an established crusader, Edward was regarded as the natural leader of any crusade and therefore the leading prince of Christendom; second, his power base in England enabled him to resist the Capetian policy, continued by Philip, of extending their powers at the expense of their vassals. This led to war between France and England and England's ally, Flanders. Peace was made with Edward I in 1298, but the war in Flanders proved a morass. In May 1302, the French in Bruges were massacred and Philip's subsequent campaign to avenge them ended in a defeat at Courtrai during which Peter Flote was killed.

These wars incurred enormous expense, adding to the liability that Philip had inherited from his father's war against Aragon – around 1.5 million *livres tournois*. Every expedient available to the monarch was used to raise funds. Feudal obligations were exploited to the limit, and force used to extract taxes from the towns. When all the accepted and legitimate sources had been exhausted, the King's ministers turned to rich but unpopular minorities. First came the Lombard merchants living in Paris who, early in Philip's reign, had acted as his bankers, securing loans on the basis of future taxation: they were progressively fleeced through fines and seizures culminating with outright expropriation and expulsion from France. In July 1306, it was the turn of the Jews. Their property was seized and they were thrown out of France.

Another expedient was debasing the currency of *livres, sous* and *denirs*. Between 1295 and 1306 the royal mint drastically reduced the value of specie in circulation. In June 1306, King Philip blithely proposed the return to the good money of the time of his grandfather, Louis IX. Money circulating in France lost two-thirds of its value, which led to riots in Paris from which the King only escaped by taking refuge in the Paris Temple.

By far the most promising source of additional revenue was the Catholic Church. Hitherto, it could only be taxed with the Pope's permission but both Edward I in England and Philip IV in France had done so without it. Already, by 1296, attempts by the Pope, Boniface VIII, to mediate in the war between the two kings had alienated the French. Now, in a bull entitled *Clerico laicos*, Boniface reiterated the ban on the taxation of the clergy without papal consent. Philip's response was to forbid the transfer of all funds from France to the Pope in Rome. Since the Pope depended on his French revenues, he had no alternative but to back down and, to set a seal on this reconciliation, on 11 August 1297, he declared Philip's grandfather, Louis IX, a saint.

Like popes Innocent III and Gregory IX, Boniface VIII had been born in the small town of Anagni, south of Rome. His family, the Caetani, were not as grand as the Segni who had provided the earlier popes, but he was a man in the same mould, a graduate in canon law from Bologna, who in the 1260s had gone on diplomatic missions to France and England, becoming a cardinal under Nicholas IV. His predecessor, Pietro del Morrone, who had reigned as Celestine V, had once been a hermit. Leaving the seclusion of his cave, Pietro had founded the monastery of Santa Spiritu in Naples and had formed links with the Franciscan 'spirituals' who wished to observe the absolute poverty of the Order's founder. In 1294 when he was chosen as Pope he was aged eighty-four and was once again living alone in a cave.

Celestine V's election had come after a long impasse in the College of Cardinals, and in the hope that the choice of a genuinely spiritual person would revitalise the Church. However, he had also been the favoured candidate of Charles II, the French King of Naples, who, against the will of the cardinals, installed Celestine V in the Castel Nuovo in Naples and packed the College of Cardinals with his own nominees. Though no doubt holy, Celestine was also naive, uneducated and incompetent, with insufficient knowledge of Latin to follow the day-to-day administration of the Church.

Celestine V had been reluctant to accept the papal tiara and by the end of 1293 it had become clear to him that he could not cope. After attempting to hand over the government of the Church to a committee of three cardinals, he asked the leading canon lawyer among the cardinals, Benedetto Caetani, if it was possible for a pope to resign. Citing false precedents, the Cardinal drew up a formula for his abdication. At a consistory on 13 December, Celestine V laid down the papal insignia, hoping to return to the life of a hermit, but his successor, fearing that he might form the focus for a schism, had Celestine confined in Castel Fuome near Ferentino where he died in 1296. That successor was Benedetto Caetani who took the name Boniface VIII.

The reconciliation of Pope Boniface VIII and King Philip IV which led to the canonisation of Saint Louis in 1297 was put under renewed strain by a bitter dispute between the Pope and the powerful Colonna family over land in the Campagna. The two Colonna cardinals who had supported Boniface VIII's election now turned against him, alleging that the abdication of Celestine had been uncanonical and that he had been murdered by the new Pope. After the Colonnas had seized a consignment of papal treasure, Boniface moved against them, demolishing their castles and giving their land to members of his own family. The Colonna cardinals fled to the court of King Philip in France.

The year 1300 marked the high point in the pontificate of Boniface VIII and seemed at the time the acme of papal claims to universal jurisdiction. Not only had the Pope prevailed over the Colonnas, but he seemed on the brink of a triumph in the East: a crusade was under way to retake Tortosa, while Jerusalem was to be returned by the Mongols to the Church. It was also the thirteen-hundredth anniversary of the birth of Christ and, to mark the occasion, Pope Boniface pronounced it a jubilee year, promising full remission of sins to those who visited Saint Peter's basilica and the Lateran after confessing their sins. This was the most dramatic demonstration of a pope's power to 'bind and loose' since Urban II had preached the First Crusade. The offer was taken up by as many as 200,000 pilgrims: the crowd was so dense that a breach had to be made in the Leonine walls to let it through. Pope Boniface, exultant, appeared before the pilgrims sitting on the throne of Constantine holding sword, crown and sceptre, shouting 'I am Caesar.'[326]

Pride comes before a fall. In 1301, Bernard Saisset, Bishop of Pamiers, whose scornful remarks about King Philip IV have already been noted, was arrested by order of the King, thrown into prison and, with evidence gained after torturing his servants, charged with blasphemy, heresy, simony and treason. This was a blatant trespass on ecclesiastical jurisdiction and an affront to the authority of the Pope. In the bull *Ausculta fili* published on 5 December 1301, Pope Boniface condemned this violation of the Church's prerogatives and summoned the French bishops to a synod in Rome. Thirty-nine dared to attend and on 18 November 1302, Pope Boniface published a bull, *Unam sanctam*, that reiterated all the claims to papal supremacy that had been made since the reign of Gregory VII: 'it is altogether necessary for salvation', he wrote, 'that every human creature be subject to the Roman Pontiff'.

The bull quoted freely from the writings of previous popes and from Thomas Aquinas and Bernard of Clairvaux who now, like King Louis IX, had been declared a saint. With no sign that King Philip was ready to accept the claims of *Unam sanctam*, bow to the will of the supreme pontiff, and repent of his errors, Pope Boniface prepared a bull of excommunication. However, before it was published he was stopped in his tracks by a coup of stupendous audacity. While Boniface was staying in his palace at Anagni, a force of French soldiers led by King Philip's minister, William of Nogaret, and including friends of the two Colonna cardinals and their partisans, burst into the Papal Palace to make a prisoner of the Pope.

Guarded by only a token force of Templar and Hospitaller knights, Pope Boniface, in full papal regalia, defied his captors to kill him. 'Here is my neck,' he shouted, 'here is my head.' Nogaret and the Colonnas drew back from such an irrevocable act: instead, they meant to take Boniface back to France to stand trial before a Church Council on the charges laid against him by their propagandists – heresy, sodomy and the murder of Pope Celestine V. However, news of the outrage spread among the people of Anagni who rallied to the defence of the Pope. The French were driven out of the city and Pope Boniface VIII returned to Rome; but he was broken in spirit by the humiliation. He died four weeks later, and with him died the aspirations of popes to universal rule.

sixteen

The Temple Assaulted

The 'outrage' at Anagni scandalised Europe and was compared by Dante, despite his dislike of Boniface VIII, to the recrucifixion of Christ. Horrified by the sacrilege, the conclave that gathered to choose a successor excommunicated the two Colonna cardinals and excluded them from its deliberations. Unanimously, the remaining cardinals chose Niccolò Boccasino, the Cardinal Archbishop of Ostia, but within a year of his accession he fell ill with dysentery and died.

The cardinals reassembled to choose a successor but there was a deadlock between those who wanted vengeance for the outrage at Anagni and those who sought accommodation with the Colonnas and the King of France. The former were in a majority but were divided by the personal ambition of two cardinals from the Orsini family. After eleven months of inconclusive deliberations, the cardinals decided to consider candidates from the wider Church. They were subject to overt outside pressure: King Charles II of Naples came to Perugia to join a delegation sent by King Philip IV of France.

In June 1305, ten of the fifteen cardinals agreed on a Frenchman, the Archbishop of Bordeaux, Bertrand of Got. The third son of Béraud of Got, Lord of Villandraut, his was a family deeply entrenched in the political and ecclesiastical establishment of Gascony. Esteemed by their suzerain, King Edward I of England, members of the Got family had been sent on delicate diplomatic missions, and Bertrand's elder brother, Béraud, had risen to become a cardinal and Archbishop of Lyons. Bertrand rose in his wake, becoming his brother's Vicar-General, a papal chaplain, a bishop and finally Archbishop of Bordeaux.

Taking the name Clement V, Bertrand of Got was no doubt aware that his elevation to the throne of the supreme pontiff was not due to any positive qualities but because he was the least objectionable candidate to the different parties concerned. King Philip IV of France had reason to think that the new Pope would be amenable to his bidding. King Edward I of England showed his approval of the elevation of the son of one of his vassals with rich gifts to him both in Bordeaux and in Lyons at the time of his coronation. To the Italians, however, Clement V was the puppet of King Philip of France, a perception substantiated, in their eyes, by the fact that never as pope did he set foot in Rome.

Certainly, in the previous two centuries, popes had only resided there for eighty-two years, often preferring for reasons of health or security to hold court in Orvieto, Viterbo, Anagni or Naples; but on the whole, they had chosen cities within the Papal States, or at any rate in Italy: Clement V was never to cross the Alps; and though he would sojourn in cities such as Lyons, Vienne, and finally Avignon, which were technically outside the jurisdiction of the French King, they were not beyond the reach of his armed forces as he was to discover at the Council of Vienne.

Why did Clement V remain so close to France? Two Italian chroniclers, Agnolo of Tura and Giovanni Villani, wrote that Cardinal Niccolò da Prato had arranged a meeting between Bertrand of Got when he was still Archbishop of Bordeaux and Philip the Fair, at which the King had specified four conditions for his support: reconciliation with the Colonnas and all those involved in the outrage at Anagni; a formal denunciation of Boniface VIII; the nomination of Francophile cardinals; and a secret clause, 'mysterious and great', which the King would communicate to Bertrand of Got at a later date.

According to these conspiracy theorists, Bertrand's response to Philip's command was 'You will command and I will obey'; and even though the story is now considered imaginary, 'it reflects the background of Clement's election as perceived on the Italian peninsula'.[327] It also appears from his later actions that Clement V met the King's demands: in December 1305, he appointed ten new cardinals, nine of them from the Kingdom of France, including Angevin possessions, and one from England. Four of the new cardinals were the Pope's relatives and one, Arnaud of Poyanne, an old friend. Their choice was not just a matter of favouritism but secured for the new Pope a team he could trust.[328] The balance in favour of cardinals from the Kingdom of France was confirmed by a second nomination of five cardinals in 1310, two of them the Pope's nephews and all from France.

But this preponderance of French churchmen was not simply to pay off a debt. Rather, the Pope's cultivation of Philip the Fair was because 'collaboration with the king of France was ... imperative for the realisation of Clement's dearest goal, the crusade'.[329]

The heady optimism about the Holy Land that had prevailed in the Papal Curia in 1300 had been exposed as wishful thinking. The Mameluks had reoccupied Palestine; Ruad had fallen and the Mongol Il-khan, Ghazan, who was to have delivered Jerusalem into the hands of the Christians, proclaimed in 1304 that the official faith throughout his dominions was to be Islam. The last Christian principality on the mainland of Asia, Cilician Armenia, was assailed by both Mongols and Mameluks. On 14 November 1305, Clement was crowned with the papal tiara in the Church of Saint-Just in Lyons in the presence of King Philip the Fair, his brother Charles of Valois, Jean II, Duke of Brittany, and Henry, Duke of Luxembourg: two days later he issued an encyclical that proclaimed a new crusade.

To Clement, who had taken the name of the earlier Pope who had worked in such harmony with Saint Louis, a crusade could only succeed if it was led by the King of France. To this end, he not only persuaded Philip the Fair to take the Cross, which he did in Lyons on 29 December 1305, but he also worked assiduously to resolve the disputes that might prevent the fulfilment of his vow such as that between France and England. He brokered a treaty between Philip IV and Edward I and, appreciating the strains on Philip's financial resources, he granted him a tenth of the income of the Church in France to fund the crusade – five or six times the revenue of the King.

King Philip's intention at this juncture was to fulfil his vow, not simply to gain glory by delivering the Holy Places from the infidel but also to establish a French empire in the eastern Mediterranean. The weakness of the Byzantine Emperor that had enabled the Hospitallers to seize the island of Rhodes now led King Philip IV to covet the throne of the eastern Empire for his brother, Charles of Valois. It might not conform to the plan of Clement V, but France, Venice, Aragon and Naples 'were openly committed to the winning of Constantinople'.[330]

In Philip's mind, a prerequisite to a successful crusade was the merger of the military orders. He would command the united order and be succeeded by one of his sons. The idea was not new and is to be found in many of the treaties written around this time to advise the Pope on the recovery of the Holy Land. Of particular significance was *De recuperatione terre sancte* by a Norman lawyer, Pierre Dubois, a propagandist for the French government, a spin doctor of his time. His proposal was in essence 'a plan for the establishment of French hegemony over the west and the east, through a crusade'.[331] Central to his scheme was the uniting of the Temple and the Hospital and the harnessing of their resources by the French King. Ominously, in a postscript to his treatise, Dubois added that it might be expedient 'to destroy the Order of the Templars completely, and for the needs of justice to annihilate it totally'.[332] However, the idea of merging the two orders was almost universal: the Mallorcan writer, Ramón Lull, who devoted much time and ultimately his life to the problems posed by Islam, actually damned to hell those who opposed it.

Almost the only man who did so was the Grand Master of the Temple, James of Molay. In response to a request from Pope Clement V, he produced a memorandum putting forward his views. He started with the pedigree of the proposal to merge the orders, tracing it back to the Second Council of Lyons in 1274 and listing the popes, among them Boniface VIII, who had decided against it. James of Molay recognised that there would be some advantages to a merger – a united order would be in a stronger position to defend itself against its enemies – but on balance he thought they would be more effective if they remained separate. Competition between the Temple and the Hospital was beneficial and, while their aims were similar, they each had a distinct ethos – the Hospital gave precedence to its charitable work while the Temple was primarily a military force 'founded especially as a knighthood'. Overall, he felt that the two orders were more likely to achieve their objectives of giving alms, protecting pilgrims, and waging war against the Saracens if they retained their independence.

A second memorandum was presented by James of Molay, at the Pope's request, on the future conduct of the crusade. Here again, the Grand Master went against the prevailing view at the time that favoured the *passagium particulare* – the limited incursion of a professional force to bolster the forces of Cilician Armenia. The lesson to be learned from the Temple's loss of Ruad, he suggested, was that such small-scale operations were bound to fail. Nor could he recommend an alliance with the Armenians. In their dealings with them over the Amanus march, the Templars had found them untrustworthy. Because they disliked the Franks and suspected their intentions, the Armenians would not allow them to enter their castles. Moreover, the climate in the region was so unhealthy that he doubted whether more than a fraction of a crusading army would survive.

What, then, was the solution? James of Molay proposed a *passagium generale*, a full-scale crusade on the classical model such as that of King Louis IX. The only way to reconquer the Holy Land was by defeating the land forces of Egypt. To do this, the kings of France, England, Germany, Sicily and Spain should raise an army of between 12,000 and 15,000 knights and 5,000 foot-soldiers which the Italian maritime republics would convey on their galleys and transport to Cyprus as a forward base for the reconquest of Palestine.

To all the other pamphleteers, particularly those of a like mind with the King of France, this was an old-fashioned and thoroughly discredited concept of crusade and, taken with his opposition to the merger of the orders, exposed James of Molay as a stubborn, unimaginative and self-interested old man. No doubt aware that his views would be unpopular, James wrote in his memorandum to Celestine V that he would find it easier to express his ideas face to face with the Pope: like most knights at the time, he could neither read nor write.

As a result, Pope Clement V summoned the Grand Masters of both the Temple and the Hospital to confer with him at Poitiers on All Saints' Day, 1 November 1306. The meeting was postponed because the Pope succumbed to a bout of an endemic gastric illness which often incapacitated him for months at a time. James of Molay reached Europe from Cyprus late in 1306 or early 1307 and was in Poitiers by the end of May. Fulk of Villaret, the Grand Master of the Hospital, was delayed by his Order's operations on Rhodes but reached Poitiers by the end of August. While in Poitiers, besides discussion of the vexed question of a crusade, James of Molay raised the matter of certain charges that had been made against members of the Temple and asked the Pope to institute an enquiry 'concerning those things, falsely attributed to them so they say, and to absolve them if they are found innocent, as they assert, or to condemn them, if they are found guilty, which they in no way believe'.

Allegations of gross impropriety appear to have been made by some knights who had been expelled from the Order – Esquin of Floyran, the Prior of Montfaucon; Bernard Pelet, Prior of the Mas-d'Agenais; and a knight from Gisors, Gérard of Byzol. Esquin had first told King James II of

Aragon of scandal within the Order and, having failed to persuade him of the truth of his charges, had gone to King Philip of France. Philip IV mentioned the rumours to Pope Clement V at Lyons at the time of his coronation in 1305, and again in May 1307 when the King was in Poitiers. On 24 August 1307, Clement V wrote to King Philip IV about these accusations, saying that though 'we could scarcely bring our mind to believe what was said at that time', he had subsequently heard 'many strange and unheard of things' about the Temple and so 'not without great sorrow, anxiety and upset of heart' had decided to institute an enquiry.[333] In the meantime, while he recovered his health, the Pope asked that no precipitate action be taken.

No doubt satisfied that his request for an enquiry had been met, James of Molay travelled from Poitiers to Paris where, on 12 October 1307, he was a pall-bearer at the funeral of King Philip's sister-in-law, Catherine of Courtenay, the wife of Charles of Valois. The next day, Friday 13 October 1307, he was arrested in the Temple compound outside Paris by William of Nogaret and Reginald Roy.

Three weeks before, King Philip had sent secret orders to his *baillis* and seneschals throughout France ordering the detention of all members of the Temple for crimes 'horrible to contemplate, terrible to hear of . . . an abominable work, a detestable disgrace, a thing almost inhuman, indeed set apart from all humanity'. These were put into effect with remarkable efficiency: around 15,000 knights, sergeants, chaplains, *confrères*, servants and labourers throughout the territories governed by the King of France were rounded up in a single day. Only around two dozen escaped, among them the Preceptor of France, Gérard of Villiers, and Imbert Blanke, the Preceptor of the Auvergne. One knight, Peter of Boucle, though he shed his habit and shaved off his beard, was recognised and arrested.

As with the Jews and the Lombards some months before, all the property of the Temple was sequestered; but the King's move against the Temple was different in kind. The Templars were not foreigners like the Lombards or infidels like the Jews. They were members of a proud and powerful corporation that came under ecclesiastical jurisdiction, subject not to the King but to the Pope. King Philip had seized the persons and the property of an exempt order, and, showing that he was only too aware of the dubious legality of his action, his warrants had implied prior consultation 'with our most holy father in Christ, the Pope'.

In fact, Pope Clement V had not been consulted and sent the King an angry rebuke.

> You, our dear son ... have, in our absence, violated every rule and laid hands on the persons and properties of the Templars. You have also imprisoned them and, what pains us even more, you have not treated them with due leniency ... and have added to the discomfort of imprisonment yet another affliction. You have laid hands on persons and property that are under the direct protection of the Roman Church ... Your hasty act is seen by all, and rightly so, as an act of contempt towards ourselves and the Roman Church.[334]

Clement did not say whether or not he believed the charges made against the Templars; his objection was principally to the usurpation of his prerogative, and the betrayal of trust implicit in the King's unilateral action; but that other 'affliction' which he rebukes Philip for adding to the discomfort of imprisonment was no doubt the torture to which the accused were immediately subjected by another ecclesiastical institution, the Inquisition.

Founded to root out heresy in Languedoc, and staffed by the friars of the Order of Preachers founded by Dominic Guzman, since 1234 a canonised saint, the Inquisition in France had become an instrument of coercion in the hands of the state. The chief Inquisitor, William of Paris, was King Philip's confessor and, given the King's piety, was no doubt privy to his plans. On the Sunday after the Templars' arrest, it was Dominican preachers who first explained the reasons for the arrests at a public meeting in the King's gardens, appearing alongside the officers of the King.[335]

To assist the Inquisitors' interrogation, torture had been authorised half a century earlier by Pope Innocent IV. It was to stop short of spilling blood or breaking limbs: favoured methods at the time were the rack, which stretched a man's limbs to the point of dislocating his joints; and the strapedo whereby a man was raised over a beam by a rope tied to his wrists that had been bound behind his back. A third technique was to rub fat into the soles of the feet and place the feet before a fire. Occasionally, the torturers miscalculated: the feet of Bernard of Vado, a Templar priest from Albi, were so badly burned that his bones fell out. A Templar knight, James of Soci, claimed to know of twenty-five fellow Templars who had died 'on account of tortures and suffering': an anonymous letter in the library of

Corpus Christi College, Cambridge, put the number at thirty-four.

Besides such specific measures to produce pain, suspects were placed in irons, fed only bread and water, and denied sleep. Given that a large number of those arrested were not battle-hardened warriors, but ploughmen, shepherds, millers, blacksmiths, carpenters and stewards, the shock and disorientation, combined with the mere threat of torture, quickly led many to admit whatever the King's officers and the Inquisitors suggested. By January 1308, 134 of the 138 Templars arrested in Paris had admitted some or all of the charges brought against them and it was the Grand Master himself, James of Molay, who within ten days of his arrest led the way.

What were the 'strange and unheard of things' that they were accused of, the crimes 'horrible to contemplate, terrible to hear of . . . an abominable work, a detestable disgrace, a thing almost inhuman, indeed set apart from all humanity'? According to the Capetian prosecutors, the Order of the Temple was given over to the worship and service of the Devil. Each new recruit, at his initiation, was told that Jesus Christ was a false prophet who had been crucified not to redeem the sins of mankind but as a punishment for his own. The postulant was ordered to deny Christ, and to spit, trample or urinate on an image of Christ on the Cross, and then kiss the Templar who received him on the mouth, the navel, the buttocks, the base of the spine, 'and sometimes on the penis'. He was told that he could have 'carnal relations' with other brothers; that this was not only licit 'but they ought to do and submit to this mutually' and it was 'no sin for them to do this'.

To mark their rejection of Christ, Templar priests were said to have omitted the words of consecration during Mass. At secret ceremonies, they worshipped a demon called Baphomet who appeared in the form of a cat, or a skull, or a head with three faces. Cords which had touched this head were tied around the waists of the Templars 'in veneration' of the idol. This was done everywhere and 'by the majority': those that refused were either killed or imprisoned.

Added to these gross iniquities were lesser crimes that confirmed existing public suspicions. The chapter meetings of the Temple were held in secret, at night, and under heavy guard. The Grand Master and other senior officers had heard the confessions and absolved the sins of their fellow Templars even though they were not ordained priests. They were covetous and avaricious: 'they did not reckon it a sin ... to acquire properties belonging to another by legal or illegal means' and sought 'to procure increase and profit to the said Order in whatever way they could . . .' A later charge accused them of treachery: it was their secret negotiations with the Muslims that had led to the loss of the Holy Land.

Clearly, when Pope Clement V and King James II of Aragon had first heard these charges, they had found them impossible to believe. Heresy and sodomy were invariably combined by the black propagandists of the time – by the Catholics in describing the Cathars, for example, or by William of Nogaret and William of Plaisans in their attack on Pope Boniface VIII. However, here the stock-in-trade charges were not only combined with the failings that had been ascribed to the Order by its critics; they also exploited a powerful public anxiety about sorcery and the power of demons that was to explode in the witch-hunts of the fifteenth and sixteenth centuries.

The scepticism of the Pope, together with the widespread acceptance of his sovereign rights over the Temple, might have hampered, if it was unable to frustrate, King Philip's assault on the Order had it not been for the admission by James of Molay that he had indeed denied Jesus Christ and spat on Christ's image at the time of his reception in Beaune. The only charge the Grand Master had rejected was that he had indulged in homosexual acts. However, blasphemy was more than enough to satisfy William of Nogaret.

The confessions of other high Templars followed: Geoffrey of Charney, Preceptor in Normandy; John of La Tour, Treasurer of the Temple in Paris, hitherto a close financial adviser to King Philip; and Hugh of Pairaud, the Templar Visitor of France, who, having received many of the French Templars, was named by others as the instigator of their corruption. Hugh's confession, made on 9 November, embraced all the charges, including an admission that 'he said to those whom he was receiving that if any heat of nature urged them to incontinence, he gave them licence to cool off with other brothers'. Refusing at first to incriminate others, he was taken away by his guards and 'afterwards on the same day' admitted to the Inquisitors that the practice was ubiquitous. 'Clearly threats or torture had been used to force the issue.'[336]

How had such diabolical practices started? Geoffrey of Gonneville, the Temple's Preceptor in Aquitaine and Poitou, claimed that 'a certain evil Master . . . was in the prison of a certain sultan, and could not escape unless he swore that if he were released, he would introduce that custom into our

Order, that all who were received henceforth should deny Jesus Christ ...': possibly Bertrand of Blanquefort or William of Beaujeu was intended. Geoffrey had refused to deny Christ and had been excused by the Preceptor, perhaps because his uncle was an influential figure in the government of the King of England. But he had to swear on the Gospel that he would not reveal that he had been let off.

Only four Templars denied the charges outright – John of Châteauvillars, Henry of Herçigny, John of Paris and Lambert of Toysi – a proportion so small that they could be disregarded. Philip's *coup* against the Order appeared to be justified and while suspicions of his motives remained, especially outside France, Pope Clement V felt that he had no alternative but to accept the King's action as a *fait accompli* and attempt to recover the initiative himself. On 22 November 1307, less than a month after James of Molay's confession, Clement V sent a letter entitled *Pastoralis praeeminentiae* to all the kings and princes of Christendom asking them 'prudently, discreetly, and secretly' to arrest all Templars and hold their property in safe-keeping for the Church. He praised the good faith and religious zeal of Philip IV but insisted that he, the Pope, was now in control.

The first to be convinced that this was the case was James of Molay who, when brought face to face with three cardinals sent by Clement V from Poitiers to Paris, revoked his confession. According to one account, he tore open his shirt to the show the marks of torture on his body, at which the cardinals 'wept bitterly and were unable to speak'.[337] Other retractions followed and it seems probable that the cardinals were not altogether surprised: the ten members of the sacred college appointed by Pope Clement in his first consistory were said to have threatened to resign because of the Pope's pusillanimous attitude towards the King of France. There was undoubtedly discontent within the Papal Curia, and lobbying by the friends of the Temple such as James of Molay's brother, the Dean of Langres. Moreover, many of the leading Templars were well known to the three cardinals sent to Paris, two of whom were Frenchmen: it was while he was dining with them that Hugh of Pairaud revoked his confession.

Considerable risks were attached to this course of action because, under the statutes of the Inquisition, relapsed heretics were handed over to the secular arm to be burned. James of Molay no doubt felt confident that he would receive justice from the Pope and at first this confidence seemed vindicated. When King Philip, *en route* for Poitiers, heard that the cardinals had refused to confirm the condemnation of the Templars, he rushed back to Paris and wrote to Clement V, threatening to charge the Pope with the same sins; but Clement V kept his nerve, replying that he would rather die than condemn innocent men; and in February 1308, he ordered the Inquisition to suspend its proceedings against the Templars.

However, while the law may have given the Pope control over the fate of the Templars, they were held in the prisons of Philip the Fair. Oliver of Penne, the Preceptor of Lombardy, was the only Templar of any standing whom Pope Clement held in Poitiers under house arrest but he absconded on the night of 13 February: a reward of 10,000 florins was put on his head. Moreover, the extensive properties of the Temple were also in the hands of royal officials and the Pope had no battalions at his command. Poitiers was nearer to Paris than Anagni, and the *de jure* powers of the Pope were paltry compared to the *de facto* powers of the King.

All the same, King Philip had to be mindful of public opinion and once Pope Clement had failed to respond to his initial threats, the King's propagandists went to work to stigmatise anyone who might appear to support the Templars. Anonymous pamphlets were printed attacking the Pope, purporting to express the outraged feelings of the people of France. One, probably written by the Norman lawyer Pierre Dubois, said that Pope Clement's nepotism had proved beyond doubt that he was corrupt and therefore incapable of dispensing justice. Only bribery could explain why he had not condemned the Templars after so many had confessed their guilt.

The two great corporations of the kingdom were enlisted to support and disseminate this royal propaganda – the University of Paris and the Estates General. In late February, 1308, King Philip IV asked the doctors of theology in Paris how he should proceed in the case of the Templars. Would he be justified in putting them on trial without reference to the Pope? And should they be found guilty, what should be done with their property? Their response was not what he wanted: while praising the King for his Catholic zeal, they confirmed that the Temple came under the papal jurisdiction, and reminded him that the King's rights did not supersede, or justify the usurpation of, the rights of others. Nor could the King take action against heretics except at the request of the Church.

Frustrated by the theologians, King Philip summoned the Estates General, representing the nobility, the clergy and the burghers – to meet at

Tours three weeks after Easter to support their king in his struggle against the heretical Templars. Royal officials were told to make sure that every town with a market sent a representative, while the King's vassals and the higher clergy were invited by a personal letter from their sovereign. No record survives of the proceedings, but almost certainly the assembly at Tours was harangued by royal ministers such as William of Nogaret on the iniquities of the Temple and Clement V's predecessor, Boniface VIII.

While their colleagues returned home to spread the word about the Templars, a number of the delegates to the Estates General remained to accompany King Philip to Poitiers. There, in the company of a powerful, even intimidating, entourage that included Philip's brother, Charles of Valois, his sons and the grandees from the Estates General, the King prostrated himself before Pope Clement who in turn raised him with every outward sign of respect and affection. On 29 May, at a public consistory held before a large assembly of cardinals, bishops, nobles and burghers, the King's minister, William of Plaisans, laid out the case against the Templars. They were not only guilty of heresy and sorcery but were responsible for the loss of the Holy Land. It was only thanks to the religious zeal of King Philip and the people of France that they had been exposed. They had done the Pope's work for him and, if he did not immediately acknowledge that the Templars were guilty, the people of France, as 'the most zealous champions of the Christian faith', would themselves exercise the judgement of God.

Pope Clement was not to be brow-beaten into precipitate action. Although William of Plaisans had specifically denied that King Philip had his eye on the Templars' property, the Pope said that he would not pass judgement until both the property and the persons of the Temple were in his hands. On the face of it, the positions were irreconcilable but it seems likely that a compromise was reached behind the scenes.

Going some way towards meeting the Pope's demands, King Philip sent seventy-two Templars to repeat their confessions before Clement at Poitiers. Although this was no doubt presented as an acknowledgement by the King of France of the Pope's jurisdiction, it could equally well have been a measure to give Clement the appearance of hearing both sides of the case. Inevitably, the seventy-two Templars had been carefully chosen, and the first to give evidence before the Papal Curia was the priest, John of Folliaco, who claimed to have alerted the authorities to the Temple's corruption prior to the time of the arrests. So too had Stephen of Troyes, a Templar sergeant, who gave a vivid description of the head that was brought in at the Temple's chapter by a priest 'preceded by two brothers with two large wax candles upon a silver candelabra'.[338] He also maintained that he had been beaten up for rejecting the homosexual advances of a Templar brother, and that when he had complained of this to Hugh of Pairaud, he was told that he should not have refused. A Templar sergeant, John of Châlons, claimed that Gérard of Villiers, the Preceptor in France, had placed recalcitrant Templars in a pit in which nine of the brothers had died. He also said that the Preceptor had been warned that he would be arrested and so had fled with fifty horses and escaped on eighteen galleys with the treasure of Hugh of Pairaud.

Forty of the extant depositions admit to one or another of the charges made at the time of the original arrests. Descriptions of the idol were inconsistent, one saying it was 'a foul and black idol', another that it 'seemed white, with a beard' while two insisted that it had three faces. An analysis of the depositions shows that sixty per cent were made by Templars who were either apostates from the Order or had been coerced through torture. None was a high official: the Pope was told that these were all too ill to come to Poitiers but were held at his disposal in prison at Chinon. However, the selection served the purpose of both the Pope and the King. Without loss of face, Clement was now able to authorise the Inquisition to proceed with its investigations, and in return King Philip officially remitted the Order's property to special curators, and acknowledged that he only held the Templars 'at the request of the Church'.

In a number of bulls issued from Poitiers in July and August 1308, in particular *Faciens misericordiam*, Pope Clement V endorsed King Philip's version of events, and accepted that he had acted 'not from avarice' but 'with the fervour of the orthodox faith, following the clear footsteps of his ancestors'. Clement authorised each bishop in his diocese to appoint provincial councils to try the miscreant Templars under their jurisdiction. These were to be composed of two Dominicans, two Franciscans and two canons of the cathedral. The Order as a whole was to be investigated by eight papal commissioners, and three cardinals were dispatched to Chinon to interview its leaders. Finally, Clement summoned a general Council of the Church to meet in Vienne in 1310 to discuss the Templars, the crusade and Church reform.

What brought about this apparent change in Clement's attitude towards the Templars? It is possible, but unlikely, that he had been persuaded by the confessions of those Templars brought to Poitiers: he knew both the Templars and King Philip's methods too well. It seems more probable that Clement decided that the Templars must be sacrificed for the sake of the Church. The phrase used in his encyclical about King Philip 'following in the footsteps of his ancestors' is revealing. Not only in his own mind, but in the mind of his subjects, Philip had inherited the prestige and the authority of his grandfather, Saint Louis, and so, unlike the Emperor Frederick II in his titanic struggle with the Papacy, could threaten to usurp not just the pontiff's temporal power but his spiritual power as well. Despite the judgement of the Parisian divines that heresy was a matter for the Church and the Church alone, the royal propaganda against the Templars indicted as equally culpable the *fautores*, those who aided and abetted their iniquity, if only through neglect.

The Capetian propagandists also played on public anxieties by associating the Templars with the other marginalised groups in European society – lepers, Jews and Muslims: it was at this moment that King Philip's cousin, King Charles II, who ruled southern Italy from Naples, chose to evict from his domain the Muslim community that the Emperor Frederick II had settled at Lucera. The success of this propaganda can be gauged by a letter sent by the Court of Foix to King James II of Aragon, asking if it was true that the Templars had converted to Islam and planned to form an alliance with the Jews and the Muslims of Granada. It was also said that some fugitive Templars had sought asylum with the Saracens, and indeed, as with all successful propaganda, it contained a germ of truth: in September 1313, the former Preceptor of Corberis, Bernard of Fontibus, was sent as ambassador by the Sultan of Tunis to the court of King James II in Barcelona.

Even more effective was the association of these marginalised groups with the forces of darkness. The charges of sorcery and devil-worship had a potent effect on the medieval mind. Images of demons were ever-present in the carvings and frescoes of cathedrals and churches: and it was not only uneducated peasants who lived in fear of their powers. James Duèze, a fellow Gascon who received a cardinal's hat from Clement V and was to succeed him as Pope John XXII, though the son of a rich merchant from Cahors and a graduate in law from Montpellier University, was terrified of being killed through sorcery and, when pope, ordered his inquisitors to expose those who had made 'a pact with hell'. He was 'convinced that there were persons, masquerading as Christians, who were joined to the devil by a secret alliance'.[339]

Could the Pope himself have been suborned by Satan? The idea was not too far-fetched for those like William of Nogaret and William of Plaisans who had the ear of King Philip the Fair: indeed, it seemed to be the only plausible way to explain the actions of those who thwarted the 'most Christian' King. Had not the servants of the Bishop of Béziers, who had called Philip as silent and stupid as an owl, admitted under torture that he communed with evil spirits? And, most significant of all, had not Philip's arch-enemy, Pope Boniface VIII, been a heretic, a sodomite and in league with the Devil?

The spiritual standing of the late Pope was of more than academic interest because, besides pressing for the condemnation of the Templars, King Philip IV was also insisting upon a posthumous trial of Pope Boniface VIII on a charge of heresy. There was a provision in canon law for such a process, and precedents such as the exhumation and trial of Pope Formosus in 897. To Philip, a conviction would justify *ex post facto* the outrage at Anagni, nullify the excommunication of William of Nogaret, and establish the King's right not just to judge, 'but also to seize and punish a heretical pope'.[340]

As part of his campaign of vilification against the dead pontiff, Philip the Fair was also pressing for the canonisation of Pietro del Morrone, the hermit Pope, Celestine V, who according to the French deposition had been forced to abdicate, subsequently imprisoned and finally murdered by his successor, Boniface VIII. To pronounce infallibly that Celestine was in Heaven would, in Philip's thinking, prove that Boniface was in Hell; and the case for Celestine was enhanced by reputed miracles and widespread popular devotion.

Under intense pressure from the powerful French monarch who regarded himself as answerable only to God, and wholly vulnerable to the forces of coercion at his command, Clement V resorted to his favoured tactic of procrastination, and at the same time edged away from King Philip's sphere of control. The political chaos in Italy made it impossible for him to return to the Papal States; but the Papacy had acquired an enclave on the edge of Provence, the country of Venaissin, and, suitably placed on the River Rhône, the city of Avignon. In August 1308, Pope Clement announced that the Papal Curia would leave Poitiers and establish itself at Avignon. It was considered a temporary measure, but the popes were to remain there for the next seventy years.

The move to Avignon, which was not completed until March 1309, did not relieve the pressure on the Pope from Philip the Fair. Already, before leaving Poitiers, Clement had agreed to a posthumous trial of Boniface VIII. He did so reluctantly, and with considerable anguish, because he understood how damaging to the authority of the Papacy it would be if Pope Boniface VIII should be condemned as a heretic. News of the trial scandalised opinion outside France, and confirmed the impression that Clement V was a pawn in the hands of Philip IV. King James II of Aragon wrote to the Pope to express his disquiet.

However, when the trial eventually opened Clement himself defended the record of Boniface VIII before the advocates of the French King, recalling his piety, his service to the Church and the many manifestations of his orthodox faith. After this, he allowed the trial to continue but, thanks to his knowledge of Roman law, was able to spin things out, either by calling for written depositions or, in December 1310, by suspending the proceedings on the grounds that he was suffering from one of the recurring bouts of his illness.

Negotiations continued out of court during his recuperation, resulting in a compromise: the Pope recognised that King Philip and his servants had acted in good faith at Anagni, intending simply to deliver a summons for Pope Boniface VIII to attend a General Council. Any violence against the person of the Pope had been the result of a personal vendetta pursued by his enemies in the Papal States. Philip was praised as 'a fighter for the faith' and 'defender of the Church', and Clement V withdrew any papal bulls detrimental to Philip or the Kingdom of France. William of Nogaret was absolved in return for a commitment to go on crusade, and to visit a number of shrines in France and Spain. In return for these concessions, King Philip IV declared his full submission to any decision that Pope Clement V should make on the question of the orthodoxy of Pope Boniface VIII.

This compromise had a bad press outside France. Dante Alighieri thought it a further instance of the prostitution of the Papal Curia to King Philip IV. The ambassador of Aragon to the Curia wrote to his sovereign that Philip was now 'king, and pope, and emperor!' There was a widespread belief that William of Nogaret's absolution had cost Philip 100,000 florins. However, to a modern historian this criticism of Clement's policy during the trial of Boniface 'is not supported in historical rescarch' but rather makes it clear 'that Clement won an irrefutable victory. The only compromise he was forced to make involved his generous praise of Philip's behaviour – but this was a theoretical concession that the Pope often found very easy to make.'[341] The same was true in the case of the hermit Pope, whom Clement V canonised in 1313, not under his papal name, Celestine, but as Saint Pietro del Morrone; and not as a martyr as King Philip had wanted, but as a confessor.

In this way, with the weapons of patience and procrastination, Pope Clement V preserved the authority and autonomy of the Church. Unlike his great predecessors such as Pope Gregory VII and Innocent III, who had fought titanic battles against the German emperors, Clement had found himself virtually powerless in a petty wrangle with a fanatic and vengeful king. On the question of Pope Boniface VIII and his predecessor, Celestine V, he had fought a successful rearguard action, compromising only on inessentials. But was the Temple an inessential? Pope Clement seemed unable to decide.

When Pope Clement V left Poitiers in August 1308, King Philip IV certainly assumed that the means were in place to settle the fate of the Order in a relatively short space of time. The Templars remained in the hands of the royal gaolers, and further confessions by the imprisoned members of the military Order could be expected now that he had authorised the Inquisition to proceed with its interrogation. The Templar leaders interviewed by the four cardinals at Chinon had all retracted their retractions and confirmed their crimes. None of them owned up to all the charges, but the combined confessions covered them all. All repented of what they had done and asked to be received back into the Church.

The presence at Chinon of William of Nogaret and William of Plaisans may well have had a bearing on what the veteran Templars chose to say. There was every incentive for the accused to admit the charges because if he continued to protest his innocence he risked further torture and life imprisonment. If he escaped, he had nowhere to hide: Clement had again written to all the kings of Christendom asking them to detain all fugitive

Templars in the lands they controlled and hand them over to the episcopal commissions. Many of the bishops, particularly those in northern France, were Philip's appointees; moreover, the Pope had warned all the clergy that helping the Templars would make them guilty of heresy by association.

King Philip could also feel confident of the outcome of the papal commission of enquiry into the Order. He himself had sent a list of suitable candidates to Pope Clement V and among the eight members were a number of supporters of the King. The president of the commission was Gilles Aicelin, Archbishop of Narbonne, who had spoken against the Templars in Poitiers in 1308. The bishops of Mende and Bayeux were also the King's men, the latter often employed by Philip on royal business. Four of the commissioners were not French but one, the Archdeacon of Trent, had worked with one of the Colonna cardinals and another, the Prévost of Aix, had been employed as a diplomat by King Philip's cousin, King Charles II of Naples.

However, the complex procedures which had been laid down by Pope Clement V, and the difficulty of bringing eight such eminent churchmen together, meant that the commission only held its first session a year after it had been formed. On 8 August 1309, at the monastery of Sainte-Geneviève in Paris, it issued a summons to all who would like to give evidence to appear before it in November; and the commission finally convened, after last-minute delays, on 22 November in the episcopal hall of the Bishop of Paris.

Among the first witnesses was Hugh of Pairaud, the Templar Visitor in France, who said nothing in defence of the Order. When James of Molay gave evidence on 26 November, he said that he would like to defend the Order because it was inconceivable that the Church should now want to destroy it, but he doubted his ability to do so without help. However, he would 'regard himself as vile and miserable and would be so regarded by others if he did not defend the Order, from which he had received so many advantages and honours'.

It was not just that James of Molay was illiterate, as he had attested at the time of his arrest; it was that the Temple under his rule had failed to adapt to the increasing legalism of the period. Other corporate bodies such as the Hospitallers and the monastic orders engaged the services of legal counsel but the Knights Templar 'seem to have made little effort either to recruit lawyers or to raise up legal experts from within their own ranks'

despite the vigilance with which they had protected their rights and immunities.[342] Emotional, confused, a Don Quixote in his own eyes as well as in
the perception of others, James of Molay no doubt regretted the omission.
When an account of his confession before the cardinals in Chinon was read
out to him, he became agitated, crossed himself twice and issued what the
commission took to be a challenge to trial by combat to 'certain persons' –
presumably the cardinals who had taken his deposition. Rebuked by the
commission, James said that he had not intended such a challenge, but that
if it should please God they should follow the practice of the Tartars and
Saracens who 'cut off the heads of such evil-doers ... or split them down
the middle'.[343]

The commissioners were unimpressed by this belligerent bluster but
agreed to a recess to enable him to prepare the defence of his Order. King
Philip's minister, William of Plaisans, who was present at the sitting, and
to whom, ironically, James of Molay had appealed for help, was disconcerted
by the spectacle of this loose cannon: after two years of torture and imprisonment, the Grand Master seemed confused about what he had confessed,
what he had revoked, and whether or not he was expected to defend the
Order. William warned him to take care not to 'perish by a noose of his
own making'.

When James of Molay came back before the commission on Friday 28
November he repeated that he felt unable to mount a defence of his Order
because 'he was a knight, unlettered and poor', and that because he had read
in one of the apostolic letters that Pope Clement had reserved judgement in
his case to himself, he had decided to remain silent until he was brought
before the Pope. To the commission, he would say only three things: first,
that the liturgy in the Templar churches was more beautiful than in any
churches other than cathedrals; second, that the Order had been lavish in
its charitable donations; and third, that no Order 'had shed its blood so
readily in defence of the Christian faith' or was more highly esteemed by
the Saracen enemy. Had not the Count of Artois placed the Templars in the
advance guard of Saint Louis's army on the Nile? And would he not have
lived if he had listened to the advice of the Grand Master?

When the commissioners drily replied that all this was worthless if faith
was absent, James of Molay agreed but insisted that he did believe 'in one
God and in a Trinity of Persons and in other things appertaining to the
Catholic faith ... and when the soul was separated from the body, then it

would be apparent who was good and who was bad and each of us would know the truth of these things which were being done at present'.

On 28 November, the commission suspended its first sitting and did not reconvene until 3 February 1310. In the interim, the defeatism that had overwhelmed most of the Templars after their first arrest had been replaced by a spirit of resolve. At the first session, the Preceptor of Payns, Ponsard of Gizy, had told the commission that all the charges made against the Order were false; that the confessions had been made 'on account of danger and fear'; and, after describing how he had been tortured, he said that if threatened with similar torments, he would admit to anything that was put to him. Between 7 and 27 February, 532 Templars from throughout France followed his example.

On 14 March, a full list of the 127 charges made against the Order was drawn up and read out before ninety of the Templars who had volunteered to defend the Order. By the end of the month, the figure had risen to 597 Templars, among them a priest, John Robert, who said that he had heard innumerable Templar confessions, none of which mentioned any of the sins imputed to the Order. Faced with such a large number, the commission asked the accused to select a manageable number as procurators and in due course two priests were chosen, Reginald of Provins, Preceptor of Orléans, and Peter of Bologna, Procurator of the Temple at the Papal Curia in Rome. Peter of Bologna was an ordained priest, aged forty-four, and had been a member of the Temple for twenty-five years. He was presumably a Lombard and had been received at Bologna where he may have studied law under the Preceptor of Lombardy, William of Noris. His appointment as the Temple's Procurator at the Papal Curia suggests an intellectual aptitude rarely found in the military Order. After his arrest in November 1307, he had confessed to denying Christ and spitting on the Cross. He had denied sodomy but admitted that it had been allowed.

Reginald of Provins was also a priest, about eight years younger than Peter of Bologna. The fact that he had thought of joining the Dominicans rather than the Templars also suggests an advanced education, and the manner in which he had avoided an overt confession when first interrogated demonstrates a nimble mind. He had been received into the Order at Brie fifteen years before.

The first submission of these two Templar priests was a protest at the conditions in which they were being held – denial of the sacraments, the confiscation of their property and religious habits, the poor food and iron fetters, and the way that those who had died in prison had been refused burial in consecrated ground. Later, when interviewed by the commission's notaries in the Paris Temple where he was incarcerated, Peter of Bologna denounced the charges as 'shameful, most wicked and unreasonable and detestable things . . . fabricated, invented and made from new, by witnesses and rivals and lying enemies'. He insisted 'that the Order of the Temple was clean and immaculate, and always was, from all the articles, vices and sins'. Any confessions were clearly false, made either as a consequence of torture or to avoid it.

On Wednesday 1 April, Peter of Bologna and Reginald of Provins, together with two knights with a record of service in Outremer, William of Chambonnet, Preceptor of Blaudeix in the Auvergne, and Bertrand of Sartiges, Preceptor of Carlat in Rouergue, appeared before the papal commission: both knights had served in the Holy Land and neither had confessed to any of the charges when first questioned by the Bishop of Clermont.

At once Reginald of Provins put the commission itself on the defensive, first by insisting that only the Grand Master and chapter of the Order were authorised to appoint procurators for the defence of the Temple; second, that the initial procedures against the Order on charges of heresy had been irregular and therefore of doubtful legality. Clearly, it was a prerequisite of a proper defence that those accused be granted money to hire advocates and placed in the custody of the Church, not the King. For the first time since the Templars' arrest in October 1307, they were mounting a cogent defence.

Even after almost seven hundred years, the words of Peter of Bologna suggest not just a skilful advocate but a timeless apologist for the rights of the accused. The initial proceedings against the Templars, he told the commission, had been pursued 'with a destructive fury', the brothers 'led like sheep to the slaughter' and driven 'by diverse and various kinds of tortures, from which many had died, many were for ever disabled, and many at that time driven to lie against themselves and the Order'. Torture, he argued, removed any 'freedom of mind, which is what every good man ought to have'. It deprived him of 'knowledge, memory and understanding' and therefore anything said under torture should be discounted. He also disclosed that Templar brothers had been shown letters with the seal of

King Philip that had promised that they would not only be spared torture but that 'good provision and great revenues would be given annually during their lifetime, always saying first to them that the Order of the Temple was altogether condemned'.[344]

Thus, all the evidence against the Order was tainted and, moreover, defied common sense. Was it credible that so many a noble, distinguished and powerful man was 'so foolish and mad' that 'to the loss of his soul, [he] would enter and persevere in the Order'? Surely knights of this calibre, if they had discovered such iniquities in the Temple, in particular the blasphemies against Jesus Christ, 'would all have shouted out, and have divulged all these matters to the whole world'?

This robust defence of the Temple and the never-ending deliberations of the papal commission exasperated King Philip IV. The Church Council called to meet at Vienne in October 1310, finally to dissolve the Temple, had had to be postponed for a year because the commission had not submitted its report. The King therefore decided to expedite matters through the agency of Philip of Marigny, the Archbishop of Sens. The Archbishop had recently been promoted from the see of Cambrai thanks to the influence of his brother, Enguerrand of Marigny, who was in the process of displacing William of Nogaret as the principal minister of the King. It was at Enguerrand's request that King Philip had obtained Philip's appointment to the see of Sens from the Pope; he was therefore in debt to both the King and his brother and in the spring of 1311 was in a position to repay it.

By reason of ecclesiastical demarcations dating back to the days of the Roman Empire, the diocese of Paris lay in the province of Sens. It was therefore the Archbishop of Sens who had the power to judge the cases of the individual Templars within his jurisdiction. On Sunday 10 May, when the papal commission was in recess, he convened a council in Paris to proceed against them. Peter of Bologna realised at once what was intended and immediately appealed to the commission to protect those Templars 'who had brought themselves to the defence of the said Order'. He asked the commission to order the Archbishop of Sens not to proceed against them.

The president of the commission, Gilles Aicelin, Archbishop of Narbonne, at once removed himself from considering this petition on the grounds that 'he had to celebrate or hear Mass'. It was left to the remaining commissioners to decide that, while they felt considerable sympathy for the Templar petitioners, the proceedings of the papal commission and council appointed by the Archbishop of Sens were 'completely different and mutually separate'. Since the Archbishop received his powers directly from the Holy See, it was not within the commission's competence to interfere.

On Monday 11 May, the commission reconvened to take the testimony of any Templar who wished to defend the Order in the absence of its president, the Archbishop of Narbonne. In a break in the proceedings, it was announced that fifty-four Templars who had retracted their confessions to defend the Order were to be burned as relapsed heretics that very day. The commission immediately sent the Archdeacon of Orléans and one of the Templars' gaolers, Philip of Voet, to ask the Archbishop to postpone the execution: Voet had told them how many Templars who had died in prison had sworn, on the brink of eternity, that the charges against the Order were false.

Their intervention was ignored. The fifty-four Templars were herded on to carts and taken to a field by the convent of Saint-Antoine outside the city. There they were burned to death. All of them, without exception, denied 'the crimes imputed to them, but constantly persisted in the general denial, saying always that they were being put to death without cause and unjustly: which indeed many of the people were able to observe by no means without great admiration and immense surprise'.[345] Those who had never admitted to the alleged crimes could not be judged to be relapsed heretics and so were sentenced to lifelong imprisonment. Only those who confirmed their confession and repented were absolved of their sins and set free.

Four days later, four more Templars were handed over by the Archbishop of Sens to be burned as relapsed heretics, and the body of the former Treasurer of the Paris Temple, John of La Tour, was exhumed so that it too could be consumed in the conflagration. The effect of these actions was apparent in the witnesses now called before the commission: a Templar from the diocese of Langres, called Aimery of Villiers-le-Duc, insisted that all the errors ascribed to the Order were false but begged the commissioners not to reveal this to the King's officers because he did not want to be burned. The commissioners were only provoked into a protest when one of the two procurators, Reginald of Provins, disappeared from prison.

The protest was effective: Reginald of Provins was returned together with the two knights, William of Chambonnet and Bertrand of Sartiges: but now it was Peter of Bologna who had gone missing and, despite the dispatch of three canons to fetch him, he was not found. After this, the proceedings of the commission limped on with many of its members absenting themselves with a variety of excuses. On 17 December, when William of Chambonnet and Bertrand of Sartiges said that they could not proceed with the defence of the Order without Reginald of Provins and Peter of Bologna because they were 'illiterate laymen', they were told that both Templar priests had renounced their defence of the Order and returned to their original confessions. Reginald of Provins had been dismissed from the priesthood by the Council of Sens, and Peter of Bologna had escaped from prison. More probably, he had been murdered by his gaolers: but, whatever the fate of the two Templar priests, the two knights felt unable to proceed without them and so 'left the presence of the commissioners'.[346]

seventeen

The Temple Destroyed

Why, in the words of Peter of Bologna, did the members of the most formidable military force in the Western world go to their deaths 'like sheep to the slaughter'? One of the reasons was undoubtedly the advanced age of most of the Templars living in France. Having served for a time in the East, many had returned to Europe to take up posts in the administration. The younger knights were sent to Cyprus: in 1307, over seventy per cent of the Templar force had been recruited since the start of the century.[347] Here they were prepared for military action: they had fought the Saracens for Tortosa and were ready for a Mameluk invasion of the island.

Pope Clement V's bull ordering the arrest of the Templars throughout Christendom, *Pastoralis praeeminentiae*, reached Cyprus in November 1307. The *de facto* ruler at the time was Amaury, the brother of King John, who had been backed by the Templars when he seized power in August 1306. The Pope's orders put Amaury in an awkward position. He was in debt to the Templars and, like most others on Cyprus, he thought the charges against the Order almost certainly untrue; however, he was also unwilling to defy the Pope or make an enemy of King Philip of France. He therefore ordered his officers to proceed against the Templars under their Marshal, Ayme of Oselier, but they met with some resistance and fighting took place.

Eventually, the Templars surrendered and eighty-three knights and thirty-five sergeants were placed under house arrest on their estates. Their property was sequestered but Amaury's officers failed to find the bulk of the Templars' treasure. No trial took place until the following May when two judges appointed by Pope Clement arrived on the island. None of the accused admitted the charges. Depositions were taken from witnesses from outside the Order, among them sixteen knights and the Seneschal of the kingdom, Philip of Ibelin, and the King's Marshal, Reginald of Soissons.

283

Most had supported King Henry II against Amaury and so might have been expected to show an animus against the Templars, but all their evidence was in their favour. Philip of Ibelin, who was the first witness, thought it was only the secrecy surrounding Templar receptions that led to a suspicion of wrongdoing. Reginald of Soissons confirmed that the Templars did believe in the sacraments and had always conducted their religious ceremonies correctly.

A knight, James of Plany, was outspoken in his defence of the Templars, reminding the court that they had shed their blood for Christ and the Christian faith, and were as good and honest men as one could find in any religious order. Lord Perceval of Mar, a Genoese, described a group of Templars taken prisoner by the Saracens who had chosen to die rather than betray their faith. Lesser witnesses, though they mentioned the secrecy of the Templar receptions and the Order's avarice, said nothing to implicate them in blasphemy or heresy. A priest, Laurence of Beirut, said that he had heard the confessions of sixty Templars and could say nothing against them. It was clear from further testimony that many Templars confessed to Dominicans, Franciscans and secular priests, and not necessarily to their own chaplains.

The only witness from among the Latins on Cyprus to give evidence against the Templars was Simon of Sarezariis, the Prior of the Hospital of Saint John, but he could produce no solid evidence, merely alluding to conversations he had had with unnamed persons in the past. With this one exception, the noble witnesses all gave evidence in favour of the Templars, despite being partisans of King Henry II.

This result was considered unacceptable by Pope Clement V who ordered a new trial under the Papal Legate in the East, Peter of Plaine-Cassagne, Bishop of Rodez. This took place after the murder of Amaury and the restoration of King Henry in the summer of 1310, and though the records are not extant, it would seem that the Pope's political imperatives prevailed: the chronicles record that the Templar Marshal, Ayme of Oselier, and many of his fellow Templars died while incarcerated in the fortress of Kerynia.

In Italy, proceedings against the Templars varied according to the political loyalties of the rulers involved. Charles II of Naples, cousin of King Philip the Fair, so far as is known from the few surviving depositions, secured the requisite confessions, thanks presumably to the use of torture. In the Papal

States, torture also produced some confessions of denial of Christ, spitting on the Cross and the worship of idols; but on the whole a perambulatory inquisition conducted by the Bishop of Sutri produced paltry results. In Lombardy, many of the bishops supported the Templars and some were brave enough to say so. The bishops of Ravenna, Rimini and Fano failed to find evidence of guilt in the few Templars who were brought before them. In Florence, after the use of torture, six out of thirteen Templars confessed.

In Germany, Burchard, Archbishop of Magdeburg, moved quickly against the Templars, among them the German Preceptor, Frederick of Alvensleben. At Trier, a provincial Church Council summoned by the archbishop came up with no evidence against the Order. A similar council held at Mainz, presided over by the archbishop, Peter of Aspelt, was interrupted by a contingent of twenty armed Templar knights led by the Preceptor of Grumbach, Hugh of Salm. The cowed archbishop was obliged to listen to their complaint that the members of the Order had not been given a fair chance to defend themselves; and that those who had insisted upon their innocence had been burned. Hugh of Salm also claimed, as miraculous proof of their innocence, that the Templars' while habits did not burn in the fire.

At a later hearing, Hugh of Salm's brother, Frederick, the Preceptor of the Rhine, offered to prove the innocence of the Order through a trial by ordeal. He said that he had served in the East with James of Molay and knew him to be 'a good Christian, as good as any could be'. Other witnesses attested to the charitable work of the Templars, among them a priest who said that during a famine the preceptory at Maistre had fed a thousand of the poor every day. At the end of the hearing, the archbishop ruled in favour of the Templars who had been brought before him, a decision that displeased the Pope.

Outside France and Cyprus, the most significant Templar presence was in Spain, in particular in Aragon, where the Order had played a prominent role in the reconquest of lands held by the Moors. The enormous privileges and substantial endowments dating from the heroic days of the *Reconquista* had for some time now been eroded by the King. Indeed, though the Order still had considerable holdings in Aragon, it had been squeezed by the need to send funds to the Order in Syria and Palestine and by the demands made by the Aragonese kings. Though the Temple still acted as a bank, it was itself in debt.

In the middle of October 1307, King James II had received a letter from King Philip IV of France listing the iniquities of the Templars and advising him to seize their property and persons as Philip had done in France. The Aragonese monarch was incredulous. The Templars, he wrote back to Philip the Fair,

> have lived indeed in a praiseworthy manner as religious men up till now in these parts according to common opinion, nor has any accusation of error in belief yet arisen in them here; on the contrary, during our reign they have faithfully given us very great service in whatever we have required of them, in repressing the enemies of the faith.

However, when the news reached Spain that James of Molay had confessed to the alleged crimes, King James II ordered the seizure of the Templars and their holdings in his kingdom. Some Templars refused to surrender their castles: in contrast to France, the Order in Aragon had a number of men under arms and time to prepare for such a defence. The fortress at Pensícola was taken, and the Templar Master in Aragon, Exemen of Lenda, arrested, but Ascó, Cantavieja, Villel, Castellote, Chalamera and Monzón remained in the hands of the Order while Ramón Sa Guardia, the Preceptor of Mas Deu in Roussillon, held out in the fortress of Miravet. From here he wrote to King James II, reminding him of the blood that had been shed by the Templars in the wars against the Moors, most recently against Granada. During a time of famine, twenty thousand had been fed by the Templars at Gardeny and six thousand at Monzón. When the French had invaded Aragon and threatened Barcelona, it had been the Templars who had stood firm. For all these reasons, the King should release the Master and other Templars who are all 'loyal, Catholic and good Christians'.

However, by now the die was cast – not because King James had been persuaded that the Templars were guilty as charged, but because he wanted to make sure of their assets before they were expropriated by the Church: he even suggested a *quid pro quo* to Pope Clement whereby two of his nephews would be given land in Aragon if the Pope relinquished his rights to the Temple's property in Spain.[348] Perhaps aware that avarice was now the King's prime motivation, Ramón Sa Guardia wrote to say how much he pitied him, 'the King of France, and all Catholics in relation to the harm which arises from all this, more than ourselves who have to endure the evil'. He feared for the King's soul if he had deluded himself that he was doing the work of God and not of the Devil. Like Peter of Bologna, he asked how, if the charges were true, so many members of the finest families should have joined the Order, some of them for as little as six years, and yet not have denounced the alleged abuses?

On 1 February 1308, King James decided to lay siege to those fortresses still in Templar hands. Unwilling or unable to mount a frontal assault, his tactic was to starve the garrisons into submission. Ramón Sa Guardia, who continued to communicate with the King, warned that they were prepared to die as martyrs unless King James guaranteed to protect them for as long as Pope Clement remained under the influence of the King of France. However, King James felt no need to compromise and by the end of November the Templars of Miravet had been starved into submission. Monzón held out until May 1309 and by the end of July, with the fall of Chalamera, the Order's resistance had come to an end.

Proceedings against the Aragonese Templars now followed but, since torture was not allowed under Aragonese law, these elicited no confessions. The captives were kept in reasonable comfort on a decent diet. Ramón Sa Guardia was as outspoken before the Inquisitors as he had been in his letters to the King. He said that receptions into the Order had been wholly orthodox, as had been the Templars' practice of the Catholic religion. The allegations of the denial of Christ were 'horrible, exceedingly heinous and diabolical' and 'any brother committing a sin against nature' (i.e. sodomy) was punished 'by the loss of his habit and perpetual imprisonment . . . with great shackles on the feet and chains on the neck . . .' The charges had arisen from 'a malign and diabolical spirit', and any who had confessed to them were liars.

In March 1311, the Pope ordered the Archbishop of Tarragona and the Bishop of Valencia to use torture to extract confessions but the methods that had proved so successful in France failed in Spain. Eight Templars tortured in Barcelona persisted with their protestations of innocence; a local Church Council in Tarragona, on 4 November 1312, found the Templars innocent 'although they were put to the torture towards the confession of their crimes'.

As in Aragon, so in the kingdoms of Castile-Leon and Portugal. Templars were arrested and arraigned before episcopal commissions but none could find evidence to substantiate the charges. Throughout the Iberian peninsula, it was only in Navarre that the predominant French influence led to some success in extracting confessions from Templars to the alleged crimes.

Like King James II of Aragon, King Edward II of England had received a letter from King Philip the Fair in mid-October, 1307, describing how he had uncovered the cesspit of corruption in the Temple and advising his son-in-law to proceed as he had done with the arrest of the miscreants and the expropriation of their assets. Like King James of Aragon, King Edward was at first incredulous. Though the Temple's presence was not as considerable as it was in the Kingdom of France, with between 144 and 230 knights in England, Scotland, Ireland and Wales, it had nevertheless played an important role in the royal government since the first Grand Master, Hugh of Payns, had come to London in 1129. It had served as banker to the Angevin monarchs; it had been trusted with the fines paid by the murderers of Thomas à Becket, and acted as an intermediary in disputes between the kings of England and France, holding fortresses in Normandy that were the dowry of Princess Marguerite of France until her husband, the son and heir of King Henry II of England, came of age.

The trust placed in the order by King Richard the Lionheart has already been recorded; the Templar Grand Master, Robert of Sablé, had been both his vassal and trusted friend. The Temple in London was a safe depository for royal revenues; and the Order was a substantial presence in the commercial life of the kingdoms, exploiting the many privileges and exemptions granted by kings and popes. Though the Temple's wealth had led to some envy, their annual income from landed property did not exceed 4,800 *livres*, not enough to inspire 'strong feelings of jealousy' or 'a general dislike'.[349] James of Molay had been warmly received by King Edward I when he visited England in 1294 and William of La More, the English Master, had been the old King's trusted adviser. Edward II, who had only ascended the throne three months before, found the charges made against the Order implausible and wrote to the kings of France, Aragon, Castile, Portugal and Naples to say so. The Order had an honourable record of service in the Holy Land and 'shines bright in religion'. He also wrote to Pope Clement insisting that the Templars had been 'constant in the purity of the faith' while those who made such vile accusations were criminals and liars.

This letter, dispatched on 10 December, crossed with the papal bull, *Pastoralis praeeminentiae*, ordering the arrest of all the Templars in Christendom, which King Edward received four days later. This left the young King with no choice and so on 26 December he ordered the detention of the English Templars in 'the quickest and best way'. By this time the news of James of Molay's confession had reached England, and Edward, like King James II of Aragon, may also have seen the advantages of taking control of the Templars' assets before they fell into other hands.

However, suspicions remained of King Philip and his influence on Pope Clement; and the treatment accorded to the Templars hardly suggests that the charges were believed. The English Master, William of La More, who was arrested on 9 January, was imprisoned in Canterbury but two Templar brothers were permitted to go with him, and he was allowed furniture, clothes, bed-linen and his personal possessions as well as a *per diem* allowance of two shillings and sixpence. Many of the preceptors were allowed to stay in their preceptories until summoned to appear before the Inquisitors almost two years later.

At the time of their arrest, an inventory was made of the Templars' possessions which gives a snapshot of their lifestyle and belies their critics' charges that they were living well off the fat of the land. In Yorkshire, the inventories show that church vestments, livestock and agricultural implements were the only assets of any value. There were no arms, very little money, and the furniture was meagre and poor. Some stores of salted mutton, bacon, salt fish, herrings, stockfish, cheese and a little salt beef were found, but almost no wine.[350]

On 13 September 1309, the two Inquisitors appointed by the Pope arrived in England – Dieudonné, Abbot of Lagny, and Sicard of Vaur, a canon of Narbonne whose archbishop was Gilles Aicelin, the president of the papal commission examining the Order in Paris. This was the first appearance of Inquisitors in England: unlike France, where the Inquisition had been accepted and used as a tool of the monarchy, it had no standing in English law. Moreover, trials were normally held before jurors and torture was not allowed. As a result, the interrogation of the English Templars that took place between 20 October and 18 November before the two Inquisitors and the Bishop of London yielded no results. None admitted to any wrongdoing. Imbert Blanke, the Preceptor of Auvergne, who had fled to England at the time of the arrests in France, said that the secrecy surrounding

Templar receptions had been 'because of foolishness' and nothing un-toward had taken place.

Frustrated by their failure to elicit any confessions, the Inquisitors per-suaded the provincial Council of Canterbury that met in London on 24 November to ask King Edward II for permission to use torture: the request was couched euphemistically as proceeding 'according to ecclesiastical con-stitutions'. Permission was granted, but torture failed to produce the desired results. The only irregularity that emerged was the widespread assumption among the Templars that forgiveness for transgressions by the Master in Chapter amounted to sacramental absolution.

An additional frustration for the two Inquisitors, which they relayed in their report to the Pope, was King Edward's reluctance to give any assur-ances about the transfer of the Templars' property to the Church. He said that he could not act without consulting the earls and barons of the kingdom, a position that was not merely procrastination: for while the Pope could legitimately point out that the original endowments had been made for the Templars' mission in the Holy Land, the King could equally well maintain that they had come from the English nobility who, if the Order was to be dissolved, were entitled to have them back. This position was vigorously supported by his barons.

Exasperated by the lack of results from England, Pope Clement V urged the archbishops of Canterbury and York to pursue the case against the Templars with greater zeal. Pressure came from other quarters: William of Greenfield, the Archbishop of York, had received a letter from King Philip IV urging his co-operation. The Church authorities did what they could, but as William of Greenfield told the provincial Council that he had con-vened in May of 1310, 'torture had never been heard of within the realm of England'. The best he could come up with was hearsay evidence from witnesses outside the Order: John of Nassington had been told that the Templars at Temple Hirst had worshipped a calf. A knight, John of Ure, said that the Preceptor of Westerdale had shown his wife a book which stated that Christ had not been born of a virgin, but was the son of Joseph. The only evidence of sodomy came from a friar, Adam of Heton, who said that when he was a child, boys used to say: 'Beware the kiss of the Templars'. Another friar knew of a woman who had found a Templar's drawers in a latrine and saw that the sign of the Cross had been sewn into the seat.[351]

Pope Clement clearly suspected that the English were being dilatory in their enquiries, and wrote to King Edward offering him a plenary indulgence if he would transfer the Templars under his jurisdiction to France. He also put pressure on the English ecclesiastics by declaring in his bull *Faciens misericordiam* that the Templars' guilt was established and that anyone who now tried to protect them was guilty by association with their sins. The provincial Council in York, feeling unable either to convict or acquit, authorised their archbishop to refer the whole matter to the Papal Court at the Council to be held at Vienne. In the meantime, they came up with a very English formula whereby each Templar should state in public as follows: 'I acknowledge that I am gravely defamed by the articles contained in the Bull of our Lord the Pope, and inasmuch as I am not able to purge myself I submit to the Divine Grace and to the decision of the Council.' Having made this statement outside York Minster, each was reconciled to the Church and sent to live in a number of monastic foundations – William of Grafton to Selby, Richard of Keswick to Kirkham, John of Walpole to Byland, Thomas of Stanford to Fountains, and Henry of Kirby to Rievaulx. The bad behaviour of Thomas of Stanford and Henry of Kirby led to complaints by the Cistercian abbots to the Archbishop of York.

Proceedings against the Templars in Scotland and Ireland were no more successful in meeting the expectations of Pope Clement and the King of France. The only worthwhile confessions were made in England by two fugitive Templars, Stephen of Stapelbrugge and Thomas of Thoroldeby, who were retaken in June 1311 and subsequently described blasphemies at the time of their reception. Both had probably been tortured. In July, a Templar priest called John of Stoke also confessed that a year after his reception he had been told by James of Molay to deny Christ. When all had expressed penitence, they were absolved and reconciled with the Church. So too were a further fifty-two Templars who accepted the formula arrived at by the Council of York. However, the two most prominent Templars in England, the Master, William of La More, and the Preceptor of the Auvergne, Imbert Blanke, continued to insist upon their innocence and that of their Order: William even denied using the words of absolution when forgiving errant Templars for their transgression of the Rule. He was sent to the Tower of London to await the Pope's mercy and died there in February 1313. Imbert Blanke was sentenced to 'be shut up in the most vile prison bound in double irons, and there be kept until it was otherwise ordained, and meanwhile to be visited for the purpose of seeing if he wished to confess to anything further'.[352] He too died in prison.

On Saturday 16 October 1311, after a year's delay, an ecumenical Council of the Catholic Church assembled at Vienne. This city on the Rhône, only twenty kilometres or so south of Lyons, had been built among the ruins of its Roman past. The Roman amphitheatre on the slopes of Mount Pipet could seat more than 13,000 spectators and the Temple dedicated to the Emperor Augustus was now used as a church. It was to Vienne that the Emperor Augustus had exiled Archelaus, the son of King Herod; and here that the unlovely Blandina had died a martyr for Christ – 'after the whips, after the beasts, after the griddle, she was finally dropped into a basket and thrown to a bull'. Another martyr of the time, a Roman officer called Maurice, had been executed upstream at Augaune in Switzerland for refusing to sacrifice to pagan gods. It was in the great cathedral on the banks of the Rhône, dedicated to this saint, that Pope Clement V welcomed the fathers from all over Christendom and opened the first session of the Council.

The turnout was disappointing. Pope Clement had summoned bishops and princes from throughout Christendom, including the four patriarchs of the Eastern Church, but of the 161 prelates invited more than a third had made their excuses, sending delegates in their stead. Those bishops who attended did so with little enthusiasm: the town was overcrowded, decent lodging consequently hard to find, and at that time of year, as the Bishop of Valencia complained to King James II of Aragon, 'the land is cold beyond measure'.

No kings appeared for the first six months of its deliberations even though the recovery of the Holy Land, one of the three items on the Council's agenda, was very much their concern. The second item, the reform of the Church, was there almost as a matter of course but the zeal for cleansing the Church of corruption that had animated earlier councils was hard to sustain with a pope who had appointed four of his relatives to the College of Cardinals and used every possible device to squeeze money out of the faithful. Cynicism was the prevailing sentiment among those who attended the Council: a French chronicler, Jean of Saint-Victor, wrote that 'it was said by many that the council was created for the purpose of extracting money'.[353]

The third item on the Council's agenda was the Order of the Temple. To Pope Clement, it was imperative that the Council should decide upon dissolution and to this end he had been gathering all the evidence from the enquiries in different countries, urging the use of torture where they did not elicit the requisite confessions from the accused. This had taken much longer than he had anticipated, and had been the reason for the postponement of the Council for a year. As late as the summer of 1311, many of the reports were not yet in. When they did arrive, and were studied by the Pope and his advisers in the Priory of Grazean, they were far from satisfactory. Only those from France contained credible confessions; those from outside France, in particular from England, Aragon and Cyprus, could only come up with hearsay evidence from non-Templars to give substance to the accusations.

In addition to preparing summaries of these reports to present to the Council, Pope Clement asked two of his cardinals to write opinions as to what should be done about the Temple: one was James Duèze, a fellow Gascon, now Bishop of Avignon, and the other William Le Maire, the Bishop of Angers. Both judged that the Order's guilt was proven and that it should therefore be suppressed, not by a vote in the Council but by the Pope in his capacity as head of the Church – *de plenitudine potestatis*. They rejected the objections 'that the Order ought to be given a defence, nor should so noble a member of the Church be cut off from its body without the rigour of justice and great discussion'; but such views were clearly prevalent outside the Papal Curia and the circles loyal to the King of France. King James II of Aragon was told by his representative at the Council that 'on the basis of what we have heard from cardinals and clergymen, it is not possible to condemn the Order as a whole, since there is no evidence of guilt on the part of the Order'. The Cistercian abbot, James of Thérines, wondered whether men of noble birth who had risked their lives to defend the Holy Land could really be heretics, and he drew attention to many inconsistencies in the inquisitorial proceedings. Walter of Guisborough, an English cleric, wrote that 'most of the prelates stood by the Templars, except for the prelates from France who, it would seem, did not dare to act otherwise for fear of the king, the source of all this scandal'.[354]

Clement was in a difficult position. He had formally invited the Templars to come to Vienne to defend the Order but clearly did not expect them to do so. However, late in October, to his astonishment, seven Templars presented themselves before the Council saying that they were there to defend the Order and that between 1,500 and 2,000 of their fellow Templars were in the vicinity ready to support them.

Pope Clement ordered that they be detained, and asked the Council to form a committee of fifty to decide whether or not the Templars should be allowed to defend the Order; if so, whether it was only those who had appeared before the Council or whether the Templars from all over Christendom should choose a proctor? And, if that proved too difficult, whether the Pope should nominate one to act for them? The conclusion of this commission was, by a large majority, that the Templars should be allowed to mount a defence. Only the French bishops close to King Philip, those of Rheims, Sens and Rouen, dissented.

This decision was all the more extraordinary in that conditions in Vienne were deteriorating, with a scarcity of food leading to high prices and the spread of disease to the deaths of a number of the Council fathers. The stubbornness of the commission in such circumstances exasperated Pope Clement V and enraged King Philip of France. To exert pressure on the Council, Philip resorted to the tactic he had used four years earlier by summoning the French Estates to meet in February – not at Tours but at Lyons, merely twenty kilometres up river.

The Pope, still dreading that Philip might return to the attack against Pope Boniface VIII, and desperate to get a new crusade under way, was in constant correspondence with the King and on 17 February received a secret and high-powered delegation consisting of Philip's son, Louis of Navarre, the counts of Boulogne and Saint-Pol, and his principal ministers – Enguerrand of Marigny, William of Plaisans and William of Nogaret. Together with the inner circle of curial cardinals, they conferred with the Pope on how to proceed.

Pressure was applied for a quick resolution from another source: King James II of Aragon was emphatic that the Order of the Temple must be dissolved and its properties in his kingdom be made over to the Spanish Order of Calatrava. The disposal of the Temple's wealth seems to have been a sticking point in the negotiations between the Pope and the French King: Philip, still holding out for the same kind of deal as King James II, wrote to the Pope from Mâcon, merely sixty miles north on the River Saône, 'burning with zeal for the orthodox faith and in case so great an injury done to Christ should remain unpunished, we affectionately, devotedly and humbly ask Your Holiness that you should suppress the aforesaid Order and wish to create anew another Military Order, on which be conferred the goods of the above-mentioned Order with its rights, honours and responsibilities'.

Knowing that King Philip had one of his own sons in mind as Grand Master for such a new order, Pope Clement remained surprisingly firm on the question, insisting that if the Temple was to be dissolved, its possessions should pass to the Hospital. To have done with the whole matter, King Philip decided to compromise, promising to accept whatever the Pope decided, reserving only 'whatever rights remain to us, the prelates, barons, nobles and various others in our kingdom'.

Still Pope Clement dithered but on 20 March his mind was made up for him by the arrival in Vienne of King Philip himself, accompanied by his two brothers, three sons and a strong force of armed men. Two days later, Clement held a secret consistory in which his special commission on the Order of the Temple was asked to revise its ruling. Seeing that the game was up, and possibly bribed or brow-beaten by the French, a majority of the prelates voted for the Order's suppression – a decision, in the opinion of one of the few dissenters, the Bishop of Valencia, 'against reason and justice'.

On 3 April, the Council fathers assembled in the cathedral of Saint-Maurice to listen to a homily preached by Pope Clement on Psalm 1, verse 5: 'The wicked will not stand firm when Judgement comes, nor sinners when the virtuous assemble.' The supreme pontiff sat enthroned with, on one side on a slightly lower pedestal, King Philip of France, and on the other King Philip's son, the King of Navarre. After the homily, and before the proceedings commenced, the convenor of the session announced that, under pain of excommunication, no one was permitted to speak at this session except with the permission of, or at the request of, the Pope.

Pope Clement now read out the bull, *Vox in excelso*, abolishing the Order of the Temple. The bull was carefully worded to avoid an outright condemnation of the Order as such: it was suppressed 'not by way of a judicial sentence, but by way of provision or apostolic ordinance' because of the 'infamy, suspicion, noisy insinuation and other things above which have been brought against the Order'. It mentioned certain incontestable facts – 'the secret and clandestine reception of the brothers of this order, and the difference of many of these brothers from the general custom, life and habits of others of Christ's faithful'; but also accepted as established the 'many horrible things' that had been done 'by very many brothers of this Order ... who have lapsed into the sin of wicked apostasy against the Lord Jesus Christ himself, the crime of detestable idolatry, the execrable outrage of the Sodomites...'

The text was self-justificatory, reminding the faithful that 'the Roman Church had sometimes caused other illustrious Orders to be suppressed from causes incomparably less than those mentioned above, even without blame being attached to the brothers'. It was even apologetic: the Pope's decision had been reached 'not without bitterness and sadness of heart'. However, the Council fathers were not asked to agree or disagree with the Pope's ruling: the Order of the Temple was abolished

by an irrevocable and perpetually valid decree, and we subject it to perpetual prohibition with the approval of the Holy council, strictly forbidding anyone to presume to enter the said Order in the future, or to receive or wear its habit, or to act as a Templar. Which if anyone acts against this, he will incur the sentence of excommunication *ipso facto*.

By a subsequent bull, *Ad providam*, published on 2 May, the Templars' property was transferred to the Hospitallers, 'who are ever placing their lives in jeopardy beyond the seas'. An exception was made of the Templars' holdings in Aragon, Castile, Portugal and Mallorca whose disposal was to be decided at a later date.

In the event, the three kings principally concerned – Edward II of England, James II of Aragon, and above all Philip IV of France – though they publicly agreed to the Pope's plans for the Temple's riches, all ensured that a proportion remained in their hands or the hands of their vassals. Edward II had already farmed out some of the Templar's properties and warned the Hospital not to take advantage of *Ad providam* to 'usurp' Templar holdings. Litigation by the Hospital and papal legates continued until 1336. The London Temple was eventually given over to the use of lawyers: the Temple church remains standing to this day.

In Aragon, King James insisted that the security of his kingdom depended upon royal possession of the Templar holdings: the Templars' resistance to arrest in 1308 had demonstrated the dangers of an armed force that did not owe its first loyalty to the King. Here again, it was only after several years of negotiation that a settlement was reached. A new military order was created based on Montesa in Valencia which was to be subject to the Master of Calatrava in conjunction with the Cistercian Abbot of Stas. In the rest of Aragon, Templar properties were to go to the Hospital but, before taking office, the Hospitaller Castellan of Amposta was to do homage to the King. The Templars themselves who were reconciled with the Church continued to live in the Order's preceptories, or went to other convents and monasteries, where they lived on pensions paid out of the Temple's resources. The dissolution of the Order did not mean that they were dispensed from their vows.

As in Yorkshire, however, the former Templars in Aragon found it difficult to switch from a military to a monastic routine. Some absconded from the monasteries, abandoned their habit and returned to the secular world. Whether disillusioned by what had occurred, or simply liberated from the strict discipline of the Order, some ex-Templars turned mercenary and took wives. In some instances it was suggested that the pensions paid were too large, enabling them to lead indolent lives. One former Templar, Berenguer of Bellvís, kept a mistress; another was charged with rape but, significantly, no charges of sodomy are extant.

Complaints against former Templars led Pope Clement V's successor, Pope John XXII, to make repeated attempts to persuade former Templars to return to the religious life. In a letter to the Archbishop of Tarragona, the Pope asked him to ensure that they 'did not involve themselves in wars or secular business' or wear luxurious clothes. Care should be taken that there should never be more than two former Templars in any one monastery and, if they should refuse to return to the enclosed life, then they should be deprived of their pension. There were some cases where this sanction was put into effect, but overall 'the survivors were not beset by financial hardship, even if some were leading a frustrating existence; and as their numbers dwindled probably the Church's concern over them grew less and they were left to end their days with little interference'.[355]

In Portugal, King Diniz was permitted to found a new military order, the Order of Christ, and endow it with the Templar possessions: the magnificent headquarters at Tomar with its rotunda remains standing today. King Sancho of Mallorca reached a compromise with the Curia, transferring Templar property to the Hospital in exchange for an annual rent. In Castile, some of the Templar holdings were seized by the King, others by barons, and some by the military orders of Ucles and Calatrava: the King's failure to ensure the transfer to the Hospital provoked a protest from the Papacy as late as 1366. A similar pattern is seen in Italy, Germany and Bohemia where local rulers seized a proportion of the Templar holdings, leaving to the Hospital what remained. In Hildesheim the Templars resisted and were ejected by force. The Dominican Order of Preachers, which ran the Inquisition, was given the Templar houses in Vienna, Strasbourg, Esslingen and Worms. In the Kingdom of Naples and Provence it was five years before King Charles disgorged the Templars' property. Only in Cyprus was the transfer swift and unproblematic, no doubt because of its position on the front line.

In France King Philip IV had been persuaded by his brother, Charles of Valois, and his chief minister, Enguerrand of Marigny, that capitulating to Pope Clement on the question of the Temple's property was a price worth paying to secure the definitive dissolution of the Order. However, the King fought a rearguard action, writing to the Pope that he agreed to the transfer to the Hospital on condition that the Pope re-formed the Order, and it would be made only 'after the deduction of necessary expenses for the custody and administration of these goods'. Like his son-in-law, King Edward II, he also reserved the rights 'of the king, the prelates, barons, nobles, and all other persons of the kingdom who had a share in the aforesaid property'. In the event, the Hospital had to pay for its rights: 200,000 *livres tournois* were transferred to the royal treasury in Paris by the Prior of the Hospital in Venice, supposedly to indemnify the Crown for the loss of treasure that had been deposited with the Temple in Paris. Even after this sweetener, a complete transfer did not take place; a further 60,000 *livres tournois* were advanced by the Hospitaller Prior in Venice in 1316 to cover the Crown's expenses in bringing the Templars to trial; and in 1318 another 50,000 in final settlement, leaving the Hospital, in the short term, worse off than before.

This was not the only profit to accrue to the King of France as a result of the Council of Vienne. On 3 April 1312, less than two weeks after he had dissolved the Order of the Temple, Pope Clement V consummated the ambition that had been the objective of his tortuous policies since his pontificate began. Preaching before the assembled prelates of Christendom in the cathedral of Saint-Maurice, and taking as his text a verse from the Book of Proverbs, 'the desire of the righteous shall be granted', the Supreme

Pontiff proclaimed a new crusade. It was not to be a *passagium particulare* as most had counselled, but the *passagium generale* whose sole proponent had been the former Grand Master of the Temple, James of Molay, now languishing in chains. It was to be led by King Philip of France but paid for by the Church through a ten-per-cent tax on all ecclesiastical income over the next six years.

In the following year, at a ceremony of great solemnity held in Paris, King Philip the Fair took the Cross. He received it from the hands of the Papal Nuncio, Cardinal Nicholas of Fréauville, and was followed by his three sons, his son-in-law, King Edward II of England, and many of the nobility of both kingdoms. Their differences behind them, the grandson of Saint Louis and the Gascon Pope were at last united in the quest to recover the Holy Land from the infidel. The two rivers of piety and chivalry converged to form an irresistible torrent; and to celebrate this great occasion, the city of Paris was bedecked with bright banners, the air was filled with the sound of music and gaiety, and festivities of an unprecedented splendour continued for more than a week.

There was only one piece of unfinished business; a short distance from the revels, the senior officers of the former Order of the Temple waited in the King's dungeons for the judgement of Pope Clement V. The former Grand Master, James of Molay, had persistently refused to give a final account of himself to anyone but the Pope, and seemed convinced that when he came face to face with the only authority that the Church had put over him, he would surely vindicate his own honour and that of his Order.

Such a personal encounter was never to take place. Towards the end of December 1313, Pope Clement appointed a commission of three cardinals to decide on the fate of the Templar leaders – the Legate, Nicholas of Fréauville, Arnaud of Auch and Arnaud Nouvel. On 18 March 1314, these three cardinals called a council of doctors of theology and canon law to meet at Paris in the presence of Philip of Marigny, the Archbishop of Sens. Before this council were arraigned James of Molay, Hugh of Pairaud, Geoffrey of Gonneville and Geoffrey of Charney. Judgement was then given that 'since these four, without any exception, had publicly and openly confessed the crimes which had been imputed to them and had persisted in these confessions and seemed finally to persist in them ... they were adjudged to be thrust into harsh and perpetual imprisonment'.[356]

Two of the accused, Hugh of Pairaud and Geoffrey of Gonneville, submitted to this judgement without protest; but the severity of the sentence, coming at the end of seven years of incarceration, was finally too much for James of Molay. Now an old man, well into his seventies, what profit was there in submission if the reward was a lingering death? The Pope had betrayed him; all he could hope for now was justice from God. Therefore, just when the three cardinals felt that the case of the Temple was finally settled, James of Molay, together with the Preceptor of Normandy, Geoffrey of Charney, stood finally to retract their confessions and insist that both they and their Order were wholly innocent of all the charges.

This turn of events dumbfounded the cardinals, and threw the carefully choreographed finale into confusion. The two recalcitrant knights were taken away by the royal marshal while news of what had happened was hurried to the King. No sooner had it reached him than King Philip summoned the lay members of his Council where it was decided that the two knights, as relapsed heretics, must suffer the prescribed fate. That very evening, 'around the hour of vespers', James of Molay and Geoffrey of Charney were taken to a small island in the River Seine called the Ile-des-Javiaux to be burned at the stake.

Before they died, it was later said, James of Molay made one last demand of Pope Clement and King Philip: he summoned them to appear before the year was out before the tribunal of God. It was also reported that 'they were seen to be prepared to sustain the fire with easy mind' which 'brought from all who saw them much admiration and surprise for the constancy of their death and final denial'. The two old men were then tied to the stake and burned to death. Later, under cover of dark, friars of the Augustinian monastery on the bank of the river and other pious people came to collect the charred bones of the dead Templars as relics of saints.

As the cynics at the Council of Vienne had predicted, Pope Clement V's projected crusade never took place. Pope Clement died on 20 April 1314, a little over a month after the death of James of Molay. The inventory of the few possessions found in his bedchamber included 'two small books in the "romance" language, covered with tanned leather with an iron lock ... containing the Rule of the Templars'.[357] King Philip the Fair followed him to the grave on 29 November of the same year after an accident out hunting. The large sums of money that had been raised to pay for a crusade were either swallowed up by the French exchequer or used for the private purposes of the deceased Pope. In his will, Pope Clement V left 300,000 florins to his nephew, Betrand of Got, Viscount of Lomagne, in return for a vow to go on crusade, a vow never fulfilled. As an anonymous chronicler put it at the time, 'the pope guarded the money, and his cousin, the marquis, had his share; and the king and all who had accepted the Cross remained here; and the Saracens live in peace there, and I believe they can continue to sleep in security'.

The Verdict of History

What has been the verdict of history on the Templars? From the time of their trial, opinion was divided on whether or not they had really committed the crimes ascribed to them. Dante Alighieri thought they were the innocent victims of King Philip IV's greed while Ramón Lull, the Mallorcan poet, mystic, missionary and crusade theoretician, though initially dubious, came to accept that the charges made against the Order were true. However, both were partisan: Dante had been expelled from Florence by the party backed by Charles of Anjou while Lull, like Philip the Fair, was fanatically determined upon the merger of the two major military orders.

In the centuries that followed, retrospective judgements of the Temple were similarly distorted by political considerations: partisans of the Roman popes and the French kings were unwilling to concede that their sovereigns' predecessors had perpetrated a gross injustice while democrats and constitutionalists tended to portray the Templars as the victims of tyranny. Thus, in the early sixteenth century, in *De occulta philosophia* by Henry Cornelius Agrippa, the Templars were coupled with witches while later in the same century the French political thinker, Jean Bodin, cites them, together with the Jews, as an example of a vulnerable minority marginalised and then expropriated by a rapacious king.

In the seventeenth and eighteenth centuries, a presumption of guilt in the case of the Templars was used as a stick with which to beat the Roman Catholic Church by Protestants and sceptics alike. The Anglican divine, Thomas Fuller, wrote that it was 'partly their vitiousnesse, and partly their wealth' that caused the Templars' 'final extirpation'; while Edward Gibbon, in his *History of the Decline and Fall of the Roman Empire*, referred to 'the pride, avarice, and corruption of these Christian soldiers'.[358] It was such a perception of the Templars that inspired the Templar characters of Sir Walter Scott.

However, with the advent of the Enlightenment in the seventeenth century there emerged a third view of the Templars as neither orthodox nor heretical Christians but rather as the high priests of an ancient and occult religion that predated the birth of Christ. It might be thought that an intellectual movement that prided itself on supplanting superstition with common sense would blow away the cobwebs of obfuscation that surrounded the story of the Templars: but the Enlightenment, as Peter Partner pointed out in his book on the Templars, *The Murdered Magicians*,

> was far from being the simple exercise of the rational faculties which some of its protagonists liked to suggest. The transformation of ideas about the Templars during the eighteenth century shows how far from stern scientific rationalism the men of the Enlightenment could wander. In the very body of Church history which was the prime target for rationalisation and demystification, eighteenth-century men found the Templars, and turned them into a wild fantasy which for mystagogy and obfuscation equalled anything that the old Catholic historiography could offer. So successful was the enterprise that to this day it is impossible to approach the Templars without encountering the remnants, or even the full and gaudy robes, of eighteenth-century prejudice.[359]

The chief agents of this 'Templarism', the metamorphosis of the Templars from history into myth, were the Freemasons, secret confraternities pledged to mutual support whose imprecise deism made them inimical to the Roman Catholic Church. They were not the first to make the Templars characters in fiction: even before the Order's dissolution, Templars had started to figure in epics and romances, frequently as the champions of lovers, consoling them if their passion is unrequited, facilitating its con-summation if it is not. Far more than the Hospitallers or the Teutonic Knights, the Templars captured the imagination of chroniclers and poets alike. The Knights of the Grail in Wolfram von Eschenbach's *Parzival* are depicted as Templars, but 'there is no evidence in his poem that he, a poor German knight, possessed any secret knowledge about the order of the Temple, which at that time still held very little property in Germany, and most of whose members were French'.[360]

The Freemasons' hypothesis was quite as fanciful as *Parzifal*. Andrew

Ramsay, a Scottish Jacobite exiled in France who was Chancellor of the French Grand Lodge in the 1730s, claimed that the first Freemasons had been stonemasons in the crusader states who had learned the secret rituals and gained the special wisdom of the ancient world. Ramsay made no specific claim for the Templars, probably because he did not wish to antagonise his host, the King of France; but in Germany another Scottish exile, George Frederick Johnson, concocted a myth that transformed 'the Templars ... from their ostensible status of unlearned and fanatical soldier-monks to that of enlightened and wise knightly seers, who had used their sojourn in the East to recover its profoundest secrets, and to emancipate themselves from medieval Catholic credulity'.[361]

According to the German Freemasons, the Grand Masters of the Order had learned the secrets and acquired the treasure of the Jewish Essenes which were handed down from one to the other. James of Molay, on the night of his execution, had sent the Count of Beaujeu to the crypt of the Temple Church in Paris to recover this treasure which included the seven-branched candelabra seized by the Emperor Titus, the crown of the Kingdom of Jerusalem and a shroud. It is undisputed that in evidence given at the trial of the Templars, a sergeant, John of Châlons, maintained that Gérard of Villiers, the Preceptor in France, had been tipped-off about his imminent arrest and so had escaped on eighteen galleys with the Templars' treasure. If this were so, what happened to this treasure? George Frederick Johnson said that it had been taken to Scotland, one of his followers specifying the Isle of Mull.

Speculation did not end with the eighteenth century; in fact it has never been more feverish than it is today, creating, in the words of Malcolm Barber, Britain's foremost Templar historian, 'a very active little industry, profitable to scientists, art historians, journalists, publishers, and television pundits alike'.[362] Starting with the esoteric claims of the Freemasons, the Templars are claimed to have been the guardians of the Holy Grail which is in turn the chalice used by Christ in the Last Supper, the blood line of the Merovingian kings descended from the union of Christ with Mary Magdalene,[363] or simply the Templars' most precious relic, the Shroud of Turin.[364]

Spare facts are fleshed out with speculation. In *Les Templiers. Ces Grands Seigneurs aux Blancs Manteaux* (1997), the French writer Michel Lamy goes back beyond the founding of the Poor Fellow-Soldiers of Jesus Christ in

1118 to the Saxon Cistercian and Abbot of Citeaux, Stephen Harding, the friend and mentor of Bernard of Clairvaux. Lamy reminds us how Abbot Stephen sought the help of Jewish rabbis in his translations of the books of the Old Testament from Hebrew. 'What reason was there for such a sudden interest in Hebrew texts?' he asks. According to Lamy, they revealed that a hidden treasure lay buried beneath the Temple Mount. This is why the lay patron of the Cistercians, Count Hugh of Champagne, went to Jerusalem and instigated his vassal, Hugh of Payns, to establish his order of Poor Fellow-Soldiers of Jesus Christ on the Temple Mount: 'One may think that the documents probably brought to Palestine by Hugh of Champagne (who no doubt discovered them in the company of Hugh of Payns) were not without some kind of connection to the place which later became the dwelling place of the Templars.'[365]

The same hypothesis is found in two books by British writers, *The Holy Blood and the Holy Grail* by Michael Baigent, Richard Leigh and Henry Lincoln (1982), and *The Head of God* by Keith Laidler (1998): the slow pace of recruitment in the early years of the Order is explained by the need to confine this search for the buried treasure to the few initiates. 'The Templars' apparent lack of activity in their formative years', wrote Laidler, 'seems to have been due to some form of covert project beneath the Temple of Solomon or nearby, an operation that could not be revealed to any but a few high-ranking nobles.'[366]

To these writers, there is no doubt that something extraordinary was found. Was it, asks Michel Lamy,

> the Ark of the Covenant? A means of communicating with external powers; gods, elementals, genies, extra-terrestrials or other things? A secret about the holy use and so one might say the magic of architecture? The key of a mystery linked to the life of Christ and his message? The Grail? The means to recognise the places where the communication with heaven as with hell is made easy at the risk of delivering Satan or Lucifer?

No, claims Laidler: what they found was no less than the embalmed head of Christ.

This was the head known as Baphomet that was supposedly worshipped in secret by the Templars. If it was not found under the Temple by Hugh of Payns, then it may have been brought to France by Mary Magdalene where it came into the possession of the Cathars and was held in their fortress of

Montségur. When it was about to fall to the crusaders, three *parfaits* escaped with their treasure. 'But what was this treasure of the Cathars? How much gold and silver could three perfecti carry? It could not have been monetary ... It had to be something else, something that had been held in Montségur until the very last moment, something that had been essential for the ritual that took place on the vernal equinox, the day before the castle capitulated' – in other words, the head of Christ. And where could the fugitive Cathars take it but to 'the only place in France that was beyond the reach of the king, an organisation that was to all intents and purposes autonomous and which shared essentially the same Gnostic world-view as the Cathars: the Order of the Temple'.[367]

Thus, when Gérard of Villiers fled from the Paris Temple in 1307, he took this relic-to-end-all-relics with him. The fleet of Templar galleys that sailed from La Rochelle split up, half going south to Portugal where they were later absorbed into King Diniz's Order of Christ, the other half sailing north to Scotland where they weighed anchor in the Firth of Forth. South of Edinburgh was the castle of Rosslyn held by a family, the Saint-Clairs, with long links with the Templars, where the chapel was 'an alternative Temple of Solomon'. It is here, beneath a pillar, that the fugitive Templars buried 'the Head of God'.

Intriguing though such speculations may be, they betray by their use of language the lack of a plausible historical foundation: 'the answer would seem to lie ...'; 'it seems very likely that ...'; 'it is known that ...'; 'could well have ...'; 'it seems certain that ...' 'After some research', writes Andrew Sinclair in his book *The Discovery of the Grail*, 'these fantasists put forward a hypothesis. Was Christ or the Grail buried under a mountain in the south of France? Did Jesus marry Magdalene and provide the blood line of the Merovingians? Within a few pages, the assertion becomes the actual, the idea is changed into the proof ...'[368] Or, as Peter Partner succinctly puts it in relation to the Templars, 'Templarism ... was a belief manufactured by charlatans for their dupes.'[369]

The enigma of the Order of the Temple has not been left wholly to the charlatans but has also been the subject of serious study by professional historians. The French Revolution of 1789 which brought down the two institutions that had a vested interest in the Templars' guilt – the monarchy and the Catholic Church – opened the way for a less partial investigation.

The fact that the French royal family were imprisoned in the keep of the Paris Temple, and from there went to their execution, was seen by the Templars' defenders as a symbolic revenge for the death of James of Molay: in March 1808, a requiem Mass was held on the anniversary of his death. In the same year, the Temple *donjon* was demolished: it had become a place of pilgrimage of royalists loyal to the memory of their martyred king.

Three years before, in 1805, a play entitled *Les Templiers* by a lawyer from Provence, François Raynouard, which maintained the innocence of the Templars, had been staged at the Théâtre français. The play was of sufficient interest to Napoleon for him to compose a critique while on campaign for the benefit of his chief of police. When the papal archives were brought to Paris in 1810, Raynouard was allowed to look for documents that might throw new light on the Templars' trial. The material he uncovered proved nothing conclusive, but shifted the balance in favour of the Order's inno-cence. It certainly 'gave no support to those holding dark suspicions of the Templar magical practices or of their Gnostic religious rites'.[370]

Later in the nineteenth century, however, the German historian Hans Prutz, after an exhaustive study of the Templar depositions, concluded that many of the Templars had been contaminated by Catharism and were guilty of devil-worship.[371] On the other hand, the American historian of the Inquisition, Henry Charles Lea, writing about ten years after Prutz, decided that the Templars were almost certainly innocent: none had been prepared to die for their heretical beliefs; no concrete evidence of devil-worship had been found; and the confessions, made under torture, merely dem-onstrated, as Peter of Bologna had said at the time, 'the helplessness of the victim, no matter how highly placed, when once the fatal charge of heresy was pressed against him, and was pressed through the agency of the Inqui-sition'.[372]

Experience of Stalin's show trials in the twentieth century has dem-onstrated the efficacy not just of torture, but of lesser means of coercion such as sleep deprivation, in inducing people to give false evidence against themselves. Philip the Fair's gaolers showed the same brutality as the agents of the NKVD and the Gestapo; and his propagandists, like William of Nogaret and William of Plaisans, showed a talent worthy of Goebbels. The exaggeration and perversion of what actually happened can persuade the subject of interrogation, particularly one 'insufficiently instructed to be able to see the difference between ... the inoffensive and the criminal',[373] to alter his perception of what he remembered. Thus the veneration of images of Christ or John the Baptist can be presented as worship of an idol; the cord tied around the waist, common practice among the Templars, is perverted from a pious talisman into a diabolical charm; and the symbolic kiss that was common as 'the climax in sequences of actions in both monastic and secular life'[374] becomes the indulgence of homosexual passion.

Was the Temple a hotbed of homosexuality? Inevitably, in the decades of the late twentieth century during which attitudes towards homosexuality in Europe and America have changed from condemnation to tolerance, it appears almost 'homophobic' to suggest that many of the Templars were not gay. Thus the French historian, Jean Favier, judged that the 'absence of women, the influence of the east, all contributed to the fact that sodomy had entered deeply into the customs of the Temple'. And the American historian, Joseph Strayer, concurs, believing that homosexuality is always found in all-male institutions: perhaps he was thinking of the British public schools.

Are these twentieth-century assumptions useful in reaching a verdict on this particular charge? There can be no doubt that homosexuality was not unknown in medieval society: it was rife in the court of William Rufus and while it now seems that Richard the Lionheart was not homosexual, the Emperor Frederick II's promiscuity was alleged to have embraced boys as well as girls; and his Seneschal in the Holy Land, Richard Filangieri, was accused by his Ibelin enemies of a homosexual liaison with the imperial *bailli* in Acre, Philip of Maugustel.[375]

That sodomy was found among the Templars is also established by the case history cited in the 'Details on Penances' in their Rule.[376] However, it is significant that the 'the deed was so offensive' that the Master and 'a group of worthy men of the house' decided that it should not be brought to chapter: and this same repugnance is found in the willingness of many of the Templars, among them James of Molay, to confess to almost anything but sodomy. If, therefore, one can avoid the distortions of late-twentieth-century prejudice, one can be fairly certain that there was no institutionalised sodomy in the Temple; and at the same time reject the accusations of heresy, blasphemy and idolatry as unproven. There is, wrote Malcolm Barber in a recent paper, 'The Trial of the Templars Revisited', a 'fairly general consensus among modern historians that the Templars were not guilty as charged'.[377]

What should be the wider verdict of history on the Knights of the Order of the Temple? To Peter Partner who, in *The Murdered Magicians*, so effectively salvaged the Templars' reputation from both Philip the Fair's diabolism and the 'mystagogy and obfuscation' of the Masons, we are left with some-thing quite dull. 'The most striking characteristics of the medieval Templars was their ordinariness; they represented the common man, and not the uncommon visionary.' The fall of the Order came about as a result of their 'mediocrity and lack of nerve ... most, including their leaders, at the moment of trial proved to have nothing much to say'.[378]

In some ways, this verdict on the Templars is quite as damning as that of the Masons or Philip the Fair. Were they really mediocre? Certainly, if one compares the raw material of a Templar, a Frankish knight such as the Count of Eu, with a Muslim knight such as Usamah Ibn-Munqidh, the Muslim appears to have many more of the qualities that appeal to us today. Usamah is not only pious, brave and a skilled hunter but he is also a poet. The Count of Eu, as described by John of Joinville, rather than write poetry, 'rigged up a miniature ballistic machine with which he could throw stones into my tent. He would watch us as we were having our meal, adjust his machine to suit the length of my table, and then let fly at us, breaking our pots and glasses,'[379] and he slaughtered Joinville's poultry – the kind of crude horseplay that might be found in some officers' messes in the British Army today.

Were the warrior monks of the Temple any different from knights like the Count of Eu? To what extent did the religious aspect of their vocation elevate them above their kind? If the Templar knight showed the same prodigious courage in battle as his secular counterpart, he also shared his lack of learning and sophistication. In a satirical poem written in the late thirteenth century by the Flemish troubadour, Jacquemart Giélée, *Renart le nouvel*, the Templar is portrayed as considerably less sophisticated than the Hospitaller: he 'is not a trained speaker, his argument is simple and unskilfully delivered, repeating again and again: "we are defenders of the Holy Church", and emphasising the danger to Europe from the Muslims ...'[380] – an image that matches almost exactly the impression we gain over the centuries from James of Molay. But this lack of sophistication does not exclude a certain sanctity. The high regard for the Templars of the Franciscan, John Peckham, Archbishop of Canterbury at around the time Giélée wrote his satire, and 'a man of great integrity and personal austerity', suggests a high standard of holiness in the Order.

Thus, a final verdict on the Templars must depend upon our judgement of Catholic Christianity, and in particular of its long war against Islam, the crusades. By and large, the crusades – like the Inquisition – are perceived today to have been a bad thing. Here again we encounter Peter Partner's 'full and gaudy robes ... of eighteenth-century prejudice'. Diderot, in his entry on the crusades in his *Encyclopaedia*, described the Holy Sepulchre as 'a piece of rock not worth a single drop of human blood'; to him, the crusaders were motivated by greed, 'imbecility and false zeal'. To the Scottish philosopher, David Hume, they were 'the most signal and most durable monument of human folly that has yet appeared in any age or nation'.[381]

This judgement has descended through Edward Gibbon to the most renowned historian of the crusades in our own day, Sir Steven Runciman: his verdict at the end of his monumental work was that the Holy War waged by the Catholic Church was 'nothing more than a long act of intolerance in the name of God, which is the sin against the Holy Ghost'.[382] Runciman was particularly outraged by the sack of Constantinople by the Latins, declaring that 'there never was a greater crime against humanity than the Fourth Crusade' – a curious judgement, as the historian Christopher Tyerman points out, to make less than ten years after the close of World War II. But Runciman is not alone. To the Israeli historian, Joshua Prawer, the Kingdom of Jerusalem was an early example of European colonialism; and to the theologian, Michael Prior, the crusades are a striking example of how 'the Bible has been used as an agent of oppression'.[383]

It is only more recently that historians have taken a second look into the minds of the crusaders and have reached a less damning conclusion. 'Crusade historians', wrote Jonathan Riley-Smith, the Dixie Professor of Ecclesiastical History at the University of Cambridge, 'suddenly discovered ... the fundamental weakness of the arguments for a general materialistic motivation and the paucity of the evidence on which they rested became much clearer. The adventurous younger sons began at last to ride off the scene. Few historians appear to believe in them any longer.'[384]

The truth which has emerged from recent research is that the crusader frequently sold or mortgaged all his worldly wealth in the hope of a purely spiritual reward. Unlike the Muslim *jihad*, the crusade was always voluntary. For a secular knight, a period of adventure and subsequent chivalrous renown may have been an inducement to take the Cross: but for the knight who joined a military order, the austere rule of the barracks-cum-cloister was quite likely to lead either to a long period in captivity or to an early death.

From the very start, the rate of attrition in the Templar Order was high. Six of the twenty-three Templar Grand Masters died in battle or in captivity. The year's postulancy originally envisaged was abandoned because of the urgent need for men to serve in the East. In evidence at their trial, it was said that 20,000 Templars died in Outremer. Some were killed in battle but others, after being taken captive, chose to die rather than renounce their faith. 'To appreciate how startling it is to find these martyrs,' wrote Jonathan Riley-Smith of those who went on crusade,

> one should remember that martyrdom, involving the voluntary accept-ance of death for the sake of the faith and reflecting the death of Christ, is the supreme act of love of which a Christian is capable and is the perfect example of a Christian death. It is the martyr's gift of his own life and is so great an act of merit that it justifies him at once in God's sight.[385]

From the Christian perspective, one could therefore apply to the Templars the words of John in the Book of Revelation: 'These are the people who have been through the great persecution, and ... they have washed their robes white again in the blood of the Lamb.'[386]

Of course, the Knights of the Temple also took life, but here again there is a common misconception about the motivation of those who fought the crusade. Because of the anti-Catholic animus dating from the Enlight-enment, and because most histories of the crusades tend to start with the First Crusade, it is common to see it as the first of many waves of aggression of the Christian West against the Islamic East. However, it was Islam, not Christianity, that from its inception promoted conversion through conquest; and even if Christianity, at certain times and in certain places, also baptized at the point of a sword, its growth in its first three centuries to encompass the whole Roman Empire was almost wholly pacific. Therefore, from the time of the Prophet Muhammad's first *razzia*, the Christians' perception was that wars against Islam were waged either in defence of Christendom or to liberate and reconquer lands that were rightfully theirs.

This is explicit in the *Reconquista*, in the preaching of Pope Urban II after the Byzantine defeat at the Battle of Manzikert, and in that of the Dominican Humbert of Romans in the following century. Humbert's appeal 'rested in great part upon the argument that Islam had expanded aggressively at the expense of Christian rulers and that Christian armies had both a right and an obligation to halt Islamic expansion and to repossess the lands that the Muslims had occupied'.[387] The idea that a man could achieve martyrdom when he himself was perpetrating violence was no innovation but is clearly established in Western Christendom from the end of the eighth century.

Why, then, though there are some canonised Hospitallers, are there no Templar saints? This can be partly explained by the self-effacement of the individual knight but also by the involvement of the Church in the Order's end. Its final destruction, as we have seen, the cruel death of a number of its members, was not the work of Muslims but of the forces of coercion of the Inquisition in the service of the 'most Christian' King of France. The two-hundred-year life-span of the Order of the Temple coincides almost exactly with the claim of the Papacy to a paramount sovereignty over the whole world. It is a token of the Order's single-minded devotion to its original charism that, though a multinational force, it was never enlisted by the popes in their constant struggle to enforce their claims against their rivals for universal dominion, the German emperors.

So intent were the popes, however, on winning this contest that they failed to see, until it was too late, the threat posed by the predatory nation-state. The danger posed by Frederick II of Hohenstaufen had been obvious, and his pagan megalomania plain for all to see. But who could have envisaged that the grandson of Saint Louis would be the instrument for the downfall of the Roman pontiffs – a man 'whose religious devotion ... sometimes bordered on mysticism' and 'often dictated his policy even in clear antagonism to royal interests'?[388] Pope Boniface VIII, as he sat on Constantine's throne during the centenary celebrations in 1300, demonstrated the height of papal pretensions: Clement V, only a few years later, declared that he had lost 'the moral, spiritual and authoritative leadership which the papacy had built up in Europe over the centuries of minute, consistent, detailed, dynamic, forward-looking work'.[389]

In England, more than two hundred years later, King Henry VIII was to despoil the monasteries just as King Philip IV of France had despoiled the

Temple, exploiting the self-interest of new social forces; but, unlike King Philip IV, he failed to bend the Pope of his time to his will and repudiated the authority of the Holy See. As with the Enlightenment view of the crusades, so the Whig view of English history sees in this the genesis of the English nation-state. The Reformation which followed in England, Scotland and on the Continent of Europe led to the fragmentation of that unified Christendom which the successors of Saint Peter had tried so long to preserve. The French Revolution in 1789 also despoiled and almost destroyed the Catholic Church, leaving monasteries such as Cîteaux and Molesme in ruins and converting Clairvaux into a prison. Napoleon succeeded where William of Nogaret had failed, in bringing a captive pope to Paris to watch impotently as the Corsican adventurer crowned himself Emperor in the cathedral of Notre-Dame.

With this ceremony the Vicar of Christ was once again humbled by the power of brute force. European history finally abandoned the restraints inherent in Christian aspirations and hurtled towards the modern era. Whether or not the balance of suffering endured by humanity tilts towards the Middle Ages under the weight of the crusades, the Inquisition and the wars of religion, or towards the era of the nation-state under the carnage of the trenches, the gulags and the concentration camps, is for each one of us to decide.

APPENDICES

The Later Crusades

The wars between Christians and Muslims continued for many centuries after the dissolution of the Order of the Temple. In the course of the fourteenth century, the Mamelukes of Egypt were replaced as the principal force driving Islamic expansion by the Ottoman Turks. Named after the Seljuk Emir, Oman, whose fief was to the south of Nicaea in Anatolia, they rapidly expanded in the course of the fourteenth century to conquer the whole of Asia Minor and, bypassing Constantinople via the Dardanelles, swept through Macedonia and Bulgaria to the Danube. The Christian Serbs were defeated at the Battle of Kosovo in 1386.

The Christian imperative then became not the recapture of Jerusalem but the relief of Constantinople. In 1396, a major expeditionary force from western Europe led by King Sigismund of Hungary and Count John of Nevers was annihilated at Nicopolis on the Danube. In 1443, a crusading army summoned by Pope Eugenius IV was defeated at Varna. Ten years later, Constantinople fell to the Ottoman Turks.

This catastrophe for Christendom had the same impact as the fall of Jerusalem more than two centuries before. John Capistrano was sent by Pope Nicholas V to preach a new crusade in Hungary, raising an army which in 1456 defeated a superior Ottoman force besieging Belgrade. However, the respite was only temporary. Belgrade fell in 1521 and the Hungarians were finally defeated at the Battle of Mohács in 1526.

A parallel advance by Islam under the Ottomans took place in the Mediterranean. The Knights of the Hospital lost Rhodes in 1522 and the Latin Kingdom of Cyprus fell in 1571. The victory of a Christian fleet at the Battle of Lepanto in the same year enabled the Venetians to hold on to Crete until 1669. The only advance made by the Christians before the seventeenth century was in Spain: between 1482 and 1492, the *Reconquista* was completed with the fall of the last Islamic principality on the Iberian peninsula, Granada.

From the fourteenth century onwards, the idealism of the early crusades had given way to cold calculations by Christian rulers on the one hand, and a deep cynicism among their subjects on the other. Erasmus, in the sixteenth century, condemned the whole concept of the crusade, and the Reformation which followed wholly undermined the penitential value of crusading by denying the power of popes to remit penances and forgive sins. The principal forces ranged against Islam came from those nations whose interests they threatened: the Venetians in the Mediterranean, the Hapsburgs of Austria in the eastern Europe.

The high tide of Islamic expansion into Christendom which had started in the lifetime of the Prophet in the eighth century came in 1683 when an Ottoman army besieged Vienna, the capital of the Holy Roman Emperor, Leopold of Austria. Neighbouring German states and the Poles under Jan Sobieski formed an army which relieved the siege; and in 1684, a Holy League was formed under the auspices of the Pope to push back the Ottoman advance. In the eighteenth century, Russia took on the championship of the Orthodox Christians living under Muslim rule. Buda was retaken in 1686, Belgrade in 1688, and, by the Peace of Karowicz in 1699, large parts of central Europe and Greece were recovered by the Christian powers. The Serbs, who had remained loyal to the Orthodox Church over five centuries of Ottoman rule, regained their independence under the Treaty of Berlin in 1878. After the Balkan wars of 1912 and 1913, the frontiers of the Ottoman Empire, now the state of Turkey, were pushed back into Thrace where they remain today.

In the nineteenth and twentieth centuries, Spanish, French and Italian colonies were established in North Africa, and Britain became the virtual overlord of Egypt and the Sudan, but these conquests were inspired by mercantile and political rivalry, not by religious zeal. The concept of Christendom had lost its meaning. When General Allenby took possession of Jerusalem after defeating the Turks at Gaza in 1917, he was aware of the historical significance of what he did: a cable from the British War Office said: 'Strongly suggest dismounting at gate. German emperor rode in and the saying went round "a better man than he walked". Advantages of contrast will be obvious.'[390] The 'better man' referred to by the War Office was not Jesus Christ, who entered the city on the back of a donkey, but

Mohammed's father-in-law, the Caliph Umar. General Allenby dismounted and entered the Holy City on foot.

The British rule over Outremer after 1917 was shared by the French who exercised a protectorate over Syria until 1941. In 1947, the British withdrew from Palestine whose Jewish inhabitants, in the following year, proclaimed a Jewish state. Jerusalem was governed by the Hashemite Kingdom of Jordan until June 1967, when it was taken by Israeli forces during the Six-Day War. Its exact status under international law is unresolved. The Temple Mount remains in the hands of the Muslims. The Church of the Holy Sepulchre is shared, often acrimoniously, by six different Christian denominations.

What role was played by the military orders in the later crusades? After the fall of Acre, the Teutonic Knights abandoned the cause of the Holy Land to concentrate on campaigns against the pagan Prussians and Lithuanians on the Baltic. In 1309 they moved their headquarters from Venice to Marienburg south of Danzig and, having absorbed a smaller military order in Livonia, the Sword Brothers, in the thirteenth century, they gained control of the Baltic littoral as far north as the Gulf of Finland. Frequently criticised by the popes in Rome for being more interested in enslaving than converting their pagan captives, they imported peasants from Germany to colonise the conquered Prussian lands and profited from trading as a member of the Hanseatic League. Now that the Holy Land was inaccessible to Western knights, the seasonal campaigns of the Teutonic Knights against the pagan Lithuanians, called *Reisen*, became a fashionable way for European knights to prove their worth. Henry Bolingbroke joined a number of these *Reisen* before seizing the English throne as Henry IV.

In 1386, Jagiełło, the Grand Duke of Lithuania, led his whole people into the Catholic Church and married the Crown Princess of Poland, Jadwiga. In 1410, the armies of this newly unified state defeated the Teutonic Knights at the Battle of Tannenberg: 400 knights and the Grand Master were killed. Thereafter, the Order went into decline – losing its powers on the one hand to the secular Germans who had colonised the country and on the other to their stronger neighbour, the King of Poland. In 1525, the last Grand Master, Albert of Brandenburg-Ansbach, converted to Protestantism, dissolved the Order and transformed its territory into a secular duchy. Of the fifty-five knights left in Prussia, few remained Catholic. Most took wives and became absorbed into the local nobility – the Prussian *Junkers*. In 1561, the last *Landmeister* of the Livonian branch of the Teutonic Knights followed suit, becoming the secular Duke of Courland. A residual Order with possessions in Catholic Germany remained extant until it was abolished by Napoleon in 1809. It was revived as an honorary ecclesiastical corporation by the Austrian Empire in 1834.

On the Iberian Peninsula, the military orders continued to fight the Moors but under the direction of kings. In Castile, the orders of Santiago, Alcántara and Calatrava continued to defend and settle land conquered from the Moors. The Order of Alcántara also guarded the frontier with Portugal in Extremadura. All the Hispanic orders contributed to the Christian victory at the River Saldo in 1340 which led to the capture of Algeciras in 1344. In the subsequent one-and-a-half centuries, the *Reconquista* was limited to a number of raids into the last Moorish principality, Granada. All took part in the final campaigns which in 1492 finally completed the *Reconquista*, driving the Muslims out of Spain.

Thereafter, the Spanish orders remained as rich and powerful corporations within the Iberian states. In Aragon, the Hospital was the largest single landowner and in Castile the Order of Alcántara owned half of Extremadura. The power of the Masters inevitably involved them in political intrigue. Kings and nobles repeatedly secured masterships for the candidates they favoured who were often their legitimate or illegitimate sons. Between 1487 and 1499, the Castilian orders came under the control of the King, and Montesa was incorporated into the Crown of Aragon in 1587.

In Portugal, the Order of the Temple had, with papal permission, been reconstituted as the Order of Christ. Here, too, it was controlled by the Portuguese kings who were able to install royal princes or other favourites as Master. Its most significant achievements came under its Master, Prince Henry, appointed in 1418, who used the wealth of the Order to finance exploratory voyages down the coast of Africa, around the Cape of Good Hope and eventually to Asia. In the sixteenth century, control of the orders passed to the Crown and, as progressive papal bulls relaxed the vows of poverty, chastity and obedience, membership became merely a matter of honour and prestige.

The only order to continue to make a substantial contribution to Christendom's Holy War against Islam was the Hospital, the Knights of Saint John. Under their Grand Master, Fulk of Villaret, they had been notably silent during the Templars' trial, partly from fear of what might happen to them if they antagonised Philip the Fair, and partly because they hoped to profit from the Temple's demise. Why were they spared? If William of Nogaret was indeed the grandson of Cathars, perhaps he was influenced in their favour by the Order's sympathetic attitude towards the heretics during the Albigensian Crusade. On the face of it, the likelihood that blasphemy, heresy and sodomy would infect one Order but not the other seems small. However, the Hospital had a number of advantages: it had more trained lawyers on its payroll, its headquarters on Rhodes was beyond the reach of any other power. Its readiness to take a leading part in any future *passagium particulare* was consistent with both King Philip IV's and Pope Clement V's crusade thinking.

Despite the rivalry between the Temple and the Hospital, there is no evidence that the Hospitallers gloated over the fate of their brethren. The two orders had always had fewer differences than points in common, and the Hospitallers continued to hold the Templars in high regard. 'Their inheritance of former Templar properties added to their prestige, not so much because they became greater landlords but because it was an honour to follow in the footsteps of so noble a body.'[391] The addition of the Templars' estates to those they already possessed, despite the 'deductions' made by King Philip IV and other European kings, considerably augmented the Hospital's resources but over time, as James of Molay had predicted, the lack of competition led to decline and stagnation. In 1343, Pope Clement VI wrote that it was 'the virtually unanimous and popular opinion of the clergy and laity' that the Hospitallers were doing nothing for the defence of the faith. Proposals were made to create a new order endowed with some of the Hospital's wealth.[392]

In 1522, the Hospitallers lost Rhodes to the Ottoman Turks and in 1530 they were given the island of Malta by the Emperor, Charles V. In 1565, their capital of Valletta was besieged by the Turks but they put up an heroic resistance under their Grand Master, John Parisot of La Valette, leaving almost 250 knights among the 1,500 dead. After a five-month siege, the Turks withdrew. Six years later, Hospitaller galleys contributed to the defeat of the Ottoman fleet at the Battle of Lepanto.

Throughout the seventeenth century, the Hospitallers, now more commonly known as the Knights of Malta, provided a useful naval force either for campaigns against the Islamic powers or for small-scale privateering at the expense of ships from the ports of North Africa. The oarsmen were slaves; the officers young aristocrats from the different *langues* of the Order who later retired to manage the numerous commanderies in Europe. Membership of the Order secured 'a sinecure within a privileged aristocratic corporation providing a comfortable benefice for life'.[393] Life in Valletta, the Order's capital on the island of Malta, was described by the historian Roderick Cavaliero as dull. 'Dullness was the keynote of life in the island. The tone set at the top was of mild urbanity with a meticulous and fussy insistence on discipline and precedence.'

By the end of the eighteenth century, the decay of the Hospital had reached a point where its impregnable fortress of Valletta could be taken by Napoleon Bonaparte after a siege of only one day. Of the 332 knights in the garrison, fifty were too old to fight. As Napoleon commented afterwards, 'the place certainly possessed immense physical means of resistance, but no moral strength whatever'. By the time Napoleon was finally defeated at the Battle of Waterloo, Malta was occupied by the British who had no intention of handing it back to the rump of the Hospitaller Order. After deposing the Grand Master who had lost Malta, Ferdinand of Hompesch, the Knights of Saint John chose as his successor the Tsar of Russia, Paul I, 'who was not Catholic or celibate, or a professed brother, but was certainly mad'.[394]

There followed what a historian of the Hospital has called 'the worst twenty years of the Order's history: twenty years of opportunity squandered by petty self-interest, which made permanent the temporary disasters of the revolutionary period'.[395] However, later in the nineteenth century it returned to the benevolent purpose for which it had originally been founded – a body of devout Roman Catholics whose aristocratic members worked to help the sick, the poor and the dispossessed. As such, it remains extant today.

That today's Knights of Malta should abandon their military calling was inevitable once the Catholic Church had renounced the concept of an armed crusade: indeed, since the Second Vatican Council it has shown a respect for the heretic and the infidel that would have baffled Saint Bernard of Clairvaux. However, it cannot be said that this spirit of tolerance has meant the end to any enmity between Christians and Muslims. Mosques are built in the heartland of what was once called Christendom – in Paris, London and Rome itself – but the practice of the Christian religion remains forbidden in Arabia, the heartland of Islam. A number of states such as Iran, Sudan, Afghanistan and Pakistan govern according to the teaching of the Koran. Armed conflicts between Christians and Muslims continue in Africa, the Balkans, Indonesia and the Philippines. Islamic fundamentalists in recent years have murdered Christian missionaries in Pakistan, Coptic monks in Egypt, and Trappist monks and a Catholic bishop in Algeria.

Conflict also continues in the Holy Land between the Palestinians, mostly Muslims, and the Israelis, mostly Jews. After long hesitation, the Vatican came to recognise the state of Israel and, though it continues to argue that Jerusalem should be placed under international jurisdiction, it no longer advocates the Christian reconquest of the Holy City that had been a prime objective of so many popes over so many years. Yet the Church witnesses in dismay the exodus from the Holy Land of indigenous Christians who feel that they have no future in the country that saw the birth of their religion. In the next millennium, if present trends continue, the only significant body of Christians to be found worshipping in the Church of the Holy Sepulchre in Jerusalem will be the pilgrims flown in on jumbo jets.

Grand Masters
of the Temple

Hugh of Payns	1119–1136
Robert of Craon	1137–1149
Everard of Barres	1149–1152
Bernard of Trémélay	1152–1153
Andrew of Montbard	1153–1156
Bertrand of Blanquefort	1156–1169
Philip of Nablus	1169–1171
Odo of Saint-Amand	1171–1179
Arnold of Torroja	1180–1184
Gérard of Ridefort	1185–1189
Robert of Sablé	1191–1193
Gilbert Erail	1194–1200
Philip of Plessiez	1201–1209
William of Chartres	1210–1219
Peter of Montaigu	1219–1232
Armand of Périgord	1232–1244
Richard of Bures	1244–1247
William of Sonnac	1247–1250
Reginald of Vichiers	1250–1256
Thomas Bérard	1256–1273
William of Beaujeu	1273–1291
Theobald Gaudin	1291–1293
James of Molay	1293–1314

Bibliography

Karen Armstrong, *Muhammad: A Biography of the Prophet*, London, 1991.

Saint Augustine, *Confessions*, translated by Henry Chadwick, Oxford, 1991.

Michael Baigent, Richard Leigh and Henry Lincoln, *The Holy Blood and the Holy Grail*, London, 1982.

Malcolm Barber, *The Trial of the Templars*, Cambridge, 1978.

Malcolm Barber, *The New Knighthood: A History of the Order of the Temple*, Cambridge, 1994.

Malcolm Barber (ed.), *The Military Orders: Fighting for the Faith and Caring for the Sick*, Aldershot, 1994.

D. Barker (ed.), *Studies in Church History*, Oxford, 1978.

T. S. R. Boase, *The Cilician Kingdom of Armenia*, Edinburgh, 1978.

John Boswell, *Christianity, Social Tolerance and Homosexuality: Gay People in Western Europe from the Beginning of the Christian Era to the Fourteenth Century*, Chicago, 1980.

A. Bothwell-Gosse, *The Templars*, London, 1918.

Adriaan H. Bredero, *Bernard of Clairvaux: Between Cult and History*, Edinburgh, 1996.

Christopher N. L. Brooke, *The Medieval Idea of Marriage*, Oxford, 1989.

E. A. R. Brown, 'The Prince is Father of the King: The Character and Childhood of Philip the Fair of France', *Medieval Studies*, 49.

Peter Brown, *The World of Late Antiquity: From Marcus Aurelius to Muhammad*, London, 1971.

James Bryce, *The Holy Roman Empire*, London, 1904.

G. K. Chesterton, *The Everlasting Man*, London, 1925.

Dan Cohn-Sherbok, *The Crucified Jew: Twenty Centuries of Christian Anti-Semitism*, London, 1992.

Roger Collins, *Early Medieval Europe, 300–1000*, London, 1991.

Thomas Curtis van Cleve, *The Emperor Frederick II of Hohenstaufen, Immutator Mundi*, Oxford, 1972.

Philippe Delacroix, *Vrai Visage de Saint Bernard, Abbé de Clairvaux*, Angers, 1991.

Ives Dossat, *Gillaume de Nogaret, petit-fils d'hérétiques, Annales du Midi*, no. 212, Toulouse, October 1941.

Eamon Duffy, *Saints and Sinners: A History of the Popes*, New Haven, CT, 1997.

Peter W. Edbury, *The Kingdom of Cyprus and the Crusades, 1191–1374*, Cambridge, 1991.

Peter W. Edbury and John Gordon Rowe, *William of Tyre*, Cambridge, 1988.

Amos Elon, *Jerusalem: City of Mirrors*, London, 1989.

Eusebius, *The History of the Church from Christ to Constantine*, translated by G. A. Williamson, London, 1965.

J. Favier, *Philippe le Bel*, Paris, 1978.

Richard Fletcher, *The Conversion of Europe: From Paganism to Christianity, 371–1386 AD*, London, 1997.

A. J. Forey, *The Templars in the Corona de Aragon*, Oxford, 1973.

Alan Forey, *The Military Orders: From the Twelfth to the Early Fourteenth Centuries*, London, 1992.

F. L. Ganshof, *Feudalism*, translated by Philip Grierson, Toronto, 1996.

Edward Gibbon, *The Decline and Fall of the Roman Empire*, London, 1960.

John Gillingham: *Richard the Lionheart*, London, 1978.

Gustave E. von Grunebaum, *Medieval Islam: A Study in Cultural Orientation*, Chicago, 1946.

F. Holmes Duddon, *The Life and Times of Saint Ambrose*, Oxford, 1935.

Norman Housley, *The Later Crusades: From Lyons to Alcazar, 1274–1580*. Oxford, 1992.

Stephen Howarth, *The Knights Templar*, London, 1982.

Ann Hyland, *The Medieval Warhorse: From Byzantium to the Crusades*, Stroud, 1994.

Paul Johnson, *A History of the Jews*, London, 1987.

Jean de Joinville, *The Life of Saint Louis*, translated by M. R. B. Shaw, Harmondsworth, 1963.

Alexander Jones (ed.), *The Jerusalem Bible*, London, 1966.

Josephus, *The Jewish War*, translated and with an introduction by G. A. Williamson, London, 1959.

Gabriel Josipovici, *The Book of God: A Response to the Bible*, London, 1988.

Benjamin Z. Kedar, *Crusade and Mission: European Approaches towards the Muslims*, Princeton, 1984.

Benjamin Z. Kedar (ed.), *The Horns of Hattin*, London, 1992.

Maurice Keen, *The Penguin History of Medieval Europe*, London, 1968.

Maurice Keen, *Chivalry*, London, 1984.

David Knowles, *Christian Monaticism*, London, 1969.

Ronald Knox, *Enthusiasm*, Oxford, 1950.

Keith Laidler, *The Head of God: The Lost Treasure of the Templars*, London, 1998.

Michel Lamy, *Les Templiers. Ces Grand Seigneurs aux Blancs Manteaux*, Bordeaux, 1997.

Robin Lane Fox, *The Unauthorised Version: Truth and Fiction in the Bible*, London, 1991.

H. C. Lea, *A History of the Inquisition in the Middle Ages*, New York, 1888.

Bernard Lewis, *The Assassins: A Radical Sect in Islam*, London, 1967.

Ferdinand Lot, *The End of the Ancient World and the Beginnings of the Middle Ages*, translated by Philip and Mariette Leon, London, 1931.

Amin Maalouf, *The Crusades through Arab Eyes*, translated by Jon Rothschild, London, 1984.

Hyam Maccoby, *The Mythmaker: Paul and the Invention of Christianity*, London, 1986.

E. Martin, *The Templars in Yorkshire*, York, 1929.

Hans Eberhard Mayer, *The Crusades*, translated by John Gillingham, Oxford, 1972.

Marion Melville, *La Vie des Templiers*, Paris, 1978.

Sophia Menache, *Clement V*, Cambridge, 1998.

Colin Morris, *The Papal Monarchy: The Western Church from 1050 to 1250*, Oxford, 1989.

Jerome Murphy-O'Connor, OP, *The Holy Land: An Archaeological Guide from Earliest Times to 1700*, Oxford, 1986.

Janet L. Nelson (ed.), *Richard Coeur de Lion in History and Myth*, London, 1992.

Helen Nicholson, *Templars, Hospitallers and Teutonic Knights: Images of the Military Orders, 1128–1291*, Leicester, 1993.

Helen Nicholson (ed.), *The Military Orders*, vol. 2, Aldershot, 1998.

John Julius Norwich, *Byzantium: The Apogee*, London, 1991.

John Julius Norwich, *Byzantium: The Decline and Fall*, London, 1995.

Zoe Oldenbourg, *Massacre at Monségur*, translated by Peter Green, London, 1961.

Peter Partner, *The Murdered Magicians: The Templars and their Myth*, Oxford, 1982.

Joshua Prawer, *The Latin Kingdom of Jerusalem: European Colonialism in the Middle Ages*, London, 1973.

Michael Prior, *The Bible and Colonialism*, Sheffield, 1997.

H. Prutz, *Geheimlehre und Geheimstatuten des Templerherren-Ordens*, Berlin, 1879.

Raimonde Reznikov, *Cathares et Templiers*, Portet-Sur-Garonne, n.d..

Jonathan Riley-Smith, *The Feudal Nobility and the Kingdom of Jerusalem, 1174–1277*, London, 1973.

Jonathan Riley-Smith, *The Atlas of the Crusades*, New York, 1991.

Jonathan Riley-Smith, *The First Crusade and the Idea of Crusading*, London, 1986.

Jonathan Riley-Smith (ed.), *The Oxford Illustrated History of the Crusades*, Oxford, 1995.

Steven Runciman, *A History of the Crusades*, vol. 1: *The First Crusade and the Foundation of the Kingdom of Jerusalem*, Cambridge, 1951.

Steven Runciman, *A History of the Crusades*, vol. 2: *The Kingdom of Jerusalem and the Frankish East 1100–1187*, Cambridge, 1952.

Steven Runciman, *A History of the Crusades*, vol. 3: *The Kingdom of Acre and the Later Crusades*, Cambridge, 1954.

E. P. Sanders, *The Historical Figure of Jesus*, London, 1993.

Sylvia Schein, *Fidelis Crucis: The Papacy, the West, and the Recovery of the Holy Land, 1274–1314*, Oxford, 1991.

Bruno Scott-James (ed.), *The Letters of Saint Bernard of Clairvaux*, London, 1953.

Andrew Sinclair, *The Discovery of the Grail*, London, 1998.

H. J. A. Sire, *The Knights of Malta*, New Haven and London, 1994.

R. C. Smail, *Crusading Warfare, 1097–1193*, Cambridge, 1995.

R. W. Southern, *Western Society and the Church in the Middle Ages*, Harmondsworth, 1970.

R. W. Southern, *Saint Anselm: A Portrait in a Landscape*, Cambridge, 1990.

Jonathan Sumption, *The Albigensian Crusade*, London, 1978.

Christopher Tyerman, *England and the Crusades, 1095–1588*, Chicago, 1988.

Christopher Tyerman, *The Invention of the Crusades*, London, 1998.

J. M. Upton-Ward, *The Rule of the Templars: The French Text of the Rule of the Order of the Knights Templar*, translated and introduced by J. M. Upton-Ward, Woodbridge, 1992.

Geza Vermes, *Jesus the Jew: A Historian's Reading of the Gospels*, London, 1973.

W. Montgomery Watt, *Muhammad, Prophet and Statesman*, Oxford, 1961.

A. N. Wilson, *Paul: The Mind of the Apostle*, London, 1997.

Ian Wilson, *The Blood and the Shroud*, London, 1998.

Robert S. Wistrich, *Anti-Semitism: The Longest Hatred*, London, 1991.

Endnotes

1 Alexander Jones (ed.), *The Jerusalem Bible*, London, 1966, Genesis, 18:13, 14.

2 Ibid., Genesis, 22:12–18.

3 See Paul Johnson, *A History of the Jews*, London, 1987, pp. 6–7.

4 *The Jerusalem Bible*, Exodus, 32:1–6.

5 Ibid., 2 Judges.

6 Ibid., 1 Samuel, 15:19–20.

7 Ibid., 2 Samuel, 11:14–15.

8 Josephus, *The Jewish War*, translated and with an introduction by G. A. Williamson, London, 1959, p. 40.

9 Quoted in Robert S. Wistrich, *Anti-Semitism: The Longest Hatred*, London, 1991, p. 8.

10 *The Jewish War*, p. 80.

11 Ibid., p. 174.

12 *The Jerusalem Bible*, Jeremiah, 23:5–6.

13 Ibid., Psalm 72:8, 11.

14 *The Jewish War*, p. 255.

15 Ibid., p. 319.

16 Gabriel Josipovici, *The Book of God: A Response to the Bible*, London, 1988, p. 230.

17 G. K. Chesterton, *The Everlasting Man*, London, 1925, p. 233.

18 E. P. Sanders, *The Historical Figure of Jesus*, London, 1993, p. 280.

19 Geza Vermes, *Jesus the Jew: A Historian's Reading of the Gospels*, London, 1973, p. 129.

20 *The Jerusalem Bible*, Isaiah 53:3–4.

21 Ibid., Psalm 109:25.

22 See Robin Lane Fox on the Gospel of Saint Luke in *The Unauthorised Version: Truth and Fiction in the Bible*, London, 1991, p. 31.

23 *The Jewish War*, p. 406.

24 Ibid., p. 407.

25 *The Jerusalem Bible*, Luke, 21:5–6.

26 Ibid., John, 2:19.

27 Ibid., Matthew, 26:61.

28 Eusebius, *The History of the Church from Christ to Constantine*, translated by G. A. Williamson, London, 1965.

29 *The Jerusalem Bible*, Matthew, 27:25.

30 Ibid., John, 11:50.
31 Ibid., Acts of the Apostles, 9:15.
32 A. N. Wilson, *Paul: The Mind of the Apostle*, London, 1997. See also Hyam Maccoby, *The Mythmaker: Paul and the Invention of Christianity*, London, 1986.
33 *The Jerusalem Bible*, Acts of the Apostles, 18:16–17.
34 Ibid., Acts of the Apostles, 24:5–6.
35 Quoted in Edward Gibbon, *The Decline and Fall of the Roman Empire*, London, 1960, p. 197.
36 Eusebius, *The History of the Church from Christ to Constantine*, p. 171.
37 Ibid., p. 341.
38 Ibid., pp. 200, 202.
39 *The Jerusalem Bible*, 2 Peter, 2:1.
40 F. Holmes Duddon, *The Life and Times of Saint Ambrose*, Oxford, 1935.
41 Saint Augustine, *Confessions*, translated by Henry Chadwick, Oxford, 1991.
42 *The Jerusalem Bible*, Romans, 13:13–14.
43 Peter Brown, *The World of Late Antiquity: From Marcus Aurelius to Muhammad*, London, 1971, p. 122.
44 Roger Collins, *Early Medieval Europe, 300–1000*. London, 1991, p. 91.
45 James Bryce, *The Holy Roman Empire*, London, 1904, p. 12.
46 Brown, *The World of Late Antiquity*, p. 174.
47 Ibid., p. 135.
48 Maurice Keen, *The Penguin History of Medieval Europe*, London, 1968, p. 78.
49 *The Jerusalem Bible*, Matthew, 19:12.
50 Eusebius, *The History of the Church from Christ to Constantine*, p. 343.
51 *The Jerusalem Bible*, Luke, 18:23–4.
52 David Knowles, *Christian Monasticism*, London, 1969, p. 12.
53 Ibid., p. 23.
54 Ferdinand Lot, *The End of the Ancient World and the Beginnings of the Middle Ages*, translated by Philip and Mariette Leon, New York, 1931, p. 395.
55 Ibid., p. 394.
56 Ibid., p. 389.
57 Richard Fletcher, *The Conversion of Europe: From Paganism to Christianity, 371–1386 AD*, London, 1997, p. 213.
58 Bryce, *The Holy Roman Empire*, p. 69.
59 Ibid., p. 49.
60 W. Montgomery Watt, *Muhammad, Prophet and Statesman*, Oxford, 1961, p. 51.
61 Ibid., p. 129.
62 Ibid.
63 Gustave E. von Grunebaum, *Medieval Islam: A Study in Cultural Orientation*, Chicago, 1947, p. 68.
64 Watt, *Muhammad, Prophet and Statesman*, p. 220.
65 Karen Armstrong, *Muhammad: A Biography of the Prophet*, London, 1991, p. 139.
66 Von Grunebaum, *Medieval Islam*, p. 78.

67 Ibid., pp. 79–80.

68 Wistrich, Anti-Semitism: The Longest Hatred, p. 20.

69 Fletcher, *The Conversion of Europe*, p. 341.

70 Von Grunebaum, *Medieval Islam*, p. 201.

71 Joshua Prawer, *The Latin Kingdom of Jerusalem: European Colonialism in the Middle Ages*, London, 1973, p. 4.

72 Von Grunebaum, *Medieval Islam*, p. 182.

73 Gibbon, *The Decline and Fall of the Roman Empire*, p. 721.

74 Keen, *The Penguin History of Medieval Europe*, p. 47.

75 Jerome Murphy-O'Connor, OP, *The Holy Land: An Archaeological Guide from Earliest Times to 1700*, Oxford, 1986, p. 78.

76 F. L. Ganshof, *Feudalism*, translated by Philip Grierson, Toronto, 1996, p. 1.

77 Ibid., p. 19.

78 Eamon Duffy, *Saints and Sinners: A History of the Popes*, New Haven, CT, 1997, p. 82.

79 Hans Eberhard Mayer, *The Crusades*, translated by John Gillingham, Oxford, 1972, p. 4.

80 Bryce, *The Holy Roman Empire*, p. 78.

81 Keen, *The Penguin History of Medieval Europe*, p. 12.

82 Bryce, *The Holy Roman Empire*, p. 93.

83 Gibbon, *The Decline and Fall of the Roman Empire*, p. 723.

84 John Julius Norwich, *Byzantium: The Apogee*, London, 1991, p. 131.

85 Fletcher, *The Conversion of Europe*, p. 232.

86 Prawer, *The Latin Kingdom of Jerusalem*, p. 7.

87 Jonathan Riley-Smith, *The First Crusade and the Idea of Crusading*, London, 1993, p. 21.

88 Marcus Bull, in *The Oxford Illustrated History of the Crusades*, edited by Jonathan Riley-Smith, Oxford, 1995, p. 15.

89 See Christopher Tyerman, *The Invention of the Crusades*, London, 1988, p. 9.

90 Michael Prior, *The Bible and Colonialism*, Sheffield, 1997, p. 35.

91 Mayer, *The Crusades*, p. 7.

92 Norman Housley, 'Jerusalem and the Development of the Crusade Idea, 1099–1108', in *The Horns of Hattin*, edited by B. Z. Kedar, London, 1992, p. 32.

93 Riley-Smith, *The Oxford Illustrated History of the Crusades*, pp. 77.

94 Mayer, *The Crusades*, p. 321.

95 Bull, in *The Oxford Illustrated History of the Crusades*, p. 17.

96 Riley-Smith, *The First Crusade and the Idea of Crusading*, p. 52.

97 Fletcher, *The Conversion of Europe*, p. 31.

98 Quoted in Dan Cohn-Sherbok, *The Crucified Jew: Twenty Centuries of Christian Anti-Semitism*, London, 1992, p. 40.

99 Mayer, *The Crusades*, p. 44.

100 Quoted in Riley-Smith, *The First Crusade and the Idea of Crusading*, p. 96.

101 Quoted in R. C. Smail, *Crusading Warfare, 1097–1193*, Cambridge, 1995, p. 115n.

102 Quoted in Amin Maalouf, *The Crusades through Arab Eyes*, translated by Jon Rothschild, London, 1984, p. 39.

103 Riley-Smith, *The First Crusade and the Idea of Crusading*, p. 154.

104 Michel Lamy, *Les Templiers: Ces Grand Seigneurs aux Blancs Manteaux*, Bordeaux, 1997, p. 26.

105 Christopher N. L. Brooke, *The Medieval Idea of Marriage*, Oxford, 1989, p. 136.

106 Ibid., p. 138.

107 R. W. Southern, *Western Society and the Church in the Middle Ages*, Harmondsworth, 1970.

108 'Traité du Précepte et de la dispense', cited in Philippe Delacroix, *Vrai Visage de Saint Bernard, Abbé de Clairvaux*, Angers, 1991, p. 52.

109 Quoted in Adriaan H. Bredero, *Bernard of Clairvaux: Between Cult and History*, Edinburgh, 1996, p. 95.

110 Knowles, *Christian Monasticism*, p. 78.

111 See A. J. Forey, *The Templars in the Corona de Aragon*, Oxford, 1973, p. 5.

112 Prawer, *The Latin Kingdom of Jerusalem*, p. 254.

113 R. W. Southern, *Saint Anselm: A Portrait in a Landscape*, Cambridge, 1990, p. 169: Anselm modified this line when he wanted to get rid of a troublesome brother-in-law.

114 Quoted in Malcolm Barber, *The New Knighthood: A History of the Order of the Temple*, Cambridge, 1994, p. 13.

115 *The Rule of the Templars: The French Text of the Rule of the Order of the Knights Templar*, translated and introduced by J. M. Upton-Ward, Woodbridge, 1992, p. 20.

116 Marion Melville, *La Vie des Templiers*, Paris, 1978, p. 3.

117 Upton-Ward, *The Rule of the Templars*, p. 19.

118 Ibid., p. 36.

119 Ibid., p. 28.

120 Colin Morris, *The Papal Monarchy: The Western Church from 1050 to 1250*, Oxford, 1989, p. 280.

121 Quoted in Barber, *The New Knighthood*, p. 49.

122 Maurice Keen, *Chivalry*, London, 1994, p. 8.

123 Forey, *The Templars in the Corona de Aragon*, p. 271.

124 Rev. Dr E. Martin, *The Templars in Yorkshire*, York, 1929, p. 380.

125 Alan Forey, *The Military Orders: From the Twelfth to the Early Fourteenth Centuries*, London, 1992, p. 189.

126 H. J. A. Sire, *The Knights of Malta*, New Haven and London, 1994, p. 4.

127 Nicolo de Martoni, quoted in Sire, *The Knights of Malta*, p. 8.

128 Quoted in Barber, *The New Knighthood*, p. 27.

129 Forey, *The Templars in the Corona de Aragon*, p. 22.

130 Riley-Smith, *The First Crusade and the Idea of Crusading*, p. 44.

131 Forey, *The Military Orders: From the Twelfth to the Early Fourteenth Centuries*, p. 213.

132 *The Jerusalem Bible*, Matthew, 16:24–5.

133 Quoted in Barber, *The New Knighthood*, p. 261.

134 Alan Forey, in *The Oxford Illustrated History of the Crusades*, p. 204.

135 Helen Nicholson, *Templars, Hospitallers and Teutonic Knights: Images of the Military Orders*, Leicester, 1995, p. 62.

136 Upton-Ward, *The Rule of the Templars*, p. 22.

137 Brooke, *The Medieval Idea of Marriage*, p. 267.

138 John Boswell, *Christianity, Social Tolerance and Homosexuality: Gay People in Western Europe from the Beginning of the Christian Era to the Fourteenth Century*, Chicago, 1980.

139 Southern, *Saint Anselm*, p. 150.

140 *The Jerusalem Bible*, Romans, 1:26.

141 Saint Augustine, *Confessions*, III, 8.

142 Southern, *Saint Anselm*, p. 130.

143 Forey, *The Military Orders: From the Twelfth to the Early Fourteenth Centuries*, p. 189.

144 Upton-Ward, *The Rule of the Templars*, p. 112.

145 Denys Pringle, 'Templar Castles on the Road to the Jordan', in Malcolm Barber (ed.), *The Military Orders: Fighting for the Faith and Caring for the Sick*, p. 148.

146 Imad ad-Din al Isfahani, quoted by Judi Upton-Ward, in 'The Surrender of Gaston and the Rule of the Templars', in Barber (ed.), *The Military Orders: Fighting for the Faith and Caring for the Sick*, p. 181.

147 John Julius Norwich, *Byzantium: The Decline and Fall*, London, 1995, p. 107.

148 Mayer, *The Crusades*, p. 99.

149 Riley-Smith, *The Oxford Illustrated History of the Crusades*, p. 81.

150 Quoted in Steven Runciman, *A History of the Crusades*, vol. 2, *The Kingdom of Jerusalem and the Frankish East 1100–1187*, Cambridge, 1952, p. 254.

151 *The Letters of Saint Bernard of Clairvaux*, edited and translated by Bruno Scott-James, London, 1953, p. 461.

152 Ibid.

153 Stephen Howarth, *The Knights Templar*, London, 1982, p. 199.

154 Melville, *La Vie des Templiers*, p. 92.

155 Christopher Tyerman, *England and the Crusades, 1095–1588*, Chicago, 1988, p. 182.

156 Barber, *The New Knighthood*, p. 66.

157 Jane Martindale, 'Eleanor of Aquitaine', in Janet L. Nelson (ed.), *Richard Coeur de Lion in History and Myth*, London, 1992, p. 40.

158 Quoted in Bredero, *Bernard of Clairvaux*, p. 150.

159 Von Grunebaum, *Medieval Islam*, p. 58.

160 R. C. Smail, *Crusading Warfare, 1097–1193*, Cambridge, 1995, p. 43.

161 Prawer, *The Latin Kingdom of Jerusalem*, p. 67.

162 See Jonathan Riley-Smith, *The Feudal Nobility and the Kingdom of Jerusalem, 1174–1277*, London, 1973, p. 81.

163 Prawer, *The Latin Kingdom of Jerusalem*, p. 506.

164 Ibid., p. 504.

165 Jonathan Phillips, in *The Oxford Illustrated History of the Crusades*, p. 116.

166 Prawer, *The Latin Kingdom of Jerusalem*, p. 238.

167 Ibid., p. 383.

168 Quoted in Malouf, *The Crusades through Arab Eyes*, p. 129.

169 Susan Edgington, 'Medical Knowledge in the Crusading Armies: The Evidence of Albert of Aachen and Others', in Barber (ed.), *The Military Orders: Fighting for the Faith and Caring for the Sick*, p. 326.

170 Robert Irwin, 'Islam and the Crusades', in *The Oxford Illustrated History of the Crusades*, p. 235.

171 Quoted in Barber, *The New Knighthood*, p. 93.

172 Ibid., p. 93.

173 Jaroslav Folda, 'Art in the Latin East, 1098–1294', in *The Oxford Illustrated History of the Crusades*, p. 150.

174 Prawer, *The Latin Kingdom of Jerusalem*, p. 416.

175 Jaroslav Folda, in *The Oxford Illustrated History of the Crusades*, p. 416.

176 Ann Hyland, *The Medieval Warhorse: From Byzantium to the Crusades*, Stroud, 1994, p. 153.

177 Nicholson, *Templars, Hospitallers and Teutonic Knights*, p. 117.

178 Upton-Ward, *The Rule of the Templars*, p. 91.

179 Knowles, *Christian Monasticism*, p. 84.

180 Smail, *Crusading Warfare*, p. 39.

181 Helen Nicholson, 'Before William of Tyre: European Reports on the Military Orders' Deeds in the East, 1150–1185', in Helen Nicholson (ed.), *The Military Orders*, vol. 2, Aldershot, 1998, p. 114.

182 Runciman, *A History of the Crusades*, vol. 2, *The Kingdom of Jerusalem*, p. 366.

183 Barber, *The New Knighthood*, p. 76.

184 Smail, *Crusading Warfare*, p. 201.

185 Runciman, *A History of the Crusades*, vol. 2, *The Kingdom of Jerusalem*, p. 178.

186 Bernard Hamilton, 'Queens of Jerusalem', in D. Barker (ed.), *Studies in Church History*, Oxford, 1978, p. 157.

187 Bernard Lewis, *The Assassins: A Radical Sect in Islam*, London, 1967, p. 27.

188 William of Tyre, *Historia Rerum in partibus transmarinis gestarum*, quoted in Bernard Hamilton, 'The Elephant of Christ: Reginald of Châtillon', in Barker (ed.), *Studies in Church History*, p. 98.

189 Runciman, *A History of the Crusades*, vol. 2, *The Kingdom of Jerusalem*, p. 348.

190 Kamal al-Din, quoted in Lewis, *The Assassins*, p. 111.

191 Quoted in Barber, *The New Knighthood*, p. 103.

192 See ibid., p. 104.

193 Runciman, *A History of the Crusades*, vol. 2, *The Kingdom of Jerusalem*, p. 398.

194 'The Elephant of Christ: Reginald of Châtillon', in Barker (ed.), *Studies in Church History*, p. 99. Sir Steven Runciman in his *History of the Crusades* does not mention a ransom.

195 Ibid., p. 100n.

196 Quoted in Barber, *The New Knighthood*, p. 109.

197 Tyerman, *England and the Crusades*, p. 46.

198 Runciman, *A History of the Crusades*, vol. 2, *The Kingdom of Jerusalem*, p. 406, n. 4.

199 Ibid., p. 448.

200 Ibid., pp. 441–2.

201 'The Elephant of Christ: Reginald of Châtillon', in Barker (ed.), *Studies in Church History*, p. 104.

202 Ibid., p. 107.

203 Peter of Blois, quoted by Michael Markowski in 'Peter of Blois and the Concept of the Third Crusade', in Kedar (ed.), *The Horns of Hattin*, p. 264.

204 Prawer, *The Latin Kingdom of Jerusalem*, p. 81.

205 William J. Hamblin, 'Saladin and Muslim Military Theory', in Kedar (ed.), *The Horns of Hattin*, p. 236.

206 Smail, *Crusading Warfare*, p. 38.

207 Barber, *The New Knighthood*, p. 117.

208 Michael Markhowski, 'Peter of Blois and the Conception of the Third Crusade', in Kedar (ed.), *The Horns of Hattin*, p. 13.

209 Mayer, *The Crusades*, p. 136.

210 See Tyerman, *The Invention of the Crusades*, p. 28.

211 Alfred Richard, *Contes*, II, p. 457, quoted in Jane Martindale, 'Eleanor of Aquitaine', in Nelson (ed.), *Richard Coeur de Lion in History and Myth*, p. 210.

212 Prawer, *The Latin Kingdom of Jerusalem*, p. 185.

213 Tyerman, *England and the Crusades*, p. 58.

214 Steven Runciman, *A History of the Crusades*, vol. 3, *The Kingdom of Acre*, Cambridge, 1954, p. 11.

215 Norwich, *Byzantium: The Decline and Fall*, p. 129.

216 Runciman, *A History of the Crusades*, vol. 3, *The Kingdom of Acre*, p. 54n.

217 Peter W. Edbury, *The Kingdom of Cyprus and the Crusades, 1191–1374*, Cambridge, 1991, p. 17.

218 Runciman, *A History of the Crusades*, vol. 3, *The Kingdom of Acre*, p. 73.

219 See John Gillingham, *Richard the Lionheart*, London, 1978, p. 161.

220 H. E. Marshall, *Our Island Story*, London, p. 167.

221 J. O. Prestwich, 'Richard Coeur de Lion: *Rex Bellicosus*', in Nelson (ed.), *Richard Coeur de Lion in History and Myth*, p. 16.

222 Gillingham, *Richard the Lionheart*, pp. 285, 288.

223 A. Bothwell-Gosse, *The Templars*, London, 1918, p. 11. Alternatively, Richard 'married' these vices to the religious orders when commanded to abandon them by the preacher, Fulk of Neuilly. See Runciman, *A History of the Crusades*, vol. 3, *The Kingdom of Acre*, p. 109n.

224 Duffy, *Saints and Sinners*, p. 110.

225 Tyerman, *The Invention of the Crusades*, p. 89.

226 Norman Housley, in *The Oxford Illustrated History of the Crusades*, p. 266.

227 Quoted in Peter Partner, *The Murdered Magicians: The Templars and their Myth*, Oxford, 1982, p. 30.

228 Nicholson, *Templars, Hospitallers and Teutonic Knights*, p. 102.

229 Michael Gervers, '*Pro defensione Terre Sancte*: The Development and Exploitation of the Hospitallers' Landed Estate in Essex', in Barber (ed.), *The Military Orders: Fighting for the Faith and Caring for the Sick*, p. 5.

230 Nicholson, *Templars, Hospitallers and Teutonic Knights*, p. 131.

231 Barber, *The New Knighthood*, p. 267.

232 Forey, *The Templars in the Corona de Aragon*, p. 349.

233 Ibid., p. 351.

234 Ibid., p. 48.

235 Nicholson, *Templars, Hospitallers and Teutonic Knights*, p. 21.

236 Peter W. Edbury and John Gordon Rowe, *William of Tyre*, Cambridge, 1988, p. 128.

237 Alan Forey, in *The Oxford Illustrated History of the Crusades*, p. 213.

238 Forey, *The Templars in the Corona de Aragon*, p. 136.

239 Edbury and Rowe, *William of Tyre*, p. 148.

240 Mayer, *The Crusades*, p. 188.

241 Ibid., p. 189.

242 Quoted in ibid., p. 191.

243 Peter Lock, 'The Military Orders in Mainland Greece', in Barber (ed.), *The Military Orders: Fighting for the Faith and Caring for the Sick*, p. 333.

244 Norman Housley, *The Later Crusades, 1274–1580*, Oxford, 1992, p. 153.

245 Forey, in *The Oxford Illustrated History of the Crusades*, p. 189.

246 Jonathan Sumption, *The Albigensian Crusade*, London, 1978, p. 38.

247 Zoe Oldenbourg, *Massacre at Monségur*, translated by Peter Green, London, 1961, p. 27.

248 Père D'Avrigny, quoted in Ronald Knox, *Enthusiasm*, Oxford, 1950, p. 319.

249 Quoted in Sumption, *The Albigensian Crusade*, p. 53.

250 Ibid., p. 31.

251 Raimonde Reznikov, *Cathares et Templiers*, Portet-Sur-Garonne, n.d. p. 21.

252 Ibid., p. 13.

253 Ibid., p. 46.

254 Sumption, *The Albigensian Crusade*, p. 208.

255 Tyerman, *The Invention of the Crusades*, p. 75.

256 James M. Powell, 'The Role of Women in the Fifth Crusade', in Kedar (ed.), *The Horns of Hattin*, p. 301.

257 Quoted in Barber, *The New Knighthood*, p. 163.

258 Quoted in ibid., p. 130.

259 Quoted in Thomas Curtis van Cleve, *The Emperor Frederick II of Hohenstaufen, Immutator Mundi*. Oxford, 1972, p. 64.

260 Maalouf, *The Crusades through Arab Eyes*, p. 230.

261 Van Cleve, *The Emperor Frederick II of Hohenstaufen*, p. 239.

262 Maalouf, *The Crusades through Arab Eyes*, p. 230.

263 Quoted in Van Cleve, *The Emperor Frederick II of Hohenstaufen*, p. 421.

264 Quoted in ibid., p. 335.

265 Ibid., p. 420.

266 Quoted in ibid., p. 101.

267 Quoted in ibid., p. 217.

268 Quoted in Maalouf, *The Crusades through Arab Eyes*, p. 228.

269 Barber, *The New Knighthood*, p. 240.

270 Runciman, *A History of the Crusades*, vol. 3, *The Kingdom of Acre*, p. 193.

271 Prawer, *The Latin Kingdom of Jerusalem*, p. 75.

272 T. S. R. Boase, *The Cilician Kingdom of Armenia*, Edinburgh, 1978, p. 110.

273 Smail, *Crusading Warfare*, p. 101.

274 For a comprehensive list, see Riley-Smith *The Feudal Nobility and the Kingdom of Jerusalem 1174–1277*, pp. 62–3; or Prawer, *The Latin Kingdom of Jerusalem*, p. 404.

275 Quoted in Riley-Smith, *The Feudal Nobility and the Kingdom of Jerusalem*, p. 63.

276 See Prawer, *The Latin Kingdom of Jerusalem*, pp. 509–10.

277 See Benjamin Z. Kedar, *Crusade and Mission: European Approaches towards the Muslims*, Princeton, 1984, p. 157.

278 Quoted in ibid., p. 126.

279 Upton-Ward, *The Rule of the Templars*, p. 148.

280 Forey, *The Templars in the Corona de Aragon*, p. 323.

281 Quoted in Forey, *The Military Orders: From the Twelfth to the Early Fourteenth Centuries*, p. 208.

282 Prawer, *The Latin Kingdom of Jerusalem*, p. 93.

283 Quoted by Jonathan Phillips in 'The Latin East', in *The Oxford Illustrated History of the Crusades*, p. 119.

284 'Le Templier de Tyre', quoted in Prawer, *The Latin Kingdom of Jerusalem*, p. 326.

285 Nicholson, *Templars, Hospitallers and Teutonic Knights*, p. 30.

286 Barber, *The New Knighthood*, p. 230.

287 Malcolm Barber, 'Supplying the Crusader States: The Role of the Templars', in Kedar (ed.), *The Horns of Hattin*, p. 319.

288 Prawer, *The Latin Kingdom of Jerusalem*, p. 197.

289 Keen, *Chivalry*, p. 120.

290 See Prior, *The Bible and Colonialism*, p. 34.

291 Keen, *Chivalry*, p. 56.

292 Runciman, *A History of the Crusades*, vol. 3, *The Kingdom of Acre*, p. 220.

293 Quoted in Barber, *The New Knighthood*, p. 142.

294 Jean de Joinville, *The Life of Saint Louis*, translated by M. R. B. Shaw, Harmondsworth, 1963, p. 175.

295 Keen, *The Penguin History of Medieval Europe*, p. 133.

296 Joinville, *The Life of Saint Louis*, p. 201.

297 Ibid., p. 222.

298 See Robert Irwin, 'Islam and the Crusades', in *The Oxford Illustrated History of the Crusades*, p. 238.

299 Joinville, *The Life of Saint Louis*, p. 277.

300 Ibid., p. 288.

301 Prawer, *The Latin Kingdom of Jerusalem*, p. 414.

302 Mayer, *The Crusades*, p. 253.

303 *Flores Historiarum*, quoted in Barber, *The New Knighthood*, p. 157.

304 See Judi Upton-Ward, 'The Surrender of Gaston', in Barber (ed.), *The Military Orders: Fighting for the Faith and Caring for the Sick*, pp. 186–7.

305 Sylvia Schein, *Fidelis Crucis: The Papacy, the West, and the Recovery of the Holy Land, 1274–1314*, Oxford, 1991, p. 20.

306 James A. Brundage, 'Humbert of Romans and the Legitimacy of Crusader Conquests', in Kedar (ed.), *The Horns of Hattin*, p. 311.

307 Schein, *Fidelis Crucis*, p. 25.

308 Ibid., p. 41.

309 See Peter Edbury, 'The Templars in Cyprus', in Barber (ed.), *The Military Orders: Fighting for the Faith and Caring for the Sick*, p. 193.

310 Barber, *The New Knighthood*, p. 176.

311 Quoted in Schein, *Fidelis Crucis*, p. 67.

312 Runciman, *A History of the Crusades*, vol. 3, *The Kingdom of Acre*, p. 420.

313 Quoted in Schein, *Fidelis Crucis*, p. 115.

314 Ibid., pp. 125–6.

315 Quoted in ibid., p. 126.

316 Nicholson, *Templars, Hospitallers and Teutonic Knights*, p. 125.

317 Norwich, *Byzantium: The Decline and Fall*, pp. 264–73.

318 Edbury, 'The Templars in Cyprus', in Barber (ed.), *The Military Orders: Fighting for the Faith and Caring for the Sick*, p. 194.

319 Quoted in Tyerman, *England and the Crusades*, p. 233.

320 Schein, *Fidelis Crucis*, p. 140.

321 Quoted in ibid., p. 145.

322 E. A. R. Brown, 'The Prince is Father of the King: The Character and Childhood of Philip the Fair of France', *Medieval Studies*, 49, pp. 282–334.

323 See Reznikov, *Cathares et Templiers*, p. 21; and Ives Dossat, *Gillaume de Nogaret, petit-fils d'hérétiques, Annales du Midi*, no. 212, Toulouse, October 1941.

324 From William of Nogaret's eulogy during the posthumous proceedings against Boniface VIII, quoted in Malcolm Barber, *The Trial of the Templars*, Cambridge, 1978, p. 29.

325 Ibid., p. 30.

326 Bryce, *The Holy Roman Empire*, p. 109.

327 Sophia Menache, *Clement V*, Cambridge, 1998, p. 19.

328 see ibid., p. 40.

329 Ibid., p. 86.

330 Schein, *Fidelis Crucis*, p. 180.

331 Ibid., p. 210.

332 Quoted in Barber, *The Trial of the Templars*, p. 16.

333 Quoted in ibid., p. 48.

334 Quoted in Menache, *Clement V*, p. 207.

335 Jean of Saint Victor, *Prima Vita*, quoted in Menache, *Clement V*, p. 206.

336 Barber, *The Trial of the Templars*, p. 67.

337 Ibid., p. 76.

338 Quoted in ibid., p. 100.

339 Ibid., p. 184.

340 Menache, *Clement V*, p. 192.

341 Ibid., p. 199.

342 James Brundage, 'The Lawyers of the Military Orders', in Barber (ed.), *The Military Orders: Fighting for the Faith and Caring for the Sick*, p. 351.

343 Quoted in Barber, *The Trial of the Templars*, p. 125.

344 Quoted in ibid., p. 148.

345 From the chronicle of William of Nangis, quoted in Barber, *The Trial of the Templars*, p. 157.

346 See ibid., p. 161.

347 Forey, *The Military Orders: From the Twelfth to the Early Fourteenth Centuries*, p. 87.

348 See Barber, *The Trial of the Templars*, p. 206.

349 Menache, *Clement V*, p. 229.

350 Martin, *The Templars in Yorkshire*, p. 142.

351 Ibid., p. 147.

352 Quoted in Barber, *The Trial of the Templars*, p. 202.

353 Jean de Saint-Victor, p. 656, quoted in Barber, *The Trial of the Templars*, p. 221.

354 Chronicle of Walter of Guisborough, p. 396, quoted in Menache, *Clement V*, p. 236.

355 Forey, *The Templars in the Corona de Aragon*, p. 364.

356 *The Chronicle of William of Nangis*, quoted in Barber, *The Trial of the Templars*, p. 241.

357 See Simonetta Cerrini, 'A New Edition of the Latin and French Rule of the Temple', in Nicholson (ed.), *The Military Orders*, vol. 2, pp. 211–12.

358 Quoted in Barber, *The New Knighthood*, p. 316.

359 Partner, *The Murdered Magicians*, p. 100.

360 Nicholson, *Templars, Hospitallers and Teutonic Knights*, p. 94.

361 Partner, *The Murdered Magicians*, p. xix.

362 Barber, *The New Knighthood*, p. 331.

363 See Michael Baigent, Richard Leigh and Henry Lincoln, *The Holy Blood and the Holy Grail*, London, 1982.

364 See Ian Wilson, *The Blood and the Shroud*, London, 1998.

365 Lamy, *Les Templiers. Ces Grand Seigneurs aux Blancs Manteaux*, p. 28.

366 Keith Laidler, *The Head of God: The Lost Treasure of the Templars*, London, 1998, p. 177.

367 Ibid., p. 199.

368 Andrew Sinclair, *The Discovery of the Grail*, London, 1998, p. 264.

369 Partner, *The Murdered Magicians*, p. 112.

370 Ibid., p. 138.

371 H. Prutz, *Geheimlehre und Geheimstatuten des Templerherren-Ordens*, Berlin, 1879, pp. 62, 86, 100, cited in Malcolm Barber, 'The Trial of the Templars Revisited', in Nicholson (ed.), *The Military Orders*, vol. 2, p. 330.

372 H. C. Lea, *A History of the Inquisition in the Middle Ages*, New York, 1889, p. 334, quoted in Barber, 'The Trial of the Templars Revisited', p. 329.

373 J. Favier, *Philippe le Bel*, Paris, 1978, p. 447; quoted in Barber, 'The Trial of the Templars Revisited', p. 330.

374 Southern, *Saint Anselm*, p. 153.

375 See Riley-Smith, *The Feudal Nobility and the Kingdom of Jerusalem*, p. 201.

376 See Upton-Ward, *The Rule of the Templars*, Article 573, p. 148.

377 Barber, 'The Trial of the Templars Revisited', p. 331.

378 Partner, *The Murdered Magicians*, p. 180.

379 Joinville, *The Life of Saint Louis*, p. 310.

380 Nicholson, *Templars, Hospitallers and Teutonic Knights*, p. 74.

381 David Hume, *History*, i, p. 209, quoted in Tyerman, *The Invention of the Crusades*, p. 111.

382 Runciman, *A History of the Crusades*, vol. 3, *The Kingdom of Acre*, p. 480.

383 Prior, *The Bible and Colonialism*, p. 35.

384 Jonathan Riley-Smith, 'The Crusading Movement and Historians', in *The Oxford Illustrated History of the Crusades*, p. 7.

385 Riley-Smith, *The First Crusade and the Idea of Crusading*, p. 115.

386 *The Jerusalem Bible*, Book of Revelation, 7:15.

387 'Humbert of Romans and the Legitimacy of Crusader Conquests', in Kedar (ed.), *The Horns of Hattin*, p. 306.

388 Menache, *Clement V*, p. 177.

389 Ibid., p. 86.

390 Quoted in Amos Elon, *Jerusalem: City of Mirrors*, London, 1989, p. 167.

391 Michael Gervers, '*Pro defensione Terre Sancte*: The Development and Exploitation of the Hospitallers' Landed Estate in Essex', in Barber (ed.), *The Military Orders: Fighting for the Faith and Caring for the Sick*, p. 20.

392 See Schein, *Fidelis Crucis*, p. 245.

393 Anthony Luttrell, 'The Military Orders, 1312–1798', in *The Oxford Illustrated History of the Crusades*, p. 347.

394 Jonathan Riley-Smith, *The Atlas of the Crusades*, New York, 1991, p. 156.

395 Sire, *The Knights of Malta*, p. 250.

Index